AMERICA'S ETHICAL
ARCHETYPE

AMERICA'S ETHICAL ARCHETYPE

*Establishing the Psychology of Moral Authority
and Correcting Our Country's Broken Politics*

Damien Terrence Dubose

ISBN: 979-8-9906668-1-8 (paperback)

ISBN: 979-8-9906668-2-5 (ebook)

ISBN: 979-8-9906668-0-1 (hardcover)

To my parents for raising me in a way that led to my passion for values and morals. Your guidance set the stage for everything I am today.

And to my beautiful wife Munkhzaya for diligently supporting me during this journey. You wanted this book as much as I did. Thank you for your patience and encouragement, which helped me get through to the end.

Contents

$\equiv\!\!\!\equiv\!\!\!\equiv \star \bigstar \star \equiv\!\!\!\equiv\!\!\!\equiv$

PREFACE

═══════════ ★ ★ ★ ═══════════

In my daily experiences and conversations with people from diverse backgrounds, I often encounter fellow citizens who express dissatisfaction with the current state of American culture, but also struggle to articulate their discontent and often fear social backlash for even attempting to do so. The perception of moral decay seems widespread, though most are at a loss to identify the actions required to redress it in a tangible way.

As an individualist, I tend to project a similar attitude onto others, and this leads me to downplay the importance of culture and its effect on all. But it occurs to me that outside the realm of business, American culture is bereft of real leaders—and it has been this way for an extraordinarily long time. When I say we have no real leaders, I mean we have no moral leaders. None. Zero.

In fact, America has withdrawn from the space of morality altogether—save for spiritual mysticism (religion), in which active participation is also dwindling. This void in moral leadership signals disaster for the future of ethics because it is morality that informs it.

With such a large part of everyone's lives influenced by culture, there must be someone to inform the culture, someone who develops the ideas that program others—this is the territory of philosophy. However, history shows that there must also be someone who leads, someone who guides the culture toward the acceptance and application of better ideas; yet, embracing this responsibility does not require that one does it for culture's sake.

Among the dominant philosophies in contemporary American culture, each is rooted in mysticism, where spiritual mystics are intellectually bankrupt, and secular mystics, bankrupt morally. Societies have fallen into these same patterns of moral and intellectual impoverishment throughout time. Nevertheless, in the case of America, something entirely unprecedented emerged: A rational set of principles, based on individualism, and applied through capitalism. Yet, there exists a growing sense among us, a disquiet felt but not always articulated, signaling a departure from these ideals. This is not merely nostalgia for a bygone era; it is an acute awareness of a shift away from the rigorous application of reason and the valorization of the individual which are the bedrock of American culture.

The brilliance of America's founding lay in its commitment to reason as the guiding light for governance and personal conduct, a stark contrast to the mystical approach that has often clouded human history. Nonetheless, the gradual encroachment of less rational methodologies on public discourse and decision-making processes marks a significant departure from the original blueprint. The very culture America's early vibrancy helped to create is diluting the intellectual DNA that sparked its initial vibrancy.

This drift from our foundational principles is not just an intellectual curiosity; it is a tangible loss felt by those who sense, even if subconsciously, the fading of the nation's foundational ideals. We stand at a crossroads, witnessing the erosion of the principles that once defined us, yet lacking a clear path forward. It is here, in this moment of cultural introspection, that we must find our bearings. The task ahead is to recalibrate our cultural compass, integrating the rigor of reason with the insights of psychology, to forge a path that not only honors our past but also informs our future. We need a revitalized culture that embraces the complexity of human nature while steadfastly adhering to the principles of rights and rational thought.

I am certain America's founders were applying reason as they conceived of the principles for this country, but after decades of the culture's continuous distancing from that reasoning—much in part to the mystical approach used to perpetuate that culture—we need to revisit reason and reset the culture to evolve it for current and future generations. We need a culture that acknowledges psychology in moral philosophy, to set a sustainable path forward.

As a child growing up in Baltimore, Maryland, my family raised me as a Christian, and they frequently involved me in church activities. That upbringing significantly shaped my intimate awareness of and concern for values and morality from an early age. Although it was not clear to me at that time, I could sense a slight difference in those raised with an explicit "belief system" versus those who had not received that kind of training.

During those early years I also sensed differences between myself and others within my immediate circle, in response to many of the common references I would hear. For example, people would talk about things like "higher powers," "angels," "demons," and "God's purpose." People would also talk about miracles, and all of this became very confusing to me. It was clear that some people "understood" these things in a way that I did not.

Though I could sense values were important, the way in which people tried to communicate these messages to me was unacceptable; spirits and the supernatural were not convincing, to my mind. What many people regarded as miraculous seemed to me rather to be complex applications of logic and human ingenuity. To illustrate, a friend once recounted an instance of two women watching an airplane take off; one had marveled, "I still can't understand how they do that" to which the other responded, "I guess we'll never know." This exchange reflects how people can perceive even commonplace technological feats as miraculous, even though these feats are based on scientific principles. At that time, I had no knowledge of philosophy or psychology as fields of study, nor of their developments.

Fast forward to my final year of graduate school: In pursuit of an MBA with a specialization in finance, I took advantage of some of the resources offered by the school's career development center, particularly the array of aptitude tests designed to align one's skills and interests with a career path. Given my nature, the abstract insights gleaned from these tests immediately intrigued me and improved my ability to narrow down the career trajectories I should consider.

Driven by this newfound clarity and always inquisitive about abstract ideas that help explain the world on a deeper level, I would eventually take another test online, which I now know to be a version of the Myers-Briggs Type Indicator (MBTI), a widely recognized personality-assessment tool designed to measure how people perceive the world and make decisions. The assessment provided me with a written psychological profile over 150 pages long. Amazed by what I was reading, I completed the entire profile in one evening. Even when I disagreed with something, the very next line would say, "The person is likely to disagree with this assessment"—which made me extremely curious about the conceptual framework driving these apparent insights.

I had always been fascinated by psychology because it explained people to me in a way that I could understand, but this was the first time I would go into the details so deeply. This discovery marked a pivotal moment. Knowing and understanding my MBTI-type shed light not just on my idiosyncrasies but also on how I relate to the world around me.

For starters, it eased my long-standing feelings of being "different," putting many previously indescribable aspects of my personality into words. More importantly, it made me aware of my need for conceptual understanding before action, explaining my natural hesitancy to jump into situations without first grasping the underlying logic. The profile also highlighted that my type is rare, which helped me reconcile some of the social disconnects I had previously experienced. This discovery made explicit what I had subconsciously known: I am inherently more of a conceptual thinker than a perceptual observer. This newfound self-awareness has been instrumental in enhancing not only my understanding of myself but also my interactions with others.

But I did not stop there. Intrigued by the accuracy of the MBTI profile, I began to search the internet to see what other information I could get to better understand how this profile I had just read seemed to be so accurate. Before long, I became aware that the creators of this test developed it using Carl Jung's psychological-type theory—a theory that serves as the foundation for many psychological-typing systems.

At that time, my knowledge of Jung was quite limited, mostly confined to what I had learned through the lens of the MBTI. However, as I encountered various sources, some did mention Jung's concept of cognitive functions. It became increasingly clear through my research that a significant element was missing from most of these typing systems: They conspicuously omitted Jung's cognitive functions, an aspect I found to be the linchpin of the entire framework. Recognizing this gap led me to be more discerning in my research, gradually distancing myself from material that focused solely on the MBTI without engaging with the more complex concepts of Jung's cognitive functions.

Understanding my personality type freed me from the inner conflict I had experienced. I came to accept that I habitually think in principles, which empowered me to treat ideas not just as abstract concepts, but as tools for action. This newfound acceptance enhanced the confidence I had in decisions I was making, while ensuring they remained grounded in perceptual evidence. This shift reverberated throughout all aspects of my life.

Although this transformation became evident in my everyday demeanor, I still lacked a unified conceptual framework to integrate my ideas—a gap the significance of which I only came to understand at a subsequent pivotal moment.

One day, a friend mentioned in passing that I reminded her of a book called *The Fountainhead* by Ayn Rand, and suggested I read it. Not thinking much of it at the time but always interested in examining novel ideas, I decided to check out the book. About three minutes in, I can recall sensing: This is it; this is me; and this is how I see the world. I "understand" exactly what the writer means.

After finishing *The Fountainhead*, and because of how much I identified with its message, observations, and main character, I looked for more of Rand's work and quickly found the nonfiction book *The Virtue of Selfishness*. This was a different, ideologically-revealing experience for me because in this book Rand explains some of the philosophical premises at the root of her fiction. For me, Rand's nonfiction was more exciting than her fiction, and I would come to find out that there were several additional nonfiction collections by her. Before long, I had consumed most of the published titles in her catalog and become intimately knowledgeable about her philosophy: Objectivism.

As an adult, instinctively concerned with morality yet removed from the belief system I had in my youth associated with moral and ethical tenets and values, these issues still concerned me on a spiritual level, especially as they pertained to the noticeable changes I was seeing in American culture. And much of what Rand wrote about in her nonfiction was how she considered America's system to be the only moral system in the world. Knowing I needed to continue to research to gain a wider perspective, I began reading John Locke, Adam Smith, Karl Marx, John Maynard Keynes, the Federalist Papers, the Anti-Federalist Papers, economics, political theory, the U.S. Constitution, Plato, Aristotle, even Booker T. Washington and Frederick Douglass— anything that could give me an understanding of the fundamental reason why America and its system seemed to be so important to the history of the world—and why Rand would come to conclude that America embodies the principles of individual liberty more purely and fundamentally than any other nation.

I gained the insight that I needed from this research, which fortified my conclusions on the issue of America's importance, but a continued interest in personality motivated me to read Carl Jung's *Psychological Types* in addition to these other titles. I was immediately struck by some connections between his and Rand's work. For me, the interconnection of these two frameworks brought everything together, but I needed to better understand the overlap between the two that I sensed.

The answer was in the two branches of philosophy at the foundation of Objectivism: metaphysics and epistemology; and their psychological equivalents, what Rand terms "sense of life" and "psycho-epistemology."[1] Jung's work addressed these areas specifically in meticulous and explicit detail.

The two frameworks—Objectivism and Psychological Types— significantly enhanced my understanding of both the world and myself. I came to realize that key concepts—namely morality, value, and even the concept of an individual—consistently shape my thoughts and actions. These themes, at the forefront of my concern, act as filters for my engagement with the world and self-perception. They are not merely intellectual pursuits; they anchor every decision I make, guide every relationship I maintain, and even influence my own sense of

---

[1]   (Peikoff 1991, 417)

well-being. These ideas resonate with me emotionally, shaping my aspirations and my sense of responsibility. However, crucially, these are not merely personal benchmarks; they are foundational American principles that inform the broader societal context in which I operate.

I must reiterate that the core concepts I have mentioned are not just abstract ideas for me. The concept of morality is an internal compass that guides whether I lend a helping hand to a stranger or stand up for what I believe is right in a heated work meeting. Similarly, when I talk about the concept of value, I am not speaking in solely financial or economic terms, even though these contexts are manifestations of the same overarching principle. Value to me is the inherent worth of an action, idea, or relationship, as in the value derived from a meaningful conversation with a friend or implementing a successful project that benefits my team. The concept of the individual goes beyond that expressed as or by a single unit in society; it is about the autonomy to make choices, to pursue one's own values, to have the freedom to innovate, to contribute, to disagree, or to opt-out.

In exploring the complexities of human psychology, Carl Jung's typological theory offers a compelling framework. It suggests that specific psychological attitudes—namely extroversion and introversion— shape our approach to key life concepts as well as the way we process information through our cognitive processes. Upon learning this, it was undeniable to me that engaging with any concept at the root of my deepest concerns requires a certain psychological attitude. This attitude can operate at distinct levels of cognitive processing—either perceptual or conceptual—each leading to distinct methods of exploring and understanding the world.

At the perceptual level, there is a propensity to focus on individual, isolated experiences—what Jung called "phenomena"—as definitive proof of a spiritual or mystical concept, without integrating a broader conceptual framework. This approach is more enigmatic, tapping into the subconscious to result in methodologies steeped in mysticism, intuition, and spiritual insight.

Conversely, the conceptual level typically shuns such methods of thinking. It, with conscious direction, aligns with reason, grounding its understanding in logical analysis and empirical evidence. However, it might still exhibit an over-reliance on specific data points or studies while ignoring overarching theories or principles that provide broader, more nuanced understanding.

In the summer of 2022 in Washington, DC, while attending a talk at the Objectivist Conference, or OCON—an annual week-long conference hosted by the Ayn Rand Institute and dedicated to discussing her philosophy of Objectivism—I heard professional intellectual Onkar Ghate discuss the leaked U.S. Supreme Court decision in Dobbs v. Jackson Women's Health Organization, 597 U.S. ___ (2022). Ghate, who argued that abortion is a fundamental right, critiqued the Supreme Court's unofficial draft opinion, which suggested that the court might no longer federally protect abortion. His talk primarily focused on the intellectual flaws and fallacies in the court opinion that could potentially lead to the overturning of the landmark half-century-old Roe v. Wade, 410 U.S. 113 (1973) decision.

In one of his arguments, Ghate utilized one aspect of the Supreme Court's reasoning, particularly their claim that the individual derives their right to privacy "from no fewer than five different constitutional provisions" to illuminate a deeper concern, the type of "concrete-bound mentality" witnessed in the court justices.[2] The Objectivist term "concrete-bound" refers to a way of thinking that focuses too narrowly on specific details without adequately considering the broader principles or context of decision-making.

---

[2]   (Ghate 2022)

Ghate stated, "Liberty is a principle, it's a right, an abstraction. The whole constitution has to do with liberty. The idea that it's, 'oh, you have to appeal to five different clauses, you're overwhelming me'… that is what their attitude is and that is a concrete-bound attitude."[3]

As I sat and listened to the rest of the talk, that small reference just kept eating away at me… "concrete-bound"—I just could not let it go. Though I had no disagreement with Ghate's critique on the issue as a whole or how it pertains to the label he places on the mentality in question, it raised several questions for me, the first being: Why is he waging this criticism at all? As I had learned, most people think in a concrete-bound manner as a feature of their psychological type. My question then became: Why do philosophers and intellectuals fail to account for the predominant way of thinking for the masses?

It seems redundant to me to argue about the concrete-bound nature at the root of most people's mentality; a mentality associated with a certain attitude toward the psychological process of thinking, according to Jung. In fact, Jung's psychological types were based on the very criteria of people's attitude towards the four psychological processes he names—sensation, intuition, thinking, and feeling. And if certain types have this concrete-bound mentality linked to them, what would be the point of harping on that characteristic if psychology addresses it already? In other words, if one can link a particular way of thinking to specific psychological types, as per Jungian theory, then addressing this at the level of those types might be more effective than repeatedly pointing it out in individual cases.

I then began to ask myself: Is this understanding of psychology not acknowledged or accepted within the intellectual community? I concluded this could not be the case because the core principles of Jung's psychological types are frequently used in places like schools and

---

[3] ibid

workplaces. The MBTI, which heavily draws from Jung's typological theory, is frequently used in these official settings to aid individuals in comprehending their own preferences and working styles. This widespread application of Jungian principles indicates that they are not only acknowledged and accepted, but also embraced, within various communities, including the intellectual one. At minimum, I see uses of the basic concepts of introversion and extroversion in all types of organizational psychology. Educators use it. The military uses it. I leveraged it in graduate school to successfully tailor a career path for myself. So why is it so rare for philosophers and intellectuals to take this understanding into consideration when thinking, reasoning, and philosophizing? Why are we having this disconnect?

As mentioned previously, Jung identifies two psychological attitudes: extroversion and introversion. However, my frustration with much of philosophy lies in its tendency to blindly adopt a one-sided, "universal" approach, leaning either toward extroversion or introversion when formulating theories and examining questions of moral significance, thereby completely neglecting the other. This narrow focus overlooks the complex interplay between these two attitudes and how they collectively contribute to human experience.

Take the ideologies of individualism and socialism: Individualism, with its focus on rights and liberties, closely aligns with an introverted perspective that values the individual's internal world. It values the internal qualities of ingenuity, hard work, and freedom. Socialism, on the other hand, leans toward an extroverted perspective, emphasizing collective well-being and social equality over individual distinctions. In both cases, understanding the psychological foundation on which these systems rest provides a clearer insight into their implicit underlying principles.

Such an oversight makes it easier to conflate the subject-object relationship, a tension I find to be crucial between the two types. The subject-object relationship refers to the way an individual (the subject) interacts with and perceives their external environment or other entities (the objects). For those with an extroverted orientation, the "subject" often encompasses the group they identify with, such as their community. This implies that their actions and decisions are primarily influenced by the norms, values, and expectations of the collective. Conversely, individuals with an introverted perspective maintain themselves as the "subject"; they filter their interactions with the external world through personal reflection and internal values. This fundamental difference in orientation shapes how each party perceives and prioritizes rights and responsibilities.

Understanding this, the question I was then led to is: Are individuals obligated to prioritize their own rights in all instances, addressing the wants and needs of others in the wider society only when they themselves desire or choose to fulfill them? Or does the individual serve at the behest of the group, able or forced to carve out an existence solely from the scraps of others? Logic dictates that a political philosophy must lean one way or the other, even though individuals or theorists can never completely ignore the needs of both perspectives. A better approach would present any philosophical stance by first acknowledging the psychological foundation it rests upon. This would provide a clear and solid starting point for further discussion.

Next, I researched other books tangentially related to this subject and found a common thread among most analyses. While numerous discussions focus on one's political party or surface-level ideologies, they often overlook the psychological roots of the individual involved. Objectivism, as expounded by Ayn Rand, zeroes in on this foundational aspect. Rand posited that an individual's "psycho-epistemology" shapes their views on ethics and, by extension, politics, since these share an intrinsic link. The reality of this understanding as it pertains to the United States' attitude toward politics is that the opposing philosophies at the root of these "disagreements" simply and absolutely cannot coexist. There is no way to bridge these divides, nor is there any reason to attempt it, because its very attempt is at the heart of what destroys the fabric of America. An anti-conceptual, collectivist approach is antithetical to the country's core principles.

Understanding the root causes of political debates is not the main objective of my endeavor; that ground has been well-covered. Instead, my purpose is to offer actionable recommendations based on a deep understanding of these foundational issues.

Observing what I considered to be profound American injustices during the COVID-19 pandemic catalyzed the impetus for my deeper journey into the subject matter of this book. The mishandling of politics and policy seemed not just a failure of governance but a moral failing that led to an unjust devaluation of human life. During this era, a health crisis and the pervasive spread of misinformation and propaganda characterized the situation, further deepening the sense of uncertainty and helplessness. The political climate exacerbated the situation by prioritizing its own narrative over addressing the palpable human cost of the crisis.

Policies that enforced both physical and emotional distancing at a time when closeness was most needed not only prevented many, including myself, from being with loved ones in their last moments or mourning their deaths in traditional ways, but also set the stage for further governmental overreach with questionable effectiveness. The election period's abrupt rule changes, as documented in the Congressional Research Service report, *COVID-19 and Election Emergencies: Frequently Asked Questions and Recent Policy Developments*,[4] significantly affected the democratic process. Although the report does not explicitly allege systemic corruption, it details rapid changes that readers may interpret as facilitating or revealing vulnerabilities that political opportunists within the system might exploit, implying a disturbing level of potential corruption. Moreover, a systematic review

---

[4] (Congressional Research Service 2020)

and meta-analysis found that lockdowns, a major component of the government's response, had little to no effect on reducing COVID-19 mortality while imposing significant economic and social costs.[5] Compounding this, the subsequent government response to the crisis—exacerbated by shutdowns—lacked clear, rational justification. Arbitrary financial handouts aimed at crisis mitigation merely served as a reckless band-aid for a self-inflicted wound, further undermining trust in leadership. Meanwhile, a notable surge in crime during this period, particularly in homicides and gun violence, compounded these issues. According to various reports, homicide rates increased by 26% in 2020 compared to the previous year.[6] This surge has continued, with homicides still about 24% higher than pre-pandemic levels by the first half of 2023, illustrating the profound destabilization of community and safety. This underscores the profound consequences of a governance approach that prioritized immediate relief without addressing the underlying issues it had itself created.

The collective impact of these experiences—ranging from personal loss to societal instability during the pandemic—underscored a profound crisis of morality and leadership, compelling me to delve deeper into its causes. This crisis was not just a backdrop of grief and upheaval; it was a clarion call to examine the philosophical, ethical, and cultural underpinnings that have led us here. It illuminated a deeper problem: a neglect in the development of humans into individual citizens who are ethically grounded and civically engaged.

America's essence—rooted in self-governance and personal responsibility—cannot sustain itself without a societal commitment to fostering the evolution of its citizens from their primitive origins to a more civilized state of being. From birth, humans possess a nature that is primitive and inclined toward collectivism. Throughout history,

---

5   (Herby, Jonung and Hanke 2022)
6   (Blumgart 2021); (Associated Press 2023)

society has refined the process of developing civilized individuals who can uphold the ideals of self-governance and personal responsibility. Yet, it has become apparent that many of our leaders have abandoned this essential journey of guiding development, opting instead for policies and rhetoric that pander to primitive and childlike mentalities. This abandonment has pushed America to a precipice, rendering its current societal model untenable.

On reflection, I conclude that nowhere is the consideration of these attitudes more vital than in political philosophy. In a country founded on individual rights, understanding the balance between extroverted and introverted attitudes is crucial. A system that hinges on individual rights, especially one characterized, as Rand argued, as "the only moral system in the world," would ideally be based on an introverted orientation, permitting collective actions only when necessary. This adherence to an introverted orientation would align with the principles laid down by America's Founding Fathers, who I argue employed an introverted approach to secure individual freedoms for the country's citizens, because prioritizing the sovereignty and autonomy of the individual is the only way unalienable rights can be achieved. However, much of what we have seen over the last nearly 250 years—from elected officials in our political institutions to American culture in general—has been a distancing from and abandonment of that introverted attitude.

The extroverted mentality, in its quest for objectivity, often limits its understanding to experiences that are directly observable, aiming to base judgments solely on what can be immediately perceived. This approach, however, overlooks the crucial need for abstract reasoning and the application of principles to navigate complex concepts like "rights" and "freedom." Such an approach leads to intellectual chaos, despite their unwavering confidence in it. It becomes evident that those resistant to abstract thought, or those entrenched in a concrete-bound mindset, fundamentally struggle to engage with nuanced ideas. The lack of capacity for abstract reasoning acts as a barrier to meaningful dialogue; individuals who have formed judgments find themselves locked within a narrow perspective, unable to consider wider contexts or the possibility of revising their views.

Our nation's very survival and prosperity hinge on our collective commitment to fostering the evolution of its citizens from primitive beginnings to a more civilized state. In the pages that follow, I detail my exploration into these foundational issues, offering both a critique of our current state and a roadmap toward a moral and rational society. My aim is to highlight the critical need for developing individuals into reasoned and ethical citizens, essential for navigating our way out of our current crises and toward a future that respects the dignity and potential of every person, underscoring the urgency of addressing not just the symptoms of our crises but their moral and philosophical underpinnings.

While the examples provided will hopefully illuminate these ideas and the concepts underlying them to anyone journeying through these pages, I authored this work for a specific purpose and set of audiences. My intent is not to validate or give respect to the implicit political ideologies of all psychological types, but rather to provide a conceptual framework for those who seek greater clarity and actionable insights into navigating and transforming our societal landscape.

This book addresses three primary audiences: conceptual thinkers, individuals deeply concerned with morality, and those feeling unsettled by mainstream narratives. Conceptual thinkers will find the analytical depth they crave, exploring the nexus of psychology and ethics. Morality-conscious readers will find this exploration offers a novel lens through which to examine ethical foundations and their impact on societal structures. Meanwhile, unsettled mainstream individuals, sensing a discord but lacking the tools to articulate it, will discover frameworks to understand and engage with the root causes of our era's challenges. Together, these groups form the core readership, united by a common journey toward uncovering the ethical and psychological underpinnings essential for navigating America's political landscape. Through this exploration, the book aims to foster a dialogue that encourages a deeper, principled understanding of the issues at hand, challenging all to consider the foundational ideals that should guide our collective future.

The moral conclusions provided herein are for those who seek to gain a conceptual understanding of the principles governing that realm, but not all people in society need undertake the task of deep philosophical inquiry. A conceptual understanding of ethics and politics, while fundamentally enriching and intellectually empowering for anyone who embraces the endeavor, is basic for a political system's creators and guardians (e.g., philosophers, political theorists, policy makers, etc.) in addition to those who choose to study the topic. It is from these citizens that collective morality ensues. Based on history, most people will adopt their views from the leaders of the group with whom they identify and will accept what the group considers normative.

Introduction

——— ★ ★ ★ ———

I n the heart of America's current political landscape lies a pervasive sense of "dysfunction," a phenomenon widely recognized, yet which few can thoroughly dissect or agree on an origin therein. This book aims to unearth the conceptual root of this dysfunction, tracing it back to a crisis of moral and intellectual decay; a decay amongst the country's thought and political leaders specifically. At the forefront of this exploration is the intersection of psychology and ethical philosophy, underpinning the belief that ethics—how a country distributes moral authority between government and citizens—is the bedrock upon which the politics of any country, especially America, rests.

Through an analytical lens, this work aims to demonstrate that a singular psychological method and philosophical stance are essential to uphold an ethical framework conducive to America's foundational ideals. It is here we introduce a guiding theme that underscores the belief in human agency as a determinant of the psychological and ethical landscapes individuals navigate: that "choice defines perspective." This principle has evolved into a mantra illuminating our central thesis: The choices we make, grounded in our belief in personal agency, shape our psychological dispositions and, by extension, our ethical and political philosophies.

We tackle pivotal questions central to the American ethos: How can we truly know? What does it mean to possess an individual identity?

And crucially, how should we actualize ethics within the political and social spheres to honor and protect the abstract concept of a "right" in its proper sense?

Drawing from the insights of Carl Jung and Ayn Rand—two seminal figures whose works delve into the depths of human psyche and moral philosophy—we navigate the interplay between objective and subjective realities, and the inherent challenges in achieving a balanced perception. Jung illuminates the subjective lenses through which we view the world with his perspectives on psychological types, suggesting that individual mental frameworks invariably color our grasp of "objectivity." In complement, Rand's advocacy for rational egoism and her critique of mysticism, central to her philosophy of Objectivism, underscores the philosophical underpinnings of capitalism and individualism, challenging us to reconsider the ethical basis of political systems.

This book not only scrutinizes the philosophical and psychological dimensions of American politics but also addresses the contemporary issues of mental health, leadership, and rationality versus irrationality in societal decision-making. By examining the societal implications of Jung's classification of rational and irrational types, and Rand's observations on psycho-epistemology, we uncover the profound influence of psychological dispositions on political ideologies and governance.

As we venture into this inquiry, we invite readers to re-evaluate the ethical foundations that guide political discourse and policymaking in America. This examination is not just an academic endeavor but a call to recognize and embrace the diversity of psychological orientations within our society. However, it also prompts a critical reflection on the nature of leadership and the alignment of personal philosophies with the nation's foundational principles, fostering a political environment that respects and uplifts every individual, guided by a philosophy that marries the best of psychology and ethics for the betterment of all.

Nevertheless, we must first ask why this topic and the answers to these questions are of any importance to Americans, or anyone aspiring to become an American. The answer resides in the foundational principles upon which America established itself.

Our nation's founders embedded philosophical principles of individualism into the very fabric of our society, principles that can only emerge from a fundamental understanding and psychological acceptance of human agency. This emergence marked a critical transformation in the arc of human history, signifying a decisive shift toward a society founded on reason and the intrinsic value of human life. It heralded the dawn of an era where the concepts of liberty, autonomy, and rights became not just ideals but foundational principles that guided the development of laws, governments, and societal norms. This pivotal moment in history brought into focus the attributes of human dignity, freedom of thought, and the capacity for self-determination—qualities that, before this point, were often subordinate to the demands of collective survival, tradition, or authoritarian rule.

This evolution toward a society that cherishes individualism and human rights represents a significant departure from a pre-rational, instinctive existence, a transformation that was neither inevitable nor straightforward. Instead, it emerged from a protracted journey, where, throughout much of history, the immediate, tangible needs of survival often overshadowed abstract concepts such as rights or individual agency. One cannot overstate the fragility of this accomplishment. Reaching a recognition and valuation of individual rights and agency at this advanced level of cognitive and social development is a delicate and hard-won achievement, not a universal given. It underscores the necessity of continual vigilance and dedication to preserve these principles against the forces that threaten to undermine them.

A review of philosophical and psychoanalytic history suggests that most people fail to fully grasp and appreciate the profound impact of these advances, as well as their transformative power over societies and individuals alike. Thus, those who assume the country's leadership positions bear the critical responsibility of not only adhering to, but also fully comprehending, these principles and their utmost importance. This comprehension enables such leaders to properly defend, explicate, and perpetuate these principles for future generations. Furthermore, should the U.S. government falter in maintaining this principled stance, we risk a complete regression to a primitive state in which these advancements are obscured or lost. Such a regression would jeopardize America's position as the world's premier destination for those seeking political and economic freedom.

Given this backdrop of societal evolution toward cherishing individualism and human rights, it becomes imperative to examine the psychological foundations that underpin such principles.

Psychologically speaking, all rational judgment derives from one's view of morality: a system of values and principles that guides decision-making and behavior, distinguishing between actions deemed right or wrong, good or bad, based on their implications for individual well-being. However, any genuine philosophical study or theory of morality must include the abstraction and analysis of observations regarding how morality manifests and functions within groups.

Such an abstraction results in ethics—a branch of philosophy that involves systematizing, defending, and recommending normative concepts of right and wrong behavior, in consideration of the collective societal impact and the broader implications of moral principles on human interaction and social structures. Therefore, a society's ethical philosophy is a result of the dominant moral disposition of the individuals comprising it, and it is for this reason that the ethics of a society reflect the fundamental thinking undergirding every political system of governance.

Because morality is at the root of rational judgment for all humans, ethics is an unavoidable preoccupation for any group, dictating how humans interact and treat one another. Furthermore, just as the final backstop for morality is one's willingness to defend oneself—with force—against opposing forces trying to violate, confiscate, or destroy one's values, ethical philosophy examines that force at a collective level. In other words, given that force underpins morality and, by extension, ethics, which flow downstream to influence politics, shaping government, its laws, and policies, we see its influence extend into the realm of political philosophy.

Political philosophy, deriving but distinct from ethical philosophy, relies on explicit and stated force rather than implicit consent or moral persuasion. Politics involves the governance and organization of communities and states, dealing with the distribution of power and resources. Political philosophy, therefore, examines the foundational principles and ethical considerations underlying political systems and behaviors.

Like all philosophical disciplines, political philosophy necessitates two distinct mental processes, achievable only by an individual possessing consciousness: abstraction and thinking. Abstraction involves isolating essential characteristics from vast amounts of sense data to discern a thing's essence. Thinking, then, is the articulation of these abstractions into coherent theories and concepts.

One's actions, whether verbal or nonverbal, stem from both judgment and perception, which precede action. Perception, the primary psychological process, precedes and influences all thinking. These mental processes—perception and judgment—are taken up in two parallel branches of philosophy: metaphysics, the study of existence, reality, and the universe at its most fundamental level; and epistemology, which examines the nature and scope of knowledge and belief. This relationship is crucial, as one's theory of knowledge (epistemology) is grounded in one's understanding of reality (metaphysics). Therefore, one's rational judgment is based on one's perception of reality—the perception that conditions the thinking underlying any ethical philosophy.

This book, recognizing the significant impact of psychology on philosophy, builds on the premise that a thorough exploration of ethics requires delving deeply into both fields. I adopted this interdisciplinary approach to urge philosophers to refine and enhance their contributions by integrating psychological insights. Despite extensive research, existing literature often overlooks the crucial intersection of ethics and psychology, failing to address it in a sufficiently intellectual or culturally relevant way. This oversight is not entirely new; classical works by figures such as Plato and Aristotle, while groundbreaking in ethical philosophy, naturally did not engage with psychology as we understand it today, given that the historical development of psychology as a distinct field came much later. They embedded their inquiries into human behavior and motivation within a broader philosophical discourse, laying important groundwork but leaving room for further exploration of and with modern psychological insights. This gap persists in more contemporary works, such as in John Rawls's *A Theory of Justice* (1971) or Robert Nozick's *Anarchy, State, and Utopia* (1974), which, despite their insights, do not fully contextualize ethics within the framework of psychological diversity and individual dispositions.

Specifically, there seems to be little philosophical accounting for the various known psychological dispositions universally observed across societies, such as one's preference for either collectivity or individuality, or one's tendency to favor emotional rationalization over intellectual explanation. These preferences and tendencies, crucial for understanding ethical and political motivations, have profound implications and biases that inevitably influence ethical and political considerations. Moreover, the theory of knowledge itself, which informs whether people believe they can know something definitively, is foundational in shaping our philosophical approaches to ethics and justice. Given psychology's immense influence, it is pertinent to consider these aspects when discussing political or socioeconomic systems, culture, or morality itself, because psychology factors heavily in a person's judgments on these topics.

In exploring psychology and philosophy, two of the most intelligible and useful frameworks that I have come across are Ayn Rand's Objectivist philosophy and Jung's theory of psychological types. Rand's exploration into capitalism, individual rights, morality, and ethics deeply resonated with my worldview, presenting a philosophy that not only aligns with my perceptions but also is rich in detail and depth. Conversely, Jung's work significantly enhanced my understanding of human behavior through his analysis of psychological types, sharpening my self-awareness and improving my interactions with others.

While Rand articulated a story that spoke to normative ideals without compromising on intellectual rigor, Jung adopted a descriptive method, focusing more on understanding human behavior than prescribing ways to live. Jung's reluctance to offer private opinions contrasted with Rand's forthrightness. The synthesis of Rand's philosophical precision and Jung's psychological insights has enriched my perspective, offering a comprehensive understanding of the interplay between human nature and the philosophical principles that can guide our lives.

It is because of this complementary yet contrasting nature of their insights—Rand's philosophical clarity and advocacy for individualism versus Jung's deep psychological understanding of human nature—that I present here the theories of these two thinkers, and their respective systems of thought, as well as related ideas to contrast against each other throughout this examination. This contrast not only highlights their distinct views but also serves as a basis for presenting subsequent and original thoughts related to their philosophies. I examine the writings of Rand and other Objectivist authors such as Nathaniel Branden and

Leonard Peikoff in this investigation because they most accurately and intelligibly explain the individualistic essence of American political philosophy. In a similar vein, I chose as my other core theme the psychological types of Jung because I believe his system of attitudes and functions, along with the framework he places them in, most accurately and intelligibly provides a means to a basic understanding of the inner workings of human psychology at the most fundamental level.

Ayn Rand was a writer and influential figure throughout the 20th century known for bestselling novels such as *The Fountainhead* (1943) and *Atlas Shrugged* (1957); her works have since been translated worldwide into dozens of languages. In these books, she adopts a philosophical approach in her effort to explain from both a psychological and moral standpoint what she saw as the culture of independence stemming from reason—uniquely embedded in America—a culture that she argues led to the United States' meteoric rise and dominance on the world stage. On the heels of *Atlas Shrugged*'s success in particular, Rand began to author essays on the topics of morality, psychology, economics, politics, government, eventually creating the philosophical system of Objectivism.

Leonard Peikoff, Rand's protégé and leading authority on Objectivism at the time of her death in 1982, elucidates that her philosophy meticulously addresses five core branches of philosophy: metaphysics (the study of existence), epistemology (the study of knowledge), ethics (the study of right and wrong), politics (the study of government and society), and esthetics (the study of art and beauty).[7] Objectivism unifies elements of both rationalism and empiricism and holds that one is not exclusive of the other.

---

[7] (Peikoff 1991, 417)

While pure rationalists often view ideas as separate from our sensory experience, Rand recognizes concepts as abstractions from the perception of reality's facts. She also denounced the pure empiricist view which considers sensory experience the sole source of knowledge, neglecting the role of concepts in understanding reality. Rand argued that our intellect is our primary survival tool, with reason as our main method used in making judgments. This means we experience reality externally, through our senses, but we must use our intellect to truly comprehend it and make informed decisions.

Crucially, for our purposes and as it pertains to psychology, Rand's writings include two psychological concepts she titles "sense of life" and "psycho-epistemology."

She defines a sense of life as,

> *A pre-conceptual equivalent of metaphysics, an emotional, subconsciously integrated appraisal of man and of existence.*[8]

The definition given for psycho-epistemology is,

> The study of man's cognitive processes from the aspect of the interaction between man's conscious mind and the automatic functions of his subconscious.[9]

She would also add,

> *Men's epistemology—or, more precisely, their psycho-epistemology, their method of awareness—is the most fundamental standard by which they can be classified.*[10]

---

[8] (Rand, Philosophy and Sense of Life 1966, 15)
[9] (Peikoff 1991, 419)
[10] (Rand, For the New Intellectual 1963, 21)

These are the concepts within Objectivism that unlock our ability to contrast the ideas of Rand with the other major contributor in this investigation.

Carl Jung is a quite different figure: a Swiss psychiatrist and close collaborator with Sigmund Freud over a five-year period who became widely known for founding analytic psychology and for his work focusing extensively on the human unconscious. He published several books over his career detailing the many findings he identified through cases in his psychiatric practice.

In his book *Psychological Types*, Jung maintained that there are eight psychological archetypes—abstracted from his experience as a psychiatrist—into which each person would fall into only one or another of. The two foundational concepts at the base of his archetypes were what he called attitude and functional types.

Additionally, Jung developed the new concepts of attitude types, namely introversion and extroversion, in order to further categorize a person. He posited that everyone possesses both mechanisms. Extroversion categorizes a mentality conditioned by the objects of one's interests and is heavily reliant on sensation. Introversion categorizes a mentality conditioned by one's inner self. It is idea oriented and heavily reliant on the subjective factor.

The more intricate functional types categorize people based on their tendency toward one of four psychological functions he names: sensation or intuition, labeled irrational functions, and thinking or feeling, labeled rational functions. Jung also holds that everyone possesses all these functions as well, though to different degrees and in various combinations.

Jung intended his psychological archetypes and descriptions to offer a means of understanding how people's conscious and subconscious minds interact, examining the way they perceive the world and make judgments.

While exploring the lives and works of Ayn Rand and Carl Jung, it is crucial to understand their distinct backgrounds and the eras they navigated, each significantly shaping their philosophical and psychological explorations. Ayn Rand, born in Russia in 1905 and later emigrating to the U.S. in 1926, witnessed firsthand the rise of the Soviet Union, which deeply influenced her advocacy for individualism and her critique of collectivism. Her seminal work, *Atlas Shrugged*, published in 1957, articulates these themes amidst the backdrop of America's evolving societal and political landscape.

Carl Jung, born in Switzerland in 1875, carved his path in psychoanalytic theory during a time of burgeoning interest in the human psyche's depths. His publication of *Psychological Types* in 1921 introduced a groundbreaking approach to understanding human personality, predating Rand's philosophical contributions.

Although there is no evidence to suggest if or how Rand and Jung might have influenced each other, the contemporaneous development of their ideas within the tumultuous 20th century provides fertile ground for comparison. Rand, with her focus on the philosophical implications of individual psychology within the context of American liberalism, and Jung, with his deep dive into the complexities of the human psyche from a more clinical and analytical standpoint, both contributed uniquely to our understanding of the individual's role within society.

Their positionalities—Rand as a Russian immigrant influenced by the rise of totalitarianism, and Jung, as a Swiss psychiatrist developing the foundations of psychoanalysis—offer distinct perspectives that, when juxtaposed, enrich the dialogue between psychology and philosophy. This book seeks to bridge these perspectives, exploring how their conceptions of human nature and morality can inform a more nuanced understanding of ethics, especially in the context of America's political philosophy and its foundational emphasis on individual rights.

At their core, the concept of psychological types from Jung, and sense of life and psycho-epistemology from Rand, address the human mind's automatized methods of functioning. In *Psychological Types,* Jung outlined his observations on personality archetypes, delving into the conscious and subconscious aspects of the mind influenced by individuals' attitudes and psychological functions. Rand, in her exploration of sense of life and psycho-epistemology, similarly observes automatized mental processes. Her nonfiction often discusses rationalists, empiricists, concrete-bound thinking, "secondhandedness," and integration—themes that echo the psychological functions Jung described. However, while there is significant overlap in their ideas, Rand's treatment of these concepts often adopts a more idealized approach, particularly evident in her essays "Philosophy and Sense of Life" and "The Comprachicos," where she elaborates on one's sense of life and psycho-epistemological development and application.

Contrasting Rand's detailed exploration with Jung's analytical approach reveals both common ground and divergent paths in their examination of the psyche. Jung provides a comprehensive analysis of the psyche's functional components, offering a professional psychiatric perspective that complements and helps expand one's understanding of the subsequently-developed Randian concepts sense of life and psycho-epistemology. This comparison not only highlights their contributions but also illustrates the richness that a dialogue between psychology and philosophy can bring to understanding the human condition.

The works of both thinkers have many similarities, and it is this intersection of psychology and philosophy, particularly in their approaches to human nature and morality, that first led me to the idea of using a comparison of the two to examine the proper method of conceiving ethics. In the subsequent sections of this book, I will go on to compare Jung's findings, including some cases he cites throughout history in his book *Psychological Types* supporting his conclusions, with various nonfiction essays and passages from some of Ayn Rand's novels—all to show where and how their concepts within psychology and philosophy intersect.

My goal is to change the expectation as it pertains to philosophical conclusion, from generalizing principles that overlook individual psychological orientations, to an approach that integrates these orientations, recognizing the diverse contributions of each type. Understanding issues from more than one rational standpoint is essential, and in Jung's framework, extroversion and introversion represent these standpoints.

While it is true that psychological types have faced scrutiny—for example, society often stereotypically labels introverts as withdrawn or antisocial, and extroverts as overly dominant or superficial—such critiques miss the underlying value each type brings to society. Instead of criticizing a type for their intrinsic characteristics, a more enlightened philosophical approach should acknowledge the intrinsic value of all types, recognizing that each contributes positively to societal dynamics in their own unique way. Indeed, the pathway to a more harmonious society lies in a philosophy that leverages the strengths of all types to uplift everyone, respecting individual values and rights.

If we are to truly acknowledge the core American tenet of individual value and rights for all, then our philosophical underpinnings must account for these varying perspectives, offering a cohesive intellectual framework that reduces conflicts between them in the broader society. This approach establishes an environment in which individuals, regardless of their automatized psychological functioning, hold themselves accountable for the impact of their actions on others. The endurance of types within this framework suggests that they are not only purposeful but also necessary; their mere existence indicates this possibility.

The efforts of my argument in this book are to acknowledge the legitimacy of each type and promote their acceptance in social engagement. However, this social acceptance does not automatically extend to leadership roles within American government because true fulfillment of those roles demands a perspective in line with the country's principles.

There are some important things to remember throughout the reading of this book.

First, much of the material used here comes from philosophers and intellectuals, with the result it focuses heavily on the thinking function, as opposed to its rational counterpart, feeling, or the irrational functions of sensation or intuition.

Secondly, I tend to interchange some words throughout the text: I often use introverted, abstract, subjective, and individual synonymously, while I also use extroverted, concrete, objective, and collective in an equivalent manner. In a later examination of the concept of force, I use the terms sensation, experience, consequence, and force interchangeably.

Additionally, it is crucial to clarify the terminology used regarding consciousness. Jung extensively discussed the "unconscious," which includes both the personal and collective aspects that influence our behavior without our direct awareness. In this text, I will use "subconscious" to describe phenomena that occur without conscious intention, as this term is more commonly understood and avoids any neuro-cognitive confusion that might arise from the use of "unconscious." This choice is consistent with everyday usage and helps maintain clarity, while "unconscious" will be specifically used to refer to Jung's psychological constructs.

When discussing Jung's psychological types, I speak of each as Jung does, as a pure type—but this is never the case in real life. The specific psychological function—in other words, the mental process that influences how an individual perceives the world and makes decisions—that predominates in the subject's psyche dictates that person's type.

It is also important to acknowledge what we will soon examine in the writings of Rand speaks mostly about psychology from a philosophical standpoint, while what we will be investigating in the work of Jung is a scientific account of the dynamics of the psyche and the processes underlying personality development based on analytical psychology. Jung rarely let slip any of his moral positions on the different personality types, while Rand was forthcoming and outright with such judgments.

Though the ideas here may initially seem complicated, the goal is that the book's message finishes clearly and simply.

PART I

Basic Principles, Axioms, and Definitions

Part I of this book equips the reader with an essential understanding of the concepts and principles foundational to Americanism, Objectivism, and Jungian psychology. These themes weave throughout the narrative, serving as the backbone for deeper explorations of ethics, politics, and the psyche in the subsequent chapters. The interplay among these three main themes enriches our discussion, allowing for a nuanced examination of the individual's role in society and governance, the philosophical underpinnings of personal freedom and responsibility, and the psychological dynamics that influence our perceptions and decisions.

America's Foundational Principles

$$\star \bigstar \star$$

The founding fathers established the United States on the core principles that emphasize the role and rights of the individual. The architects of America laid the cornerstone of what would become not merely a democracy but a constitutional republic, firmly rooted in these axioms. These guiding principles reflect the vision and values that the founders intended to instill within the framework of the nation. This section delves into the core principles, which today still stand as pillars of the nation, which highlight the significance of the individual within America's foundational structure.

Liberty and Individual Rights

Central to America's foundational principles is the concept of liberty as the foundation for individual rights. The Declaration of Independence (US 1776) enshrines these concepts; the U.S. Constitution (US 1787) and its amendments protect them. Liberty, in this context, refers to the freedom of individuals to pursue their own lives, make their own choices, and fulfill their own potential, limited only by the necessity to respect the equal rights of others.

The U.S. recognizes and protects individual rights, which are natural, inalienable entitlements not bestowed by any government. These rights encompass, among other things, the rights to life, liberty, and the pursuit of happiness. Ensuring the protection of these rights is paramount, as society considers them inherent to the dignity and worth of every individual.

The Constitutional Republic

The founders established the U.S. as a constitutional republic, a crucial distinction from Great Britain's constitutional monarchy, which reflects their dedication to individual rights. In this system, the U.S. Constitution is the supreme law, designed to protect the individual from the tyranny of the majority and the overreach of governmental powers. The role of elected representatives is not merely to enact the will of the majority but to safeguard the rights of all individuals, especially minorities.

This governance structure emphasizes the rule of law, checks and balances, and the separation of powers, all aimed at ensuring that no single entity or group can easily undermine the rights of the individual. The system recognizes the potential for power to corrupt and endeavors to distribute authority in a manner that upholds the freedoms of individuals.

The Principle of Equality

Inextricably linked with the notions of liberty and individual rights is the principle of equality. This principle asserts that all individuals are equal before the law and have the same intrinsic value regardless of their background, beliefs, or socioeconomic status. Equality does not imply identical treatment or outcomes but equal consideration and respect for the rights of each person.

The axiom of equality challenges the polity to continuously strive toward a more inclusive and fair society, one in which every individual can succeed and contribute to the community's wellbeing. It serves as a reminder and a goal, guiding the evolution of laws and policies to better reflect the ideals of fairness and justice.

Conclusion

The foundational principles of liberty, individual rights, the nature of a constitutional republic, and the ideal of equality constitute the bedrock upon which America stands. The nation's very identity and its vision of governance intertwine with these principles. They compel not only the protection of the rights and freedoms of each person but also the perpetual effort to refine and improve the republic in accordance with these enduring values. This commitment to the individual and their inherent rights and freedoms is what defines the American political landscape, distinguishing it as a unique experiment in self-governance and liberty.

Axioms of Objectivism

═══════════════ ★ ★ ★ ═══════════════

Objectivism, the philosophical system developed by Ayn Rand, places the individual at the center of its ethical, metaphysical, and epistemological frameworks. This philosophy asserts a few fundamental axioms as self-evident truths, serving as the foundation upon which all its principles rest. This section explores the core Objectivist axioms.

Existence Exists

The primary axiom of Objectivism is that "existence exists." This assertion forms the base of Objectivist metaphysics, recognizing reality as objective and independent of human feelings, wishes, hopes, or fears. For the individual, this means acknowledging that one cannot alter reality by mere desires but must be engaged with and understood as it is. The acknowledgment of an objective reality is crucial for guiding rational behavior and decision-making.

Consciousness

Closely related to the axiom that existence exists is the axiom of consciousness: the faculty of perceiving that which exists. Consciousness does not create reality but is a means of becoming aware of reality. This axiom highlights the role of the mind in identifying and interpreting the facts of the world. Objectivism asserts that individuals attain knowledge through reason, engaging in a process of concept-formation and logical deduction rooted in sensory evidence.

Identity: A is A

The Law of Identity states that everything is what it is, that entities have specific natures and attributes that define them. This principle, encapsulated in the formula "A is A," is an axiom of Objectivism and serves as the basis of its metaphysical view. It implies that contradictions cannot exist and that to attempt to deal with reality by embracing contradictions is to invite declination and failure.

Implications of Objectivist Axioms

These axioms lay the groundwork for the entire Objectivist philosophy, which logically extends these fundamental truths into a comprehensive worldview:

Epistemology

Objectivism holds that reason is man's only means of acquiring knowledge. This stance builds on the axioms by emphasizing a reality that exists independently of perceptions and a consciousness that must adhere to the law of identity.

Ethics

The axiom that "existence exists" leads to the recognition of the fact that life is the standard of value. The Objectivist ethics, then, is based on rational self-interest, with happiness as the moral purpose of one's life. This ethical framework arises naturally from the axioms advocating for actions in accordance with reality and one's nature as a rational being.

Politics

Objectivist politics derives its principles of individual rights and laissez-faire capitalism from its ethical stance, which, in turn, rests on its axioms. Objectivism proposes a political system where the rule of law protects the freedom of the individual, grounded in the acknowledgment of objective reality and the sovereignty of the individual's mind.

Conclusion

The axioms of Objectivism form the foundation of a philosophy that inherently values the individual. While not explicitly laid out for individuals, the logical extensions of these axioms culminate in a worldview that champions individual rights, freedom, and rational self-interest. This framework provides a compelling argument for a society structured around the recognition of objective reality and the vital role of the individual's mind in navigating it.

Jungian Psychological Types

★ ★ ★

Carl Jung structures his psychological-type framework around four basic dichotomies. The first dichotomy explores attitudes, specifically differentiating between introversion (i) and extroversion (e). These attitudes set the direction of one's libido, which Jung conceptualizes as psychic energy. This psychic energy represents the intensity or psychological value of a psychic process, devoid of any moral, aesthetic, or intellectual considerations.

The second major classification places psychological functions into rational and irrational categories. Within these categories lie the third set of dichotomies: thinking (T) and feeling (F) under rational functions, and sensation (S) and intuition (N) under irrational functions. According to Jung, reflection decisively shapes rational functions as they conform to established laws of reason. These functions aim for decisions and judgments and are expressions of human adaptability to commonly recurring experiences. In contrast, irrational functions are rooted in pure perception. These functions operate beyond the limits of reason, capturing the entirety of direct sensory experiences and intuitive insights. It is essential to note that the term "irrational" here does not signify something contrary to reason, but rather pertains to processes that are driven by perceptions and intuitions that do not adhere to conventional logical reasoning, such as spontaneous emotional responses or instinctual reactions to environmental stimuli.

The fourth and final dichotomy concerns the conscious and unconscious realms of the mind. Together, these central concepts and dichotomies serve as the foundational building blocks for Jung's psychological archetypes. Subsequent sections of this primer will offer a deeper exploration of each term, introduce character notation for easier reference, and clarify how these foundational concepts integrate to form Jungian archetypes.

Attitudes

The fundamental premise of Jung's work on psychological types rests on the differences between introversion and extroversion, or what he calls attitude types. A common misconception today is that these attitudes center solely on superficial ideas, for example that extroverts derive their energy from engaging with people, whereas introverts recharge through time alone. While there is some truth to these observations, this interpretation is an oversimplification of Jung's intended meaning. Jung's true definition of introversion and extroversion centers on the subject's attitude toward the external world or internal world, respectively. This orientation shapes their attitudes toward all objects of perception, not just social interactions, and includes a wide range of external and internal stimuli.

For example, consider two individuals at a social gathering. The extroverted individual may engage eagerly with the environment, focusing on external details like conversations, food, and music. They are likely to initiate interactions and share opinions, validating their experiences through the external world. In contrast, the introverted individual might engage less with the environment and more with their internal reactions to it—thoughts, feelings, or sensory experiences. They validate their experience not through the object or external world but through internal reflection.

According to Jung, the person who habitually prioritizes themselves—i.e., the subject—over the object is an introverted type. Conversely, the person who habitually prioritizes the object of their interest over themselves is an extroverted type. This tendency, in combination with one's inclination toward a specific psychological function, dictates how a person is likely to perceive reality and make judgments.

While one aspect or side of this relationship will dominate, creating a "type," the side's counterpart never completely vanishes, as both processes are indispensable to the psychological makeup of a socialized human. There can never be a pure type for this reason.

Jung's explanation of the attitudes is as follows:

> *The introvert's attitude is an abstracting one; at bottom, he is always intent on withdrawing libido[11] from the object, as though he had to prevent the object from gaining power over him. The extrovert, on the contrary, has a positive relation to the object. He affirms its importance to such an extent that his subjective attitude is constantly related to and oriented by the object. The object can never have enough value for him, and its importance must always be increased.[12]*

Of the attitudes of extroversion and introversion respectively, Jung writes,

> *The one achieves its end by a multiplicity of relationships, the other by monopoly.[13]*

---

[11] Jung used the term "libido" to refer to the general psychic energy that drives all human behaviors and motivations, not just sexual ones. He saw libido as a transformative and creative force that could be channeled into various pursuits, and he associated it with the collective unconscious and the process of psychological growth and self-realization.

[12] (Jung 1923, 307)

[13] (Jung 1923, 309)

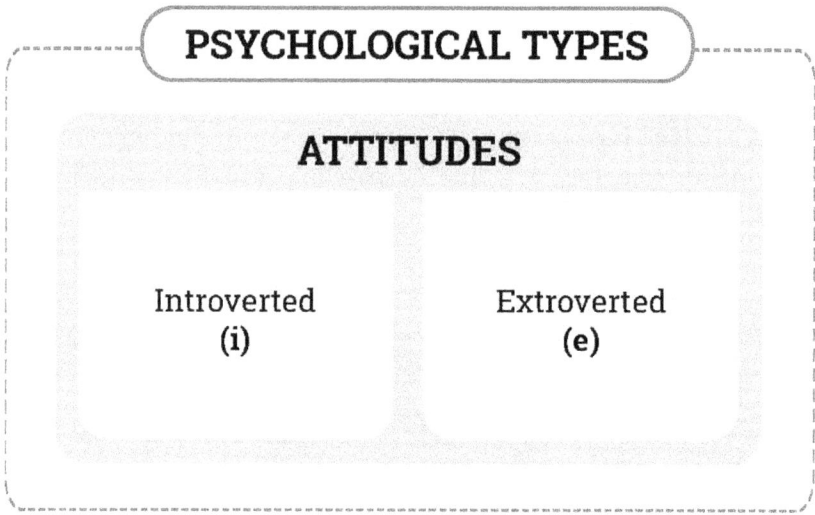

PSYCHOLOGICAL TYPES

ATTITUDES

Introverted
(i)

Extroverted
(e)

Functions

The second core element of Jung's typological framework involves psychological functions, categorized as sensation, intuition, thinking, and feeling. I concur that Jung's list of functions provides an exhaustive catalog of the basic ways in which humans process psychic information.

Broadly, these functions fall into two groups: rational and irrational. The rational functions, which encompass thinking and feeling, primarily aim to make judgments. In Jung's framework, judgment involves evaluating information and making decisions based on certain principles or values. This capacity to judge is what renders these functions "rational," as they rely on structured reasoning or emotional valuation.

In contrast, the irrational functions—sensation and intuition—are concerned with perception. Perception, in this context, refers to the way we become aware of things, people, occurrences, or ideas. These functions do not aim to evaluate or judge what one perceives, but rather to simply take in the information as it is. This is why Jung termed these functions "irrational," signifying not a lack of reason but a form of engagement not strictly governed by rational evaluation.

Each group contrasts the functions diametrically: Sensation opposes intuition, and thinking opposes feeling.

To better conceptualize these functions and their interactions, it may be useful to consider them in terms of axes. Envisioning the functions in this way illuminates how a dominant function takes the lead in one's psychological orientation, while the subordinate function serves a supportive, secondary role. This binary structure provides the foundation for understanding the complex interplay of psychological types, as we will explore in subsequent sections.

The term "binary" in this context indicates a pair of opposing functions within their respective categories. That is, one either employs thinking or feeling to make judgments, and either uses sensation or intuition for perception. There is no additional possibility that blends these functions; they are mutually exclusive in their operation. In this manner, the framework remains strictly dichotomous, underlining the absence of a middle ground or hybrid functional orientation.

It is important to note, however, that although the framework is dichotomous, individuals often display varying degrees of preference for one function over the other within each pair. This gradient of preference adds another layer of complexity to one's psychological profile. While the functions themselves operate in a binary fashion, the degree to which one function dominates can vary, making the psychological landscape of each person uniquely nuanced.

Irrational Functions

Jung refers to sensation and intuition as irrational functions, commonly known today as perceiving functions. According to Jung,

15

these functions are fundamental to both infantile and primitive psychology, which operate independently of rational evaluation.

Sensation

Sensation serves as our direct channel to both the external and internal worlds and is the entry point of all percepts, or sense-data, we encounter. This includes not just what we can see, touch, smell, hear, or taste, but also involves our awareness of internal physiological changes such as a fluctuation in heart rate or stomach discomfort. Jung's definition of sensation is comprehensive. He states,

> Sensation is the psychological function that mediates the perception of a physical stimulus. It is, therefore, identical with perception.[14]

In Jung's view, sensation extends beyond external stimuli to encompass internal stimuli, specifically, changes in internal organic processes. Sensation is an element of ideation and feeling, since it conveys perceptual images of external objects to the mind and, through the perception of bodily changes, influences the character of affect, or the outward expression of inner feelings and emotions.

Concrete versus Abstract in Sensation

Jung makes a critical distinction between "concrete" and "abstract" sensation. Concrete sensation always mixes with other psychic elements such as ideas, feelings, and thoughts, and it primarily reacts. In contrast, abstract sensation is a differentiated form of perception that focuses solely on a particular sensory attribute, for instance the vivid redness of a flower, entirely removed from all other influences.

---

[14] (Jung 1923, 423)

This abstract form is often associated with artists and is a product of functional differentiation.

- **Concrete**: When you touch a hot stove, the immediate sensation of pain leads to a quick withdrawal of your hand. This is a concrete sensory reaction that prompts an immediate response.
- **Abstract**: An artist might focus solely on the interplay of light and shadow on a landscape, contemplating how these elements contribute to the overall aesthetic experience, without immediately reacting to it.

Intuition

The intuition function serves to transform and counterbalance the strong sensory impressions by mediating perceptions of mythological images, which are the forerunners of rational ideas. Much like sensation, intuition is a characteristic feature of both infantile and primitive psychology. The mind subconsciously processes these impressions to construct what we can term an "ideational concrete" way of thinking—wherein a structure of meaning attached to raw sense data.

Example: Imagine a scientist who suddenly grasps the solution to a complex mathematical problem. She may not immediately be able to explain how she arrived at the solution but feels a deep sense of certainty about her conclusion. This demonstrates Jung's idea of intuition as a form of "instinctive apprehension."

Jung defines intuition as follows:

> It is the function that mediates perceptions in an unconscious way... In intuition a content presents itself whole and complete, without our being able to explain or discover

> *how this content came into existence. Intuition is a kind of*
> *instinctive apprehension, no matter of what contents.*[15]

According to Jung, intuitive knowledge possesses an intrinsic certainty and conviction, allowing some philosophers to consider it a form of highest knowledge. This certainty arises from a particular state of psychic "alertness," whose origins remain unconscious to the individual.

Jung also delves into subjective and objective forms of intuition. Subjective intuition is a perception of subconscious psychic data originating in the individual, whereas objective intuition perceives data dependent on subliminal perceptions of the object and the thoughts and feelings they evoke.

Concrete versus Abstract in Intuition

As with sensation, Jung distinguishes between concrete and abstract forms of intuition. Concrete intuition mediates perceptions related to the actuality of things, and is reactive. In contrast, abstract intuition, like abstract sensation, requires a directed focus and aims to mediate perceptions of ideational connections.

- **Concrete**: Consider a detective who arrives at a crime scene. He immediately senses something is off about the placement of objects in the room, although he cannot initially articulate why. This is concrete intuition at work.
- **Abstract**: A philosopher pondering ethical theories might suddenly grasp a deep interconnection between concepts that seem unrelated on the surface, even if they cannot immediately rationalize this understanding. This would be an example of abstract intuition.

---

[15] (Jung 1923, 415-416)

Although Jung classifies intuition as an irrational function, one can often break it down into its component elements to align with the laws of reason, making it a complex and nuanced element of Jung's typological framework.

Rational Functions

Thinking and feeling, as delineated by Jung, are rational functions—commonly referred to today as judging functions. Both functions are engaged in imparting judgments on the contents of ideation and sensations but do so following different laws and norms.

Thinking

Thinking, in Jung's framework, is a conscious and directed intellectual judgment that is an apperceptive activity, or an assimilative process. Its primary aim is to establish conceptual relations among ideas, adhering to its inherent laws of logic. Jung importantly distinguishes this from mere ideation or what he later terms "intuitive thinking," which is the association or stringing together of ideas without active conceptual judgment. He categorizes thinking into the following forms:

- **Active Thinking**: An act of will, a directed function that voluntarily evaluates and organizes thoughts according to known, rational norms.
  - ○ **Example**: In a financial analysis, utilizing predetermined financial models and metrics to assess the profitability of a new project exemplifies active thinking.

- **Passive Thinking**: This is an undirected form of thinking that organizes and evaluates content autonomously, often following norms not consciously recognized.
  - ○ **Example**: In a strategic planning meeting, a financial analyst might spontaneously realize that a proposed cost-saving measure would risk long-term profitability,

even without immediate data to back this insight. This "gut-feeling" is subject to later validation through active, deliberate analysis.

Concrete versus Abstract in Thinking

In the realm of thinking, "concrete" often refers to dealing with facts, data, and observable phenomena, while the "abstract" deals with theories, principles, and underlying frameworks.

- **Concrete**: Using predetermined financial models and metrics to evaluate the profitability of a new project.
- **Abstract**: Discerning that a particular business venture is in alignment with one's long-term ethical or personal values. To elaborate on this, consider the work of Michael Porter, a personal favorite of mine in the field of strategic management and competitive strategy. Porter's theories on competitive advantage and industry dynamics are more than merely descriptive. They require a level of abstract thinking that compels one to look beyond surface-level facts and examine the underlying forces at play. This is a form of introverted thinking that focuses on the internal consistency and logical structure of theories, rather than on simply explaining easily observable phenomena.

Feeling

The feeling function in Jung's framework is a form of subjective judgment. Its primary aim is not to establish conceptual relations, as is the case with thinking, but rather to establish a subjective criterion of acceptance or rejection. Feeling evaluates the worth of objects or ideas in terms of like or dislike, good or bad, assigning them a value based on subjective criteria. Jung distinguishes this function from "feeling-sensation," clarifying that feeling, as a form of judgment, "produces no perceptible physical innervations."[16]

- **Active Feeling**: An act of will, a conscious function that voluntarily evaluates content according to personal values or emotional criteria.
  - **Example**: When negotiating a business deal, consciously considering the trustworthiness of the other party, and factoring it into the decision-making process is an example of active feeling.

- **Passive Feeling**: This form of feeling is less directed and more spontaneous, often arising unbidden. It evaluates content autonomously based on internal or less consciously recognized norms.
  - **Example**: An executive might have an immediate sense of discomfort or discord when considering a proposed company direction, even if all the logical parameters seem sound.

Concrete versus Abstract in Feeling

In the realm of feeling, the "concrete" may involve immediate emotional responses to specific situations or stimuli, whereas the "abstract" involves more generalized emotional or value-based frameworks that guide decision-making.

- **Concrete**: Trusting a business partner based on their consistent, positive behavior in past transactions.
- **Abstract**: Sensing that a particular business venture is in alignment with one's long-term ethical or personal values.

---

[16]   (Jung 1923, 399)

Additional Points

Feeling, passive thinking, and intuition share some similarities: Each involves less consciously directed processes and is more spontaneously emergent. These functions often draw on subconscious or preconscious mechanisms to offer insights, judgments, or ideas. By understanding these cognitive functions in both their active and passive states, and in their concrete and abstract dimensions, we can gain a more holistic view of human decision-making and cognition.

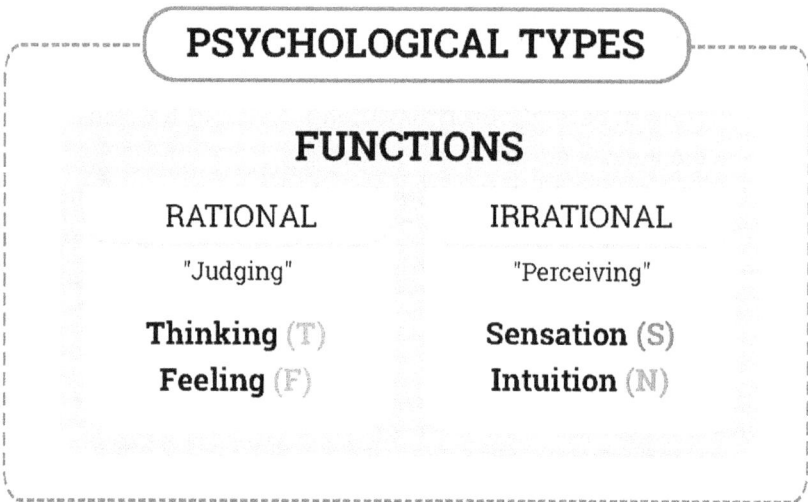

```
┌─────────────  PSYCHOLOGICAL TYPES  ─────────────┐
│                                                 │
│                    FUNCTIONS                    │
│                                                 │
│        RATIONAL              IRRATIONAL         │
│                                                 │
│        "Judging"            "Perceiving"        │
│                                                 │
│      Thinking (T)           Sensation (S)       │
│      Feeling (F)            Intuition (N)        │
│                                                 │
└─────────────────────────────────────────────────┘
```

Functional Attitudes

Jung proposed that each function can manifest as either introverted or extroverted (i.e., abstract or concrete) resulting in two binary functional attitudes for each of the four psychological functions. This creates eight total functions in all.

When thinking about the orientation of these psychological functions in axial form, the dominant side of the orientation is under relative conscious control, while the opposing side remains a subconscious process.

FUNCTIONAL ATTITUDES

	THINKING (T)	FEELING (F)
Rational	Introverted Thinking (**Ti**)	Introverted Feeling (**Fi**)
	Extroverted Thinking (**Te**)	Extroverted Feeling (**Fe**)
	Extroverted Thinking (**Te**)	Extroverted Feeling (**Fe**)
	Introverted Thinking (**Ti**)	Introverted Feeling (**Fi**)
	SENSATION (S)	**INTUITION (N)**
Irrational	Extroverted Sensation (**Se**)	Extroverted Intuition (**Ne**)
	Introverted Sensation (**Si**)	Introverted Intuition (**Ni**)
	Introverted Sensation (**Si**)	Introverted Intuition (**Ni**)
	Extroverted Sensation (**Se**)	Extroverted Intuition (**Ne**)

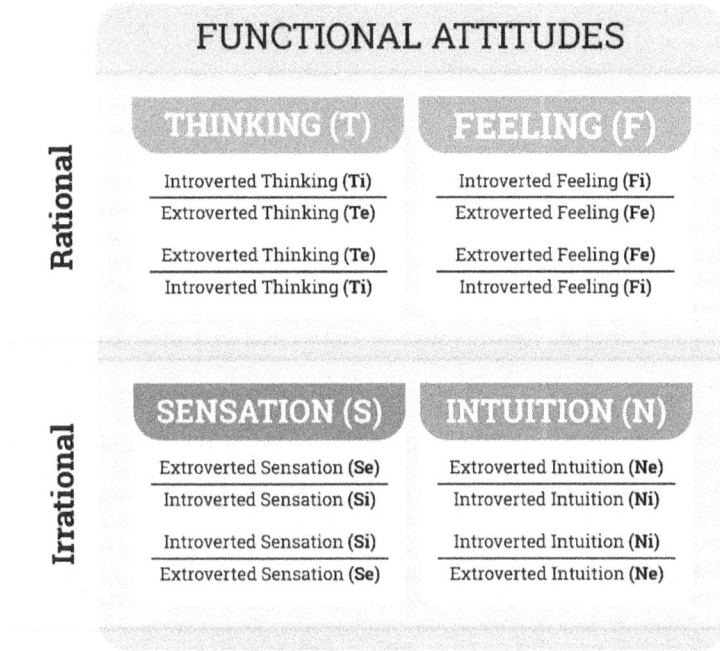

Function Axes

Employing the axial form for visual illustration, each psychological function exists in two orientations: introverted and extroverted. This dual nature results in eight total orientations: Four are rational, also known as judging functions (Thinking and Feeling), and four are irrational, also known as perceiving functions (Sensation and Intuition).

FUNCTIONAL AXES

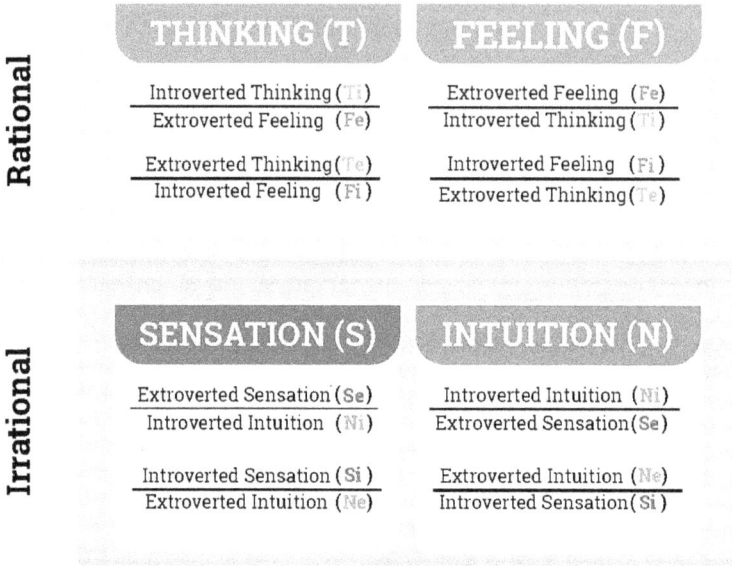

	THINKING (T)	FEELING (F)
Rational	Introverted Thinking (Ti) / Extroverted Feeling (Fe)	Extroverted Feeling (Fe) / Introverted Thinking (Ti)
	Extroverted Thinking (Te) / Introverted Feeling (Fi)	Introverted Feeling (Fi) / Extroverted Thinking (Te)

	SENSATION (S)	INTUITION (N)
Irrational	Extroverted Sensation (Se) / Introverted Intuition (Ni)	Introverted Intuition (Ni) / Extroverted Sensation (Se)
	Introverted Sensation (Si) / Extroverted Intuition (Ne)	Extroverted Intuition (Ne) / Introverted Sensation (Si)

The Conscious Mind

Carl Jung argues that every individual uses all eight psychological functions to varying degrees. However, one's psychological type—defined as the pattern of priority given to the functions—is determined by the four functions primarily used in the conscious mind. These functions make up what Jung referred to as the ego, or the part of the mind that mediates between the individual and the external world.

Conversely, the unconscious part of the mind houses the remaining four functions, rendering them less accessible for deliberate action or "command," as it were. They operate more autonomously, often without our conscious intention or awareness. Taking the example of a person who is categorized as an INTJ, which refers to someone who primarily utilizes introverted intuition and extroverted thinking, these unconscious functions include extroverted intuition, introverted thinking, extroverted feeling, and introverted sensation. These functions may manifest in numerous ways, often unpredictably, and usually in response to specific triggers such as stress or excitement.

The conscious mind, responsible for determining one's psychological type, consists of one rational axis and one irrational axis. Meanwhile, the unconscious mind houses the remaining two axes, functioning more autonomously. In everyday life, an INTJ may use their dominant function, introverted intuition, for long-term planning or solving complex problems, while their inferior function, extroverted sensation, can manifest in overindulgence or impulse actions under specific conditions such as high-stress situations.

In each psychological type, one encounters a primary functional axis that harbors the dominant and the inferior functions. Jung terms the latter "inferior" because it lags in the process of differentiation, often becoming less completely identified than the most favored function. The term differentiation in this context refers to the maturing and specialization of psychological functions. The dynamics of societal demands usually compel an individual to hone the function with which they are naturally best equipped, or that which grants the most social success. This one-sided development inevitably retards one or more other functions, rendering them "inferior" in a psychological, but not psychopathological sense. Although the inferior function can be conscious as a phenomenon, its significance often remains underappreciated, functioning as a complex that is partly conscious and partly unconscious.

Additionally, a secondary functional axis exists, composed of the auxiliary and tertiary functions, which form another set of binary functions. The auxiliary function supports the dominant by providing a supplementary mode of adaptation, while the tertiary function offers an additional, albeit less developed, perspective that helps further balance the individual's overall psychological orientation. For instance, in a type where thinking is dominant and feeling is inferior, intuition might serve as the auxiliary function, and sensation as the tertiary, contributing to a more balanced interaction with the world.

Together, these axes not only form both a rational and an irrational axis but also populate the ego-complex at the center of one's field of consciousness. This configuration is exemplified in the INTJ personality type, where the auxiliary function of extroverted thinking helps them organize their environment and achieve objectives, while the tertiary function of introverted feeling serves as a moral compass. This illustrates how different functions play distinct roles in shaping a person's interactions and internal moral framework.

Consciousness, in Jung's terms, maintains the relationship of these psychic contents to the ego. In this manner, individuals become conscious of these functional axes as they perceive them in relation to the ego complex.

The ego-complex itself is but one of many complexes within the broader psyche and represents only the subject of one's consciousness, not the entire self, which also comprises unconscious elements. The inferior function, if not sufficiently integrated into conscious life, can sink wholly or in part into the unconscious, becoming a source of regressive, archaic fantasy formations. The conscious realization of these unconscious elements allows for the potential further development of the inferior function, and by extension, a more balanced ego-complex and self.

Thus, the ego-complex and the functional axes that contribute to it should be viewed as a portion of the psyche that is directly related to consciousness, distinct from the more holistic concept of the "self." This understanding incorporates both the nature of the inferior function and its potential impact on the ego and consciousness. Continuing with the example of the INTJ, the following graphic illustrates the functions and axes of the conscious mind.

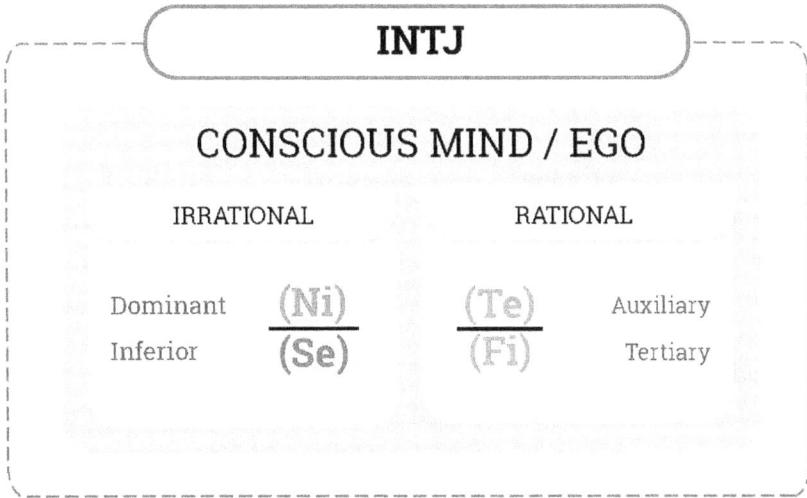

INTJ			
CONSCIOUS MIND / EGO			
IRRATIONAL		RATIONAL	
Dominant	(Ni)	(Te)	Auxiliary
Inferior	(Se)	(Fi)	Tertiary

The Types

Today, many people encounter Jungian psychological types through the four-letter code provided by the Myers-Briggs Type Indicator (MBTI). Isabel Briggs Myers and Katharine Cook Briggs created this test, inspired by Carl Jung's theories, to identify an individual's psychological type.

While fundamentally anchored in Carl Jung's original theories, the MBTI introduces refinements and complexities that were not present in Jung's framework. Originally, Jung identified eight psychological types, based on what he called the dominant function, be it thinking, feeling, sensation, or intuition, each coupled with an orientation of introversion or extroversion. Isabel Myers, drawing from Jung's foundational ideas, extended this schema by adding a fourth dichotomy of "Judging" (J) and "Perceiving" (P), which her mother, Katharine, had previously posited as an implicit but unexplored aspect of Jung's typology.[17]

---

[17] (Emre 2018, 131)

Myers articulated that every cognitive act is either an act of perception—becoming aware of something—or an act of judgment—forming a conclusion about something. She used this J/P dichotomy to clarify the roles of "dominant" and "auxiliary" functions in an individual's personality. In her model, if a person is a perceiving type, their dominant function is one of the two perceptive functions: sensation or intuition. Conversely, if a person is a Judging type, their dominant function is one of the two judging functions: thinking or feeling.[18]

This addition expanded the number of types to sixteen and added a layer of intricacy, allowing for nuanced insights but also creating areas for confusion, especially when attempting to align this framework with Jung's original categorizations of rational and irrational types.

In the MBTI system, one considers an INTJ a judging or "rational" type because of the recognition of their utilization of extroverted thinking. However, Jung would classify an individual with an INTJ personality type as an irrational or "perceiving" type because the dominant function is introverted intuition, an irrational function.

The discrepancy I observe in the MBTI's classification method stems from its being set from the perspective of an observer, classifying individuals as either judgers or perceivers based on their extroverted function, which Myers recognizes as being "dominant." If their dominant extroverted function is rational, manifesting as either extroverted thinking or extroverted feeling, we categorize a subject as a judging type. This occurs because individuals express the extroverted rational function externally and in a manner that is easily observable, such as making decisions, organizing, or engaging with the world in a structured manner.

---

[18] ibid

On the other hand, if a subject's extroverted function is irrational, expressed as either extroverted sensation or extroverted intuition, the MBTI system classifies the subject as a perceiving type. In these cases, the rational function operates within the internal psychological landscape of the individual; an outside observer may find it challenging to readily observe the process of reasoning, judging, or valuing, as individuals internally engage in that process and may not overtly express it. This contrasts with extroverted rational types, whose external actions readily reveal their rational functions.

Interpreters could view this adjustment to Jung's original concept in multiple ways—either as an enhancement that addresses a previously neglected area, or as a modification that might distort the original theoretical intent. The J/P classification negates an introverted subject's preferred attitude and detaches it from the preferred function. This adds an unnecessary layer of confusion to typing with Jung's concepts. Jung's work does not substantiate Myers's claim that extroversion dictates the dominant function.

In contrast to the MBTI, Socionics—a psychological theory originating from Lithuania and popular in Eastern Europe—adheres more closely to Jung's original framework concerning the judging and perceiving classifications. Unlike the MBTI, which adjusts these categories based on the orientation of the dominant extroverted function, Socionics maintains the classification according to the individual's dominant function, whether introverted or extroverted. This means that, in Socionics, an INTJ remains a "perceiving" or "irrational" type due to the dominance of introverted intuition, consistent with Jung's original categorization. This approach avoids the potential for confusion that arises from the MBTI's method of assigning judging or perceiving labels based on extroverted functions. Therefore, while the MBTI diverges from Jung's original concepts in this aspect, Socionics offers a system that remains more faithful to them.

The MBTI-typing mechanism does deliver some analytical value, however, particularly in how it reveals the auxiliary function of an individual, extending beyond Jung's initial framework which focused primarily on the dominant function itself. Jung hinted at the significance of this secondary function, which pairs with the dominant function to influence one's psychological state.

According to Jung, the auxiliary function serves a supportive role, enhancing the dominant function by offering a complementary perspective. For example, if thinking is the dominant function, it can effectively partner with either intuition or sensation but never with feeling. This is because, unlike feeling, which competes directly with thinking, intuition and sensation are perceptive functions that align well with and augment the thought process.

This complementary relationship becomes particularly salient when considering the array of daily cognitive activities that necessitate both judgment and perception. Observations reveal that the auxiliary function is beneficial to the extent that it remains subordinate to the dominant function, without seeking its own autonomy.

Should the auxiliary functions of intuition or sensation attain a level of differentiation comparable to the dominant thinking function— whereby they become separated from other functions and operate independently—they could disrupt the cognitive orientation by shifting it from a judgment-focused to a perception-focused mindset. This would compromise the essential rationality underpinning the thinking function. Therefore, the auxiliary function's value lies in its ability to bolster the dominant function while maintaining a collaborative rather than competitive relationship.

In considering the auxiliary function, Jung himself did not explicitly incorporate this concept into his typological framework, leaving a gap that the MBTI effectively addresses. Given that individuals must employ perception and judgment constantly in their daily lives, the MBTI's emphasis on identifying both dominant and auxiliary functions adds a layer of nuance absent from Jung's original types. Specifically, it reveals the distinct perception and judgment functions one prefers for these activities.

Moreover, one should not overlook the role of the auxiliary function as it serves the dominant function. This relationship is particularly noteworthy when considering that the MBTI framework might imply a false equivalence between the dominant and auxiliary functions, potentially diluting the distinct servitude relationship posited by Jung.

It is important to consider that Isabel Briggs Myers's aim was not to overwrite Jung's conceptual groundwork but rather to build upon it. Therefore, one could see the MBTI's addition of the judging and perceiving dichotomy as refining or extending Jungian theory, rather than directly contradicting it.

In summary, while the MBTI builds on Jung's work, it also diverges in notable ways, especially in the introduction of the judging and perceiving categories and the emphasis on auxiliary functions. Whether one views these changes as refinements or distortions may depend on perspective, but they undeniably contribute a layer of complexity to the discussion of psychological types.

To offer a nuanced global perspective on the variation and prevalence of MBTI types, the following percentages delineate the distribution of personality types based on a study spearheaded by NERIS,[19] the organization behind the widely used 16personalities.com platform. Distinguished for its melding of the Big Five personality traits with the acronymic nomenclature popularized by Myers-Briggs, NERIS has, to date, amassed data from over forty million respondents in thirty-six languages across numerous countries. The U.S.'s 4,645,382

---

[19] (16personalities.com 2016)

respondents made a significant contribution to the data set. In the diagram below, I have categorized the types in line with the original groupings posited by Jung, whose theories underpin the foundational philosophy of both NERIS and 16personalities.com.

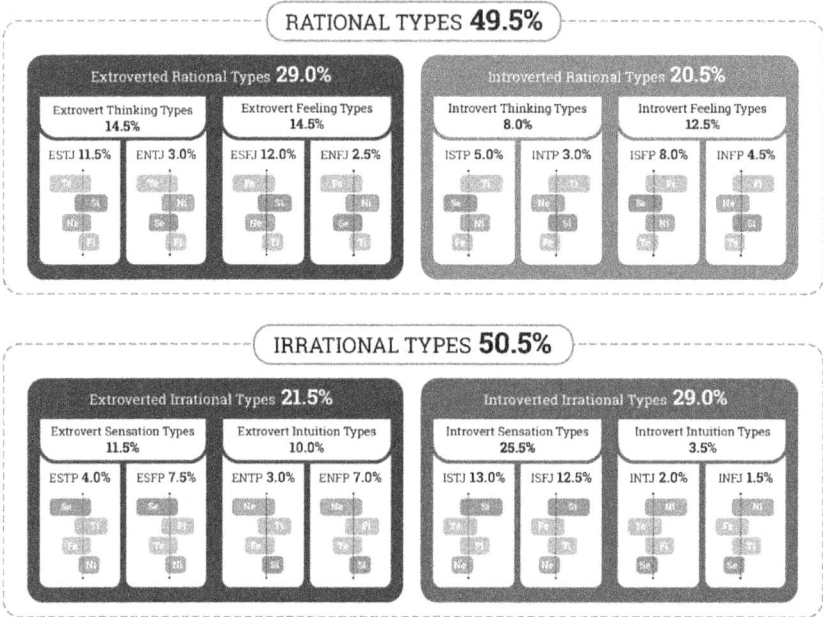

PART II

OBSERVATION

In the following sections of the book, which form the crux of my arguments, I have aimed to provide an in-depth analysis of the synergies between Ayn Rand's Objectivist philosophy and Carl Jung's psychological theories. The journey we embark on through the landscape of psychology and ethics as seen through the lens of Jung and Rand's philosophies, begins with "Philosophy and Sense of Life" and extends through essays including "The Psycho-Epistemology of Art," "Faith and Force: The Destroyers of the Modern World," and others. Weaving a narrative that connects cognitive styles, ethical philosophy, and their political implications, it is my hope to present a critical examination of how our psychological make-up influences our moral and political beliefs, shaping the world we live in. This inquiry aims to assert that integrating the ideas of Rand and Jung can enable us to establish a comprehensive ethical framework, uniquely qualified to support American political philosophy and elucidate the basic concepts laid out in previous sections for a broader audience. Chosen for its comprehensive exploration of American ideals, Objectivist philosophy serves as the catalyst for this nuanced discussion of America's ethics and politics.

Structure and Questions

Each subsection within Part II: Observation will focus on a group of specific essays or texts. At various points, a set of questions will be posed, which a close examination of the texts will strive to answer. These questions aim to promote deeper understanding and stimulate thoughtful analysis. As you read this section, I invite you to engage critically with the material presented. The material, along with the questions will serve as a guide to help you integrate the principles of Objectivist philosophy with Jungian psychology, clarify the intersection between the two, and challenge you to consider their wider implications in the realms of cognition, ethics, and society.

Selection Criteria for Essays

To achieve this synthesis, we will examine several essays written primarily by Rand using Jungian psychology to expand on the psychological aspects implied, thereby providing essential detail, and further clarifying the role individual psychology plays in collective issues in society. We carefully selected each essay in this section based on specific criteria to ensure a comprehensive comparison between Objectivism and Jung's theories. The criteria for selection include:

1. **Relevance to Thematic Categories**: Each essay must align with one of the three overarching themes—Psychology, psychology as it relates to ethics, and ethics as it relates to politics. This pattern ensures a structured exploration from individual psychological underpinnings to their implications in broader ethical and political contexts.

2. **Psychological Implications**: The essay should reveal significant psychological dimensions of Objectivism, offering insights that facilitate a meaningful comparison or contrast with Jung's theories on the psyche.

3. **Contribution to Synthesis**: The selected works must contribute to our understanding by demonstrating how individual psychology informs and reflects collective societal issues, particularly in the realms of ethics and politics.

With these criteria guiding our selection, we organize these essays into the mentioned themes, each serving as the foundation for the intricate discussion that follows. This meticulous approach allows us to delve deeply into the interconnections between individual psychology and societal constructs, shedding light on the nuanced interplay between personal beliefs and collective ethical and political practices.

Foundational Texts

The Romantic Manifesto: A Philosophy of Literature (1969) by Ayn Rand

- **Introduction**: This examination commences with a focus on what may initially seem like an unrelated topic: art. *The Romantic Manifesto*, like many of Ayn Rand's nonfiction works, is a compilation of essays primarily written for and published previously in various outlets, most notably her magazine, *The Objectivist*. Within this publication, two essays are particularly pertinent to the overarching theme of this book, and one essay, "Philosophy and Sense of Life," penned in 1966, serves as the foundational starting point for the discussions that will follow. The book serves as a segue from the realm of art into the deeper territories of psychology and philosophy, making it an often overlooked yet critical subject for examinations such as mine here.

- **Selected Essays**:
  - "Philosophy and Sense of Life" (1966)
  - "The Psycho-Epistemology of Art" (1965)

Philosophy: Who Needs It (1982) by Ayn Rand

- **Introduction**: Published posthumously, this book is a collection of essays written by Rand between 1970 and 1975—most of which first appeared in her newsletter, "The Ayn Rand Letter." With one exception, "Faith and Force: The Destroyers of the Modern World," originally a speech given at Yale University in 1960, these essays serve as essential material for addressing specific psychological questions at the root of Objectivist philosophy. I have selected the following four essays from the book for this examination, emphasizing their pivotal role in exploring the psychological foundations of Objectivism.

- **Selected Essays**:
  - "The Missing Link" (1973)
  - "Selfishness Without a Self" (1974)
  - "Causality Versus Duty" (1974)
  - "Faith and Force: The Destroyers of the Modern World" (1960)

Return of the Primitive: The Anti-Industrial Revolution (1999) by Ayn Rand

- **Introduction**: Originally published in 1971 as *The New Left,* this book, which was primarily intended for contemporary college students, analyzes the political state of the era. In this collection of essays, our focus is on one article, "The Comprachicos," a piece which was, according to Rand, incomplete upon first publication in this volume. Modified substantially for the revised edition, the essay serves to provide a nuanced understanding of the cultural and political climate of that time.

- **Selected Essays**:
  - "The Comprachicos" (1970)

The Voice of Reason: Essays in Objectivist Thought (1990) by Ayn Rand

- **Introduction**: Published posthumously by Rand's estate and her protégé, Leonard Peikoff, this book serves as the final collection of Rand's work, and features a selection of previously unpublished essays, articles, and speeches. Apart from one article published in 1971, each of the pieces in this compilation had never appeared in written form. The essay selected for this examination focuses on the crucial distinction between psychological diagnosis and moral judgment, underscoring the paramount importance of keeping psychology and moral philosophy separate.

- **Selected Essays**:
  - "The Psychology of Psychologizing" (1971)

The Virtue of Selfishness (1964) by Ayn Rand and Nathaniel Branden

- **Introduction**: Focused on the ethics of Objectivism, this collection includes essays by Ayn Rand and Nathaniel Branden, who was a close associate and intellectual partner of Ayn Rand, that originally appeared in "The Objectivist Newsletter." The book explicitly articulates Objectivism's ethical perspective and contains two articles selected to further examine the intersection of philosophy and psychology, one by Rand and one by Branden. These articles serve to explore the psychological concepts employed in Objectivism as well as their relation to Carl Jung's psychological types.

- **Selected Essays**:
  - "Mental Health versus Mysticism and Self-Sacrifice" (1964)
  - "Collectivized Ethics" (1964)

PSYCHOLOGY

Foundational Psychology

The following section establishes crucial groundwork for our exploration of ethics and politics. It examines the role of subconscious beliefs and rational judgment in shaping our moral perspectives, bridging Objectivist philosophy with Jungian psychology. This integration is key to understanding the psychological underpinnings of ethical and political theories. We will probe how deep-seated beliefs, often subconscious, influence our views; and consider if deeper psychological insight can lead to stronger ethical and political frameworks. Designed for both seasoned and new enthusiasts in philosophy and psychology, this section provides a unique perspective on the interplay of mind, morality, and society, aiming to connect our inner psychological world with our external ethical and political realities.

Guiding inquiries for this exploration include:

1. What is the result if one never transitions from an implicit to an explicit view of reality?
2. Is individual rationality required to adapt to a rational environment?
3. How does the transition from a subconscious to a conscious mode of thinking influence one's ethical decision-making?
4. Can an individual's "sense of life" evolve over time to align with their rational philosophy more closely, or is it a static entity?

"Philosophy and Sense of Life"

The theories of Ayn Rand and Carl Jung offer complementary frameworks for understanding individual behavior. Rand's philosophical concept of a "sense of life" and Jung's psychological theory of "irrational functions" both delve into the primal, non-rational forces that shape our rational faculties. By exploring Rand's idea of a sense of life as a pre-conceptual metaphysical value judgment and emotional generalization, alongside Jung's focus on the perceptual level of consciousness through his irrational functions, we aim to present a cohesive understanding of how subconscious emotional patterns influence our worldview and ethical reasoning.

Defining Rand's Sense of Life and Its Psychological Implications

Ayn Rand defines **sense of life** as a "pre-conceptual equivalent of metaphysics," which shapes our choices, values, and character. This emotional response pattern serves as an automatic guide for navigating life from an early age.[20] It is a subconscious appraisal one has of the world and themselves, and which informs the emotional reactions one has to different scenarios or objects. To elaborate, Rand poses:

> *A new neighborhood, a discovery, adventure, struggle, triumph—or: the folks next door, a memorized recitation, a family picnic, a known routine, comfort... Which particular emotions will be invoked by the things in these examples, as their respective common denominators, depends on which set of things fits an individual's view of himself.[21]*

Jung's Irrational Functions and Their Interplay with Rand's Concepts

As we explore the foundational elements that shape an individual's sense of life, the theories of Carl Jung offer additional insights to

---

[20] (Rand, Philosophy and Sense of Life 1966, 14)
[21] (Rand, Philosophy and Sense of Life 1966, 14)

enrich our understanding. By examining the subconscious processes outlined by Jung, particularly the role of the irrational functions—sensation and intuition—we can better discern how these primal forces influence an individual's conceptual development and, in turn, how they reconcile their instinctive emotional responses with their conscious values and beliefs.

As discussed in Part I, according to Jung, instinctual patterns, conditioned both by individual aptitudes and early childhood environments, establish a preferential psychological attitude. This attitude leans toward either introversion or extroversion—with introversion focusing on the internal world of thoughts and feelings, and extroversion oriented toward the external world of objects and people—and further specializes in either sensation or intuition, which he categorizes as irrational functions. This orientation outlines a habitual flow of psychic energy, or what Jung refers to as "libido," setting the foundation for how one engages with the world.

Integration of Rand and Jung: The Underlying Frameworks

Rand and Jung converge on the idea that these foundational frameworks—shaped by emotional generalization and psychological tendencies—become the lens through which we interpret life and make decisions. These frameworks inform both our specific decisions and our broader understanding of existence. In the context of Jungian psychology, one's dominant irrational function—such as introverted sensation, extroverted intuition, introverted intuition, or extroverted sensation—serve as key descriptors that categorize this emotional, subconscious appraisal.

Having laid the theoretical groundwork, we can now proceed to practical examples that demonstrate the integration of these frameworks in real-life situations.

Example: Illustrating the Interplay of Rand's "Sense of Life" and Jung's Irrational Functions

Consider four individuals—Emily, David, Sarah, and Mark—each of whom is an irrational type going through a significant life change: relocation to a new city for work.

Emily is an **introverted sensation** (ISTJ or ISFJ) type. Upon arriving in the new city, Emily's Saturdays are a blend of quiet observation and gentle social interaction. In the morning, she visits a local historical museum, where she enjoys learning about the city's past through artifacts and exhibits, occasionally sharing insights with other visitors in hushed, thoughtful exchanges. Afterwards, she heads to a nearby bistro known for its serene garden patio. There, she enjoys a light lunch, often joined by a close friend or two, discussing their finds of the day and planning their next outing together. Her "sense of life" is introspective, grounded, and practical.

David is an **extroverted intuition** (ENTP or ENFP) type. He perceives the world through abstract possibilities and what could be, rather than what is immediately present. When he moves to the new city, David fills his weekends with activities that stimulate his imagination and broaden his social network. On a typical Saturday, he might attend a creative workshop downtown, followed by a meet-up with a local entrepreneur group at a lively happy hour spot, where they discuss potential business ventures over cocktails. His evenings could be spent at an underground music event, where he thrives on the energy and the possibility of making new connections that could lead to exciting opportunities. His "sense of life" revolves around external engagement, ideas, possibilities, and future achievements.

Sarah is an **introverted intuition** (INTJ or INFJ) type. She often engages in deep reflection about the abstract implications and future possibilities of her unfamiliar environment. Instead of jumping into social activities like David, Sarah spends her Saturdays rejuvenating

43

with a solo morning jog in a scenic park, followed by thoughtful discussions on emerging trends with a select group of intellectuals at a quiet café. These meetings are crucial for her, allowing her to engage deeply with like-minded individuals. Her "sense of life" centers on internally conceptualizing ideas, envisioning long-term possibilities, and experiencing a profound need for intellectual coherence.

Mark is an **extroverted sensation** (ESTP or ESFP) type. He relishes the immediate experiences that his unfamiliar environment offers, quickly joining local sports teams or engaging in community activities that allow him to feel a direct connection with his surroundings. His ideal Saturday starts with a sunrise group hike, engaging equally with both the landscape and his fellow hikers. Afterward, he joins a casual volleyball game at the beach, reveling in the sensation of the sand under his feet and the competitive spirit of the game. Evenings are for exploring the city's nightlife, tasting new foods, and dancing, each moment embraced with his characteristic zest for life. His "sense of life" revolves around immediate, external experiences and he finds fulfillment in active, hands-on engagement with the world.

In each of these cases, the individual's irrational functions shape their "sense of life," much in the way Rand's concept articulates an individual's implicit philosophy and emotional core. These underlying psychological traits operate mostly in the subconscious and serve as a lens through which they view the world.

To connect this analysis of personality types and "sense of life" back to our earlier discussion, the experiences that resonate with Emily, David, Sarah, and Mark act as manifestations of their dominant irrational functions, in which the judgment functions—thinking and feeling— are not only implicitly integrated but also operate from a layer that is less consciously controlled. Whether someone finds appeal in immediate, concrete experiences or in abstract, future possibilities not only reflects these psychological traits but also their underlying "sense of life," which serves as the emotional and psychological foundation for their rational and ethical faculties.

Sense of Life and Rationality

After Rand presents sense of life, she introduces another layer of complexity, explaining that to the extent a person is mentally active and motivated by the desire to know and understand, this mental activity serves as the "programmer" of their emotional responses. Their sense of life, in turn, evolves to mirror a rational philosophy.[22]

While sense of life is a psychological concept related to human perception, it is its integration with rational judgment that completes what in Objectivism is termed one's "psycho-epistemology," forming what is comparable to a Jungian psychological type.

Building on this framework, Rand emphasizes the unique human capability for conceptualization. Unlike non-human animals, who rely solely on immediate perception for survival and decision-making, humans possess an innate capacity for integration and conceptual thought. This cognitive ability allows them to consider past and future events, formulate a philosophy, and guide long-term actions. Both Rand and Jung assert that these faculties can be either consciously activated or serve as subconscious drivers of behavior. Failure to consciously engage these faculties results in stagnant psychological development, comparable to that of a young child, or animal.[23]

The Battle Between Rationality and Instinct in Decision-Making

In the initial stages of life, emotions function as intellectual tools, guiding individuals to instinctually sort and categorize their experiences. This forms an initial sense of life, malleable and subject to

---

22 (Rand, Philosophy and Sense of Life 1966, 15)
23 (Rand, Philosophy and Sense of Life 1966, 15-16)

change as one gains further knowledge and experience. For example, a child might initially find comfort in familiar routines and known environments, but as they encounter new and varied experiences, they may start to integrate these into their sense of life, potentially expanding their comfort zones and adjusting their emotional responses to novelty.

However, as individuals mature, this method of perceptual integration becomes increasingly insufficient. At a certain stage, individuals can transition from functioning instinctually to embracing a more conscious and conceptual approach. This shift signifies the development of a deliberately chosen philosophy of life—a set of rational principles that serves as a yardstick for one's emotional values. Rand emphasizes that while the sense of life continues to function automatically, a well-defined and coherent rational philosophy should guide emotional integrations, making emotions subordinate to cognitive judgments: The mind sets the course, and the emotions follow.[24]

Tracing the Developmental Journey: From Sense of Life to Rational Philosophy

To fully grasp the impact of Rand and Jung's theories, one must consider the developmental stages that shape a person's sense of life and rational philosophy. Despite not being the central theme of Rand's work, the stages of childhood and adolescence are posited as periods in which psychological types typically become established. This occurs as individuals gain confidence in their habitual approaches to life, having used them successfully to navigate various challenges. Although a psychological type rarely changes in a significant way after this point, an individual will always be capable of adjusting their behavior to a rational environment when the situation demands it.

---

[24] (Rand, Philosophy and Sense of Life 1966, 19)

According to Rand, the maturation process necessitates a shift from an implicit, to an explicit metaphysics, where individuals transition from an instinctual mode of functioning to a more conscious, conceptual approach. For instance, a young adult may begin to question the religious or cultural beliefs instilled in childhood, seeking a personal understanding rather than accepting inherited truths.

As individuals mature, their sense of life—or what equates to their preferred conscious attitudes toward the processes of sensation and intuition, per Jung's typology—should gradually yield to rational, conceptual faculties. For example, when an individual chooses a career path by systematically assessing their strengths and market conditions, rather than conforming to career choices influenced by familial expectations or an impulsive interest.

This shift implies that one should increasingly incorporate rational deliberation as the guiding force in decision-making and value formation, rather than relying solely on instinctual emotional responses. Rand goes on to explain how, in many, this process fails to complete over the developmental period,

> *For most men, the transition is a tortured and not fully successful process, leading to a fundamental inner conflict—a clash between a man's conscious convictions and his repressed, unidentified (or only partially identified) sense of life. Very often, the transition is incomplete, as in the case of a man whose convictions are not part of a fully integrated philosophy, but are merely a collection of random, disconnected, often contradictory ideas, and, therefore, are unconvincing to his own mind against the power of his subconscious metaphysics. In some cases, a man's sense of life is better (closer to the truth) than the kind of ideas he accepts. In other cases, his sense of life is much worse than the ideas he professes to accept but is unable fully to practice.*[25]

---

[25]   (Rand, Philosophy and Sense of Life 1966, 19)

The journey from early emotional development to mature rational thinking is complex but crucial for understanding the interplay between Rand and Jung's theories. To elucidate this, let us consider specific examples illustrating the conflict between sense of life and rational philosophy.

Case Study: The Religious Woman's Ethical Dilemma

A woman raised in a deeply religious environment learns from an early age to value faith, divine destiny, and the significance of community within her religious group. These principles shape her sense of life or subconscious metaphysics. As she matures and starts exploring philosophy and science through her university studies and personal reading, engaging in discussions with peers who hold diverse beliefs, she becomes curious about, or even attracted to a worldview that values empirical evidence, skepticism, and rational inquiry.

Now she faces an internal dilemma. On one hand, her rational mind is inclined toward skepticism and empirical thinking. On the other hand, her deeply ingrained sense of life pulls her toward faith and the sense of divine destiny. Every time she thinks about acting based on her newfound rational principles, she might experience a sense of guilt, shame, or even fear of divine retribution, rooted in her early upbringing.

In this situation, she faces a dilemma between her consciously embraced rational philosophy and her subconscious sense of life, influenced by her religious upbringing. This disconnect can manifest in many aspects of her life—career choices, relationships, moral decisions, etc.—and cause significant inner turmoil.

To align her sense of life with her consciously chosen rational principles, she would have to undergo a process of intense introspection and emotional recalibration. This would involve questioning her ingrained beliefs, re-evaluating them through the lens of rationality, and striving to integrate them in a way such that her rational mind leads, and her emotions follow, as Rand would put it.

Case Study: The Altruistic Entrepreneur's Ethical | Balancing Act

Mark has learned that he should prioritize the needs of others over his own as the highest moral virtue. He consciously accepts this idea and often advocates for altruistic causes and policies. However, his sense of life operates differently. As an entrepreneur, Mark understands that to create jobs, innovate, and contribute to society, he must make decisions that are both in his best interest and the best interest of his business, but not necessarily in the best interest of others, per se. For instance, while he might increase the price of a product to maintain business sustainability, he simultaneously struggles with the idea that this decision could make it less affordable for some consumers. Another example is when he chooses to automate a part of his production process to enhance efficiency and cut costs, knowing that it may result in layoffs, which contradicts his altruistic inclination to maximize employee welfare. While he donates a portion of his profits to charitable causes, he knows that blindly putting others' needs before his own would jeopardize not only his livelihood but also the livelihoods of his employees and stakeholders.

This case study serves as a poignant example of the tension that can arise between a person's sense of life and their consciously accepted philosophical principles. Rather than suggesting a need for balance between self-interest and altruism, it highlights how one's innate emotional attitudes may diverge significantly from one's intellectual convictions, thereby complicating the ethical landscape. This divergence underscores the necessity of achieving coherence between one's intuitive sense of life and a rationally-chosen set of guiding principles.

Case Study: The Paradox of Romantic Attraction— Jasmine and Taylor's Introspective Journey

Jasmine and Taylor, a couple who value clear communication and progressive ideals, have come to agree on the naturalness of attraction outside their relationship. Jasmine has always maintained a philosophical stance that recognizing someone's attractiveness is a rational acknowledgment and does not detract from their bond or mutual fidelity.

One evening, Taylor comments on the attractiveness of a new colleague, Alex, sparking an unexpected and intense feeling of jealousy in Jasmine. This emotional reaction is at odds with her professed beliefs about trust and attraction, revealing a stark incongruence between her conscious philosophy—that attraction to others is a benign reality of human nature—and her visceral sense of life response, which reflects more traditional or possessive views on romantic commitment.

Disturbed by her own reaction, Jasmine realizes the need for personal reflection. She begins to delve into her past experiences and unspoken fears, attempting to unearth the underlying causes of her emotional response. This process of self-examination is challenging, as it forces her to confront aspects of her subconscious that are misaligned with her conscious understanding of romantic ethics.

Through continuous introspection and open dialogue with Taylor, Jasmine works to reconcile her instinctual emotions with her intellectual convictions. This ongoing effort is vital for her to achieve internal harmony, where her sense of life not only aligns with but also supports her chosen philosophical outlook. Only then can Jasmine interact with her relationship dynamics in a way that is consistent with her rational values, free from the disquieting discord of conflicting emotions.

Jung's Types as a Lens for Rand's Sense of Life

The functions of Jung's psychological types—because he places them in a structured format and provides extensive detail from a professional psychotherapist's view—better define the nuances of the distinct types of people Rand describes. In fact, the durability of his systematic framework is, in part, a driving factor behind the synthesis I attempt in this book. He presents four distinct types oriented toward their sense of life, and four distinct types oriented toward rational functions. Our journey will later in Part II show the specific inner workings of these types in more depth.

We turn our attention back to Rand as she continues,

> *Whether he corrects it or not, whether it is objectively consonant with reality or not, at any stage or state of its specific content, a sense of life always retains a profoundly personal quality; it reflects a man's deepest values; it is experienced by him as a sense of his own identity.*
>
> *A given person's sense of life is hard to identify conceptually, because it is hard to isolate: it is involved in everything about that person, in his every thought, emotion, action, in his every response, in his every choice and value, in his every spontaneous gesture, in his manner of moving, talking, smiling, in the total of his personality. It is that which makes him a "personality."*[26]

Rand's emphasis on one's sense of life as a foundational element of "personality" provides a clear parallel to Jung's theories of psychological types. This foundational sense of life is pervasive, affecting everything an individual does. To further solidify this concept, let us explore another example.

---

[26]   (Rand, Philosophy and Sense of Life 1966, 20-21)

Case Study: Tim's Adventurous Sense of Life

Tim's sense of life is notably adventurous. This disposition is not just present when he is doing something explicitly adventurous like skydiving or traveling; it permeates every part of him. You can observe it in the way he approaches his work with enthusiasm and a willingness to take on new challenges. You see it in his social interactions, where he is open to meeting new people and quickly engages in deep conversations. It is even apparent in smaller gestures, like his spontaneous decision to try a new route on his walk home or his vibrant way of narrating a simple story. He may not even be consciously aware of this adventurous streak when making everyday choices, but it manifests in his eagerness to explore new cuisines, in the way he smiles when faced with the unfamiliar, and in his general optimistic outlook.

This adventurous sense of life shapes his entire personality and is evident in every thought, emotion, and action he exhibits. The embedding runs so deep that isolating it as a single element proves challenging, yet it is what makes Tim, Tim.

"The Psycho-Epistemology of Art"

Building on the detailed exploration on the concept of a "sense of life" in Rand's essay "Philosophy and Sense of Life," our objective in this section aims to firmly establish the interface between Rand and Jung's psychological theories. This will deepen our understanding of psycho-epistemology and demonstrate how it serves as a bridge between metaphysics and ethics, an essential step for the assumptions underlying our subsequent analysis. We will explore concept formation, and its varying styles, emphasizing the implied and applied judgment in Jung's irrational and rational types. By examining the correspondence between Rand's "**psycho-epistemology**" and Jung's psychological types, we lay the groundwork for applying these distinct yet complementary paradigms together in a cohesive approach that informs ethical considerations at both individual and collective levels.

To achieve this, we find it necessary to revisit Rand's discourse in "The Romantic Manifesto," which offers an analysis of how art reflects cognitive processes—enhancing our understanding of the concept.

Psycho-Epistemology: Navigating the Junction of Jungian Types and Objectivist Thought

According to Rand, psycho-epistemology—one's "method of awareness"—is the most fundamental criterion for classifying people.[27] More precisely, psycho-epistemology is the study of the interaction of one's conscious reasoning with their subconscious automated processes. In this book's framework, it is the discipline that interfaces Jung's psychological types with Rand's Objectivism.

In Objectivist thought, one's psycho-epistemology informs one's "sense of life," thereby grounding their basic understanding of the metaphysical world. This relationship establishes a foundation for comprehending

---

[27] (Rand, For the New Intellectual 1963, 21)

53

the formation and integration of cognitive abstractions. Here, Jung's psychological functions transcend mere descriptive categories; they represent the operational dynamics within one's psycho-epistemology that facilitate the conceptualization process. In this context, Jung's framework elucidates the "how" of concept formation, complementing the "what" provided by psycho-epistemology.

Conceptualism: Bridging Historical Philosophy with Modern Psychology

To deepen our understanding of this framework, we introduce the work of Peter Abelard, a 12th–century French theologian and poet, whose contributions to the field of philosophy have bearing on Jung's psychological theories. Specifically, Abelard's "conceptualism" serves as a bridge between nominalism, which suggests that general ideas are mere names without real existence, and realism, which posits that general ideas or universals have an independent existence.

Abelard, as noted by Jung, blended these two approaches. He acknowledged that universals are intellectual constructs articulated through language, agreeing with nominalism. Concurrently, he also accepted realism's notion that categories and classes emerge from the recognizable similarities among individual objects and facts. In Abelard's view, conceptualism offered a mediatory perspective between these two extremes.[28] Jung writes on the topic of conceptualism:

> *This is to be understood as a function which apprehends the individual objects perceived, classifies them into genera and species by reason of their similarities, and thus reduces their absolute multiplicity to a relative unity. However indisputable the multiplicity and diversity of individual things may be, the existence of similarities, which makes their combination possible in a concept, is equally beyond dispute.*[29]

---

[28]   (Jung 1923, 42)
[29]   (Jung 1923, 42)

This achievement of Abelard is relevant to our discussion because of its importance to the development of Jung's psychological attitudes. The concepts of nominalism and realism are antecedents to Jung's concepts of extroversion and introversion, respectively.

Introversion and Extroversion: Perceiving the Similar and the Diverse

Jung elucidates the process that would eventually serve as the beginnings of how we understand human psychology today. This starts with percepts—the information associated with objects perceived through the senses: touch, taste, hearing, sight, or smell—and the integration of these percepts into concepts. He continues,

> For anyone who is psychologically so constituted as to perceive chiefly the similarity of things, the inclusive concept is, as it were, given from the start; it forcibly obtrudes itself with the undeniable actuality of a sense-perception. But for one who is psychologically so constituted as to perceive chiefly the diversity of things, their similarity is not clearly given; what he sees is their difference, which forces itself upon him with as much actuality as similarity does upon the other.[30]

Understanding Conceptualism in Jungian Psychology

Jung shares his thoughts, demonstrating how he came to consider these processes essential to human psychology and, consequently, to the psychological functions of his types:

> It seems as if empathy into the object were the psychological process which brings the distinctiveness of the object into more than usually clear focus, and as if abstraction from the object were the psychological process most calculated to blind one's eyes to the distinctiveness of individual things in favor of their

---

[30] (Jung 1923, 42)

> *general similarity, which is the actual foundation of the idea.*
> *Empathy and abstraction combined produce the function that*
> *underlies the concept of conceptualism. It is grounded, therefore,*
> *on the only psychological function that has any real possibility of*
> *bringing nominalism and realism together on the middle way.*[31]

Jung articulates the significant role conceptualism plays in shaping his psychological theories, standing at the crossroads of nominalism and realism. He identifies empathy and abstraction as pivotal processes that not only underpin these historical philosophical concepts but also form the foundational mechanisms driving the psychological dynamics of extroversion and introversion.

To illustrate the workings of empathy and abstraction in everyday life, consider a family dinner. An extroverted family member might thrive on directly engaging with everyone, noticing unique reactions to the meal or the ongoing conversation, thus emphasizing the "distinctiveness of the object." An introverted family member, however, might sit back and observe the general mood of the gathering, the "similarities" in how people are enjoying themselves or not, and may even abstract those observations into a broader understanding of family dynamics. In this setting, both empathy toward individual experiences and abstraction into broader understanding are at play, validating Jung's concept of a "middle way" between nominalism and realism.

Jung's functions help us to understand the conceptualization process of one's psycho-epistemology. In other words, psycho-epistemology outlines the overarching process—giving us the "car"—while Jung's psychological types provide the detailed mechanics and the engine that power this vehicle. This interfacing of theories under the umbrella of psycho-epistemology enables a more comprehensive understanding of human cognition and its relationship to ethics.

To illustrate this interface in action, we revisit the real-world scenarios outlined in the previous section.

---

[31] (Jung 1923, 42)

Revisiting the Cognitive Journey: From Sense of Life to Psycho-Epistemology

In our previous discussions, we observed Emily, David, Sarah, and Mark as they used their primary psychological functions of sensation and intuition to navigate new environments. Now, we will explore how their auxiliary rational functions of thinking and feeling contribute to the formation of their cognitive abstractions. These **cognitive abstractions** are the mental representations that enable individuals to process complex information, make judgments, and devise plans. Specifically, they form the concepts where these abstractions are employed to create generalized ideas or categories. Sensory data (sensation), insights (intuition), logical analysis (thinking), and value-based assessments (feeling) form these categories. This integrative approach demonstrates how Jung's psychological functions collectively contribute to the dynamic process of understanding and categorizing the world around us.

Emily sought out quiet sensory experiences in her unfamiliar environment as an expression of her introverted sensation type. The rational aspect of her psycho-epistemology addresses how she uses extroverted thinking or feeling to organize and socially navigate her surroundings. If Emily uses extroverted thinking (ISTJ), she might organize her new life with a focus on efficiency and objectivity, creating lists and plans to optimize her adjustment to the new city. She might choose her living situation based on criteria like cost, distance to work, and convenience. If Emily's auxiliary function is extroverted feeling (ISFJ), on the other hand, she would instead seek to create harmonious social environments and establish connections with her neighbors and colleagues, focusing on building a network of support.

David's extroverted intuition led him to seek out social networks and conceptual possibilities in his new city. With a closer look at his psycho-epistemology, we focus on how introverted feeling or introverted thinking guides David's rational judgment. If his auxiliary function is introverted feeling (ENFP), David would make decisions based on his internal values and feelings, pursuing possibilities that feel true to his identity and personal ethics. For instance, he might choose to work with a company whose mission aligns with his values. If introverted thinking (ENTP) guides him, he will analyze the abstract information he gathers to develop an internally consistent framework, choosing projects or jobs that allow him to explore innovative ideas that resonate with his internal logic.

Our initial examination of Sarah highlighted her introspective nature, driven by her introverted intuition. As we explore her psycho-epistemology, we see how Sarah's auxiliary function might manifest as extroverted thinking or extroverted feeling. If extroverted thinking is her guide (INTJ), Sarah's judgment would involve structuring her insights into actionable plans by setting strategic long-term goals for her career progression in the new city. She may also evaluate the practical steps needed to integrate her vision into her new surroundings. If Sarah leans on the extroverted feeling function (INFJ), she might focus on how her decisions impact others and strive to contribute to the community, or to find a role that aligns with her perception of the collective good.

Mark's extroverted sensation was evident in his active participation in local activities. From the psycho-epistemological perspective, we can identify that Mark's rational auxiliary may align with either introverted thinking or introverted feeling. If he uses introverted thinking (ESTP), Mark will look for internal consistency and logical understanding in his immediate experiences, choosing hobbies or jobs that challenge his problem-solving skills. If introverted feeling is his auxiliary function (ESFP), he would seek authenticity in his experiences and align his choices with his personal values, for example by working for an organization that he feels represents his identity or allows him to express himself.

One's psychological type is a composite of both one's irrational (perceptive) and rational (judging) functions. These functions work together to form cognitive abstractions: the mental constructs that allow individuals to understand concepts, discern patterns, and derive meaning from their experiences.

The Nature of Cognitive Functions in Psycho-Epistemology

In understanding the psycho-epistemology of our participants—Emily, David, Sarah, and Mark—it is crucial to distinguish their primary irrational functions from the auxiliary rational functions they employ.

While psycho-epistemology examines the totality of mental operations, Jung's typology classifies these individuals as irrational types due to their dominant perceptive functions.

In the broader context of psycho-epistemology, the rational functions serve as crucial because they facilitate the integration of experiences into a coherent worldview, enabling ethical decision-making. The rational functions—thinking and feeling—interact closely with the irrational functions, contributing to a balanced and holistic cognitive process.

As we transition from discussing these primarily perceptive individuals to examining the example of an introverted intuitive thinker with perceiving tendencies (INTP), we observe a shift in cognitive priority. The INTP's dominant thinking function displays a psycho-epistemology that is rational in its approach to processing information and making judgments. This contrast allows us to explore a different orientation of psycho-epistemology, where a rational function leads the cognitive process; and the intuitive function enriches it with depth and insight.

Applying Psycho-Epistemology to Financial Analysis: An INTP Perspective

The role of financial analyst benefits from thorough logical analysis alongside an intuitive grasp of market dynamics. Considering Jung's psychological types, this analyst may exemplify an INTP personality—distinguished by a pronounced introverted thinking function used methodically to analyze complex financial information.

Simultaneously, INTPs, with their well-developed extroverted intuitive function, can subconsciously detect patterns and potentialities that are not readily apparent in the raw data.

Psycho-epistemology enables us to understand the INTP's conscious, rational employment of the thinking function as reflective of their logical, analytical, and data-driven approach to decision-making. On the other side, the subconscious, intuitive pattern recognition signifies the automated mental operations that the INTP has cultivated through experience, shaping their "sense of life."

Jung's cognitive functions thus serve to elucidate the inner workings of the INTP financial analyst's mind as it oscillates between analytical tasks and the processing of abstract market trends. The thinking function provides a structured method for detailed analysis, while the intuitive function enriches this with a depth of insight born from a less tangible, yet equally critical, cognitive domain.

In this manner, Jung's framework of psychological types not only adds depth to the description but also offers a systematic perspective for a clearer understanding, measurement, and potential development of the abstract concept of psycho-epistemology.

Cognitive and Normative Abstractions

Building on this foundational framework, we now note that Rand argues that the next step is to apply this understanding to evaluate the world around us and make goal-oriented choices. This application requires a secondary, albeit interconnected, series of notions Rand calls **normative abstractions**. While the primary series, called cognitive abstractions, help individuals recognize what is factual, normative abstractions go a step further. They offer essential assessments of these facts, directing us to discern not only what exists but also what we should strive for or avoid within the spheres over which we have control.[32]

---

[32] (Rand, The Psycho-Epistemology of Art 1965, 6)

Understanding cognitive and normative abstractions is crucial to our discussion because they guide how individuals and societies make ethical decisions. For instance, in the realm of business finance, cognitive abstractions might help one understand the factual basis of market trends, while normative abstractions can guide investment decisions based on ethical considerations such as unfair labor practices.

In the case of a polluted river, cognitive abstractions allow one to understand the factual state, "This river is polluted." Normative abstractions come into play when deciding which ethical course should be taken, for example, "Polluting a river is wrong, and measures should be taken to clean it."

Rand explores the significance of both types of abstractions in the context of human psychology and ethics. She distinguishes cognitive abstractions as falling within the domain of individual psychology, which in turn encompasses our perception of reality.

Jung on Rationality and Values: Complementing Rand's Objectivism

Incorporating Jung's perspective into this discussion reveals that individual reasoning does not solely shape these normative abstractions; instead, they are deeply rooted in humanity's collective history. We now bring in Jung's ideas about rationality as an "attitude" that aims to align the inherently subjective nature of judgment and action with "objective values." He writes,

> *The rational is the reasonable, that which accords with reason. I conceive reason as an attitude whose principle it is to conform thought, feeling, and action to objective values. Objective values are established by the everyday experience of external facts on the one hand, and of inner, psychological facts on the other.* [33]

---

[33] (Jung 1923, 420)

61

Consider the concept of "family values." Jung asserts that these values do not solely originate from individuals but are rooted in societal norms and collective history. In many cultures, individuals pass down these values as "firmly established complexes of ideas," which in turn shape the moral compass of the society's members. In this way, Jung adds another layer to our understanding into the shaping of objective values and reason, complementing Rand's focus on the individual's role.

Jung acknowledges established norms, while Rand posits her method for the formation of these norms. Thus, collective history serves as the "data," while the living individual plays "analyst" in how this data relates to their lives. Rand demonstrates her awareness of this fact in the evolutionary tail of collective history, which serves as the source of what she identifies as normative abstractions:

> Consider the long conceptual chain that starts from simple, ostensive definitions and rises to higher and still higher concepts, forming a hierarchical structure of knowledge so complex that no electronic computer could approach it. It is by means of such chains that man has to acquire and retain his knowledge of reality.[34]

In this context, the saying "With time comes wisdom" resonates strongly. It captures the essence of how collective history and individual experiences contribute to evolving standards of reason and rationality.

Reason and Rationality: A Crucial Distinction of this Framework

Interfacing Rand and Jung's theories effectively requires distinguishing between "reason" and "rationality," terms frequently interchanged but maintaining distinct meanings within these frameworks. One could assert that Rand's conceptualization of reason aligns with Jung's concept of the thinking function, however, it is crucial to consider the attitude—whether introverted or extroverted—one exhibits toward

---

[34]   (Rand, Philosophy and Sense of Life 1966, 6)

this process. The ethical and political implications arising from this orientation will become increasingly evident over this book's course.

According to Rand, "reason" is the faculty that identifies and integrates the material provided by an individual's senses. It is an epistemic process that operates at the level of individual cognition. Rand expands this definition to emphasize reason as the faculty enabling one to discover the nature of existents. Thus, reason, as defined by Rand, organizes perceptual units into conceptual terms, following the principles of logic. In this context, "existents" refers to all entities or items that have existence. When Rand uses "existence" as a collective noun, she is denoting the totality of all individual entities—each an "existent"—that are present in reality. This use emphasizes the scope of reason's function, which is to conceptualize and understand every individual existent through logical organization, thereby making sense of the entire spectrum of existence.[35]

In contrast, Jung's concept of "rationality" extends beyond an epistemic process to focus on it as an "attitude," influenced by both individual cognition and collective history. This broader approach to rationality encompasses both the thinking and feeling functions, whether directed inwardly (introversion) or outwardly (extroversion).

In Jung's framework, reason—as articulated by Rand—aligns closely with the types who consciously employ introverted thinking as their dominant function. These types engage in a reflective, analytical processing of information, emphasizing internal logical consistency and structure—resonating with Rand's conception of reason as a conceptual, introspective process.

This is not to say the Objectivist's and introverted thinking type's method of concept formation are the same, but only to say that the introverted thinking type is the only type where the Objectivist method of concept formation is natural and inherent.

---

[35] (Peikoff 1991, 152)

Jung's other rational types present rationality in diverse ways; one can consider these as alternative "styles of reason." While introverted thinking types reflect an introspective, conceptual approach, extroverted thinking types, for example, focus on the logical organization of external structures, such as concrete objects and secondhand ideas. Introverted and extroverted feeling types emphasize personal and interpersonal value-based considerations over logical consistency, further expanding the spectrum of rational types.

The Symbiosis of Reason: Unpacking Rand and Jung's Interpretations

Rand and Jung place significant emphasis on the role of reason, albeit in different contexts. This contrast will be a recurring and necessary theme throughout our examination. The foundational difference in their perspectives is Jung, as a psychologist, takes a descriptive stance, focusing on what "is," while Rand, adopting a philosophical and prescriptive stance, emphasizes what "ought to be."

Rand focuses on the individual's use of reason to form cognitive and normative abstractions, which in turn guide one's interactions with reality. Jung extends this idea by discussing how humanity has honed rationality throughout its history, influencing what society regards as objective and valuable.

While Rand's focus on individual reasoning, and Jung's emphasis on collective history might seem to diverge, it is worth noting that their viewpoints are not mutually exclusive but rather complementary. Both frameworks imply that the understanding of what is rational rests on a certain "average"—in Rand's view through the aggregate of individual cognitive abstractions, and in Jung's, through that method, in addition to a collective history that has given shape to what we consider to be rational functions today. Both thinkers accord reason a pivotal role in shaping our understanding of ethical norms.

The apparent differences are less about the importance of reason itself, and more about the context in which reason operates, whether within the individual psyche as in Rand's case, or within the extended collective historical context as in Jung's. In summary, while the contexts in which Rand and Jung discuss reason may differ, their theories converge on one pivotal point: the vital role of reason in shaping our ethical norms.

The Foundation of Rationality and Metaphysics in Ethics

As we venture deeper into the realms of ethics and normative science, it becomes progressively more apparent that one's approach to rationality, reflecting one's implicit and automatized "means of cognition," serves as a crucial foundation. Both Rand and Jung recognize that this rationality—the process by which we align our thoughts, feelings, and actions with objective values—constitutes the cornerstone of ethical philosophy. Equally significant is the role of metaphysics, the branch of philosophy concerned with the nature of reality. Rand explains:

> *Ethics, the normative science, is based on two cognitive branches of philosophy: metaphysics and epistemology. To prescribe what man ought to do, one must first know what he is and where he is—i.e., what is his nature (including his means of cognition) and the nature of the universe in which he acts. (It is irrelevant, in this context, whether the metaphysical base of a given system of ethics is true or false; if it is false, the error will make the ethics impracticable. What concerns us here is only the dependence of ethics on metaphysics.)[36]*

To underscore the weight of these philosophical and psycho-epistemological foundations in ethics, Rand poses key questions that we ought to consider:

---

[36] (Rand, The Psycho-Epistemology of Art 1965, 6)

Is the universe intelligible to man, or unintelligible and unknowable? Can man find happiness on earth, or is he doomed to frustration and despair? Does man have the power of choice, the power to choose his goals and to achieve them, the power to direct the course of his life—or is he the helpless plaything of forces beyond his control, which determine his fate? Is man, by nature, to be valued as good, or to be despised as evil?[37]

What one believes about the universe and human cognition shapes what one deems to be morally right or wrong. The answers to these metaphysical questions, although not normative in themselves, serve as the foundation for the ethical systems that individuals accept and practice.[38]

Case Study: The Metaphysical Underpinnings of Soviet Russia

In Soviet Russia, the metaphysical view that individual existence is secondary to the collective's well-being led to an ethical system that severely curtailed individual rights and freedoms. This metaphysical stance posited the collective—rather than the individual—as the primary unit of moral concern, thereby shaping ethical norms which called for individual sacrifices permissible for the so-called "greater good." The impracticality of this ethical system eventually became apparent, contributing to the downfall of the societal structure. It serves as an illustrative example of how a foundational metaphysical belief can directly shape, and potentially distort, ethical norms and practices.

Ethical systems are rooted in metaphysical and rational premises. The nature of reality and human cognition form the foundational beliefs upon which ethical principles stand, influencing their coherence, applicability, and whether they succeed or fail.

---

[37] (Rand, The Psycho-Epistemology of Art 1965, 6-7)
[38] ibid

Answers to Questions

As we conclude this subsection, we revisit our initial questions:

1. **What is the result if one never transitions from an implicit to an explicit view of reality?**

    Not transitioning from an implicit to an explicit view of reality confines individuals to unexamined beliefs and subconscious assumptions. This limitation restricts understanding to automatic emotional responses and unarticulated perceptions, potentially leading to misunderstandings and a lack of critical self-awareness. The absence of this transition hampers personal development by preventing the cultivation of a consciously reasoned worldview, essential for comprehensive understanding and rational decision-making.

2. **Is individual rationality required to adapt to a rational environment?**

    Individual rationality, while beneficial, is not a prerequisite for adapting to rational environments, underscoring the complexity and adaptability of human psychology.

3. **How does the transition from a subconscious to a conscious mode of thinking influence one's ethical decision-making?**

    The shift from subconscious to conscious thinking significantly enhances ethical decision-making. It allows for a more deliberate, reasoned approach, where choices are not merely reactions to subconscious impulses or unexamined beliefs. This conscious deliberation leads to more responsible and ethical actions, as it involves actively weighing consequences and considering the broader implications of one's choices, aligning actions more closely with one's explicit values and principles.

4. **Can an individual's "sense of life" evolve over time to align with their rational philosophy more closely, or is it a static entity?**

An individual's "sense of life" can indeed evolve over time to align with their rational philosophy more closely. While individuals initially form their core perceptions and emotional responses subconsciously, they can examine, understand, and even alter them through introspection and deliberate philosophical inquiry. This evolution is a dynamic process, reflecting the ongoing interaction between an individual's deep-seated emotional responses and their developing rational understanding of the world.

Applied Psychology

This section embarks on a critical, holistic examination of individual psychology, particularly the profound implications of conceptual versus concrete thinking on ethical decision-making and societal values. While education plays a role in this discourse, it is not the central focus; instead, we delve into how the contrast between these two thinking styles leads to dire ethical consequences in society, with educational practices being a contributing factor.

We anchor our discussion with key texts such as "The Comprachicos" and "The Missing Link," which offer essential insights into the intersection of cognitive development and ethical reasoning. The emphasis is on understanding deficiencies in conceptual thinking that often stem from flawed educational methodologies, precipitating ethical dilemmas and societal challenges.

The guiding inquiries in this exploration include:

1. How does the absence of conceptual thinking impact ethical reasoning and decision-making in society?
2. In what ways do educational systems contribute to or mitigate this absence, and what are the broader societal repercussions of this absence?

"The Comprachicos"

The first five or six years of a child's life are crucial to his cognitive development. They determine, not the content of his mind, but its method of functioning, its psycho-epistemology.[39]

Our analysis shifts to examining the development of one's cognitive habits, as reflected in their psycho-epistemology, and the influential role of education in this process. Having previously established the relationship between psycho-epistemology and psychological types, we use the attributes of Jung's cognitive functions to better understand how these mechanisms manifest in everyday life. This approach provides a comprehensive view of human cognition, highlighting its societal implications and assessing the impact of both historical and current educational methods on today's societal climate.

In this section, we examine Ayn Rand's critique of certain educational methodologies, using the metaphor of the Comprachicos. These 17th–century figures, known for their disturbing practice of physically mutilating children for entertainment, serve as a parallel to the psychological shaping imparted by certain educational approaches. Rand's metaphor illustrates how educational systems can mold young minds, much as the Comprachicos altered physical appearances.

The Debate: Tabula Rasa versus Inherited Cognitive Structures

First in our exploration, we investigate Ayn Rand's perspective on the mind's initial state, a viewpoint crucial in setting the stage for our discussion on cognitive development and psycho-epistemology. Rand articulates a distinctive stance on the nature of the human mind at birth:

At birth, a child's mind is tabula rasa; he has the potential of awareness—the mechanism of a human consciousness—but no content. Speaking metaphorically, he has a camera with an extremely

---

[39] (Rand, The Comprachicos 1970, 54)

sensitive, unexposed film (his conscious mind), and an extremely complex computer waiting to be programmed (his subconscious). Both are blank. He knows nothing of the external world. He faces an immense chaos which he must learn to perceive by means of the complex mechanism which he must learn to operate.[40]

Rand asserts that every human begins as an "empty slate," their minds susceptible to molding through experience, whereas Jung agrees with Immanuel Kant, a philosopher known for his critical philosophy, and disputes this notion as flawed. According to Jung, the human mind comes preloaded with inherited cognitive structures that have evolved over generations, and these structures do more than passively perceive; they actively organize experiences and guide thought processes from the outset.

In contrast, Rand suggests that any inherent capabilities humans possess—symbolized by the camera in her analogy—do not indicate pre-programming but rather the potential for conscious development. This divergence in opinion between Rand and Jung necessitates a crucial discussion on objectivity and subjectivity in psychological interpretation.[41]

Balancing Objectivity and Subjectivity in Psychological Interpretation

When examining Rand and Jung's differing perspectives on the human mind, it becomes clear that the root of their disagreement lies not in the facts they consider, but in the interpretive lenses they each apply.

The word **objective**, as defined in Webster's dictionary, means "expressing or dealing with facts or conditions as perceived without distortion by personal feelings, prejudices, or interpretations."[42] But

---

[40] (Rand, The Comprachicos 1970, 54)
[41] (Jung 1923, 283-284)
[42] (Merriam-Webster.com n.d.)

from a psychological standpoint, we can never see things as *they* are; we can only see things as *we* are.

According to Jung, our observations and perceptions of objects necessarily build subjectivity. The ability to see things purely objectively is impossible and one must understand that both objective and subjective processes are at play in our observations and communication of any idea. The optimal scenario consists of us being "satisfied" if we do not see "too subjectively."[43]

Rand, while firmly grounded in the philosophy of Objectivism that champions an objective understanding of reality, implicitly navigates the realm of psychological subjectivity when addressing moral issues. Within this framework, individuals do not just see scientific conclusions as detached objective truths but integrate them into a rational, value-oriented life as tools for individual betterment. This perspective recognizes the essential role of objective reality while highlighting the individual's agency in applying rational principles for personal and moral growth. Conversely, Jung, operating within the realm of psychiatry, adheres more strictly to an objective or scientific stance, treating inherited cognitive structures as given. This approach aligns with his profession's requirements, where the clear distinction between scientific observation and moral judgment is crucial for maintaining professional integrity and credibility.

This divergence between objective and subjective viewpoints is not merely academic; it has significant implications for our understanding of human cognition and subsequently, ethical decision-making. Specifically, the way we acquire and process knowledge shapes not only our understanding of the world but also our moral and ethical interpretations.

Intellectually and realistically, the value of matter is determined in relation to a subject, underscoring the subjective nature of value assessment. This principle highlights that an observing individual, or

---

[43] (Jung 1923, 8)

an "actual human," assesses the importance or worth of matter based on its relevance or utility to their unique experiences, choices, and agency.

For example, "people" can perceive the development of a new pharmaceutical drug as a significant scientific breakthrough with immense objective value. However, its true value becomes subjective when considering its utility to "actual humans." For a patient suffering from a disease that the drug can treat effectively, it represents a life-changing or even life-saving advancement. Conversely, for someone without that specific health condition, the same drug holds little to no personal utility, despite its scientific significance.

In its purest form, people often perceive science as exercising sovereignty in the realm of knowledge and discovery. However, this perception changes when science is applied by individuals. In such contexts, science transforms from a ruling entity to a subordinate role, serving as a tool or instrument rather than an end. Its facts and findings possess no inherent value beyond their applicability and usefulness to real, living individuals. This perspective contrasts with abstract notions like "people" or "some person," which often represent collective stand-ins that lack consideration for individual variances. Thus, individuals' tangible and diverse experiences directly influence the value of scientific knowledge, as opposed to it being an objective measure in a vacuum. This shift underscores the transition of science from a purely intellectual pursuit to a practical, life-oriented activity. As Jung puts it:

> *Science must prove her value for life; it is not enough that she be mistress, she must also be the maid. By so serving she in no way dishonors herself.*[44]

This is the difference between the subjective and practical stance on the one hand and the objective and scientific stance on the other. The former retains individual life as the standard of value in all decisions,

---

[44] (Jung 1923, 52)

while the latter evaluates facts in a vacuum, disconnected from their role in human life—the role from which they derive their value.

Abstract versus Concrete Thinking: The Nominalist and Realist Debate

To better clarify the concepts of psychological subjectivity and objectivity and their relationship to abstract and concrete thinking, let us examine how Rand's concept of cognitive development in children aligns with or contrasts against the attitudes of Jung's psychological types.

Rand posits that cognitive development is a dynamic process of automatization, where initial encounters with the world—encounters such as recognizing a table not merely as an object with four legs but as a man-made item designed for a specific purpose within human settings—become imbued with an integrated network of conceptual knowledge. This integration, once consciously learned, becomes automatic, transforming the way we perceive everyday objects into a unified, inseparable experience. She suggests that this process underpins all perception and experience, highlighting that adults cannot perceive or experience in isolation but do so within an "automatized context" sculpted by previously assimilated knowledge.[45]

Building on Rand and Jung's frameworks, my analysis suggests that the concept of automatization and the resulting "automatized context" in cognitive development closely mirrors the fundamental dynamics of Jung's psychological types. In this interpretation, the interplay and balance of individuals' cognitive functions, as outlined by Jung, shape their perception and judgment in ways that resonate with the automatization process described by Rand.

Returning to her detailed exploration of cognitive processes, Rand explains that this automatization extends beyond mere object recognition to all forms of learning, including language acquisition,

---

[45]   (Rand, The Comprachicos 1970, 55)

which is the use, meaning, and application of concepts. She argues that learning involves a transition from conscious, focused attention and observation to the creation of mental connections that render this knowledge automatic, thereby enabling the mind to engage with more complex concepts without the burden of reprocessing foundational knowledge.[46]

In this light, Rand exemplifies the mindset of an abstract thinker, adept in the realm of conceptualization. Her explanation of concept formation and application, particularly in language, underscores the stark differences between abstract and concrete cognitive approaches. This divergence in thought process, especially the neglect of the hierarchical aspect of, or proper context for concept formation by concrete thinkers, forms a pivotal point of debate between these two cognitive styles.

Through her examination of cognitive development via automatization, Rand not only reflects on individual learning processes but also bridges the understanding of the broader concepts of subjectivity and objectivity in psychological types. Her discourse complements Jung's framework by illustrating how our early and ongoing learning experiences shape the content and structure of our subconscious, thereby influencing our psychological orientation and the efficiency of our mental operations. This integration of Rand's concept of automatization with Jung's psychological types highlights the complexity of cognitive development and its significant implications for abstract and concrete thinking in ethical decision-making and societal values.

Jung's Insights into Cognitive Styles

In Jung's perspective, sensory experiences and observable facts ground concrete thinking, whereas innate mental frameworks steer abstract thinking without relying on tangibles. These frameworks—what Jung

---

[46] (Rand, The Comprachicos 1970, 55)

calls "primordial images"—are dormant until activated by a shift in focus away from specific objects. Once active, they act as invisible directors shaping our thought processes.[47]

Empirical thinkers often perceive the abstract thinkers' apparent vagueness as puzzling. Nonetheless, both groups build their reasoning on premises that they have not fully developed. An empirical thinker gradually develops a theory through accumulated experiences, whereas an abstract thinker subconsciously follows intrinsic mental frameworks.[48]

The most distinct difference between empirical and abstract thinkers lies in their focus. Individuality of objects or experiences captivates empirical thinkers. They often find general similarities distracting, believing that such commonalities impede their understanding of each object's uniqueness. In contrast, abstract thinkers concentrate on the shared traits among objects or experiences, approaching these commonalities from a detached, generalized perspective.[49]

For example, imagine two individuals visiting an art museum: one, an abstract thinker, and the other, a concrete thinker. The concrete thinker focuses on the details in each painting—the brushstrokes, the color palette, or the realism of the imagery, for example. They appreciate each artwork based on its visible attributes and the skill demonstrated in its creation. For them, every painting is a separate and unique entity, and their appreciation of each hinges on the tangible aspects of the artwork.

In contrast, the abstract thinker looks for underlying themes and ideas that connect the artworks. Different artists might intrigue them with their diverse styles in expressing similar emotions like sadness or

---

[47] (Jung 1923, 284-285)
[48] ibid
[49] ibid

joy. This individual sees beyond the physical canvas, pondering the artist's intentions, the historical context, or the philosophical messages conveyed. They perceive the artworks not just as isolated creations but as part of a larger tapestry of human expression and thought.

Jung's detailed exploration serves as an extension of the insights Rand and his psychological types provide. It emphasizes the idea that deeply ingrained perceptual and cognitive frameworks, acting much like "automatized contexts," profoundly influence the efficiency of our mental processes and our ability to learn and comprehend increasingly complex information.

Jung delves more deeply into the differences in these cognitive styles; styles that would eventually underlie his concepts of extroversion and introversion. Specifically, he discusses how empathy with external objects, or abstraction from them, shapes the ways in which concrete and abstract thinkers process information. In the following passage, Jung contrasts the slow, detailed-oriented approach of the concrete thinker with the swift, generalized approach of the abstract thinker:

> It is because he empathizes first one object and then another—always a time-consuming procedure—that the concrete thinker is very slow to recognize the similarities between them, and for this reason his thinking appears sluggish and viscid. But his empathy is fluid. The abstract thinker seizes on similarities quickly, puts general characteristics in the place of individual objects, and shapes the stuff of experience by his own mental activity, though this is just as powerfully influenced by the shadowy primordial image as the concrete thinker is by the object.[50]

The primordial images Jung refers to in this passage are what Rand identifies as concepts and what Plato would recognize as the forms. These images suggest timelessness because we cannot trace the origins

---

[50] (Jung 1923, 284-285)

of the ideas back to anything else. Human cognition inevitably involves the development of these ideas, but the method by which individuals develop them significantly impacts the outcome.

Each type faces its own danger if the process of development is purely one-sided. The abstract thinker faces the danger of prematurely shaping objects into forms without substantiating evidence. The concrete thinker risks making logical conclusions too late. Because of these differences, each attitude—introversion or extroversion—serves as a check and balance for the other.

Psycho-Epistemology and Cognitive Habits

Rand emphasizes the volitional nature of conceptual development, which mirrors Jung's description of the intrinsic mental frameworks that guide abstract thinking, arguing that cognitive skills are not innate but rather acquired through deliberate effort. The creation, combination, and application of concepts necessitates engagement with both new insights and previously understood material in a purposeful manner. Individuals do not inherently master this capability at birth but must intentionally cultivate it through practice, marking a critical juncture in the learning process upon which all other intellectual abilities depend. Success or failure in developing this skill profoundly influences an individual's overall capacity for thought and learning.[51]

Moreover, the importance of this skill transcends the immediate facts or knowledge a person possesses at any stage of life, focusing instead on how one acquires and structures knowledge. This approach to processing information effectively "programs" the subconscious, significantly impacting the quality of cognitive operations. From this understanding emerges the insight that how a person learns to think—

---

[51]   (Rand, The Comprachicos 1970, 56)

how they develop and organize concepts—lays the groundwork for their entire cognitive framework.[52] As Rand crisply puts it,

> *The programming of a man's subconscious consists of the kind of cognitive habits he acquires; these habits constitute his psycho-epistemology.*[53]

Rand's delineation of the process above encapsulates the essence of abstract thinking, highlighting its dynamic, integrative nature.

In our analysis, we can complement Rand's discussion of cognitive habits by examining how Jung's psychological dichotomies— introversion versus extroversion; rational versus irrational functions; sensation versus intuition; and thinking versus feeling—enhance our understanding of them. These Jungian dichotomies provide a nuanced framework for understanding the programming of one's "subconscious computer," as Rand puts it, thereby affecting the efficiency and effectiveness of cognitive processes. This approach demonstrates how Jung's detailed classification of psychological types can deepen our comprehension of Rand's prescriptive insights into cognitive development and psycho-epistemology.

Rand's words also indicate her views on the process of a proper education, which she appears to consider reserved strictly for conceptual development. Her statement that the "skill does not pertain to the particular content of a man's knowledge" stands in contrast to the approach of the concrete thinker, who relates all thinking to the experience of sensation, meaning that thinking never detaches from specific content. The method of acquiring and organizing knowledge that Rand mentions is about forming and shaping the content. For concrete thinkers, this abstract thinking occurs subconsciously.

---

[52] (Rand, The Comprachicos 1970, 56)
[53] (Rand, The Comprachicos 1970, 56)

Rand's focus on psycho-epistemology suggests she believes there is a "proper" cognitive style, as the method she advocates would significantly influence a person's cognitive development. This sets the stage for the two existential questions that shape a child's understanding of the world and their place within it.

"Where am I?" And "Is It Worth It?": Unveiling a Child's Cognitive Journey

In her exploration of cognitive development, Rand offers a thoughtful inquiry into the early formation of a child's sense of self and their understanding of the surrounding world. Highlighting silent but pivotal inquiries that underpin a child's emerging psyche, Rand identifies foundational questions that inherently shape their cognitive habits and overall sense of life. The essence of a child's internal dialogue and its significant impact on their worldview, according to Rand, revolves around two central yet unarticulated questions: "Where am I?" and "Is it worth it?"[54]

She argues that the child answers these formative queries not through explicit verbalization but by developing habitual responses. These responses, in turn, are not mere reflections on the benevolence of the universe or the importance of cognition but manifest as a natural curiosity and a relentless quest for understanding. Implicitly, these reactions lay the early layers of what will become the child's metaphysical and epistemological foundations—their psycho-epistemology—long before they possess the capacity to engage with such abstract concepts consciously.[55]

This observation may be the strongest evidence for the view that Rand thoroughly understood or at least intuitively grasped the fundamental principles of psychological types. Her insights into the formative stages of a child's mind and the role of automatized processes closely

---

[54] (Rand, The Comprachicos 1970, 57)
[55] (Rand, The Comprachicos 1970, 57)

mirror Jung's ideas about the development of cognitive functions. This parallel suggests that Rand, regardless of her explicit familiarity with Jung's model, had a profound understanding of the intricate dynamics of psychological development, and which aligned remarkably with the foundational concepts of Jungian psychology.

In Jung's model of psychological types, the human ego or conscious mind operates along two axes: one for rational functions, which pertain to how we think and judge (epistemology); and the other for irrational functions, which pertain to how we perceive and gather information (metaphysics). These axes create a matrix outlining an individual's preferred methods for acquiring knowledge and making decisions, reflecting their underlying metaphysical view of reality and their epistemological approach.

Each person has a dominant function, which is their primary way of interacting with the world, and this can be either rational or irrational. They also have a secondary auxiliary function, which serves to support and balance the dominant function. Importantly, the dominant and auxiliary functions must be opposite in terms of their rationality and attitude. These functions and their opposites create a sort of cognitive "map." The ordering of these functions determines the typical way in which the person will process information throughout life. A visual representation below illustrates how this process works, using the INTJ personality as an example.

```
┌─────────────────────────────────────────────────┐
│               ┌──────────────────┐               │
│               │       INTJ       │               │
│               └──────────────────┘               │
│                                                   │
│            CONSCIOUS MIND / EGO                   │
│                                                   │
│         IRRATIONAL            RATIONAL            │
│                                                   │
│    Dominant   (Ni)       (Te)     Auxiliary       │
│    Inferior   (Se)       (Fi)     Tertiary        │
│                                                   │
└─────────────────────────────────────────────────┘
```

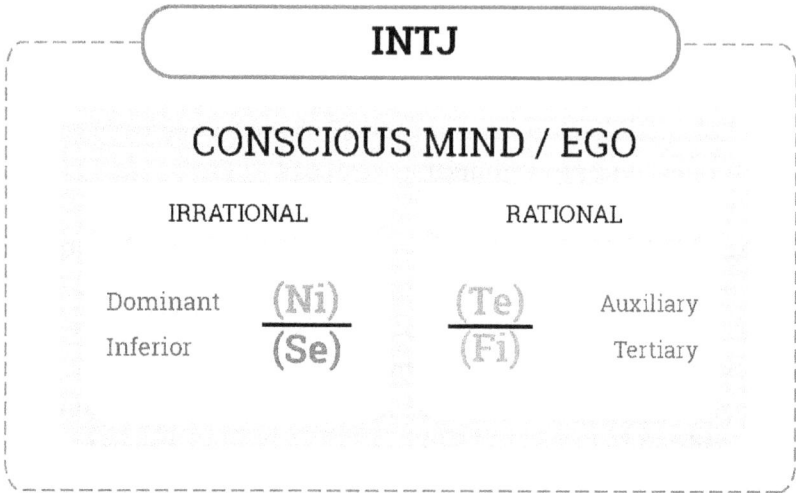

The Influence of Education on Cognitive Styles

Having explored the theoretical frameworks of Jung's personality types and Rand's concept of psycho-epistemology, we now turn our attention to the practical implications of these theories. Both historical and contemporary educational methods have shaped and continue to influence cognitive styles. However, these influences also have broader societal implications.

Taken to its logical conclusion, Rand's optimal strategy for education would be to develop every child into a rational, conceptual type, because to her, those are the essential qualities of a human.

In Jung's terms, what this suggests is the development of every child into an introverted thinking type; however, while I would agree with Rand's proposed strategies for a formal education, I would add that such an education would not necessarily result in all children becoming introverted thinking types. Nothing in history indicates this kind of social modeling is likely or even desirable. The dominant views of an era can highly influence—as we will see shortly in the case of John Dewey—but never dictate one's type.

Jung recognizes the inherent diversity of psychological types among individuals, positing that through his experience, he came to understand that individuals exhibit a vast spectrum of cognitive preferences stemming not only from the dichotomy of introversion versus extroversion but also from their dominant psychological functions. Just as external conditions and personal dispositions can lead to a preference for introversion or extroversion, they can also encourage the dominance of certain fundamental psychological functions over others. He states that it is clear from his experiences that these core functions—thinking, feeling, sensation, and intuition—distinguish themselves in their uniqueness and essential roles, each leading to the emergence of distinct types. Depending on which of these functions is most prevalent, a person may develop into a thinking, feeling, sensation, or intuitive type, further nuanced by their orientation toward introversion or extroversion, dependent upon their relation to the object.[56]

Manufacturing the Tribal Mindset: An Education in Concrete Thinking

Rand accuses John Dewey—known for his pragmatic philosophy and Progressive Education movement, which emphasized experiential learning, democratic classroom environments, and a focus on the social aspects of education rather than rigorous intellectual development—of being the chief person responsible for the modern education system she contends educates children in a manner that intentionally destroys their conceptual ability. She writes,

> To stunt a mind means to arrest its conceptual development, its power to use abstractions—and to keep it on a concrete-bound, perceptual method of functioning.[57]

---

[56] (Jung 1923, 6)
[57] (Rand, The Comprachicos 1970, 67-68)

Dewey, as the progenitor of modern education, including its application in progressive nursery schools, fundamentally challenged the emphasis on theoretical (or conceptual) learning. He advocated instead for an educational approach centered around concrete, "practical" experiences facilitated by "class projects" aimed at nurturing the students' collective spirit and engagement. This method, according to Dewey, would shift the educational focus from the solitary acquisition of knowledge to a more communal learning experience. He expressed this idea by noting,

> *The mere absorbing of facts and truths,' he wrote, 'is so exclusively individual an affair that it tends very naturally to pass into selfishness. There is no obvious social motive for the acquirement of mere learning, there is no clear social gain in success thereat.*[58]

In terms of thinking, this passage illustrates the distinction between extroversion and introversion. Extroversion focuses on concrete aspects, while introversion abstracts the details. This is what Rand meant when she said Dewey attempted to manufacture the tribal mindset in children.

Neglecting the validity of the opposite thinking style is highly destructive in any education process, however, I argue that Dewey commits this egregious error in his stance on education, where Rand does not. An education rooted in the progressive style is a replication of everyday human life, to such an extent that one should not even label it as education, at least not in the formal sense.

My reading of Rand is that she wanted a formal education to include only development of the student's conceptual faculty and to have no intrusion into their cultural learning and experience. In that way, a student is permitted two different educations: a formal conceptual and a practical cultural education, whereby one would not intrude on the other. Thus, regardless of his awareness, Dewey's educational

---

[58] (John Dewey, The School and Society, Chicago, The University of Chicago Press, 1956, p. 15.) as quoted in (Rand, The Comprachicos 1970, 67-68)

philosophy aims to cultivate a collective mindset at the expense of individual conceptual development.

Maria Montessori and Rand: A Shared Educational Philosophy

Developed in the early 20th century by Dr. Maria Montessori, an Italian physician and educator, the Montessori Method is an educational approach that emphasizes independent, self-directed learning. It is designed to foster natural learning and the holistic development of children through environments that encourage exploration and hands-on interaction. Dr. Montessori's method has been celebrated worldwide for its innovative, child-centered approach that believes in nurturing each child's potential according to their own pace and interests. Ayn Rand explicitly recognized the merits of the Montessori method, finding it aligned with her ideals of education. Both Rand's ideal educational methodology and the Montessori system share a focus on nurturing the conceptual faculties of the individual. Rand spoke of the importance of what she termed "psycho-epistemological training," which aims to develop intellectual faculties through an ordered process of attention, observation, comparison, and classification. Similarly, the Montessori method emphasizes self-directed learning and provides children with concrete materials to manipulate and engage with, such as wooden blocks, which are used for mathematical exercises. These materials act as catalysts for guided exploration, leading to an understanding of the abstract principles they represent. This hands-on experience gradually evolves into a deeper, conceptual grasp of various abstract principles. In this way, the Montessori system not only aligns with, but also operationalizes, Rand's philosophy, emphasizing disciplined intelligence as the cornerstone of human achievement while accommodating individual learning styles.[59]

In contrast, when implemented, Dewey's progressive educational system tends to prioritize the social aspects of these interactions,

---

[59] (Rand, The Comprachicos 1970)

neglecting the development of the child's individual intellectual capabilities. A classroom designed according to Dewey's principles might focus on a group project that emphasizes social collaboration, but leaves little room for individual conceptual development.

Contrary to Dewey's approach, the Montessori method offers a unique perspective on education that aligns more closely with Rand's philosophy. By segregating both conceptual and cultural learning, Rand's ideal educational system would aim to produce individuals who are not only intellectually capable but also socially aware, without one intruding on the other. A concrete method of education, as displayed in Dewey's method, intrudes on the student's ability to think, and arrests the development of independent thought.

The Plight of the Conceptual Child in Progressive Education

A conceptual child will struggle in a classroom that teaches in the progressive style. This perspective is born out of my own personal experience and struggles during childhood, which I have previously mentioned. Echoing this observation, Ayn Rand articulates the challenges faced by such individuals within the modern educational system. She highlights what she calls one of the most tragic aspects of modern schools: The spectacle of a thinking child trying to "adjust" to the pack, attempting to conceal his intelligence to fit in with his peers. She elaborates:

> He never succeeds, and is left wondering helplessly: "What is wrong with me? What do I lack? What do they want?" He has no way of knowing that his lack consists in thinking of such questions. The questions imply that there are reasons, causes, principles, values—which are the very things the pack mentality dreads, evades and resents. He has no way of knowing that one's psycho-epistemology cannot be hidden, that it shows in many subtle ways, and that the pack rejects him

because they sense his factual (i.e., judging) orientation, his
psycho-epistemological self-confidence and lack of fear.[60]

The Individual Nature of Cognition

Addressing this concern, Rand continues with a decisive argument about the inherently individual nature of cognition, asserting that understanding reality, acquiring knowledge, and discerning truths from falsehoods are capacities that belong solely to the individual. The realm of the mind is a personal domain, underscoring the absence of a shared or collective consciousness. Furthermore, she emphasizes that maintaining intellectual integrity—upholding one's convictions and truth against societal influences—is an act of personal integrity and self-interest. She adds,

> *The goal of modern education is to stunt, stifle and destroy*
> *the students' capacity to develop such an attitude, as well as its*
> *conceptual and psycho-epistemological preconditions.*[61]

These reflections resonate with the characteristics of an introverted thinking personality, epitomizing a staunch safeguarding of rational capabilities against the encroachment of collective norms. An extroverted individual would not resonate with this defensive posture, finding alignment with collective objectives more natural and less objectionable.

The Impact of Education on Organizational Culture

In my view, we can attribute the intense and pervasive tribalism characterizing our current society to the collective nature of concrete thinking. The rise of social media echo chambers and increasing political polarization are manifestations of an educational system

---

[60] (Rand, The Comprachicos 1970, 73)
[61] (Rand, The Comprachicos 1970, 68)

that has prioritized—explicitly and implicitly—social conformity over individual intellectual growth. Instead of teaching students to be independent thinkers, many schools have promoted tribal allegiance, discouraging the questioning of prevailing, or desired group norms.

In my experience within corporate America, I have noticed a deficit in conceptual thinking that significantly impacts organizational culture. This deficit manifests in several ways:

1. **Team Dynamics**: Collaborative meetings frequently become endless circles of discussion without rational conclusions.
2. **Office Politics**: The focus on image over substance hinders productivity and complicates decision-making processes.
3. **Data Management**: Managers frequently overlook the importance of structured data flow, opting for quick fixes rather than addressing root issues. They often fail to consider the long-term effects of this approach, which is indicative of a concrete thinking mentality that lacks foresight.
4. **Ineffective Leadership**: Leaders lacking a conceptual framework provide erratic and inconsistent guidance. Their meetings often reflect personal whims or moods, rather than being based on a carefully considered, logically generated strategy.

In summary, the dearth of conceptual thinking not only stifles individual growth but also undermines collective efficiency and effective leadership. This is not just a trend but a pervasive issue with far-reaching implications.

Beyond Memorization: Cultivating Conceptual Understanding

Graduates of progressive schools often still emerge with a limited framework for thinking, heavily reliant on concrete methods. This trend permeates not only general education but also specialized disciplines like medicine, where students frequently rely on mnemonics—patterns of letters, ideas, or associations—as a crutch to memorize vast amounts of information. Although effective for passing tests, this technique falls short of nurturing a profound understanding of medicine's scientific and artistic dimensions. Such reliance on rote memory serves as a stark example of an educational ethos that favors recollection over true comprehension.

Rand critiques this approach by contrasting two distinct learning methodologies: memorization and understanding. Memorization, she argues, operates at the perceptual level of consciousness, utilizing repetition and direct association without engaging with the material's content or significance. She illustrates this point by using the example of a catchy song from decades past, noting that memorized information often fades when people contemplate its meaning. This method, shared with animals, underscores a basic form of learning based on repetition and simple connections.[62]

Conversely, understanding represents a uniquely human capability, demanding an engagement with the substance of a subject rather than simply memorizing its sensory form, distilling its core elements, and relating it to existing knowledge. This process of integration is pivotal, moving beyond mere collection of data to a thoughtful, self-guided synthesis of ideas. Rand positions conceptual thinking as a fundamental human trait, distinguished by the capacity for such integration. This form of thinking elevates beyond accepting the given, encouraging a reflective and abstract approach to knowledge.[63]

Such thinkers challenge the passive acceptance of facts and norms, embodying an independent stance that resists conformist pressures and authoritative dictates. As Rand passionately notes,

---

[62] (Rand, The Comprachicos 1970, 68-69)
[63] (Rand, The Comprachicos 1970, 68-69)

A thinking child cannot conform—thought does not bow to authority.[64]

This perspective emphasizes the critical role of education in shaping psycho-epistemological habits from an early age. By training the mind to automate certain cognitive processes, education can instill habits that last a lifetime, steering individuals away from superficial perceptual thinking toward a deeper, more introspective conceptual approach.[65] Thus, the influence of education extends beyond the classroom, molding psychological types and setting the foundation for lifelong conceptual engagement with the world.

Education's Ripple Effect: Fostering Tribalism and Shaping Society

The prevalence of concrete-bound psycho-epistemologies in young students, as Rand critiques, has significant ramifications, contributing to the tribalism evident in today's American politics and culture. She observes:

> *In keeping with their concrete-bound psycho-epistemology— what the students regard as "relevant" are such things as courses in "community action," air pollution, rat-control and guerrilla warfare. Their criteria for determining a college curriculum are the newspaper headlines of the immediate moment, their hierarchy of concerns is established by tabloid editorials, their notion of reality does not extend beyond the latest TV talk-show.*[66]

This passage reveals how an educational system, focused on immediate and emotionally charged issues, fosters a tribal mindset. Such an

---

[64] (Rand, The Comprachicos 1970, 72)
[65] (Rand, The Comprachicos 1970, 72)
[66] (Rand, The Comprachicos 1970, 88)

approach, driven by the urgency of the moment and the influence of media narratives, fails to cultivate independent and critical thinking. Instead, it encourages students to align themselves with collective beliefs and emotional responses, which leads to a societal climate where group consensus and reactive discourse often overshadow critical individual thought.

While the issues she mentions—like "community action," air pollution, and guerrilla warfare—may have been pertinent at the time she was writing, one can draw parallels to today's hot button topics like gender studies, climate control, and race relations. It is not that these issues are unimportant or unworthy of attention; quite the contrary. Rather, it is that these "hot button" topics are not disparate issues but different facets of the same underlying conceptual challenges, where the key concern is that individuals often address them from a perceptual, emotional, and collective perspective, rather than approaching them from a conceptual, rational, and individualistic standpoint. Their perceptual focus distracts from addressing these challenges at a deeper level. As a result, public discourse remains mired in a cycle of reactivity, failing to progress toward meaningful, long-term solutions.

For example, climate change is not a unitary phenomenon, but rather an intricate set of issues that unquestionably merit serious attention. However, addressing it not only necessitates a nuanced, scientific approach but also calls for an informed citizenry capable of independent thought. This is crucial because individual citizens must bear the ethical and civic responsibilities that come with collective actions to combat climate change.

In a society of independent thinkers, people would naturally and automatically relate these collective actions to their own lives, recognizing their personal stake and responsibility in such broad initiatives. However, the current educational setting often encourages concrete, collective thinking that fails to establish this vital link between collective action and individual responsibility. As a result, climate change discussions are frequently reduced to mere sound bites and slogans, promoting tribalism over intellectual rigor. Such an approach fails to foster an environment where students can critically examine the data, participate in meaningful debate, and most importantly, comprehend the individual implications of collective decisions.

"The Missing Link"

In "The Missing Link," we delve deeper into the cognitive limitations that often impede individual and societal progress. This section begins with Rand's analysis of four diverse stories, each illustrating a distinct aspect of what she terms the "**anti-conceptual mentality**." She dissects this mentality, characterized by a passive approach to conceptualization and an over-reliance on empirical experience, through various lenses, including business, literature, economics, and academics. We then transition to Jung's perspective, contrasting concretistic and abstract thinking, and how these cognitive approaches manifest in real-world scenarios. The section further examines the historical and psychological roots of anti-conceptual thinking, tracing it back to primitive cognitive functions. Through detailed examples and theoretical analyses, we explore how this mode of thought persists in modern times, influencing education, religion, and social norms, thereby exerting a significant influence on our ethical values and political landscape. The section seeks to illuminate the challenges and consequences of failing to engage in conceptual and abstract thinking, highlighting the importance of overcoming primitive mindsets for individual and societal advancement.

Anti-Conceptual Mentality: Rand's Theoretical Framework

To begin this essay, Rand starts with a compilation of four stories and asks the reader to identify what psychological element each story has in common. The first story features a Midwestern businessman who, despite being a conservative critic of governmental control, paradoxically thrives on the very "special pull" he denounces, closing his mind to the notion of laissez-faire capitalism. The second narrative discusses a female novelist who holds a narrow view of fiction as limited to describing empirical experiences, dismissing its capacity to encapsulate modern world complexities. The third story narrates the experience of an American efficiency expert in a South American factory. In this story, the workers themselves reject piecework incentives, revealing a mindset that hinders both their personal and the community's economic development. The fourth story is about a philosophy professor who trivializes the depth of ethical discussions, showing the erosion in the intellectual rigor of the academic sphere. Each story sheds light on how individual or societal elements contribute to cognitive limitations, be they in business, literature, economics, or academics.

After presenting the cases as examples, Rand then reveals the commonality binding them, which she identifies as the anti-conceptual mentality. She describes this mentality as characterized by a unique form of passivity:

> The main characteristic of this mentality is a special kind of passivity: not passivity as such and not across-the-board, but passivity beyond a certain limit—i.e., passivity in regard to the process of conceptualization and, therefore, in regard to fundamental principles. It is a mentality which decided, at a certain point of development, that it knows enough and does not care to look further. What does it accept as "enough"? The immediately given, directly perceivable concretes of its background—"the empiric element in experience."[67]

Rand expands on this idea, highlighting the tendency of the anti-conceptual mentality to treat abstractions as if they were concrete, directly experienced realities:

> The anti-conceptual mentality takes most things as irreducible primaries and regards them as "self-evident." It treats concepts as if they were (memorized) percepts; it treats abstractions as if they were perceptual concretes.[68]

To elucidate this point, consider a person who accepts the concept of "freedom" as inherently good, but never delves into what "freedom"

---

[67] (Rand, The Missing Link 1973, 59)
[68] (Rand, The Missing Link 1973, 60)

means. This person regards freedom as an irreducible, self-evident primary. When questioned about why freedom is good, their response might merely be, "It just is," avoiding any deeper analytical thought. This individual exemplifies Rand's notion of the anti-conceptual mentality, treating a complex abstraction as though it were a simple, directly perceptible fact.

Exploring Concretism: Rand's Critique through Jung's Lens

Continuing with Rand's argument, it is clear from her quote she is speaking from the standpoint of a rational type. Mentions of conceptualization and fundamental principles are classic signs of introverted thinking, and only such a type would take notice of this quality lacking in others.

With her mention of passivity, Rand describes her view of how irrational or extroverted types work in Jung's typological theory. The specific phenomenon Rand witnessed in her examples is concretism; what Jung calls "the antithesis of abstraction." He notes,

> In civilized man, concretistic thinking consists in the inability to conceive of anything except immediately obvious facts transmitted by the senses, or in the inability to discriminate between subjective feeling and the sensed object.[69]

Back to the Basics: The Primitive Origins of Anti-Conceptual Thinking

Jung defines concrete concepts as multiple concepts fused together: rather than being isolated thoughts in and of themselves, concrete concepts adhere to something else. Concrete thoughts are always bound up with the information received through sense perceptions.

---

[69] (Jung 1923, 387)

This style of cognition is a remnant of primitive psychology, where humans predominantly operated on a perceptual level. In his definition of concretism, Jung writes,

> *Concretistic thinking operates exclusively with concrete concepts and percepts, and is constantly related to sensation. Similarly, concretistic feeling is never segregated from its sensuous context.[70]*

Jung, borrowing the term **"participation mystique"** from French anthropologist Lucien Lévy-Bruhl, posits that the form of judgment in question harkens back to early human development, describing it as a relic of more primitive cognitive processes. According to Jung, the thought and feeling patterns of primitives orient entirely around immediate, sensory experiences. Unlike modern rational thinking, primitive cognition does not stand alone; it is inseparable from material occurrences. As such, primitive humans operate on a perceptual level, with minimal rational differentiation from their sensual experiences.[71]

Rand, in her discussion of the anti-conceptual mentality, similarly observes that this type of cognition approaches even man-made concepts through a strictly perceptual lens. She writes,

> *To such a mentality, everything is the given: the passage of time, the four seasons, the institution of marriage, the weather, the breeding of children, a flood, a fire, an earthquake, a revolution, a book are phenomena of the same order. The distinction between the metaphysical and the man-made is not merely unknown to this mentality, it is incommunicable.[72]*

With this, Rand accurately describes the characteristics of the concrete thinking mentality. Regarding things as "self-evident" along with the

---

[70] (Jung 1923, 387)
[71] (Jung 1923, 9)
[72] (Rand, The Missing Link 1973, 60)

inability or unwillingness to consistently distinguish between the metaphysical and man-made are traits of this type. This is another aspect of what Jung describes as the primitive, archaic nature of concretism—because judgment is always related to sensation, rather than differentiated as a separate process.

Living Only for the Moment: Rand on the Dangers of Anti-Conceptual Thinking

Rand's idea of the anti-conceptual mentality asserts that individuals with this mindset live solely in the present. They dismiss the importance of understanding the reasons for events (the "Why?") and ignore the future implications of their actions (the "What for?"). These people retain only disconnected fragments of their past experiences, which serve no broader purpose or meaning in their lives.[73]

Divergent Approaches, Similar Conclusions: Jung and Rand's Take on Thinking

When we juxtapose Rand and Jung's observations, it becomes clear that while each is discussing the same psychological phenomenon, they are doing so from different angles. Jung identifies the problem as an overemphasis on objective data at the expense of deeper, more abstract thinking. This fixation on the external world keeps the individual rooted in the present, neglecting both past experiences and future implications. He provides more clarity with the following statement:

> In a word, what counts for this temperament is the object: the object is empathized, it leads a quasi-independent existence in the ideational world of the subject, and comprehension follows as a kind of after-thought. It is therefore an extroverting temperament, for the thinking of the extrovert is concretistic.[74]

---

[73] (Rand, The Missing Link 1973, 60)
[74] (Jung 1923, 282)

Transitioning from Jung to Rand; it becomes evident that her observation dovetails with Jung's classification, which defines this type's thinking as "afterthought." For Rand, this sort of imitative thinking is not just unproductive but fundamentally irrational, paralleling her concept of the anti-conceptual mentality.

An excessive focus on sensory data characterizes this mentality, which not only disrupts the process of rational thinking but also impedes the formation of broader conceptual understanding. Individuals immersed in this mindset find themselves overwhelmed by immediate sensory experiences, consequently losing the capacity for deeper, more directed abstract thought.

Jung, elaborating on extroverted thinking, posits that when individuals allow external facts to dominate their thinking, their cognitive processes become shallow, serving only as an echo of observable data. This type of thinking fails to transcend the immediate facts to engage with broader ideas or theories. In such cases, individuals accumulate a disorganized mass of unrelated empirical data. To compensate for this cognitive disarray, a psychological mechanism kicks in. They may resort to basic, overarching ideas, like "matter" or "energy," as a form of psychological compensation to bring some semblance of coherence to their fragmented thoughts. While this compensatory strategy can provide a minimal level of order, it also limits the depth and richness of their understanding, often leading to what Jung describes as "sterile" thinking.[75]

Missing the Forest for the Trees: A Concrete Example

Let us say an environmental scientist is researching the effects of pollution in various lakes. If this scientist were operating under what Jung describes as a form of thinking that is over-determined by the

---

[75] (Jung 1923)

object, they might collect extensive data on the pH levels, types of pollutants found, and so on, for each individual lake, but fail to abstract this information into a broader understanding of pollution's impact on freshwater ecosystems in general. They may publish papers that are exhaustive in detail but neglect to conceptualize their findings in a way that could contribute to general theories about environmental pollution. They lose themselves in the details of each individual lake and fail to link these details to larger, more abstract concepts, such as the systemic impact of industrialization on natural resources.

As a result, their work, though factually accurate, would lack the broader insights that could make it truly impactful. It would be sterile, in Jung's terms, because it does not go beyond the immediate, observable facts to link with broader ideas or theories. Instead of forming a cohesive understanding, the scientist ends up with a mass of undigested empirical material. In trying to make sense of this material, they might resort to overly simplistic or generalized ideas, such as concluding that all human activity is detrimental to lakes, or proposing one-size-fits-all solutions like ban all synthetic chemicals, without acknowledging the complexities and variations in environmental impact.

Collective Comfort: Intellectual Evasion and Emotional Reactions to Challenges of Tradition, Institutions, and Core Beliefs

Rand argues individuals of this mindset may proclaim to have intellectual convictions or principles, but if questioned, they would be unable to substantiate their views. Their convictions, she notes, lack depth and are akin to a superficial layer hovering over an intellectual void. They never think to question the foundations of their beliefs.[76]

She asserts that questioning the origins of one's convictions can lead to emotional chaos because it challenges not just a single idea, but

---

[76] (Rand, The Missing Link 1973, 62)

the individual's entire intellectual framework. This can evoke various reactions ranging from evasion and hostility to outright panic and hatred.[77]

Rand continues to expound on the idea that individuals with an anti-conceptual mentality uncritically accept "memorized rules of behavior," often referred to as "traditions." This method of thinking, which avoids engagement with abstract principles, functions effectively only within a group sharing the same perceptual limitations, fostering a collectivist mindset.[78] Such individuals cannot see themselves apart from their social group and often seek protection, provided by the group, against outsiders or any other challenging life experiences.

Consider for example certain political positions that people take with respect to various entitlement programs funded through taxation, or regulations such as minimum wage laws. These positions are often rooted in societal norms or traditions, rather than individual critical analysis. A significant aspect of these stances involves individuals implicitly or explicitly believing that they should compel others to adhere to or follow similar rules or systems. For example, one might strongly advocate for mandatory social security contributions, not just as a personal choice, but as a policy everyone should follow, regardless of their personal circumstances or preferences. Similarly, opinions on unemployment benefits, a legal minimum wage, and taxation often carry an inherent expectation that these views should form the basis of societal norms and laws, impacting everyone.

When individuals challenge these beliefs—by proposing privatization of social security, elimination of minimum wage standards, or implementation of a different tax structure, or no mandatory tax at all—their response can become intensely emotional and defensive.

---

[77] ibid
[78] ibid

This reaction does not originate solely from a threat to personal beliefs but rather from a perceived threat to the societal order and norms that these individuals believe should have universal application. The debate then shifts from a discussion on policy specifics to a defense of a broader worldview that encompasses not only personal choices but also ethical prescriptions for others' behavior.

In these situations, these types project their psychology onto others, assuming others obtain information in the same way and should come to the same conclusions. Integrating Jung and Rand's insights, we see why these types often rely heavily on external frameworks and react strongly when these frameworks face questioning. Both the anti-conceptual mentality and extroverted thinking type exemplify a resistance to examining the logical underpinnings of their convictions, particularly as they relate to the individual. This often translates into a collectivist orientation that not only shapes personal beliefs and seeks to impose these beliefs on others but also is heavily dependent on external validation for its sustenance.

Choosing to Evolve: From Tribal Conformity to Individual Thought

Building on the point about resistance to examining the logical underpinnings of one's convictions, Rand writes,

> The word "outsiders," to him, means the whole wide world beyond the confines of his village or town or gang—the world of all those people who do not live by his "rules." He does not know why he feels that outsiders are a deadly threat to him and why they fill him with helpless terror. The threat is not existential, but psycho-epistemological: to deal with them requires that he rise above his "rules" to the level of abstract principles. He would die rather than attempt it.[79]

---

[79]   (Rand, The Missing Link 1973, 63)

101

Reflected in the adage, "Rules are for people who do not like to think," the anti-conceptual mentality avoids thinking that involves abstract principles at all costs.

The tendencies and social implications therein of the primitive mentality, Rand states, are of a psycho-epistemological nature. The above passage, in combination with the following excerpt from Rand's essay "The Missing Link," provides us with a significant clue that will unlock our ability to compare her analysis with Jung more accurately.

Just as we saw with Jung, Rand alludes to the completely concretistic nature of primitive cognition, identifying it as "preconceptual," but when she mentions "their later counterparts," this makes clear she is speaking of a developmental level beyond the perceptual. Hence, allowing us to precisely isolate and identify that her concept of psycho-epistemology specifically involves one's application of Jung's rational functions. She writes,

> *Primitive tribes are an obvious example of the anti-conceptual mentality—perhaps, with some justification: savages, like children, are on the preconceptual level of development. Their later counterparts, however, demonstrate that this mentality is not the product of ignorance (nor is it caused by lack of intelligence): it is self-made, i.e., self-arrested.*[80]

Here we see a crucial point. Modern civilized humans have evolved from a primitive and infantile mentality. Rand asserts that this evolution is "volitional," emphasizing that individuals must choose to develop their conceptual faculties; otherwise, they remain at a perceptual level shared with other animals. The concept of volition is pivotal here; it introduces an element of personal responsibility. According to Rand, one's intellectual and psychological stature is not just a result of environmental factors or deterministic elements, but also involves a conscious, willful act. It requires an individual to elevate their thinking from the perceptual to the conceptual.

---

[80]   (Rand, The Missing Link 1973, 64)

Jung echoes this sentiment in his own way, particularly when discussing judgment. He posits that the individual must consciously turn inward to engage with the inner world, a process that is both active and deliberate. This introspection, influenced by cultural background and moral education, contrasts with the less developed volition in primitive mentalities.[81]

Thus, Jung, like Rand, underscores the importance of active self-reflection in psychological development. Without it, individuals risk defaulting to a primitive state, one in which they are easily swayed by external pressures and subconscious drives. Jung delves into the characteristics of this primitive mentality, highlighting the dangers of a life led by superficial values and external motivations:

> *The further we go back into history, the more we see personality disappearing beneath the wrappings of collectivity. And if we go right back to primitive psychology, we find absolutely no trace of the concept of an individual. Instead of individuality we find only collective relationship or what Lévy-Bruhl calls participation mystique. The collective attitude hinders the recognition and evaluation of a psychology different from the subject's, because the mind that is collectively oriented is quite incapable of thinking and feeling in any other way than by projection.[82]*

Primitive groups were exclusively collective, leaving no room for individual identity. In this mindset, any deviation from shared beliefs becomes not just a differing opinion, but a fundamental flaw in the deviating member. The pervasiveness and instinctual favoring of this mentality are, as we will cover next, so strong that educators design curricula specifically to perpetuate it.

---

[81] (Jung 1923, 401)
[82] (Jung 1923, 9)

Cultivating Conformity: How Current Education Suppresses Individual Thought

According to Rand, modern educational strategies, particularly those influenced by pragmatism and John Dewey's progressive education, aim to stifle conceptual development in favor of teaching students to conform socially. In Rand's view, this is a deliberate effort to cultivate mindsets that prioritize tribal or collective thinking over individual critical reasoning.[83]

These educational philosophies have had a lasting influence and are still employed in many educational systems today, especially in the West. The focus on experiential learning, social interaction, and the "real-world" application of knowledge remains prevalent. Teaching methods that prioritize group activities, project-based learning, and student-centered classrooms are common.

This serves as an example of how prevailing educational paradigms can prescribe a tribal approach geared toward universal social acceptance and adjustment. Such paradigms operate under the projection that others are psycho-epistemologically alike, in their preference for concrete thinking over conceptual reasoning.

However, one must ask: What logical purpose can this approach to education serve, if it reverses our evolutionary progression from primitive beings to more advanced, conceptual humans? It seems to aim for comfort with the primitive and collective nature of our early ancestors, while paradoxically relying on products and advancements developed through conceptual thought. Not only does this approach stand as the antithesis of true education, but it also duplicates the socialization process that life itself provides through day-to-day experience, thereby rendering this form of "education" redundant.

---

[83] (Rand, The Missing Link 1973, 66)

Moreover, this methodology reveals an infantile aversion to engaging with complexity, and a retreat to the comfort of simpler, less developed forms of thought and interaction. Such infantilism not only stifles intellectual and emotional growth but also undermines our collective ability to navigate and innovate within an increasingly complex world.

A formal education should focus on developing a student's conceptual faculty, in line with our evolutionary advancement from perceptual, to conceptual beings. If we developed to become conceptual beings, from what was once wholly perceptual at one point, conceptuality should be recognized as holding a higher value. Therefore, there is no rational explanation to purposefully retain or recreate the original level of psychological functioning from which we have evolved.

"Never Learned to Think": A "Soul" at War with Itself

Rand further elaborates on the nuances of the anti-conceptual mentality:

> It is the subtler manifestations of the anti-conceptual mentality that are more tragic and harder to deal with. These are the "mixed economies" of the spirit—the men torn inwardly between tribal emotions and scattered fragments of thought— the products of modern education who do not like the nature of what they feel, but have never learned to think.[84]

Psycho-epistemology is Rand's term for the study of man's cognitive functions in the human psyche and the relationship of the conscious and subconscious mind. In this respect, she shared a similar focus with Jung in his work on psychological archetypes. However, in this passage, she reveals a lack of nuance that her concept of psycho-epistemology cannot fully elucidate.

---

[84]   (Rand, The Missing Link 1973, 68)

105

Herein lies the incredible value of Jung's contributions. While Rand offers a critique of anti-conceptual thinking, she does not furnish a comprehensive psychological framework to understand these "'mixed economies' of the spirit." Jung fills this void by laying out his attitude and function types in a structured framework. This level of differentiation allows one to conceptualize the specific forces competing within an individual's psychological landscape, extending beyond Rand's initial observations.

Jung articulates a fundamental psychological dichotomy between individuals who are predisposed toward rational judgment and those who are inclined to focus on the concrete, sensory elements of their experience. For the rational individual, the essence of understanding resides in logical structures and theoretical constructs. This person perceives and reacts to the world through the lens of ideas, often giving secondary importance to concrete, sensory experiences.

Conversely, individuals oriented toward tangible objects are more likely to base their understanding on sensory information and immediate, practical considerations. These sensation-oriented individuals often find rational cognition to be of less relevance, as they prioritize the here-and-now aspects of reality. The divide is not merely a question of intellectual preference but represents a foundational difference in psychological orientation toward either the conceptual or the perceptual, the abstract or the sensuous.

Rand argues that the inability to think conceptually is a result of modern education. However, I propose that this deficiency must have been an existing condition from the beginning of human history. While modern educational systems may indeed exacerbate this issue, the inherent tension between thought, feeling, and instinct predates these systems.

Nonetheless, her idea that this incapacity for thought leads to inner conflict is compelling. When there is a lack of integration between thought and feeling, the subconscious—symbolized by the "soul"—senses duplicity and that something is amiss. The experience of dissatisfaction is then the emotional result of this fundamental psychological imbalance.

Lacking the insight that thoughts serve to rationalize feelings, individuals often fail to pinpoint the root cause of this internal discord. In the absence of this realization, one remains uninformed about its origin and nature, thereby leaving one without a clue as to how to resolve it.

Conceptualization does not aim to change human nature; instead, it seeks to enhance cognitive functioning, which requires intellectual labor. Until an individual learns to align their introverted and extroverted rational functions—referring to the Jungian concept of balancing thinking and feeling within the conscious mind—the persistence of inner conflict is inevitable.

Contemporary Example: Jordan Peterson's Mixed Economy of Spirit

I will offer other examples of the **mixed economy of spirit** throughout this book but let me mention specifically here Jordan Peterson as a modern example of the subtler instances of the anti-conceptual mentality. Peterson, a psychologist and public intellectual, is clearly a man of abstract thought, engaging with philosophical and psychological concepts at an elevated level, but he struggles to reconcile his thoughts with the tribal feelings rooted in Christianity, often causing him to veer from reason to revelation.

Peterson regularly delves into Biblical stories, attempting to derive universal truths from them. He does so by applying rigorous thought and conceptual frameworks to these stories, effectively using his rational faculties to parse deeply emotional and cultural narratives. Yet, the tribal emotions, traditions, and allegiances associated with

Christianity can sometimes appear to be at odds with his more abstract ideas, revealing a tension between his thinking and feeling functions.

One can observe how much logical detail Peterson applies to any scientific idea he discusses, while he discards that same intellectual rigor when discussing Christianity. Doing so, Peterson shares a struggle experienced by many other great thinkers throughout history, becoming what Jung called, "a man of passionate feeling,"[85]a description Jung used to characterize Tertullian, an early Christian apologist known for his own intellectual struggles in reconciling faith and reason.

The Human Condition: Between Animal Instinct and Rational Thought

Rand concludes her essay with the following statement:

> *There is an enormous breach of continuity between man and all the other living species. The difference lies in the nature of man's consciousness, in its distinctive characteristic: his conceptual faculty. It is as if, after aeons of physiological development, the evolutionary process altered its course, and the higher stages of development focused primarily on the consciousness of living species, not their bodies. But the development of a man's consciousness is volitional: no matter what the innate degree of his intelligence, he must develop it, he must learn how to use it, he must become a human being by choice. What if he does not choose to? Then he becomes a transitional phenomenon—a desperate creature that struggles frantically against his own nature, longing for the effortless "safety" of an animal's consciousness, which he cannot recapture, and rebelling against a human consciousness, which he is afraid to achieve.*[86]

---

[85] (Jung 1923, 45)
[86] (Rand, The Missing Link 1973, 69-70)

Jung, while critiquing Friedrich Schiller, delves into similar territory, discussing the origins of what he refers to as "barbarism." Schiller was essential to the foundation of Jung's psychological theories, and Jung credits him with being the first to broadly conceptualize psychological functions and types.

According to Jung, Schiller questions why—despite advances in knowledge and civilization in an age of enlightenment and rational inquiry—barbarism persists. Jung suggests that the root of such barbarism is not the lack of effect of reason or truth, but rather the unreasonable expectations placed on them. According to him, the true nature of barbarism lies in this imbalance, which stems from a one-sided psychological development.[87]

The common flaw that Jung identifies in Schiller's statement—and which we also see in Rand's arguments—is the overvaluation of truth and intellect. This overvaluation results from their psychological dispositions, which fuel a propensity for such intense intellectual pursuit and analytical dominance. When we look back at history, it is clear some people have chosen to become what she calls "human"— what I assume to mean a thinking type, in Jung's terms—in even the most savage eras, but not everyone will make this choice, and neither is it one necessary for societal progress. What is often perceived as a change in human nature is only the impression we have about the dominant attitude of the times, that could lead Rand or anyone to such a thought. With that approach to the question, it is safe to say man has not "become" a transitional phenomenon, but he always has been and will forever be.

So, is the refusal to engage in conceptual thought a collective issue? Undoubtedly. Does it reduce humanity to a base, animalistic level? Indeed. But does everyone need to choose the path of conceptual thought for society to flourish? No. Not every individual needs to adopt this framework for humanity to succeed.

---

[87] (Jung 1923, 72)

Answers to Questions

As we conclude this section, we revisit our initial questions:

1. **How does the absence of conceptual thinking impact ethical reasoning and decision-making in society?**

   Lack of conceptual thinking leads to superficial ethical reasoning and short-sighted decision-making. Societal norms and decisions become reactive, overlooking long-term consequences and systemic issues.

2. **In what ways do educational systems contribute to or mitigate this absence, and what are the broader societal repercussions?**

   Educational systems play a crucial role in either fostering or impeding conceptual thinking. When education emphasizes rote memorization over critical thinking and problem-solving, it contributes to the absence of conceptual thinking. Such educational practices limit students' ability to engage in abstract reasoning and complex ethical analysis. Conversely, educational approaches that encourage inquiry, abstract thinking, and critical analysis help mitigate this absence. The broader societal repercussions include the development of a citizenry less equipped to tackle complex ethical challenges, potentially leading to societal stagnation or regression in moral and ethical standards.

PSYCHOLOGY TO ETHICS

=======★ ★ ★=======

This section transitions us from examining traits of psychological types, to focusing on their ethical implications. We first explore the connection between psychology and philosophy, not only establishing the premise that justifies investigating how individual psychological orientations influence one's philosophical beliefs, but also asserting that the area of ethics belongs to the assessment of one's actions and conscious convictions. The discussion then delves into the implicit ethical approaches of each psychological type, starting with irrational types and moving to rational types, specifically in their feeling and thinking orientations. I will introduce several case studies to illustrate these psychological tendencies in real-life scenarios. Finally, the last essay, "Collectivized Ethics" steers the discussion toward politics, marking the beginning of the journey to our ultimate topic.

Guiding inquiries for this exploration include:

1. What is a **perceptual mentality**?
2. What is **conceptual consciousness**?
3. What are the four steps in generating an emotion?
4. What is the connection between concrete thinking and collective thinking?

"The Psychology of Psychologizing"

Building on the previous section, this essay of Ayn Rand's, written in 1971, serves as a fitting transition from exploring psychological types, to examining their ethical implications, bridging psychology with philosophy. The analysis highlights the distinct natures of psychology and philosophy, emphasizing the need for them to remain separate to maintain clarity in defining human motivations and moral responsibilities. The central thesis is the importance of distinguishing between the descriptive aspects of psychology and the prescriptive nature of philosophy. While certain insights depend on their interdependence, these disciplines should not overlap in goals or methods. Rand delineates the two fields:

> *An individual's consciousness, as such, is inaccessible to others; it can be perceived only by means of its outward manifestations… The task of evaluating the processes of man's subconscious is the province of psychology. Psychology does not regard its subject morally, but medically… The task of judging man's ideas and actions is the province of philosophy. Philosophy is concerned with man as a conscious being; it is for conscious beings that it prescribes certain principles of action, i.e., a moral code.* [88]

Common Ground: Jung and Rand on Consciousness

The concept of psychologizing or rationalizing psychological dysfunction contrasts sharply with an unbiased exploration of human psychological functions, as discussed by Jung. To avoid confusion between conscious motivations and subconscious influences, he advocates separating a person's conscious self from their unconscious aspects. Only by this clear differentiation, Jung argues, can one achieve true understanding and clarity in psychological studies. He stresses:

---

[88]   (Rand, The Psychology of Psychologizing 1971, 27-28)

A clear differentiation of the conscious man from his unconscious is imperative, since only by the assimilation of conscious standpoints will clarity and understanding be gained.[89]

Objective Morality: Judging Actions, Not Psychologies

Both Jung and Rand concentrate their attention on a person's conscious mind and actions when analyzing individuals, cautioning against considering what the subject's subconscious reveals as a valid basis for judgment. Both also approach their disciplines—psychology and philosophy—from the appropriate perspective. Rand states,

Morality is the province of philosophical judgment, not of psychological diagnosis. Moral judgment must be objective, i.e., based on perceivable, demonstrable facts. A man's moral character must be judged on the basis of his actions, his statements, and his conscious convictions—not on the basis of inferences (usually spurious) about his subconscious.[90]

This passage provides more evidence that Rand separates philosophy from psychology in her analysis and even suggests that she does not see the perceptual types she discusses as inherently immoral, but rather that actions stemming from this type of mentality demonstrate the immoral characteristics she predicts. She continues,

It is not the task of philosophy to adjust the principles of proper action (i.e., of morality) to the requirements of the psychologically handicapped—nor to allow psychologizers to transform such handicaps into a moral issue, one way or the other.

---

[89] (Jung 1923, 151)
[90] (Rand, The Psychology of Psychologizing 1971, 28)

It is not man's subconscious, but his conscious mind that is subject to his direct control—and to moral judgment. It is a specific individual's conscious mind that one judges (on the basis of objective evidence) in order to judge his moral character.[91]

This is an essential point that even critics of Rand must acknowledge: Her moral judgments are based on actions, not on one's psycho-epistemological orientation. This focus on actions as the basis for moral evaluation is consistent with a rational, objective approach to ethics, which runs counter to approaches taken by anti-conceptual, emotional, or collective mentalities.

Sense of Life and Rational Functions

To give the previous quote more clarity, we must remember that for Rand, a "man's subconscious" represents their sense of life—what she views as the subconscious counterpart to a person's conscious mind. I have made the case that we can witness her sense of life concept in Jung's irrational functions, and his rational functions are what she views as the proper drivers of one's "conscious mind." However, when a person's conscious mind orients toward extroversion, it would also result in what she would view as an incorrect orientation. This consideration also holds for those who never develop their conceptual capacity, relegating it to the background. Evidence suggests she would classify both types as unconscious.

Consequently, Rand forbids judging a person based on their sense of life, but she allows judgment based on how they use their rational capacity, because these reflect a person's conscious convictions, which influence their actions and statements. She writes,

Since a man's psychological problems hamper his cognitive judgment (particularly the problems created by a faulty psycho-epistemology), it is his responsibility to delimit his problems

---

[91]   (Rand, The Psychology of Psychologizing 1971, 28-29)

as much as possible, to think with scrupulous precision and clarity before taking an action, and never to act blindly on the spur of an emotion (it is emotions that distort cognition in all types of psychological problems).[92]

When one acknowledges Rand's interpretation of emotion as a product of value judgments stemming from the cognitive process, the role of rational functions in her philosophy becomes clearer.

Her views suggest rational functions should serve as one's conscious guide toward emotion—the emotion that flows freely through the irrational functions. In this context, "flowing freely" means that within the irrational functions, the elements of thinking and feeling—from which emotion results—remain concretistic and merely implied, not directly and consciously engaged. Allowing the subconscious to lead in this manner is akin to the tail wagging the dog, where emotion, rather than rational thought, drives the person's actions. This scenario mirrors what we see in Jung's irrational types, where the subjection of emotion to perception causes emotion to predominate, due to the unengaged, underlying rational functions of thinking and feeling.

However, as Rand describes it, if any function other than thinking is to take the lead, it would produce the same emotionally driven approach. The very idea of not letting emotion lead is the idea of structuring one's mind in a way that the conceptual, rational function guides emotion into action.

We use the concept of type to classify individuals because we perceive one another as whole and indivisible entities. Humans cannot separate themselves from their thoughts and actions, although they do possess the ability to treat complex problems perceptually, as any other animal does, albeit through a fully instinctual and inefficient process—if used as the primary means to do so.

---

[92] (Rand, The Psychology of Psychologizing 1971, 30)

Regarding Rand's psychological type, she displays a clear preference for introversion and thinking, over feeling. The remark of "a faulty psycho-epistemology" implies there is an error in need of correction in any type oriented otherwise. Nevertheless, any judgment she makes is colored by that one-sidedness and thus compounded throughout all her work.

"Selfishness Without a Self"

In this essay, Rand builds on her theory of the "anti-conceptual mentality" she introduces in "The Missing Link," focusing on perceptual mentalities and their significant implications in the realms of ethics and societal behavior. We examine her concept of the "tribalist" and "tribal lone wolf," and how these align with Jung's typologies, particularly in their approach to judgment and decision-making. This exploration extends to the practical manifestations of these mentalities across different professions, highlighting examples of how they shape behaviors in finance, politics, and interpersonal relationships. The discussion further addresses the ethical dimensions of these mentalities, examining the moral challenges they pose and how they are reflected in broader socio-political contexts.

The Nature of Tribalists and Lone Wolves

As we begin, we encounter Rand's nuanced distinction between two types of individuals who embody what she identifies as an anti-conceptual mentality:

> *All tribalists are anti-conceptual in various degrees, but not all anti-conceptual mentalities are tribalists. Some are lone wolves (stressing that species' most predatory characteristics).*[93]

Rand's use of the term **"tribalist"** refers to those who align with collectivist or group mentalities, exemplifying the social manifestations of an anti-conceptual mindset. This mindset manifests in the actions of various groups, including primitive tribes, racists, xenophobes, adherents of the caste system, guild socialists, criminal gangs, and advocates of family solidarity or ancestor worship. In these groups, individual judgment and rational choice frequently take a backseat to

---

[93]   (Rand, Selfishness Without a Self 1974, 71)

group dynamics and collective identity. In such contexts, individuals conform to the group's norms and beliefs, often without critical examination or personal discernment.

In contrast to the group-conforming tribalists, Rand introduces the concept of the **tribal lone wolf**. This figure represents another permutation of the collective mentality. Whereas tribalists find comfort and identity within the group, the tribal lone wolf stands apart, often because of rejection or alienation. This distinction leads to a unique psychological and social dynamic, albeit one still anchored on dependency and an anti-conceptual approach. Rand continues,

> *The majority of such wolves are frustrated tribalists, i.e., persons rejected by the tribe (or by the people of their immediate environment): they are too unreliable to abide by conventional rules, and too crudely manipulative to compete for tribal power. Since a perceptual mentality cannot provide a man with a way of survival, such a person, left to his own devices, becomes a kind of intellectual hobo, roaming about as an eclectic second-hander or brainpicker, snatching bits of ideas at random, switching them at whim, with only one constant in his behavior: the drifting from group to group, the need to cling to people, any sort of people, and to manipulate them.[94]*

Jim Jones, initially a mainstream religious leader, epitomized Ayn Rand's tribal lone wolf through his transition to autocratic head of Jonestown, where he maintained manipulative control over his followers.

The Perceptual Mentality

Rand specifically mentions perceptual mentalities here, and some explanation is necessary to clarify what that means within the context

---

[94] (Rand, Selfishness Without a Self 1974, 71)

of Jung's types. Jung identifies the subordination of judgment to sensation as the core factor leading to tribal tendencies, because in these cases, one's judgment remains concretistic, and never fully differentiated. For example, in Jung's irrational types, particularly those who lead with either the sensation or intuition function, judgment is not the result of a reflective, rational choice but rather arises from a reflexive, instinctual necessity. Irrational types lack discernment, hindering their ability to rationally distinguish between materially relevant and irrelevant information. Of the extroverted irrational types, their perception for whom Jung describes as immediate and concrete, he writes,

> Their perception is directed simply and solely to events as they happen, no selection being made by judgment… Since these are in no way based on the principle of reason and its postulates, they are by their very nature irrational. That is why I call the perception types "irrational" by nature.
>
> As a rule it is quite hopeless to discuss these things with him as questions of principle, for all rational communication is just as alien and repellent to him as it would be unthinkable for the rationalist to enter into a contract without mutual consultation and obligation.[95]

As for the introverted irrational types, Jung adds,

> From an extroverted and rationalistic standpoint, these types are indeed the most useless of men… The irrational introverted types are certainly no teachers of a more perfect humanity; they lack reason and the ethics of reason.[96]

---

[95] (Jung 1923, 342-344)
[96] (Jung 1923, 371-373)

Real-world Manifestations of Perceptual Mentalities Across Professions and Behaviors

In the real world, the concepts of perceptual and anti-conceptual mentality, as described by Jung and Rand, manifest in various professions and behaviors, often in subtly interconnected ways. Consider the landscapes of finance, politics, philosophy, corporate strategy, and personal relationships, where immediate, sensory-driven decisions often overshadow long-term, rational judgment.

In the realm of finance, for example, day traders might embody this tendency. Their decisions, driven by market trends and gut feelings, reflect a perceptual mentality, prioritizing immediate sensory data over a systematic, conceptual analysis. This approach aligns with Rand's notion of an anti-conceptual mindset, where short-term reactions to external stimuli supplant rational, long-term thinking.

Similarly, in politics, we observe figures who, lacking a fixed ideology, shift their stances based on the prevailing winds of public opinion and expediency. This fluidity echoes the behavioral patterns of Rand's tribal lone wolves—individuals who, though seemingly independent, remain swayed by external factors and the need to manipulate or conform to their immediate social environment.

This pattern extends into the intellectual sphere, where armchair philosophers might engage with ideas more as a means of social alignment than as a pursuit of truth or understanding. Their eclectic, sometimes superficial, engagement with philosophies mirrors the erratic intellectual journey of someone driven by external validation, rather than internal conviction, a direct reflection of Jung's irrational types who fail to develop a differentiated judgment system.

In corporate leadership, a similar narrative unfolds. Leaders who constantly alter strategies in response to market fads or shareholder pressures exhibit a perceptual mentality. They make decisions that react to external circumstances instead of being based on a consistent, internal value system, exemplifying the mentality that lacks principled, conceptual thinking which Rand critiques.

Finally, in personal relationships, the behavior of those who rapidly shift from one emotional attachment to another, driven by fear or immediate need, rather than a coherent set of personal values, demonstrates this anti-conceptual approach. Such individuals, akin to Rand's description of lone wolves, navigate their emotional lives without a stable, rational framework, reflecting Jung's concept of irrational types guided by immediate perception.

In all these scenarios, the common thread is the predominance of immediate, external factors over stable, internal judgment. This overarching theme, drawn from the works of Rand and Jung, highlights the pervasive influence of a perceptual mentality across various aspects of human behavior and decision-making.

The Perceptual Mentality's Ethical Implications

Rand probes the ethical complexities associated with perceptual mentalities. She contends that individuals with this mindset are poorly equipped to manage ethical dilemmas effectively:

> *Whatever theoretical constructs he may be able to spin and juggle in various fields, it is the field of ethics that fills him with the deepest sense of terror and of his own impotence. Ethics is a conceptual discipline; loyalty to a code of values requires the ability to grasp abstract principles and to apply them to concrete situations and actions (even on the most primitive level of practicing some rudimentary moral commandments). The tribal lone wolf has no firsthand grasp of values. He senses that this is a lack he must conceal at any price—and that this issue, for him, is the hardest one to fake. The whims that guide him and switch from moment to moment or from year to year, cannot help him to conceive of an inner state of lifelong*

dedication to one's chosen values. His whims condition him to the opposite: they automatize his avoidance of any permanent commitment to anything or anyone. Without personal values, a man can have no sense of right or wrong. The tribal lone wolf is an amoralist all the way down.

The clearest symptom by which one can recognize this type of person, is his total inability to judge himself, his actions, or his work by any sort of standard.[97]

The Populist Dilemma: Ethics and Expediency in Political Leadership

Take, for example, political leaders who adapt their views to prevailing public opinion (i.e., populists). While this stance may appear pragmatic, it is symptomatic of their anti-conceptual nature. Such leaders lack foundational principles, rendering them ill-equipped for ethical or conceptual decisions when societal norms shift, or crises arise.

This brings us to Rand's observation in politics. She notes that commentators often urge politicians to place the country's interests above their own or their party's. I add that these commentators frequently invoke phrases like being on the "right side of history" for persuasion. However, as Rand notes, such appeals presuppose a conceptual consciousness that takes ideas seriously.

If a politician is genuinely convinced of the righteousness of his ideas, then compromising them would mean betraying the very country he vows to serve. On the other hand, if he operates with a perceptual mentality, his approach to ideas and principles becomes a matter of expedience rather than conviction. As Rand puts it:

---

[97]   (Rand, Selfishness Without a Self 1974, 71-72)

A perceptual consciousness is unable to believe that ideas can be of personal importance to anyone; it regards ideas as a matter of arbitrary choice, as means to some immediate ends. [98]

Consider the case of Barack Obama, who initially opposed gay marriage but later changed his position. One can view this alteration in stance in multiple ways. If shifting public opinion or the allure of being on the "right side of history" motivated this change, rather than a shift in fundamental principles, it would illustrate the pitfalls of a perceptual mentality.

This type of politician aligns closely with the amoralist Rand describes; one whose implicit pattern of all estimates is: "It's good because I like it"—"It's right because I did it"—"It's true because I want it to be true."[99] This absence of values is not subjective but indicative of a complete lack of a moral or ethical framework. The politician, like the amoralist, does not seek election to implement specific policies; rather, he adopts specific policies to get elected. This disconnect stems from the absence of a long-range goal or a foundational principle, a notion entirely alien to a perceptual mentality.[100]

Negative Thinking and Its Philosophical Implications

Rand astutely observes that perceptual types are unable to regard ideas with the seriousness they deserve. To them, ideas merely serve immediate ends, and they often reverse the relationship of cause and effect, misconstruing outcomes as origins. This behavior aligns with Jung's characterization of "negative thinking," a type of cognition that habitually diminishes and trivializes the significance of its objects. Jung encapsulates this tendency with phrases such as "nothing but" and

---

[98] (Rand, Selfishness Without a Self 1974, 72-75)
[99] ibid
[100] ibid

"cherchez la femme" (look for the woman), which dismiss complex phenomena by reducing them to their simplest, often most cynical interpretations. For instance, the phrase "nothing but" might be used to dismiss a profound emotional response as merely a chemical reaction, while "cherchez la femme" suggests that behind every problem involving a man, a woman must be responsible, underscoring a superficial understanding of human motivations. Both examples suggest a preoccupation with surface-level motivations rather than deeper principles or values. This form of thinking not only refuses to recognize the importance of a cause but also primarily focuses on what personal gains are involved, thereby reducing any conceptual or ethical matter to a transaction or a banality.[101]

Jung states that whenever a function distinct from thinking significantly prevails in consciousness, thinking, to the extent that it remains conscious and not directly influenced by the dominant function, takes on a negative character. If it is subordinate to the dominant function, it might appear to be positive. However, on closer examination, it becomes evident that it merely imitates the dominant function, backing it with reasoning that starkly conflicts with the logical principles inherent to thinking.[102]

Building on this, Jung's concept of negative thinking serves as the psychological underpinning for such philosophies as pragmatism and critical theory. Pragmatism, focused on the utility and practical application of ideas, and critical theory, aimed at deconstructing societal norms, each manifest this negativism in their lack of a stable, long-term ethical framework. By prioritizing immediate ends, these philosophies align with the anti-conceptual mentality, reversing the relationship of cause and effect and trivializing more profound ethical or conceptual matters.

---

[101] (Jung 1923, 327)
[102] (Jung 1923, 327)

The Nature of Selfishness and Perceptual Mentalities

A constant in what Rand recognizes as a perceptual type is their inability to generate goals or values firsthand. To note, there are a great many of these types who achieve very impressive goals in life, but, as she points out, they must choose them secondhand, sticking to what is objectively possible. She elaborates on this in her essay:

> *A perceptual mentality is incapable of generating values or goals, and has to pick them secondhand, as the given, then go through the expected motions. (Not all such men are tribal lone wolves—some are faithful, bewildered tribalists out of their psycho-epistemological depth—but all are anti-conceptual mentalities.)*[103]

To illustrate, consider a few examples:

1. The Corporate Ladder Climber, who rises through the ranks by conforming to the culture of the workplace achieves high status but limits their achievements to the boundaries set by external conditions.
2. The Celebrity Influencer, who gains popularity and financial success by echoing societal trends, allows public opinion to shape them rather than following personal convictions or pursuing long-term objectives.
3. The Political Opportunist, who rises to prominence by strategically aligning with popular movements or political figures, adopts policies to win votes, but lacks a consistent ethical or ideological framework.
4. The Trend-Savvy Entrepreneur, whose business endeavors succeed by capitalizing on popular demand, lacks a comprehensive understanding of market principles or a vision for long-term growth.

---

[103] (Rand, Selfishness Without a Self 1974, 75)

5. The Academic Chameleon, who reaches a position of prestige within their field by aligning with prevailing theories or popular opinions, contributes to their discipline but lacks core original thought.

These individuals, despite achieving goals deemed extravagant by society, face limitations resulting from their reliance on externally driven values and objectives, rather than developing them through rigorous conceptual analysis. Their apparent "selfishness," often recognized in the pursuit of personal gain or ambition, is misleading; it stems not from genuine self-determination but from a conformity to societal norms and external expectations. In this sense, the traditional distinction between selfishness and selflessness becomes nullified. These individuals are not acting in their own rational self-interest; they are, in effect, "selfless" in their deference to external influences.

The Illusion of Self in the Anti-Conceptual Mentality

Rand recognizes a particular characteristic in what she terms a tribal lone wolf: a lack of self. She writes,

> With all of his emphasis on "himself" (and on being "loved for himself"), the tribal lone wolf has no self and no personal interests, only momentary whims. He is aware of his own immediate sensations and of very little else.[104]

According to Rand, these individuals believe that some external force, whether it be society or reality itself, imposes their actions, work, and values upon them. They believe their "true self" is an undefined entity, detached from these worldly attributes. This sense of self is illusory because it is non-existent. A person's authentic self consists of their mind—the faculty that perceives reality, makes judgments,

---

[104] (Rand, Selfishness Without a Self 1974, 75)

and selects values. For the tribal lone wolf, the concept of "reality" is almost meaningless; they perceive life as a kind of conspiracy against them by people and circumstances. As a result, they do not act out of any authentic desire to assert themselves; instead, they act out of a need to conceal or fill the inner void created by their absence of a genuine self. Shockingly, Rand states such an individual would even walk over piles of corpses—not to assert himself, as one might think, but merely to hide or fill the emptiness within.[105]

The Abdication of Self and Its Implications

In the context of Objectivism, the "self" equates with the ego, a concept and tendency that Jung observed in introverts. Thus, Rand's reference to the "self," for her, equates to the "mind." This means that the self, in Objectivist terms, is synonymous with one's reasoning capacity, or what I have posited to be the dominant thinking function of an introverted thinking type.

According to Jung's typology, irrational types repress the thinking function, which results in its underdevelopment. Sensation or intuition drives them, emphasizing immediate perceptions or intuitive insights over logical analysis, which results in their thinking being underutilized, less mature, and concretistic.

This condition leads Rand to perceive a lack of an apparent "self" within these types. The mentality never fully develops beyond the perceptual level of functioning. Hence, her assessment of the mentality being a transitional phenomenon caught between an animal and human's consciousness.

Rand's analysis further illuminates our understanding of rational judgment in her own words:

---

[105] (Rand, Selfishness Without a Self 1974, 68)

> *The abdication and shriveling of the self is a salient characteristic of all perceptual mentalities, tribalist or lone-wolfish. All of them dread self-reliance; all of them dread the responsibilities which only a self (i.e., a conceptual consciousness) can perform, and they seek escape from the two activities which an actually selfish man would defend with his life: judgment and choice. They fear reason (which is exercised volition-ally) and trust their emotions (which are automatic)—they prefer relatives (an accident of birth) to friends (a matter of choice)—they prefer the tribe (the given) to outsiders (the new)—they prefer commandments (the memorized) to principles (the understood)—they welcome every theory of determinism, every notion that permits them to cry: "I couldn't help it!"*[106]

The abdication of self is an inevitable characteristic of a perceptual mentality because of its deterministic nature. As Rand incisively notes, individuals with this mentality "dread the responsibilities which only a self can perform," thereby avoiding independent judgment and opting for external influences. This mentality results in judgment becoming a mere "appendage" or predetermined byproduct of perception, as opposed to the independent and introspective judgment characteristic of a conceptual consciousness. Thus, a perceptual mentality denies judgment the cognitive space necessary to exercise volitional choice.

The Historical Evolution of Ethical Perspectives: From Altruism to Individualism

It is no coincidence that the concepts of choice and self-reliance are as new to human history as is the concept of an individual. These are corollaries, brought about by the evolution of humans' ability to individuate from our concretistic beginnings. Prior to developing this ability, all humans functioned on the primitive, tribal, and purely perceptual level. But here we can use this opportunity to take another

---

[106] (Rand, Selfishness Without a Self 1974, 69)

monumental step in understanding the connectivity between the theories of Jung and Rand. Rand writes:

> *It is obvious why the morality of altruism is a tribal phenomenon. Prehistorical men were physically unable to survive without clinging to a tribe for leadership and protection against other tribes. The cause of altruism's perpetuation into civilized eras is not physical, but psycho-epistemological: the men of self-arrested, perceptual mentality are unable to survive without tribal leadership and "protection" against reality.[107]*

Altruism—"the doctrine of self-sacrifice"[108]—and Rand's rational egoism are the ethical expressions of Jung's attitudes toward rational judgment: extroversion and introversion.

Rand argues that individuals with a perceptual mentality do not find the concept of self-sacrifice troubling because they lack a well-defined sense of self or personal value. They are unfamiliar with concepts such as intellectual integrity or a passion for truth, which are intrinsically related to individualism. When they receive admonishment about "selfishness," they believe it is a warning against the impulsive and unsophisticated behavior typically displayed by an isolated member of a tribe.[109]

The Paradox of Rational Compartmentalization: Einstein as a Case Study

The transition of ethical perspectives from collective to individual is a direct result of humans' psychological development. In this context, as we examine Jung's framework, it becomes apparent that our prehistoric psychological elements persist, leading to a phenomenon known

---

[107] ibid
[108] ibid
[109] (Rand, Selfishness Without a Self 1974, 76-77)

as **compartmentalization**. Compartmentalization underscores how individuals can display rationality in certain domains while simultaneously exhibiting less rational approaches in others. This duality is reflective of the broader shift from tribal altruism to individualism, marking a complex interplay between our evolutionary past and present cognitive behaviors.

In "The Missing Link," we covered what Rand called the mixed economies of spirit, a concept akin to what she also recognizes as a sort of psychological compartmentalization. When viewed through Jung's lens, we witness this compartmentalization in the heterogeneous capacities of his psychological functions.

Having defined psycho-epistemology as the method through which one gains awareness, Rand observes that consistency in this regard is rare. She points out that many individuals oscillate between different states of consciousness depending on the situation or subject matter at hand. Their mental states can vary widely, from periods of complete rationality to times when they are in a trance-like state, barely conscious of their surroundings or actions.[110]

She further emphasizes that individuals who maintain a consistent approach, those deeply committed to their chosen method of understanding and the corresponding perspective on life, shape the outcomes of human history, whether for better or worse. These committed individuals influence the course of events, eliciting reactions of support or dissent from others whose convictions may waver, manifesting as varying degrees of engagement or detachment in their beliefs and actions.[111]

This is another example of where Jungian psychology offers a valuable framework for navigating the often-turbulent changes in cognitive

---

[110] (Rand, For the New Intellectual 1963, 21)
[111] (Rand, For the New Intellectual 1963, 21)

states that leave many in a state of psycho-epistemological confusion, lacking a consistent method of cognitive processing. Understanding one's psychological type provides stability, even as individuals undergo compensatory adjustments that might temporarily mask their primary type. Jung explains as follows,

> *In respect of one's own personality one's judgment is as a rule extraordinarily clouded. This subjective clouding of judgment is particularly common because in every pronounced type there is a special tendency to compensate the one-sidedness of that type, a tendency which is biologically purposive since it strives constantly to maintain the psychic equilibrium. The compensation gives rise to secondary characteristics, or secondary types, which present a picture that is extremely difficult to interpret, so difficult that one is inclined to deny the existence of types altogether and to believe only in individual differences.*[112]

The inconsistencies seen in most people's method of awareness that Rand mentions are results of what Jung explains in the previous passage. Individuals tend to compensate for a one-sided attitude of a type because they require both empathy and abstraction in dealing with situations that challenge their dominant mode of functioning. This compensation happens via the inferior function which is opposite to the dominant function and leads to a secondary type. Sensation and intuition are the opposing functions of perception. Thinking and feeling are the opposing functions of judgment.

The method of awareness used is important because one function of an axis is always in service of the other, therefore, if one maintains their primary method of awareness, they can integrate their judgments based on the one dominant principle rather than fluctuating between the two.

---

[112] (Jung 1923, 3)

To build and maintain successful civilizations, some level of compensation is essential: a give and take between individual and collective needs. However, Rand contends that the very split psycho-epistemological process facilitating this compensation also makes possible a dangerous disconnection between rational thinking in specialized fields, and irrationality in broader human and social contexts:

> *Today, we are seeing a ghastly spectacle: a magnificent scientific civilization dominated by the morality of prehistorical savagery. The phenomenon that makes it possible is the split psycho-epistemology of "com-partmentalized" minds. Its best example are men who escape into the physical sciences (or technology or industry or business), hoping to find protection from human irrationality, and abandoning the field of ideas to the enemies of reason. Such refugees include some of mankind's best brains. But no such refuge is possible. These men, who perform feats of conceptual integration and rational thinking in their work, become helplessly anti-conceptual in all the other aspects of their lives, particularly in human relationships and in social issues. (E.g., compare Einstein's scientific achievement to his political views.)*[113]

This passage employs the example of Albert Einstein to highlight a paradox: individuals who are highly rational and analytical in specialized fields may not extend the same level of rationality to other areas, particularly in ethical and social matters. While Einstein made groundbreaking contributions to physics, some critics, as implied here, contend that he did not apply the same rigorous reasoning to his political and ethical views. This represents an example of what Rand describes as "split psycho-epistemology," where individuals selectively deploy their rational capabilities. Even the brightest minds can compartmentalize their rationality, excelling in one area but

---

[113] (Rand, Selfishness Without a Self 1974, 77)

faltering in others, which speaks to the larger tension between the psychological functions.

Rand's observations about compartmentalization closely align with the complexities described in Jung's framework. Both thinkers point to an inherent tension between individual and collective goals, a tension that history shows is unavoidable in any society.

Jung asserts that our psychological preferences emerge from natural instincts and the path of least resistance, influenced by early environmental factors. This leads individuals to develop distinct psychological types, each favoring ways of thinking and behaving. In an ideal state, people would employ a balanced range of psychological functions for optimal adaptation. However, the reality is that most people exhibit a strong leaning toward a specific function. This creates an imbalance, often resulting in a vague sense of dissatisfaction, which compels individuals to reassess and modify their existing attitudes.[114]

This idea dovetails with Rand's observations that individuals, even those of considerable brilliance like Einstein, may excel in specialized areas but falter when facing broader human matters like politics. Thus, both Jung and Rand articulate the challenges and imperatives of balancing individual potential with collective responsibility.

The Moral Imperative of Human Progress

As we consider the balance between individual and collective needs, it is worth turning to Rand's insights on the role of specialization in human progress as she concludes her essay. She contends that although specialization is necessary for the advancement of society, a rational philosophy must guide it to enable and ensure the full development of human potential. Rand articulates this point succinctly:

---

[114] (Jung 1923, 16)

133

Man's progress requires specialization. But a division-of-labor society cannot survive without a rational philosophy—without a firm base of fundamental principles whose task is to train a human mind to be human, i.e., conceptual.[115]

This statement serves as a capstone to our discussion, emphasizing that the evolution of human cognition from a purely perceptual state to one capable of abstract thought is not just a historical fact but also a moral imperative. Therefore, it is incumbent upon humanity to continue to evolve in this direction, even though not all individuals will attain a fully conceptual state of mind.

The United States, founded on a rational philosophy encapsulated in its constitution, represents what Rand describes as "the most moral country" in principle. However, the preservation of this rational philosophy requires ongoing intellectual vigilance against the enemies of reason, most notably, tribalists and tribal lone wolves.

---

[115] (Rand, Selfishness Without a Self 1974, 78)

"Mental Health versus Mysticism and Self-Sacrifice"

Having established in "The Psychology of Psychologizing" that moral judgment is the province of ethical philosophy reserved for humans as conscious beings, this article presents an exploration into the relationship between psychological well-being, the concept of the self, and ethical dimensions. Written by Nathaniel Branden, the text emphasizes how consciousness and the morality of self-sacrifice shape mental health, providing a framework for interpreting human behavior and ethical decision-making. To this, we bring in Jung's theories on rational judgment to examine the interplay between psychological types and their influence on moral reasoning and self-perception.

The author of this article, Nathaniel Branden, was a psychotherapist with a PhD in psychology and was a key collaborator and confidant of Ayn Rand. However, due to intellectual and personal disagreements, he faced ostracism from the Objectivist movement in 1970, which profoundly influenced his career. Seminal Objectivist works like "The Virtue of Selfishness" and "Capitalism: The Unknown Ideal" contain Branden's early writings. His growing interest in psychological concepts, which diverged from Rand's philosophical tenets, led him to explore psychological self-improvement and self-esteem, blending and deviating from Objectivist principles.

Branden's View on Consciousness and Mental Health

Early in the essay, Branden sets the stage for our discussion of ethics by reiterating the exact terms in which Objectivism views rationality, which has direct implications on one's understandings about mental health and the self. He writes,

Self-esteem is the consequence, expression and reward of a mind fully committed to reason.[116]

Here, it is crucial to remember that Objectivism's concept of reason takes on a particular form when considered within the wider scope of rationality as theorized in Jungian psychology. This view of reason orients specifically toward the thinking function. However, Branden provides further insight into the Objectivist perspective as he posits his unique views on the proper orientation of a human consciousness:

An unobstructed consciousness, an integrated consciousness, a thinking consciousness, is a healthy consciousness. A blocked consciousness, an evading consciousness, a consciousness torn by conflict and divided against itself, a consciousness disintegrated by fear or immobilized by depression, a consciousness dissociated from reality, is an unhealthy consciousness.[117]

In the above, Branden explicitly attributes "thinking" to a healthy consciousness, and the additional categorization of it as "unobstructed" and "integrated" distinctly reflects a rational and introverted approach. This view aligns closely with Jung's characterization of the introverted thinking type. Additionally, Branden's depiction of an unhealthy consciousness as one "torn by conflict and divided against itself" further underscores the introverted nature of his ideal, suggesting an inner struggle that is typical in introverted introspection and self-analysis.

Branden's Critique of Traditional Morality

To grasp fully the philosophical argument Branden presents here, and to demonstrate its significance in helping clarify a proper approach to ethics, it serves us well to proceed to his ensuing ruminations on

---

[116] (Branden, Mental Health versus Mysticism and Self-Sacrifice 1964, 45)
[117] (Branden, Mental Health versus Mysticism and Self-Sacrifice 1964, 45-46)

how, in his assessment, traditional moral views, particularly those generated through mysticism or a creed of self-sacrifice, significantly cripple self-esteem. He argues that these doctrines are fundamentally incompatible with both self-esteem and mental health, labeling them as existentially and psychologically destructive.[118]

This stance challenges the suitability of Jung's other rational types, particularly in relation to their alternate styles of reasoning. The conflict arises primarily in two fundamental areas of principle: one, feeling, and the other, extroversion. Branden writes,

> *The maintenance of his life and the achievement of self-esteem require of man the fullest exercise of his reason—but morality, men are taught, rests on and requires faith.*
>
> *When a man rejects reason as his standard of judgment, only one alternative standard remains to him: his feelings. A mystic is a man who treats his feelings as tools of cognition. Faith is the equation of feeling with knowledge.*
>
> *To practice the "virtue" of faith, one must be willing to suspend one's sight and one's judgment; one must be willing to live with the unintelligible, with that which cannot be conceptualized or integrated into the rest of one's knowledge, and to induce a trancelike illusion of understanding.*[119]

Emotionalism: The Ethics of Feeling Types

Branden dismisses the use of feelings as tools of cognition, suggesting that a psycho-epistemological reliance on feeling leads to irrationality and conflicts with mental health. I interpret this as his condemnation of the Jungian feeling type's approach to knowledge, and their resulting ethics. Being a completely subjective method of judgment, with little

---

[118] (Branden, Mental Health versus Mysticism and Self-Sacrifice 1964, 46)
[119] (Branden, Mental Health versus Mysticism and Self-Sacrifice 1964, 46)

regard for objective or sensory proofs, he would classify this type as mystical and one utilizing an invalid means of reason.

To delve deeper, I incorporate the Objectivist perspective on feeling, as articulated by Leonard Peikoff, particularly from his subsection titled "Emotions as a Product of Ideas" in "Objectivism: The Philosophy of Ayn Rand." He states:

> *A feeling or emotion is a response to an object one perceives (or imagines), such as a man, an animal, an event. The object by itself, however, has no power to invoke a feeling in the observer. It can do so only if he supplies two intellectual elements, which are necessary conditions of any emotion.*[120]

While the two necessary elements referred to here—identification and evaluation—are the outputs of Jung's thinking and feeling functions respectively, first it is important to make a crucial distinction which requires further clarification.

Jung uses the terms "emotion" and "affect" synonymously, referring to an intense "feeling state" often accompanied by noticeable physical innervations, distinguishing them from the "feeling" function, which is a more subtle, evaluative psychological experience. "Sensation," on the other hand, pertains to the direct perception of stimuli through the senses and is distinct from the evaluative "feeling" function, or its resulting "affect" (emotion).

Conversely, Peikoff, while aligning with Jung's definition of "emotion," uses the terms "feeling" and "emotion" indiscriminately, yet also employs the term "value judgment," a concept that aligns with Jung's feeling function. Thus, we can conclude that Peikoff identifies "emotions" as products of the "value judgments" associated with the feeling function and assume that there is a fundamental alignment in

---

[120] (Peikoff 1991, 154)

their understanding of "feeling" as an evaluative process. He details the entire cognitive chain leading to emotions as follows:

> *There are four steps in the generation of an emotion: perception (or imagination), identification, evaluation, response. Normally, only the first and last of these are conscious. The two intellectual steps, identification and evaluation, occur as a rule without the need of conscious awareness and with lightninglike rapidity.*[121]

From these steps, we immediately identify Jung's psychological functions. The area of perception consists of both sensation and intuition. The thinking function aligns with the process of identification, and the feeling function aligns with the process of evaluation; emotion remains the result.

Furthermore, according to Objectivism, feelings or emotions are not part of the logical method, and they do not constitute evidence for reaching conclusions. Thought and sensory evidence guide a rational inquiry, which relies on demonstrable, objective facts rather than any form of passion. This involves ensuring that one's feelings are set aside and not allowed to influence the course of inquiry or its outcome. However, Peikoff also makes an especially important declaration of the philosophy's tenets:

> *Objectivism is not against emotions, but emotionalism... There is nothing wrong with feeling that follows from an act of thought; this is the natural and proper human pattern. There is everything wrong with feeling that seeks to replace thought, by usurping its function.*[122]

In instances where an individual encounters a conflict between feeling and thought, Objectivism advises against disregarding these feelings. Instead, it suggests a thorough examination of the underlying

---

[121] (Peikoff 1991, 155-156)
[122] (Peikoff 1991, 161)

ideas, which might be a detailed and extensive process. This involves comparing these underlying ideas with one's conscious conclusions and objectively assessing any conflicts. The goal is not to suppress feelings through repression but to fully identify and rationally analyze the ideas at the root of these emotions. This process, when undertaken by the individual, should result in a new and noncontradictory integration of thoughts and feelings. The individual amends their viewpoint by considering the ideas judged to be true and discarding those deemed false. This approach fosters a harmonious relationship between emotion and reason, aligning with the Objectivist ethos of integrating feelings within a framework of rational thought.[123]

The above references allow us to firmly establish that Objectivism equates the feeling type's psycho-epistemological method to emotionalism.

Rational Extroversion: The Archetypes of Self-Sacrifice

The concept of extroverted rational types in Jung's framework offers another lens to examine Branden's ideas. This pertains to both the extroverted thinking and feeling types, the second of which were addressed in our examination of emotionalism.

Determinist, nominalist, and empiricist are all embodiments of extroversion; both Rand and Jung touch on the deterministic nature of the extroverted type and their tendency for compartmentalization—keeping different spheres of life, such as science and religion, separate.[124]

This relates back to the mind-body dichotomy, a concept often discussed by Rand. To summarize Jung's view, in determining if a thought process is extroverted, the key question is whether its guiding criteria come from external sources or are subjective in origin. He writes,

---

[123] (Peikoff 1991, 161)
[124] (Jung 1923, 294)

Judgment always presupposes a criterion; for the extroverted judgment, the criterion supplied by external conditions is the valid and determining one, no matter whether it be represented directly by an objective, perceptible fact or by an objective idea; for an objective idea is equally determined by external data or borrowed from outside even when it is subjectively sanctioned. Extroverted thinking, therefore, need not necessarily be purely concretistic thinking; it can just as well be purely ideal thinking, if for instance it can be shown that the ideas it operates with are largely borrowed from outside, i.e., have been transmitted by tradition and education. So in judging whether a particular thinking is extroverted or not we must first ask: by what criterion does it judge—does it come from outside, or is its origin subjective?[125]

While one might assume the extroverted thinking type, with their focus on objectivity and logic, suggests an alignment with Objectivist reason, what we witness in the thinking of this type is not one that is consciously introspective and individualistic, as Branden advocates. Instead, Jung's extroverted thinking type employs an attitude toward thinking that conforms to prevailing standards, making them likely to accept self-sacrificing traditional views of morality, precisely due to the wide and popular acceptance of those views.

Turning back to Jung for additional insight into this dynamic, he uses a historical example from the Catholic Church to contrast the opposing thinking types of the introvert and extrovert. The story explores a ninth–century debate between Abbot Paschasius Radbertus and philosopher Johannes Scotus Erigena, regarding the doctrine of transubstantiation. This doctrine asserts that during the Christian ritual of Communion, the wine and wafer undergo an actual transformation into the blood and body of Christ, rather than merely materially symbolizing them.

---

[125] (Jung 1923, 317-318)

Radbertus advocated for this doctrine, and it eventually became accepted Church dogma. Scotus Erigena, on the other hand, held a rationalist view that the Communion was a symbolic commemoration of Jesus's last supper with his disciples, and not a miraculous transformation.

The story discusses how these opposing viewpoints reflect broader psychological orientations: Radbertus's view aligns with extroverted, concrete thinking that was in tune with the desires of the society of his time, whereas Erigena represents introverted, rational thinking. The story considers both perspectives valuable for their contributions to the religious and intellectual life of their era. However, Jung concludes from this debate:

> *What we may learn from this example is that the thinking of the introvert is incommensurable with the thinking of the extrovert, since the two forms of thinking, as regards their determinants, are wholly and fundamentally different. We might perhaps say that the thinking of the introvert is rational, while that of the extrovert is programmatic.*[126]

As it relates to judgment, the fundamental difference in attitudes of the two types is solely a result of the source of their conditioning. The subject conditions the introvert, while the object conditions the extrovert. It is important to note that this dynamic implies the extrovert places a higher value on the external, effectively lowering the relative value of the subject. We can safely say this psychological difference is the crux of all persistent conflicts between the types.

This dynamic has enormous ethical significance, precisely due to the extrovert's approach to consciousness, which is the source of all personal values. Lacking full individuation, their consciousness remains undifferentiated from the collective or external viewpoints.

---

[126] (Jung 1923, 22)

Consequently, their personal values and ethical judgments may not be entirely self-derived but are often reflections of the prevailing norms and beliefs of their environment.

Examples of this mimetic and programmatically obedient thinking include devout followers who interpret religious texts literally and subordinate their own moral or rational faculties to the "will of God." Embracing sayings like, "Let go and let God," such individuals may pursue religious doctrines without questioning their implications, context, or their alignment with personal values.

On the other hand, when the objective material consists of secondhand ideas expressed through societal norms, others come to mind: for example, the high-achieving student who selects a career in medicine solely because society deems it prestigious without having a genuine interest in the field. Similarly, people may engage in charitable activities, such as volunteering at food banks or community clean-up events, primarily to boost their social standing or meet societal expectations without a deeper understanding or engagement with the issues they are addressing. Here, the secular version of subservience, "Kill your ego," signifies a similar relinquishment of personal desires and inclinations, not to a higher power, but to societal expectations.

In these cases, individuals willingly subdue their personal judgment to the empathized external factor—be it religious doctrines or societal norms—often without even realizing it, thereby detaching from, and ignoring their own firsthand experiences.

Another example serving to illustrate how extroverted thinking operates in application—and not to imply that individuals in these roles are extroverted thinkers in their overall personality—exists in the role of an American judge. A judge's task is to interpret and apply the law as designed by the legislative branch. While the judge may have private opinions or disagreements with the law itself, their professional responsibility mandates adherence to the legislative guidelines.

This form of thinking accepts legal concepts "secondhand" from lawmakers, without the judge necessarily generating independent concepts or interpretations beyond what the text of the law explicitly states. Therefore, even if a judge encounters a case for which they personally disagree with the guidelines set by legislators, their duty requires them to apply those guidelines impartially.

Jung notes that the extroverted thinking type's tendency toward adjustment grants them an appearance of "normality." However, this is a double-edged sword: Their normality confines them to what is objectively possible under existing conditions and exposes them to ethical and conceptual pitfalls when those conditions change. This is not genuine adaptation, according to Jung, which would require a commitment to more enduring, universal principles.[127]

Thus, one can understand Branden's depiction of a consciousness impaired by the uncritical acceptance of beliefs (mysticism) and the disregard for independent thought (self-sacrifice) as a philosophical reflection of the conflicts inherent in a reliance on the feeling function or a psyche dominated by rational extroversion. In this light, we can view Branden's arguments as a philosophical extension of Jung's theories, not as contradictory to them.

Branden's Examination of Rationality and Consciousness

Elaborating his views further, Branden explains the dangers of integrating non-rational ideas into one's consciousness. He warns against adopting concepts that lack grounding or reason, or that conflict with one's existing understanding of the world. Such actions, he argues, disrupt the integrative function of consciousness, weakening one's convictions and eroding the certainty in one's knowledge base. This viewpoint highlights the critical importance he places on the

---

[127] (Jung 1923, 312)

consistency and integrity of conscious thought, particularly in the realm of ethical philosophy.[128]

Furthermore, Branden emphasizes the impossibility of dividing one's consciousness between reason and faith. He asserts that any concession to faith, even in the smallest measure, leads to a total surrender of consciousness. In his view, faith and reason are mutually exclusive; to accept faith even slightly is to compromise one's commitment to reason entirely. This absolutist stance reflects Branden's conviction in the supremacy of reason and its role as the sole arbiter of judgment and morality. He writes,

> *There is only one reality—the reality knowable to reason. And if man does not choose to perceive it, there is nothing else for him to perceive; if it is not of this world that he is conscious, then he is not conscious at all.*[129]

Branden emphasizes the necessity for man to take pride in his ability to think, suggesting that self-esteem and life itself depend on the full exercise of rational thought.[130] This perspective underlines the importance of reason as the only valid tool for navigating reality and maintaining mental health.

Branden's Critique of Traditional Morality and the Role of Pride

In his discourse on rationality and consciousness, Branden delves into the concept of **pride** in intellectual achievement, challenging the negative connotations often associated with it in mystic morality. Paraphrasing his thoughts, he argues that intellectual pride is not an overestimation of one's knowledge or abilities, as mysticism might imply. Instead, it is a rightful acknowledgment of the effort

---

[128] (Branden, Mental Health versus Mysticism and Self-Sacrifice 1964, 47)
[129] (Branden, Mental Health versus Mysticism and Self-Sacrifice 1964, 47)
[130] (Branden, Mental Health versus Mysticism and Self-Sacrifice 1964, 48)

and responsibility involved in the pursuit of knowledge. True pride, according to Branden, is a recognition of one's efficacy in achieving values, not the boastful pretense of unearned accomplishments. He differentiates this genuine sense of pride from the false bravado of one who feigns virtues he does not possess, labeling the latter as a display of humility rather than pride.[131]

This interpretation of pride as a positive response to one's intellectual capabilities directly contrasts with the mystic view, which often deems such pride as evil or egocentric. Branden's assertion here aligns with Jung's observation that extroverts often mistakenly perceive introverts as egocentric or self-absorbed. This misconception, however, overlooks the essential nature of introverted adaptation—the deep, inward focus on personal values and understandings. Extroverts often engage in such misinterpretation, mirroring the condemnation of pride in mystic morality, where they often mistake self-reliance and confidence for arrogance or self-absorption.[132]

In this context, Jung's perspective bolsters Branden's view that the condemnation of intellectual pride is rooted in a misunderstanding of the introverted approach. The "selflessness" often celebrated in rational extroversion, which values collective standards and external validation, contributes to this critical view of pride. This aligns with Branden's critique, suggesting that such extroverted judgment, both in thinking and feeling types, tends to uphold a collective orientation that he finds detrimental to individual well-being and ethical integrity. Branden encapsulates this argument with a poignant statement:

> *If doubt, not confidence, is man's proper moral state; if self-distrust, not self-reliance, is the proof of his virtue; if fear, not self-esteem, is the mark of perfection; if guilt, not pride, is his goal—then mental illness is a moral ideal.*[133]

---

[131] (Branden, Mental Health versus Mysticism and Self-Sacrifice 1964, 48)
[132] (Jung 1923, 347)
[133] (Branden, Mental Health versus Mysticism and Self-Sacrifice 1964, 50)

This perspective, which emphasizes self-reliance and individual judgment as paramount, aligns with a rationally introverted attitude.

Branden's critique underscores the problematic nature of a moral framework that prioritizes doubt, self-distrust, fear, and guilt; over confidence, self-reliance, self-esteem, and pride. In contrast, a collectively oriented framework associated with extroverted judgment is fundamentally different from Branden's approach. The traits he criticizes reflect this detrimental collective orientation. His viewpoint challenges the mystic condemnation of pride and reveals the potential pitfalls of a morality designed in accordance with the values and standards of extroverted rational types.

Jung's Extroverted Judgment: A Closer Look

Jung describes extroverted judgment, both in thinking and feeling types, as heavily reliant on objective data and societal definitions of rationality. This reliance often represses subjective reasoning and individual perspectives. As the focus on external objects intensifies, the unconscious, filled with compulsive sensations and destructive intuitions, grows stronger. This creates a conflict where the overpowering unconscious disrupts the conscious adherence to collective rationality, causing inner turmoil and doubt.[134] Jung emphasizes this in the extroverted thinking type in particular:

> *The more it tries to fend off the doubt, the more fanatical the conscious attitude becomes, for fanaticism is nothing but over-compensated doubt.*[135]

Over time, this results in a highly defensive conscious stance and the emergence of an opposing, unconscious viewpoint. For example, unconscious irrationality may counter a consciously rational

---

[134] (Jung 1923)
[135] (Jung 1923, 325-326)

perspective, and an archaic and superstitious viewpoint in the unconscious may oppose a scientific stance.[136]

Exploring the complexities of Jung's concept of extroverted judgment, the following case studies illustrate how this dynamic manifests in individuals with dominant extroverted thinking and feeling functions, respectively, and the resulting inner conflicts that arise from their psychological orientations.

Case Study: The Rational Scientist's Dilemma

Dr. Smith, a scientist with a reputation as formidable, is deeply committed to a life governed by evidence-based practice and rational thought. He firmly anchors his approach in empirical data and logical analysis in both his professional and personal life. This dedication has made him a respected figure in his field, known for his intellectual precision and dismissal of anything not supported by hard evidence, including spirituality, superstitions, and subjective forms of expression like art and literature.

Despite his outward confidence in rationality, Dr. Smith begins to face an internal crisis manifested through recurring dreams, rich in mystical and archaic symbolism. This development is perplexing to him, as it starkly contrasts with his empirical and logical worldview. The content of these dreams, alongside a growing fascination with ancient folklore and myths, introduces a profound sense of doubt in Dr. Smith's mind. This doubt does not pertain solely to his professional work but extends to the very foundation of his belief system and worldview.

This emerging doubt and the accompanying interest in the irrational and mystical represent a significant shift in Dr. Smith's psyche. These subconscious contents are now challenging his long-dominant

---

[136] ibid

extroverted thinking, which has suppressed subjective and emotional aspects. The dreams and interests in mythological themes symbolize the subconscious compensatory response to the over-emphasized rationality of his conscious mind. They reveal a deeper layer of his personality that seeks expression and acknowledgment.

Case Study: The Compassionate Leader's Internal Critique

Ms. Johnson, a corporate leader, excels in her role thanks to her extroverted feeling orientation, skillfully creating a harmonious and emotionally supportive work environment. She prides herself on making decisions that reflect the emotional states and values of her team, fostering a positive and inclusive atmosphere.

Beneath a calm exterior, Ms. Johnson encounters an undercurrent of critical, analytical thoughts that sporadically surface, casting doubt on the authenticity and practicality of her emotion-driven decisions. This inner critical voice, a manifestation of her suppressed introverted thinking function, challenges the values she upholds, especially in moments when her feeling function is intensely engaged. These doubts, though often repressed and unacknowledged, start to erode her confidence and introduce a sense of inner conflict.

This scenario reveals the challenges inherent in the one-sidedness of Ms. Johnson's psychological orientation. Her unconscious mind is striving for equilibrium, bringing forth elements of doubt and critical analysis as a natural response to the dominance of her feeling-based approach. This emergence of a contrasting inner voice, although negative and self-deprecating, is a crucial process aimed at countering the potential imbalance created by her primary focus on extroverted feeling. It underscores the Jungian principle that a highly developed dominant function can lead to the surfacing of its opposite, seeking to introduce a more balanced perspective in her overall psyche.

The Pitfalls of Dogmatic Rationalism

Jung discusses the psychological tendencies that lead to dogmatism and the oscillation between fanaticism and doubt in individuals dominated by extroverted judgment. This orientation manifests as an outward display of strong confidence in either rational, intellectual formulas or emotional and relational harmony; while simultaneously repressing opposing viewpoints, such as mystical or religious perspectives within the unconscious. This dynamic creates a counter-position that can give rise to internal psychological conflicts and doubt.

Branden identifies a similar pattern in what he considers the prevailing cultural attitude—what we could term "dogmatic rationalism." According to Branden, if this dogmatic rationalism represents the dominant psycho-epistemological orientation in society, then mental illness becomes a moral ideal. The societal endorsement of a dogmatic, one-sided view of reality contributes to psychological discord and potential mental illness, as it encourages an orientation that is inherently conflicted and lacks integration of opposing psychological tendencies or viewpoints.

The Ethical Dimensions of Self-Sacrifice

Continuing with Branden, his analysis of self-sacrifice in relation to mental health highlights a crucial aspect:

> The first is the fact that self-sacrifice means—and can only mean—mind-sacrifice.

> A sacrifice, it is necessary to remember, means the surrender of a higher value in favor of a lower value or of a nonvalue.[137]

When interpreting Branden's use of the term "mind," one might construe it as referring to the ego, particularly in the context of

---

[137] (Branden, Mental Health versus Mysticism and Self-Sacrifice 1964, 51)

rational thinking. However, this interpretation once again suggests a limited view, aligned with introverted thinking, which does not fully encompass the diversity of mental orientations described in Jung's psychological types. For instance, an extroverted feeling type, who places high value on emotional connections and community engagement, might have an alternative perspective on what constitutes mental well-being. Jung's theory proposes that some psychological types prioritize the dominance of the collective function, relegating the subjective function to a subordinate role. This prioritization results in a self-identity closely intertwined with relationships to the external.

The Complexity of Self-Sacrifice: Introverts versus Extroverts

Self-sacrifice can mean different things depending on one's psychological type. The introvert sacrifices themself by forfeiting their subjective values, whether intellectual or emotional. The extrovert sacrifices themself by severing their ties with objects or social groups. Jung expands on these issues, drawing from Schiller's ideas to deepen his own insights into the ego's variable states, which differ between introverted and extroverted psychological types. Schiller, whom Jung explicitly characterizes as an introvert, states:

> To remain constantly himself throughout all change, to turn every perception into experience, that is, into the unity of knowledge, and to make each of his manifestations in time a law for all time, that is the rule which is prescribed for him by his rational nature.[138]

In this vein, both introverts and extroverts have two defining factors affecting their psychology: one being the conscious function of their ego, and the other being their relationship with the collective or external world. Introverts, such as Schiller, focus on maintaining a constant ego, often at the expense of their emotional states. Extroverts,

---

[138] (Jung 1923, 82)

however, place more emphasis on their ongoing relationships with objects or people, viewing their ego as less central. This diverging focus illustrates that what constitutes self-sacrifice can vary depending on one's psychological orientation.[139]

Based on Jung's elaboration, it becomes evident that Schiller and Branden's viewpoints share a common thread. Specifically, they emphasize the introverted orientation, particularly in their focus on the constancy and importance of the ego function.

In Jungian psychology, it is essential to clarify the role of the ego as distinct from specific psychological functions such as thinking, feeling, sensation, and intuition. The ego employs these functions to navigate both the internal and external worlds, aiming to maintain its stability and to mediate between the conscious and unconscious aspects of the psyche. It is responsible for a person's sense of identity and continuity over time, as well as for testing reality—distinguishing between internal subjective experiences and external objective realities.

In this context, the "constancy of the ego function" refers to the stable, unchanging nature of the ego in introverted individuals. These individuals often prioritize their internal world of thoughts, values, and subjective experiences over external relationships and objects. This focus on ego constancy contrasts sharply with the more variable nature of the ego in extroverted individuals, who give greater emphasis to external objects and relationships. This underscores the idea that different psychological orientations can have a profound influence on how individuals perceive and prioritize various aspects of mental well-being.

The Ethical Responsibility of the Psychological Community

In concluding his essay, Branden extends his critique by questioning the ethical responsibilities of mental health professionals. He challenges

---

[139] ibid

their neglect to address philosophical and moral issues, as he claims these doctrines have negative psychological effects:

> *There is a group who, perhaps, bears a graver responsibility still: the psychologists and psychiatrists who see the human wreckage of these doctrines, but who remain silent and do not protest— who declare that philosophical and moral issues do not concern them, that science cannot pronounce value judgments—who shrug off their professional obligations with the assertion that a rational code of morality is impossible, and, by their silence, lend their sanction to spiritual murder.*[140]

While finding merit in Branden's critique of rational extroversion— specifically that a diminished sense of self results from an overemphasis on external relationships and objects that often lead to negative mental health outcomes—I also recognize the limitations of his introverted, intellectually-oriented analysis, that neglects to fully capture the nature and complexities of extroverted individuals. Branden goes further to imply that these pitfalls of extroversion have moral implications, suggesting that the psychological community should label what equates to Jung's rational extroversion as a form of dysfunction. He posits that by not doing so, psychologists and psychiatrists are abdicating a moral responsibility, effectively endorsing what he perceives to be a damaging psychological orientation.

While it may be tempting to support this perspective, I find it problematic. Though there is a compelling argument that extroversion can sometimes lead to a dissolution of self or mental health issues, it is essential to recognize that extroversion and introversion are different orientations, with their own strengths and weaknesses. Categorizing extroversion as inherently dysfunctional would not only be reductive but it would also be to misunderstand the role of psychological diversity in human experience.

---

[140] (Branden, Mental Health versus Mysticism and Self-Sacrifice 1964, 54)

What Branden—who criticizes the one-sided nature of extroverted types—fails to recognize, and what Jung rightfully acknowledges in his work, is the evidence of their useful contributions throughout human history. Humans have achieved whatever feats they have in cooperation and combination with extroverted types, not in spite of them. Yet, the introvert finds it difficult to understand the nature of the extrovert because of their inherent intellectuality, causing the former to have a hypersensitivity to the negatively perceived and frequently innocuous traits of the latter.

The psychological community should be attentive to the ethical dimensions of their work, and it is not within their purview to make explicit moral pronouncements. The role of science, particularly psychology, is to offer objective measurements and frameworks for understanding human behavior and mental processes. While it is true that scientific findings can inform ethical discussions, science alone cannot govern the domain of morality. Science provides us with a formula—an equation of variables. However, the values that inform these variables are subjective and must be determined by the individual, not by scientific consensus.

Having science pronounce moral judgments would be just another form of collectivity, as witnessed in Auguste Comte's positivism, which advocates for the governance of society based on scientific principles and effectively erases the line between objective scientific inquiry and subjective moral values. This approach risks enforcing a one-size-fits-all morality that ignores individual variances, thus becoming a form of intellectual collectivism.

Fortunately, Jung developed the types to aid in understanding the psychological makeup of others who are dissimilar from oneself. Therefore, a psychologist or psychiatrist has no reason to protest in favor of a specific type, as Branden appears to do in his argument for a specific orientation. Each type has its right to existence and each type proves useful in society.

Individuals who demonstrate the one-sided attitude toward introversion are just as destructive in terms of social cohesion and mutual understanding as those who lean toward extroversion. The error lies in the one-sidedness.

For example, a society focusing solely on collective orientation might suppress or ignore the nuances of individual personalities, talents, and capabilities, which can result in a loss of individualism and self-actualization. On the other hand, a society that overvalues introversion might overlook the importance of community and collective welfare, resulting in disconnected individuals and a weakened social fabric. When individuals elevate their preferred cognitive orientation—be it introverted or extroverted—over a specific set of actions or behaviors, and then consider this preference as a universal standard for moral judgment, they risk unjustly imposing their personal preferences onto others.

"Causality Versus Duty"

Continuing the narrative woven throughout the previous sections, we trace the journey from psychological patterns to their ethical implications. By contrasting lives governed by duty and rooted in external authorities or societal norms, with those steered by an awareness of causality, we explore how psychological foundations influence decision-making and manifest in concrete ethical realities. Specifically, this exploration illuminates how a distorted sense of self leads to discernible ethical consequences. This approach not only unravels the impact [of what?] on individual rights but also shapes the discourse on ethical living.

"Duty": A Mystic Anti-Concept

Rand defines "duty" as the moral necessity to perform certain actions for no reason other than obedience to some higher authority, disregarding any personal goal, motive, desire, or interest. She argues that this anti-concept is a product of mysticism and not an abstraction derived from reality. In mystic theories of ethics, duty stands for the notion that humans must obey the dictates of a supernatural authority. Even when secularized and attributed to earthly entities such as parents, country, state, or mankind, this alleged supremacy still rests on a mystic foundation.[141]

Linking Duty to Rational Attitudes: The Seed of Mysticism

To expand on this in the context of themes we have explored thus far, Rand's critique of duty corresponds with her views on rationality. In Jungian terms, those who adhere to a sense of duty often orient their judgment according to societal norms or objective values rather than independent reasoning. This object-oriented method of

---

[141] (Rand, Causality Versus Duty 1974, 134)

engagement becomes their duty, a manifestation of a rational attitude that prioritizes external judgments over a conceptual understanding. In linking these themes, we see that Rand's disavowal of duty serves as a criticism against those who subjugate reason in favor of objective values, perceived through a mystic or perceptual lens.

The Kantian View of Duty: Childhood Conditioning

Rand directs her focus to a Kantian perspective on duty and asserts that parents often instill it by imposing arbitrary and inexplicable "musts" on their children. This form of upbringing prevents children from discerning realistic necessities and human whims, causing them to live in obedience to the latter and defiance with the former. As a result, they grow up without a clear grasp of reality.[142]

The Role of Education Systems in Perpetuating Mystic Philosophy

The previous perspectives illuminate the logical incoherence behind collective anti-concepts. When a society's education system is rooted in mystic philosophy—an approach that encourages collective thinking and bypasses conceptual explanations in favor of spiritual or societal absolutes—it can never expect to produce fully functional, rational human beings. In fact, such an education often creates just the opposite: It stunts children's cognitive development, which is devastating to the development of proper ethics for a rational and free society.

Bridging Philosophical Divides: Rand, Rousseau, and Jung

In juxtaposition to Rand's strong repudiation of duty, Jean-Jacques Rousseau, a seminal Enlightenment philosopher, offers an intriguing

---

[142] (Rand, Causality Versus Duty 1974, 137)

counterpoint via Jung. While Rand vehemently argues against the concept of duty, Rousseau presents additional nuance from an alternative perspective that is not entirely antithetical to Rand's views. Jung's psychological theories might serve as a bridge between these two. Therefore, what appear superficially to be contradictory philosophical viewpoints could be complementary when looked at through the lens of psychological functions and attitudes.

To broaden our understanding, Jung quotes Rousseau on comparable questions. Rousseau argues that relying on nature is not morally wrong, but relying on humans is. According to him, if human laws were as unbreakable as natural laws, then people could enjoy the benefits of both nature and society. This suggests that the concept of duty can only be a secondhand idea, as it presupposes judgment and can only mean obedience to humans rather than any abstract or divine authority.[143]

Furthering this thought, according to Jung, the individual, when left to their natural instincts, adheres to a moral code often more exacting than civilized morality, arguing that "his naturalism leads to lawgiving." This aligns with Rousseau's view of natural law over human law. Jung emphasizes,

> *Morality is not a misconception invented by some vaunting Moses on Sinai, but something inherent in the laws of life and fashioned like a house or a ship or any other cultural instrument.*[144]

This concept not only bridges Rand's critique of duty with Rousseau's naturalism but also highlights that morality, as Jung might argue, is an intrinsic part of life, echoing psychological perspectives.

The Psychological Dimensions of Duty: From Rand to Jung

Rand further elaborates that even as adults, individuals with a Kantian upbringing continue to feel obligated to perform various duties, including earning a living or being moral. She suggests that this represents a psycho-epistemological issue,[145] which, in our framework, relates to one's use of rational functions. This line of thought leads us to identify that the duty to be moral is a result of collective feeling, while the duty to be rational stems from collective thinking. A sense of duty or willingness to follow is a feature of the extroverted judgment functions.

In sum, a Kantian individual focuses not on goals but on his moral character, driven by a complex set of emotional reactions such as guilt, fear, and, as I would add, shame. This focus diminishes the importance of his goals, leading to a life plagued by self-doubt—the same self-doubt we witnessed Branden speak of in "Mental Health versus Mysticism and Self-Sacrifice." The types oriented toward collective judgment experience this fear of not fulfilling their duty in different forms. Collective feeling manifests this fear as guilt, while collective thinking experiences it as shame, which often stems from the apprehension of others finding out about their perceived shortcomings or failures.[146]

The Lifelong Impact of Duty: A Comprehensive Look

To illustrate the profound impact of a duty-bound upbringing on individual lives, let us examine several hypothetical but representative cases. Each story demonstrates how the sense of duty, as shaped by various backgrounds, can significantly influence one's life choices and psychological well-being.

---

[145] (Rand, Causality Versus Duty 1974, 137)
[146] (Rand, Causality Versus Duty 1974, 139)

John: The Altruistic Community Organizer

John grew up in a home that prioritized community service. His parents actively participated in charitable work and instilled in him the belief that dedicating his time to helping others was the highest priority. They frequently dismissed personal hobbies or interests in favor of altruistic pursuits, which cultivated a sense of guilt in John whenever he focused on himself.

As an adult, John became a community organizer, a career that aligns with his upbringing. However, he often feels guilty when faced with opportunities that could advance his career but conflict with community meetings. He chooses community over personal growth yet remains uneasy about the opportunities he forgoes.

John's life exemplifies the kind of moral servitude that Rand warns against. He sacrifices personal joys and aspirations in the name of a "greater good." Over time, this not only diminishes John as an individual but could also influence the younger generation in the community to adopt a similar, self-sacrificing approach to life. This perpetuates a cycle of moral duty at the cost of individual freedom and happiness.

Emily: The Academically Driven Perfectionist

Born to university professors, Emily grew up in an atmosphere that prized academic achievement more than anything else. She saw mistakes as shameful, which led her to become a perfectionist, constantly seeking external validation.

Emily becomes an academic and lives in fear of making mistakes. When she realizes an error in a published paper, she experiences profound shame, more concerned about the judgment of her peers than the inherent value of her work.

Emily's life is a cautionary tale about the psychological toll that a duty-driven upbringing can take. While she may produce quality academic work, her obsessive focus on duty deprives her of a well-rounded life experience. Furthermore, her perfectionism may impede innovative thinking, creating a ripple effect in the academic community she is a part of.

Sarah: The Inauthentic Life of a Transgender Woman

Growing up in a conservative, religious household, Sarah's upbringing conditioned her to conform to traditional gender roles. Her parents discouraged any non-conforming behavior, making her internalize societal norms and leading to a life of guilt and inner conflict.

Sarah continues to struggle with her identity, choosing not to come out as transgender at her conservative workplace. Influenced by a sense of duty toward societal norms, she pays a high personal cost for living inauthentically.

Sarah's story highlights the devastating impact that societal notions of duty can have on marginalized individuals. She is an example of how such constructs can lead to a life lived in fear and inauthenticity, which not only harms the individual but also deprives society of diverse and genuine contributions.

Mark: The Gay Man Bound by Tradition

Mark's conservative family impressed upon him the importance of traditional relationships and family structure. The expectation was not just cultural but considered a duty, filling him with shame and self-doubt from an early age.

Mark feels obligated to fulfill this duty, contemplating marriage and starting a family with a woman. Despite being aware that such a path contradicts his identity, the weight of societal and familial expectations continues to plague him with shame and questions of self-worth.

Mark's sense of duty toward family and societal norms trap him in a life of internal conflict. Society can also view the collective stress and emotional toll on individuals like Mark as a societal loss. When individuals live inauthentically under compulsion, the community loses the opportunity to benefit from the unique perspectives and contributions that would have arisen if they had experienced the psychological freedom to be themselves.

Through the interconnected life stories of John, Emily, Sarah, and Mark, we have explored the psychological and ethical consequences of living according to a Kantian interpretation of duty. The detrimental effects of a duty-driven upbringing on personal growth, authenticity, and mental well-being become increasingly evident. John's sense of guilt, Emily's shame, Sarah's guilt about her identity, and Mark's shame from societal expectations illustrate the binding constraints that a focus on moral character can impose on one's life.

Moreover, the implications of these life stories extend beyond the individual to broader societal repercussions. They serve as real-life illustrations of the dangers of a duty-bound life, affirming Rand's arguments for a life guided by rational self-interest instead.

Rand's Rebuttal: The Conflict Between Duty and Causality

In addition to challenging the sacrifice of independent judgment, Rand introduces a broader range of distinctions between these two opposing life principles. She articulates this as follows:

> *There are many other differences between the two principles. A disciple of causation is profoundly dedicated to his values, knowing that he is able to achieve them. He is incapable of desiring contradictions, of relying on a "somehow," of rebelling against reality. He knows that in all such cases, it is not some Kantian authority that he would be defying and injuring, but himself—and that the penalty would be not some mystic*

brand of "immorality," but the frustration of his own desires and the destruction of his values.

A Kantian or even a semi-Kantian cannot permit himself to value anything profoundly, since an inexplicable "duty" may demand the sacrifice of his values at any moment, wiping out any long-range plan or struggle he might have undertaken to achieve them.[147]

Rand's Stand: Dissecting the Illusion of Duty

As we have seen in the examples of John, Emily, Sarah, and Mark, the Kantian focus on duty stifles personal growth and opportunities. This is not merely a philosophical quandary but a practical concern affecting everyday choices and long-term planning.

With Rand's stance in the passage above, she fights against the "sacrificium intellectus" that members of her type—which I interpret as introverted thinking—have committed throughout history. Specifically, the sacrifice of their intellect for the alternative of collective feeling. Many people of her type have accepted this sacrifice: Tertullian was one, Kant was another. This is why she despised Kant so much; she understood intimately the nature of the sacrifice because she fought the battle herself. Her mind was her most valued possession and she refused to relinquish it.

---

[147] (Rand, Causality Versus Duty 1974, 139-140)

"Collectivized Ethics"

This essay concludes our journey from the depths of psychological underpinnings with ethical implications, to what we begin to see as their political manifestations. We again peer into the realm of extroverted rational types, examining their natural inclination toward an ethics of altruism and how this shapes a "collectivized soul." This journey takes us through a landscape in which emotional cognition challenges traditional notions of individualism, impacting modern political thought. By contrasting the influential perspectives of Rand and Jung, we aim to unravel the complexities of our collective ethical consciousness. This investigation is not just an academic pursuit but a relevant inquiry into the foundations of our societal values, inviting the reader to reconsider the underpinnings of individual rights and political philosophy.

Dissecting the Collectivized Soul

Rand challenges our understanding and prompts us to reflect on the deeper implications of our thoughts about society and its responsibilities. She brings this to light as she states:

> *If a man speculates on what "society" should do for the poor, he accepts thereby the collectivist premise that men's lives belong to society and that he, as a member of society, has the right to dispose of them, to set their goals or to plan the "distribution" of their efforts.[148]*

According to Rand, this underlying psychological admission in such ponderings, and similar issues, exposes at its best an intellectual disarray in a person's ethical and epistemological understanding. It brings to light an error known as "the fallacy of the frozen abstraction," wherein one replaces a broader ethical category with a narrower, specific ethical

---

[148] (Rand, Collectivized Ethics 1964, 107)

principle—like replacing the general concept of "ethics" with a specific form, such as altruism. Consequently, even if a person claims to have moved on from altruistic principles to a more rational ethical code, the lack of integration in their thought process forces them to inadvertently address moral questions using the framework of altruism.[149]

Case Study: The Business Executive

Consider a business executive who has recently read about and appreciates the ideas of Objectivist ethics, particularly the emphasis on rational self-interest. Motivated by these ideas, he officially announces that his company will now operate entirely based on principles of rational self-interest, aiming for long-term profitability rather than pursuing various social welfare programs or sustainability efforts not related to profitability.

However, when a crisis occurs—say, a significant product defect that could harm consumers—he immediately decides to donate a considerable sum of money to unrelated charities and rushes to launch a PR campaign emphasizing the company's commitment to "giving back to the community."

In this situation, the executive thinks he has adopted a new ethical framework rooted in rational self-interest. Yet, under pressure, he reverts to societal norms and expectations rooted in altruism—such as the obligation to "give back" as a form of penance or goodwill, even if it contradicts his stated principles of long-term profitability and rational self-interest.

Here, the executive demonstrates what Rand describes as "psycho-epistemological chaos." He believes he has adopted a new ethical framework, but his actions reveal a lack of integrated understanding. He still approaches ethical decisions through the lens of altruism,

---

[149] ibid

a specific ethical system, instead of applying the broader ethical principles he claims to have adopted.

Psycho-Epistemological Chaos: The Destructive Power of Altruism

While intellectual disarray poses its own challenges, Rand argues that the psychological implications of such a misaligned ethical stance often unearth a more profound and pernicious issue:

> More often, however, that psychological confession reveals a deeper evil: it reveals the enormity of the extent to which altruism erodes men's capacity to grasp the concept of rights or the value of an individual life; it reveals a mind from which the reality of a human being has been wiped out.[150]

The "collectivist premise" that Rand highlights suggests a familiarity with psychological theories, even if she does not directly engage with Jung's concept of attitude types. Yet, her take infers a darker ethical undertone, marking it as a form of psycho-epistemological chaos that perpetuates evil by eroding the concept of individual rights.

In stark contrast, Jung's identification of extroverted judgment is more descriptive and neutral, focused purely on understanding the human psyche, rather than evaluating its moral implications. Thus, what Jung identifies as a psychological characteristic, Rand interprets as a psychological disposition at the root of an ethical failing. This divergence illuminates the contrasting frameworks of Objectivism and Jungian psychology, with the former assigning moral weight to what the latter sees as a neutral aspect of human psychology.

Unveiling Collective Mentalities: The Convergence of Rand and Jung

In the following, we explore Rand's perspective, breaking down her extended commentary into digestible segments to shed light on Rand

---

[150] (Rand, Collectivized Ethics 1964, 107-108)

and Jung's remarkably similar assessments of collective mentalities. Drawing from these, Rand's commentary addresses the collective attitude prevalent in society, while Jung offers a specific critique of the extroverted thinking type. The parallels witnessed here will have direct relevance in subsequent sections, where we address American political philosophy.

The Altruism Paradox: Self-Seeking of the Selfless

Let us begin with Rand, who offers a critical analysis of the collectivized mentality's psychological underpinnings and societal implications. She posits that the practice of altruism, under the guise of service to others, can paradoxically lead to a nefarious form of self-seeking. She asserts:

> The man who is willing to serve as the means to the ends of others, will necessarily regard others as the means to his ends. The more neurotic he is or the more conscientious in the practice of altruism (and these two aspects of his psychology will act reciprocally to reinforce each other), the more he will tend to devise schemes "for the good of mankind" or of "society" or of "the public" or of "future generations" —or of anything except actual human beings. Hence the appalling recklessness with which men propose, discuss and accept "humanitarian" projects which are to be imposed by political means, that is, by force, on an unlimited number of human beings.

> If, according to collectivist caricatures, the greedy rich indulged in profligate material luxury, on the premise of "price no object"—then the social progress brought by today's collectivized mentalities consists of indulging in altruistic political planning, on the premise of "human lives no object." The hallmark of such mentalities is the advocacy of some grand scale public goal, without regard to context, costs or means. Out of context, such a goal can usually be shown to be desirable; it has to be public, because the costs are not to be

earned, but to be expropriated; and a dense patch of venomous fog has to shroud the issue of means—because the means are to be human lives.[151]

In this passage, Rand critiques the psychological motivations behind collective mentalities, highlighting the inherent contradictions and potential for moral hazard. She suggests that a neurotic adherence to altruism can lead to an impersonal and even destructive approach to humanitarianism, where the end justifies the means, often at the expense of individual rights and free choice, while also ignoring the costs borne by actual human beings.

Rand's stark observation brings to light a crucial aspect often missed in the discourse on altruistic government projects: the full cost of these initiatives. While these projects are frequently framed as societal improvements or advancements for the public good, they invariably require funds—funds sourced from the labor and resources of citizens. Many fail to acknowledge this financial burden, often concealed behind the veil of collective benefit. The irony stems from the fact that those who champion these policies under the banner of altruism often neglect the very people they claim to serve, transforming citizens into mere tools for achieving broader objectives, and at times, at great personal and economic cost.

Real-World Example: Alexandria Ocasio-Cortez and the Green New Deal

A contemporary example that resonates with Rand's critique is the advocacy of Alexandria Ocasio-Cortez for the Green New Deal. This push for environmentally friendly practices, while driven by the intent of preserving the planet, repeatedly neglects presenting these initiatives within the context of their utility to actual living humans, not just potential people and future generations. Sweeping environmental

---

[151] (Rand, Collectivized Ethics 1964, 108)

regulations, often championed as altruistic efforts for the greater good, many times lead to unintended consequences like economic hardships for small businesses or increased costs for consumers. This illustrates how a collectivized approach to ethics overlooks the needs, rights, and choices of living individuals by emphasizing collective goals over personal autonomy.

Building on Rand's critique of the psychological distortions inherent in collectivized mentalities, Jung's analysis offers a profound deepening of our understanding. He delves into the intricacies of the individual psyche, exploring how altruistic motives, when entangled with personal neuroses, can lead to complex ethical dilemmas and self-deceptive behaviors. He shifts the focus from the societal level to the level of individual psychology, providing a nuanced exploration of the inner conflicts that drive such behavior.

Jung observes that the extroverted thinking type—a personality that, while outwardly oriented toward collective standards—often grapples with internal contradictions, noting:

> *This type of man elevates objective reality, or an objectively oriented intellectual formula, into the ruling principle not only for himself but for his whole environment... His moral code forbids him to tolerate exceptions; his ideal must under all circumstances be realized, for in his eyes it is the purest conceivable formulation of objective reality, and therefore must also be a universally valid truth, quite indispensable for the salvation of mankind.*

> *The potentialities repressed by the intellectual attitude will make themselves indirectly felt by disturbing the conscious conduct of life. When the disturbance reaches a definite pitch, we speak of neurosis.*[152]

---

[152] (Jung 1923, 323)

Furthermore, Jung highlights the potential for an altruistic facade to mask underlying self-seeking intentions, where actions driven by ethical motives may stem from less altruistic undercurrents:

> *The conscious altruism of this type, which is often quite extraordinary, may be thwarted by a secret self-seeking which gives a selfish twist to actions that in themselves are disinterested. Purely ethical intentions may lead him into critical situations which sometimes have more than a semblance of being the outcome of motives far from ethical.* [153]

Altruism in Healthcare: Real-World Applications and Examples

The Affordable Care Act (ACA), with its mandate for individuals to obtain health insurance, reflects Rand's concern about imposing collective ideals through political means. The ACA overshadows personal autonomy and imposes significant burdens on individuals, such as healthcare providers and taxpayers. Prioritizing the collective goal over individual choice, we can see the intent to serve the broader public health, which parallels Rand's critique of using individuals as means to an end for societal projects.

Continuing with her argument, Rand discusses the example of Medicare as another case-in-point. She writes,

> *"Medicare" is an example of such a project. "Isn't it desirable that the aged should have medical care in times of illness?" its advocates clamor. Considered out of context, the answer would be: yes, it is desirable. Who would have a reason to say no? And it is at this point that the mental processes of a collectivized brain are cut off; the rest is fog. Only the desire remains in his sight—it's the good, isn't it?—it's not for myself, it's for others, it's for the public, for a helpless, ailing public... The fog hides*

---

[153] (Jung 1923, 324)

such facts as the enslavement and, therefore, the destruction of medical science, the regimentation and disintegration of all medical practice, and the sacrifice of the professional integrity, the freedom, the careers, the ambitions, the achievements, the happiness, the lives of the very men who are to provide that "desirable" goal—the doctors.[154]

Rand captures the moment where well-intentioned ideas transform into unexamined collective dogma. This underscores how altruistic intentions, once co-opted by a collective mindset, lead to overlooking practical consequences and ethical considerations. The focus shifts from individual reasoning to a more monolithic view that fails to question the broader impact of altruistic actions.

This is particularly evident in the context of Medicare. The unarguable good of providing care to the elderly can overshadow critical analysis of the policy's wider ramifications. Rand argues that in the collective pursuit of such a goal, people often suspend critical thinking and obscure the complexities of implementation and its effects on different stakeholders, such as healthcare providers. The desire to do good for the public leads to decisions that do not fully account for the sacrifices and burdens imposed on individuals within the system.

The ACA's expansion, including Medicare, serves as a contemporary instance where Rand's critique finds relevance. It exemplifies the challenges of balancing public health objectives with the need for individual autonomy, choice, and the recognition of potential unintended consequences.

Unraveling the Myths of "Big Pharma" and Beyond

Shifting focus slightly to provide more insight into the mind of an individual employing collectivized judgment, another relevant topic

---

[154] (Rand, Collectivized Ethics 1964, 109)

is the prevailing argument that blames "big pharma" for various issues in the medical field, often parroting media narratives, political talking points, and popularized anti-American philosophical thought. This perspective, however, misses the deeper complexity of these issues, which primarily stems from collective thinking, driving the interaction between private industry and government involvement.

In any mention of "big pharma," "big tech," "big banks," or any "big" business, the intertwining of these forces is evident. Many societal challenges observed in these industries trace directly back to government intervention. Despite widespread recognition of problems arising from this combined control, there is often a reluctance to fully acknowledge that government involvement, while frequently underestimated, certainly plays a crucial role in exacerbating the challenges faced by these industries and limiting market-driven solutions. In this discourse, personal choice and autonomy are frequently overlooked.

Collectivized thinking, which merges thoughts, feelings, and identities with group perspectives, often adds unnecessary complexity to issues. This collective judgment obscures the true nature of problems with inaccurate or falsely derived assumptions and conclusions. However, when examined from an individual standpoint, these issues are not inherently complex. An objective analysis, free from the collective mindset, reveals that what seems intricate is more a result of collective perception than actual complexity. Recognizing the influence of collective thought is crucial for understanding these issues accurately and bringing clarity to public discourse.

The Collectivized Soul: From Altruism to Tribal Mentality

Returning to Rand's argument, she provides a lens through which to view the implications of collectivized decision-making in public policy. She articulates:

After centuries of civilization, most men—with the exception of criminals—have learned that the above mental attitude is neither practical nor moral in their private lives and may not be applied to the achievement of their private goals.

There would be no controversy about the moral character of some young hoodlum who declared: "Isn't it desirable to have a yacht, to live in a penthouse and to drink champagne?"—and stubbornly refused to consider the fact that he had robbed a bank and killed two guards to achieve that "desirable" goal.

There is no moral difference between these two examples; the number of beneficiaries does not change the nature of the action, it merely increases the number of victims. In fact, the private hoodlum has a slight edge of moral superiority: he has no power to devastate an entire nation and his victims are not legally disarmed.[155]

To highlight a stark contrast, Rand draws a comparison between the societal acceptance of certain moral attitudes in public policy and their outright rejection in personal contexts. She emphasizes that society frequently tolerates or even promotes self-sacrifice for collective goals, whereas comparable behavior in personal life, such as committing a criminal act for personal gain, faces universal condemnation. In this context, "self-sacrifice" symbolizes the societal endorsement of actions taken for collective benefits, even at the expense of individual rights or interests. The young hoodlum's actions, while for personal gain and clearly immoral, serve as a metaphor for how society might overlook or even justify similar actions when presented for the claimed "greater good." Rand argues that the moral principles governing personal conduct should also apply to collective actions, highlighting the inconsistency in how society judges these scenarios. She further elaborates on the consequences of this disparity in societal ethics, stating:

---

[155] (Rand, Collectivized Ethics 1964, 109)

It is men's views of their public or political existence that the collectivized ethics of altruism has protected from the march of civilization and has preserved as a reservoir, a wildlife sanctuary, ruled by the mores of prehistorical savagery. If men have grasped some faint glimmer of respect for individual rights in their private dealings with one another, that glimmer vanishes when they turn to public issues—and what leaps into the political arena is a caveman who can't conceive of any reason why the tribe may not bash in the skull of any individual if it so desires.

The distinguishing characteristic of such tribal mentality is: the axiomatic, the almost "instinctive" view of human life as the fodder, fuel or means for any public project.[156]

In this passage, Rand underscores the dichotomy between private morality and public or political ethics. She contends that the ethics of altruism, which one might view positively in personal interactions, assumes a more sinister character in the public or political sphere. Rand suggests that people often uphold the respect for individual rights in private dealings but tend to dissipate it in the realm of public policy. This reflects a regression to a more primitive, tribal mentality where collective needs overshadow individual rights, particularly in the pursuit of lofty public projects. She illustrates her point with a series of rhetorical questions, highlighting how public policy often prioritizes grandiose projects, without fully considering their broader implications:

The examples of such projects are innumerable: "Isn't it desirable to clean up the slums?" (dropping the context of what happens to those in the next income bracket)—"Isn't it desirable to have beautiful, planned cities, all of one harmonious style?" (dropping the context of whose choice of style is to be forced on the home builders)—"Isn't it desirable to have an educated public?" (dropping the context of who will

---

[156] ibid

do the educating, what will be taught, and what will happen to dissenters)—"Isn't it desirable to liberate the artists, the writers, the composers from the burden of financial problems and leave them free to create?" (dropping the context of such questions as: which artists, writers and composers?—chosen by whom?—at whose expense?—at the expense of the artists, writers and composers who have no political pull and whose miserably precarious incomes will be taxed to "liberate" that privileged elite?)—"Isn't science desirable? Isn't it desirable for man to conquer space?"

And here we come to the essence of the unreality—the savage, blind, ghastly, bloody unreality—that motivates a collectivized soul.[157]

In Rand's examination of collectivized decision-making, she presents examples that highlight the superficial appeal of various public projects, from cleaning up slums to liberating artists. However, Rand points out that these initiatives often neglect deeper contextual considerations— such as long-term consequences including the impact on other social groups. Jung echoes this same superficiality in approaching complex societal issues when describing the extrovert.

He notes that individuals with this conscious attitude demonstrate a "prompt grasp of the immediate present in its superficial aspects, though not of its deeper meanings."[158] This observation mirrors the tendency Rand criticizes in collectivized decision-making—a focus on immediate, surface-level benefits without delving into the deeper, more nuanced implications. Projects that seem desirable on the surface may ignore underlying complexities and unintended consequences, leading to decisions that are appealing in the short term but detrimental overall.

---

[157] (Rand, Collectivized Ethics 1964, 108-110)
[158] (Jung 1923, 257)

Furthermore, Jung's insight, which states, "His rapidity of action looks like decisiveness; more often than not it is just blind impulse," depicts the collectivized soul's rush to implement grand schemes, while their "excitability and an enthusiasm that soon fades" sheds light on why once implemented, the disastrous results of such hasty, roughshod decisions dissipate into a mere afterthought, which quickly dwindle from their mind, because "as a rule, memory is considerably impaired." These actions, though appearing decisive and beneficial, stem more from an impulsive response to surface-level issues rather than a thoughtful consideration of deeper impacts. This impulsiveness, as Jung suggests, arises from a failure to fully appreciate, or understand the emotional and practical ramifications of such actions:

> *His thinking has more the character of a representation and*
> *orderly arrangement of contents than that of abstraction and*
> *synthesis.*[159]

Rand's critique of this collectivized soul, which loses sight of individual rights in favor of collective objectives, finds an echo in Jung's observations of the extroverted thinking type, who tends to codify societal "oughts" and "musts" into rigid intellectual formulas. These formulas, while aiming to address societal issues such as the care of the sick, the suffering, or the abnormal, often lead to the creation of extensive plans for humane societies, hospitals, and other welfare institutions. However, Jung highlights a critical gap in these endeavors: The motivation behind them often stems more from a rigid adherence to these collective formulas than from genuine empathy or compassion, which he attributes more greatly to feeling.[160]

In this context, the formula that Jung refers to is not just a set of guidelines but an almost instinctive compulsion to impose collective ideals at the expense of individual nuances and needs. Jung elaborates further:

---

[159] (Jung 1923, 257)
[160] (Jung 1923, 322)

Because this formula seems to embody the entire meaning of life, it is made into a universal law which must be put into effect everywhere all the time, both individually and collectively. Just as the extroverted thinking type subordinates himself to his formula, so, for their own good, everybody round him must obey it too, for whoever refuses to obey it is wrong— he is resisting the universal law, and is therefore unreasonable, immoral, and without a conscience.[161]

While Jung's elucidation provides evident insight into the moral importance of the intellectual formula for the psyche of the extroverted thinking type, it behooves us to recognize that Jung's use of the word "formula" features a special characteristic: The attitude of extroversion can only project onto others. This projection is not merely a preference but a dogmatic adherence to a collective standard, which overlooks individual differences and personal needs. In other words, the conscious attitude of the type ignores their "self," while projecting its contents onto others, and expects others to do the same. In this way, the self and the collective remain undifferentiated, reflecting the modern-day manifestation of the primitive practice participation mystique. This approach, while it may create a facade of unity and common purpose, leads to the neglect of the deeper, personal aspects of human life. Jung further elaborates on the consequences of such a mindset:

In keeping with the objective formula, the conscious attitude becomes more or less impersonal, often to such a degree that personal interests suffer. If the attitude is extreme, all personal considerations are lost sight of, even those affecting the subject's own person. His health is neglected, his social position deteriorates, the most vital interests of his family—health, finances, morals— are violated for the sake of the ideal. Personal sympathy with others must in any case suffer unless they too happen to espouse

---

[161] (Jung 1923, 324)

> *the same ideal. Often the closest members of his family, his own children, know such a father only as a cruel tyrant, while the outside world resounds with the fame of his humanity.*[162]

In closing, we view a profound statement from Rand that sums up the significance of the error made by the collective mentality:

> *It is only to the frozen unreality inside a collectivized brain that human lives are interchangeable—and only such a brain can contemplate as "moral" or "desirable" the sacrifice of generations of living men for the alleged benefits which public science or public industry or public concerts will bring to the unborn.*[163]

The sacrifice of actual life for potential life is the result of the concrete primitive mentality that lacks the ability to differentiate between the two.

In his own words, Jung strongly cites the sickness of such a brain that disregards the subjective nature of cognition and judgment:

> *We must not forget—although the extravert is only too prone to do so—that perception and cognition are not purely objective, but are also subjectively conditioned. The world exists not merely in itself, but also as it appears to me. Indeed, at bottom, we have absolutely no criterion that could help us to form a judgment of a world which was unassimilable by the subject. If we were to ignore the subjective factor, it would be a complete denial of the great doubt as to the possibility of absolute cognition. And this would mean a relapse into the stale and hollow positivism that marred the turn of the century—an attitude of intellectual arrogance accompanied by crudeness of feeling, a violation of life as stupid as it is presumptuous. By overvaluing our capacity for objective cognition we repress*

---

[162] (Jung 1923, 324)
[163] (Rand, Collectivized Ethics 1964, 111)

the importance of the subjective factor, which simply means a denial of the subject. But what is the subject? The subject is man himself—we are the subject. Only a sick mind could forget that cognition must have a subject, and that there is no knowledge whatever and therefore no world at all unless "I know" has been said, though with this statement one has already expressed the subjective limitation of all knowledge.[164]

---

[164] (Jung 1923, 346)

Answers to Questions

1. **What is a perceptual mentality?**

   A perceptual mentality is a state of consciousness primarily focused on the direct, sensory perception of reality. This mentality does not involve the higher-order abstraction of conceptual thinking. It is about experiencing the world directly through the senses—seeing, hearing, touching, etc., without integrating these experiences into more complex, abstract ideas, or concepts. Typically, people consider this a more fundamental or immediate level of awareness.

2. **What is Conceptual Consciousness?**

   Conceptual consciousness refers to a level of awareness that goes beyond mere sensory perception. It involves the ability to integrate perceptions into concepts, which are abstract representations that generalize individual instances. This form of consciousness allows for higher-order thinking, reasoning, and the capacity to deal with complex, abstract ideas. It is not just about seeing or hearing the world but understanding and interpreting it through a framework of concepts and ideas.

3. **What are the four steps in generating an emotion?**

   The four steps in generating an emotion are: Perception, where you notice a stimulus; Identification, where you recognize and label it; Evaluation, where you assess its meaning based on your experiences and beliefs; and Response, where you experience an emotional reaction based on this evaluation.

4. **What is the connection between concrete and collective thinking?**

   The connection between concrete and collective thinking is that both focus on the immediate and tangible. Concrete thinking deals with direct, observable facts, while collective thinking prioritizes group norms and values over individual abstract reasoning. Both can limit individual innovation by focusing on the practical and the accepted, respectively.

ETHICS TO POLITICS

★ ★ ★

We arrive finally at a place in how which we can see how all the preceding context undergirds the arena of political philosophy. The essay in this section will conclude our examination and provide us enough context to answer our ultimate question: What are the proper politics for America?

"Faith and Force: The Destroyers of the Modern World"

With this essay, the exploration of philosophical and psychological underpinnings to societal values is central, coming to full circle vis-à-vis this book's purpose of addressing how all this relates to our modern political realities. We juxtapose Jung's analysis of individual psychological types with Kant's mystical moral sense, suggesting a universal moral good that, if accepted, undermines the relevance of individual judgment. This conflict mirrors the dissonance in Rand's analysis, where mysticism, as the root of altruism, starkly contrasts with the rational individualism underpinning capitalism. These philosophical dichotomies highlight a crucial societal tension: the struggle between the collective moral ethos and the sanctity of individual rights and reason. This tension, in turn, shapes our understanding of freedom, ethics, and political structures, underscoring the importance of individual reasoning in confronting universalized concepts.

The Psychological Roots of Societal Ethos

As we progress on our way from ethics to politics, Rand speaks of three social values:

> *The three values which men had held for centuries and which have now collapsed are: mysticism, collectivism, altruism. Mysticism—as a cultural power—died at the time of the Renaissance. Collectivism—as a political ideal—died in World War II. As to altruism—it has never been alive.*[165]

In both Jungian psychology and Objectivist philosophy, the individual's relationship to collective or external entities holds significant weight, albeit from different vantage points. Jung's exploration of the collective unconscious—those psychological underpinnings that push individuals toward societal norms or collective values—reveals

---

[165] (Rand, Faith and Force: The Destroyers of the Modern World 1960, 90)

the foundational elements that manifest as the societal and ethical dilemmas which Rand tackles. Jung's notion of collective rational functions is the epitome of what Rand would identify as mysticism, serving as the psycho-epistemological root of the issue. In Jung's framework, this predisposition toward mysticism is not merely an intellectual error, but a psychological orientation, deeply embedded in the ancient roots of the human psyche.

It is as if Jung provides the "why," along with the vocabulary to discuss the subconscious drives at the root of mysticism, collectivism, or altruism; while Rand provides the "what," delineating the societal consequences of these orientations. When we consider the collective rational functions outlined by Jung, we can better understand the underpinnings of the ethical and political phenomena Rand critiques, thus offering a more complete understanding of why societies lean toward mysticism, collectivism, and altruism in the first place. By identifying the common ground between these two thinkers, we can forge a more robust analytical tool for dissecting the complex relationship between individual psychology and societal structure.

Rousseau and Jung on External Focus and Individual Suppression

There is an inherent conflict between the individual and collective functions within the ego, and, as we have seen from Jung, the complications of this relationship do not resolve themselves: A person must work to find an equilibrium point between their introverted and extroverted functions to relieve the conflict.

Jean-Jacques Rousseau, whom Jung credits with early explorations into what would later become his concepts of introversion and extroversion, observes that humans preoccupy themselves with externalities—time, places, people, and things—often to the point where the individual becomes the least part of their own existence. He wonders if this expansive focus away from oneself is natural. Jung counters by asserting that this is not a modern phenomenon but a manifestation of "participation mystique," an archaic collective mindset that dates to a time "when there was no individuality whatever." This has always been the case, only becoming consciously acknowledged in recent times. Jung asserts that individuals often mistakenly project this power onto institutions such as the church and state, while the actual suppressive force exists within our collective unconscious.[166]

There is a lot to digest from what Jung writes. First, Rousseau's analysis that we all concern ourselves with things outside ourselves, and that this is the collective mentality. Jung aptly explains the result of this as suppression of the individual due to the individual needing to grant power to external objects—a result of the fantasies within our minds. Jung also points out that people are likely to project this power into the "institutions of Church and State." This example not only shows how our collective psychology grants supremacy to an objective idea, but also aligns with Rand's mention of the values of mysticism and collectivism, respectively.

Participation Mystique and the Loss of Individuality

Participation mystique describes a specific psychological connection whereby the individual cannot clearly distinguish themselves from the object or secondhand concept they are engaged with. This ambiguous boundary leads to a form of partial identity between the individual and the object. According to Jung, this phenomenon stems from an archaic, pre-modern state of mind in which the division between subject and object was not as well-defined as it is today. In modern times, participation mystique often manifests in interpersonal relationships, where one individual gains a magical or absolute influence over another.[167]

---

[166] (Jung 1923, 74-75)
[167] (Jung 1923, 417)

By understanding this phenomenon, we can better grasp the underlying psychological elements that facilitate the power dynamics between individuals and institutions or ideologies, such as those critiqued by Rand. This adds another layer to our understanding of how mysticism and collectivism continue to wield their influence in society, both psychologically and structurally.

Objectivism's Philosophical Sequence: From Mysticism to Collectivism

To properly understand how all this fits together as it relates to the five philosophical branches of Objectivism—metaphysics, epistemology, ethics, politics, and esthetics—one must view mysticism, altruism, and collectivism as more than just random elements; they are fundamental building blocks that inform one another in a sequential sequence. Mysticism, being an epistemological concept, informs the metaphysical basis of one's belief system. If one adopts a mystical outlook, it is likely to lead to ethical stances such as altruism, which, when amplified on a societal scale, manifest as collectivist political systems.

Altruism's Threat to Civilization's Survival

Rand warns of the dangers of unchecked altruism for the survival of civilization, stating,

> If any civilization is to survive, it is the morality of altruism that men have to reject.[168]

Rand terms this as the "altruist morality," which emphasizes the well-being of others over the individual's own rational self-interest, effectively undermining the principle of individual rights. In her

---

[168] (Rand, Faith and Force: The Destroyers of the Modern World 1960, 91)

185

view, it serves as a foundational threat to any civilization built on the ideals of personal freedom. In Jung's psychological framework, this alignment is consistent with extroverted judgment, where external factors and collective norms condition one's rationality.

Modern civilizations, as products of human development, demonstrate our inherent drive to evolve into differentiated and rational beings. Their thriving and sustainability hinge on the foundation of rational ideas, such as those embodied in the U.S. Constitution, which safeguard unalienable rights to think and act in the pursuit of one's happiness, free from coercive forces. These rational principles are essential for establishing a coherent framework for governance, ethical considerations, and social stability. They also underpin critical societal functions like problem-solving, conflict resolution, adaptability, accountability, and civic participation. Jung's observations on the extrovert's ethics, characterized by a collective nature and a tendency toward altruism, offer insights into the psychological foundations of these societal dynamics:

> *The extrovert's philosophy of life and his ethics are as a rule of a highly collective nature with a strong streak of altruism, and his conscience is in large measure dependent on public opinion. Moral misgivings arise mainly when "other people know." His religious convictions are determined, so to speak, by majority vote.* [169]

Contrasting Jung's characterization with Rand's critique reveals a significant challenge to reconciling collective ethical systems with individual autonomy. If civilizations are to survive under Rand's framework, which posits that they suffer under altruistic morality, the inherent altruistic tendency of extroverts presents a conflict. Their collective approach leads to an ethics of mob rule—the inevitable result

---

[169] (Jung 1923, 500-501)

of altruism. While this is not a primary concern for the extrovert—because of their willingness to submit themselves to the will of an objective idea secondhand—a political philosophy resulting from ethics of this kind is an existential threat to the individual, especially the introverted thinking type, and to the idea of civilization itself. This highlights the need for a balanced approach that reconciles collective ethics with individual rational interests to sustain and nurture modern civilizations.

The Paradox of Value in Altruistic Morality

In a society governed by altruistic morality, the concept of value becomes entangled in a paradox. This form of morality often derives the worth of an individual or an object from its utility to something else, which, in turn, derives its value from yet another entity. This leads to a chain of value derivation that seems never-ending. In philosophical terms, this is akin to the problem of "infinite regress." Without a foundational, primary source of value, the system is in perpetual flux, devoid of a stable basis.

Within this framework, paradoxically, the individual—the smallest unit of society—is both the source and recipient of value, yet the overall assessment of value also ignores them. This inherent contradiction is troubling for multiple reasons, not the least of which is the negation of individual rights and the subjugation of personal freedoms for a never-ending chain of "greater goods." Such a system defies logical consistency and ethical robustness, as it perpetually postpones the identification of a primary source of value. There can be no groups without individuals, and by disregarding the individual in this value chain, the entire moral system upon which society is based becomes invalid.

Barbarians at the Gate: When Morality Becomes Manipulation

Let us ask an important question: Who is the beneficiary of the morality of altruism? Whom does this psychological tendency to inherently place the group above the individual serve best? Spiritual mystics would say God, and material mystics would say nature, but the barbarian and tribal lone wolf would say "me." The most barbarian humans use this loophole in human psychology as their opportunity to seize power over others.

As we have learned from Jung, ethics and morals are malleable to the extrovert. What is right or wrong—to them—is dependent on what the group has decided, or what they can get away with.

Collective Good versus Individual Rights: The Facade of Social Welfare

Dictatorial, authoritarian, totalitarian, socialist, communist, and even democratic systems all rest on the same flawed logic—that the collective good takes precedence over individual rights and freedoms. These systems, often presented under the guise of social welfare or equality, exploit the altruistic tendency to prioritize the group over the individual. They harness this psychological inclination to serve the interests of those in power, effectively converting a virtue into a tool for control and subjugation. The guise of collective well-being becomes a convenient mechanism for the most opportunistic to gain and maintain authority at the expense of individual autonomy and the sanctity of human life. Thus, what people present as a moral imperative for the betterment of society becomes, in practice, a means of manipulation and tyranny.

Consider the actions of politicians like California Governor Gavin Newsom and Denver Mayor Michael Hancock, who each implemented COVID-19 mandates for the public while disregarding these rules themselves.

In November 2020, photographers captured Governor Newsom attending a birthday dinner at the upscale French Laundry restaurant in Napa Valley. At the event, guests did not wear masks or practice social distancing, despite his administration's guidelines advising Californians to avoid such gatherings.

After the photographs surfaced, Newsom issued an apology, stating, "I need to preach and practice, not just preach and not practice." His apology acknowledged the discrepancy between his actions and the public guidelines, reflecting remorse only after the public became aware of the incident.

In a similar vein, Mayor Hancock flew to Mississippi for Thanksgiving after urging Denver residents to stay home if possible and "host virtual gatherings instead of in-person dinners." When his travel became public knowledge, Hancock apologized, stating, "I recognize that my decision has disappointed many who believe it would have been better to spend Thanksgiving alone... As a public official, whose conduct is rightly scrutinized for the message it sends to others... I apologize to the residents of Denver."

Public figures justified mask mandates, social distancing protocols, and business closures in the name of collective well-being, yet they violated their own guidelines—whether it was attending private dinners, traveling across state lines, or neglecting to wear masks in public settings. The duplicity exposes the underlying flaw in the altruistic argument: It provides a convenient mechanism for those in power to impose rules and exercise control over the public while exempting themselves from the same standards.

Here, the altruistic concern for the collective good becomes a smokescreen for self-interest and an abuse of power, eroding trust in governance and undermining individual freedoms. The actions of Newsom and Hancock, among others, illustrate the discrepancy between the public persona of altruistic leadership and the private disregard for the very principles espoused. Their apologies, coming in the wake of public exposure, highlight the extroverted ethical stance that moral misgivings arise mainly when "other people know," as Jung suggests.

The Eternal Moral Crisis: Humanity's Ethical Odyssey

The person or group who controls opinion rightfully controls morality where extroverts are concerned. This is a point Rand emphasizes via a speech delivered by the protagonist, John Galt, in her novel *Atlas Shrugged*:

> *Yes, this is an age of moral crisis. Yes, you are bearing punishment for your evil. Your moral code has reached its climax, the blind alley at the end of its course.*[170]

The previous excerpt is an extroverted opinion which even if accurate and based on evidence, can only come from concern about forces outside oneself. Humans will always be in an age of moral crisis. However, the perpetual moral crisis we find ourselves in is not merely an indicator of societal decay, but a hallmark of humanity's constant struggle for ethical refinement. Each generation encounters the same conflict if for no other reason than the inherent tension between introverted and extroverted perspectives, which complicates the establishment of a universally accepted moral code, making each generation's crisis both unique and familiar.

Integral to this predicament, is that human mortality and lifespan significantly influence how we perceive the past, present, and future. The limitations imposed by our finite existence often lead us to engage in narrative sense-making, a form of rationalization that serves as a coping mechanism for navigating the temporal constraints of

---

[170] (Rand, Faith and Force: The Destroyers of the Modern World 1960, 91)

human life. Given our cognitive and existential conditions, this act of constructing narratives is not merely a frequent practice but an inevitable one.

Such narratives are subject to the individual's chosen focus: One can either adopt a perspective that "things are happening to you to make you suffer," leading to a form of "negative rationalization," or choose to believe that "things are happening for you to learn from and increase your ability to thrive," constituting a "positive rationalization."

Consider the example of someone losing their job. A person inclined toward "negative rationalization" might interpret the event as further evidence that the universe is conspiring against them, thereby reinforcing their belief in a malevolent or indifferent world. Conversely, someone adopting "positive rationalization" might view the same event as an opportunity to pivot their career or to learn new skills, thereby re-framing the experience as a growth catalyst.

In each case, the underlying event is the same, but the narrative constructed around it diverges dramatically, affecting not only emotional well-being but also future actions and choices. The former frames life as a series of injustices, whereas the latter recasts challenges as opportunities for growth. Both narrative approaches serve to simplify complex human experiences into more emotionally manageable forms. However, these rationalizations—be they positive or negative—can lack nuance and fail to encompass the full complexity of human experience.

This psychological proclivity for narrative sense-making is what Jung criticizes in the works of philosophers like Friedrich Schiller, Jean-Jacques Rousseau, and, allowing for certain presumptions here, Ayn Rand. According to Jung, such rationalizations contribute to the idealization and overvaluation of the past, thereby distorting our understanding and potentially leading to an incomplete or flawed moral and philosophical framework. In this way, Jung's interpretation

191

would consider Rand as equally mistaken as Schiller and Rousseau, when he states:

> *Schiller likewise looks back, not of course to Rousseau's natural man—and here lies the essential difference—but to the man who lived "under a Grecian heaven." This retrospective orientation is common to both and is inextricably bound up with an idealization and overvaluation of the past. Schiller, marvelling at the beauties of antiquity, forgets the actual everyday Greek, and Rousseau mounts to dizzy heights with the sentence: "The natural man is wholly himself; he is an integral unity, an absolute whole," quite forgetting that the natural man is thoroughly collective, i.e., just as much in others as in himself, and is anything rather than a unity.*[171]

The eternal moral crisis described by Rand through Galt's speech in *Atlas Shrugged* reflects a deeper, enduring aspect of the human condition. This crisis is not a transient phase in societal evolution, but a fundamental characteristic of humanity's ethical odyssey. The perpetual quest for moral understanding and ethical refinement is intrinsic to our nature, fueled by the divergent narratives and perspectives that introverts and extroverts bring to our collective conscience. As such, the idea of reaching a definitive moral conclusion is an illusion, born from narratives we construct to make sense of our complex reality. Each generation, grappling with its unique ethical dilemmas, contributes to this ongoing saga. The inherent tension between varying viewpoints ensures that humanity's moral journey is not a path to a destination, but a continuous process of exploration, debate, and redefinition. Thus, the moral crisis we face is not a sign of societal failure, but a testament to our unceasing endeavor to understand and define what it means to live a moral life.

---

[171] (Jung 1923, 73-74)

The Evolution of Human Progress: From Instinct to Inquiry and Principles

There has never been a point in history at which people universally agreed on everything. These differences of thought must have existed since early human development and always will. While primitive ideas and rudimentary methods of decision-making—such as instinct and tradition—were essential for the survival of early humans and continue to serve essential functions in our daily lives, modern tools like the scientific method and philosophical inquiry serve to assist and guide these foundational approaches, providing us with a more rigorous framework for understanding and improving our lives.

The current stage of human development demonstrates our collective ability to identify and adopt principles that enhance the quality of life and improve living conditions. For instance, the principle of labor specialization has significantly contributed to this progress. Additionally, the widespread participation in organizations that embrace capitalist-leaning principles, such as the World Trade Organization and the International Monetary Fund, further exemplifies this trend. This global acknowledgment of capitalist systems in driving economic development and enhancing individual well-being is notable, even among countries with differing economic structures. For example, nations with socialist or command economies like Venezuela and Cuba still engage with these organizations. Moreover, China's incorporation of selective capitalist mechanisms, despite its communist governance, underscores the impact that even a partial adoption of capitalist principles can have on improving quality of life. These examples collectively demonstrate that, whether through conscious endorsement or practical experience, individuals and nations are inclined to embrace principles that yield tangible benefits.

Reason versus Mysticism: Navigating Narratives of Identity in Jung and Rand

Circling back to Rand's mention of "an age of moral crisis," she demonstrates, with Galt's next sentence, that her solution is forward-thinking:

> If you wish to go on living, what you now need is not to return to morality, but to discover it.[172]

It is important to emphasize that Galt's meaning here is to discover morality conceptually. In other words, a conceptual understanding of morality derived from objective evidence obtained through one's senses. In Rand's view, humans have always tried to shortcut their way to morality through a flawed method, which results from a "primacy of consciousness" premise—the belief that reality is dependent on one's consciousness or perceptions rather than the other way around. The method she points to as a threat to modern society is mysticism; altruism is simply its ethical result. In her words,

> This is the basic contradiction of Western civilization: reason versus altruism. This is the conflict that had to explode sooner or later.
>
> The real conflict, of course, is reason versus mysticism.[173]

One can witness these opposing approaches to ethics reflected in Jung's rational types. Both reason and mysticism serve as distinct psycho-epistemological methods through which individuals habitually construct narratives about reality and their identity (i.e., sense of self). These narratives are not merely luxuries but necessities for human

---

[172] (Rand, Faith and Force: The Destroyers of the Modern World 1960, 91)
[173] (Jung 1923, 92)

194

cognition, serving to simplify complex realities into manageable forms that facilitate decision-making.

Reason, in Rand's view, is an intellectual judgment based on one's perception of objective reality and the only proper method for narrative construction, or concept formation. Mysticism, conversely, manifests in diverse ways, significantly influenced by one's psychological type. For the introverted feeling type, it arises from emotional judgment. This represents a deeply subjective perspective where ideas are primary, not because of their conceptual interconnectedness or logical coherence, but because they resonate emotionally with the subject's subconscious conceptual understanding of the idea. Thus, the judgment is rational in relation to the emotions that objective reality evokes in the subject, yet it lacks the objective, conceptual framework that Rand deems necessary for proper reasoning.

For extroverted rational types, mysticism manifests in other distinct yet related ways. Extroverted feeling types align themselves with an idealistic form of mysticism, where they shape concepts and narratives not based on objective reality but on collective emotions and social norms. This process leads to the acceptance of ideas and values that are more reflective of collective consciousness than of factual, objective analysis, akin to Rand's critique of idealism.

Conversely, for extroverted thinking types—who tend to focus on empirical data and observable phenomena, often neglecting the subjective or conceptual aspects of consciousness—mysticism takes on a materialistic character. While this approach appears grounded in objective reality, it leads to a form of mysticism characterized by an uncritical acceptance of external data and concrete facts, without integrating them into a deeper, conceptual framework. This materialistic tendency in extroverted thinking types echoes Rand's critique of materialism overemphasizing the physical at the expense of the conceptual or subjective.

As we have seen in Jung's work, individuals make judgments either based on their own internal perspective (introversion) or based on external factors such as the consensus view and perceptions of how they believe they appear to others (extroversion).

Individuals are clearly better suited to understand when adopting the introverted attitude toward rationality, as their judgments have roots in their own subjective experiences. On the other hand, those exhibiting an extroverted attitude toward rationality rely more on objective data and external stimuli for their judgments. As a result, their perspectives are less detached from sensation and more aligned with a collective viewpoint.

This collective perspective naturally leads to altruistic decision-making, prioritizing the needs and values of the objective world, which often tends to be—simply—"others." In this context, the altruistic tendencies of extroverted rational types may even cause them to question their own inherent claim on an individual existence. However, it is important to note that the underpinning morality of altruism stands in contrast to the emphasis on individual independence that is foundational to American principles.

Defining Life and Death: Exploring Rand's Conceptual versus Mystical Conflict

In expanding on her critique of altruism and its contrast with reason, Rand further elucidates the implications of this conflict. She articulates the stark consequences of the clash between reason and mysticism, framing it as a fundamental battle that defines the very essence of human existence and societal progress. Rand continues:

> *The conflict of reason versus mysticism is the issue of life or death—of freedom or slavery—of progress or stagnant brutality.*

Or, to put it another way, it is the conflict of consciousness versus unconsciousness.[174]

Rand states the conflict of reason versus mysticism is the issue of life or death, but this, for her, means life or death on fully rational and conceptual terms. The terms on which she desires to live are: independence, integrity, honesty, justice, productiveness, and pride[175]—the conscious virtues resulting from her psychology. Projection could cause her to assume others share the same values, but as we have seen thus far, she understands not everyone is psycho-epistemologically alike.

If I were to restate her second sentence—"the conflict of consciousness versus unconsciousness"—in Jung's terms, as it pertains to thinking, it would be: "the conflict of the rational versus the programmatic." According to Jung, "real," abstract thinking is under direct control for the introverted thinking type while inaccessible to the conscious and direct control of the extrovert.

To further clarify what is meant by "life" in Rand's statement, let us look to another widely recognized psychological concept for assistance.

The concept of human life comprises two essential parts, as demonstrated in the first two levels of Abraham Maslow's, an American psychologist, hierarchy of needs: the physical and the psychological. Maslow's hierarchy is a psychological theory that classifies all human needs into five categories demonstrated in a hierarchical pyramid. Considered the most basic of these, physiological needs serve as the foundation for the other needs built upon them in succession. The order of needs is as follows: physiological, safety, belongingness, esteem, and finally, self-actualization. We can further categorize these

---

[174] (Rand, Faith and Force: The Destroyers of the Modern World 1960, 92-93)
[175] (Peikoff 1991, 250)

needs into three levels: physical or material needs; psychological or spiritual needs; and self-actualization. We all make concessions between the first two levels in our everyday choices, in order to then achieve the third. The more risk-averse a person is, the more emphasis they place on physical life.

For example, a risk-averse individual might prioritize financial stability over personal fulfillment, opting for a stable but unfulfilling career rather than pursuing a more uncertain path that might satisfy deeper psychological or spiritual needs. This focus on stability underscores an emphasis on the physical or material aspects of life, as outlined in the first two levels of Maslow's hierarchy.

The following—a quote whose length I consider necessary in order for its full context to be grasped—from *The Vision of Ayn Rand: The Basic Principles of Objectivism*,[176] a twenty-lecture course Nathaniel Branden gave while still collaborating with Rand, provides an explanation of the specific terms of life and death Rand speaks of in the previous excerpt:

> *When we say that the Objectivist ethics holds man's life, or the life appropriate to a rational being, as its standard of value, this means: the objective requirements of man's life qua man in the full context. It does not mean—it does not mean—that in any value choice, one's only or foremost consideration should be one's immediate physical self-preservation. Man's life as the standard of value does not mean that, in any moral choice, the primary consideration is only, or first of all, your physical self-preservation through the span of the next moment of your existence. Indeed, such a policy not only is not entailed by the principle of man's life as the standard. More than that: it's actively incompatible with the standard of man's life. Why?*

---

[176] (Branden, The Vision of Ayn Rand: The Basic Principles of Objectivism 2011)

Well, remember: life, as I have said, is a process of self-sustaining and self-generated action. The life proper to man, as we have seen, is a process of pursuing, achieving, and enjoying values—the values which his life as a rational being requires. But in the nature of reality, in the nature of life, the pursuit of values entails a struggle, and struggle entails risk. The pursuit of values necessarily involves the possibility of failure and defeat. A rational man does not rebel against this fact. He does not rebel against any metaphysical fact of reality. Therefore, to choose to act for one's values only when no risk is involved is to give up values, is to forsake values—and, of course, to forsake values is to forsake life.

A rational man does not venture senselessly. He does attempt the impossible. He does not indulge in grandiose, empty gestures that can result only in his destruction. But when crucial values are at stake, he accepts the fact that the risk of his life itself may be necessary.

Thus, the man who—to choose an obvious example—the man who consciously and willingly risks his life in the attempt to escape a dictatorship, the man who dies in the effort to achieve freedom, is acting on the principle of man's life as the standard of value. He knows what human existence is, and he will not accept anything less. He is unwilling to endure, and regard as normal, a non-human state of being—that is, a state where men act and function with a gun aimed at their heads, with destruction aimed at their values, and with escape from death, not the achievement of life, as the best they can hope for. It is in the name of the life proper to man that a rational person may be willing to die—not as treason to his life, but as the only act of loyalty possible to him.[177]

---

[177] (Branden, The Vision of Ayn Rand: The Basic Principles of Objectivism 2011)

Here, Branden states, life is not merely a matter of physical existence. The basic requirements one places on "life" establish the lower boundary of what one considers life to be. Consequently, "death" in this context is more multifaceted. It can signify intellectual death marked by the abandonment of reason—ethical death due to a loss of principles—or emotional death characterized by enduring isolation. It may also extend to social, economic, or political death under various adverse circumstances. Thus, "death" is anything antithetical to these various interpretations of life.

Rationality and Reality: Rand's Definitions

We must remember that, according to Jung, the thinking of the introvert is rational, while the thinking of the extrovert is a byproduct of the sensed external factor—leading to their deterministic attitude. Rand's claims of people's cries of "I couldn't help it!," in "Selfishness Without a Self" comes to mind here.

Next, Rand provides unequivocal definitions of the key terms that anchor her philosophy:

> *What is reason? Reason is the faculty which perceives, identifies and integrates the material provided by man's senses. Reason integrates man's perceptions by means of forming abstractions or conceptions, thus raising man's knowledge from the perceptual level, which he shares with animals, to the conceptual level, which he alone can reach. The method which reason employs in this process is logic—and logic is the art of non-contradictory identification.*

> *What is mysticism? Mysticism is the acceptance of allegations without evidence or proof, either apart from or against the evidence of one's senses and one's reason. Mysticism is the claim to some non-sensory, non-rational, non-definable, non-identifiable means of knowledge, such as "instinct," "intuition," "revelation," or any form of "just knowing."*

Reason is the perception of reality, and rests on a single axiom: the Law of Identity.

Mysticism is the claim to the perception of some other reality— other than the one in which we live—whose definition is only that it is not natural, it is supernatural, and is to be perceived by some form of unnatural or supernatural means.[178]

Rand's definition of reason matches Jung's description of the conscious mind—containing both perceiving and judging processes. The dominant judgment function of a person's ego—thinking or feeling— performs the integrating process she describes. But as Rand puts it, thinking is the only orientation that makes a person human—because it is the process that makes humans conceptual beings, as opposed to other animals who can only operate on the perceptual level.

Building on this, we witness mysticism employed through the rational extroversion of extroverted thinking types. To better understand this in Jungian typology, it is crucial to consider the balance between their conscious orientation toward external facts and the unconscious influences that also play a significant role. Jung notes that the lives of these types are not solely dependent on rational judgment; unconscious irrationality equally influences their decision-making.[179] We examined these influences in depth in "Mental Health versus Mysticism and Self-Sacrifice." This dynamic suggests that, although these types lean toward objective realities and collective norms, subconscious factors that may not strictly adhere to rational or empirical standards, also shape their perceptions and decisions.

Extroverted thinking types face a significant challenge in assimilating higher-level, abstract conceptions derived from facts. While adept at managing and organizing a wide array of external facts, their

---

[178] (Rand, Faith and Force: The Destroyers of the Modern World 1960, 93)
[179] (Jung 1923, 332)

intrinsic approach often leads them to accept and utilize these facts as they appear, without questioning the deeper principles or theories underlying them. This tendency reflects a form of mysticism, as critiqued in Objectivism, arising from the negation of consciousness in understanding reality. In prioritizing observable material reality over introspective self-awareness, they align with the materialist's dismissal of consciousness as a critical faculty in cognition.

Their focus on practical utility and application in real-world scenarios, rather than exploring underlying conceptual meanings, aligns with the extroverted attitude of consciousness described by Jung. This orientation toward objective systems and established thought patterns leads to a reliance on collective conceptual frameworks, which limits their engagement in deep, rational analysis and scrutiny of these frameworks.

Jung observes that for extroverts, there is a significant oversight of their own subjective needs and physical health. This occurs because they direct their focus outwardly to such an extent that they neglect even their most fundamental personal needs, including their physical health, unless those needs become unavoidably pressing: "The body is not sufficiently objective."[180] This inclination to overlook the internal for the external does not just affect physical health but extends to psychological well-being, in which they are usually unaware of its neglect. The extrovert's bias toward the external world leads to a disregard for the necessary balance between internal needs and external realities.[181]

This external focus results in a paradoxical situation whereby extroverted thinking types attempt to be conscious of reality, while simultaneously negating the very role of consciousness, central to thought and perception. Their approach leads to a flawed perception

---

[180] (Jung 1923, 310)
[181] ibid

of reality, one that is out of context and misaligned with the principles of Objectivism.

Jung's Intuition: The Role of Unconscious Perception

Before we move on, we should address Rand's reference to intuition in this excerpt because it is crucial to the understanding of Jung's definition of intuition in his psychological types.

Intuition is a direct connection to the subconscious, characterized by an attitude of expectancy, vision, and penetration. It represents the immediate inkling of an idea or hypothesis, fueled by information from the subconscious. This function operates at a lightning-fast pace, offering instinctual guesses and perceptions that extend beyond the immediately apparent. Intuition not only involves subconscious relationships and pattern recognition but also plays a crucial role in feeding anticipation, allowing one to sense potential outcomes before they occur.

In the conscious mind, this forward-looking attitude represents intuition, where the intuitive function actively interprets information into the object or situation, drawing on more than just the objective data presented. This process often leaves others puzzled about how intuitive individuals arrive at certain conclusions when the proof is not immediately visible. Individuals who adopt a sensation-oriented approach primarily concentrate on the object and its immediate qualities, restricting their understanding to what they have consciously learned. In contrast, for those oriented toward intuition, the object acts merely as a stimulus, triggering the mind to retrieve metaphysical implications and associations from the subconscious. The more developed an individual's intuitive ability, the clearer their understanding of these deeper, often unseen connections.

Importantly, intuition does not inherently conflict with reason. In rational types, it is an irrational secondary function used to

203

support rational decision-making. While it provides initial insights and hypotheses, individuals can and often do verify these insights through objective evidence, a step not required in mysticism. This understanding underscores the value of intuition in the reasoning process.

A person's prior thinking and the associations they have formed influence their perception and judgment in any given moment. As time flows continuously, judgments made at earlier points influence all perceptions and actions. Therefore, intuition, as a complex and forward-looking function, plays a significant role in shaping an individual's reasoning and decision-making processes.

According to Jung, any practical observer of humans must always be an intuitive type.[182] Considering this, one would certainly classify Rand as such; although, as she shows a tendency for introverted thinking, extroverted intuition would serve as her auxiliary function. This inclination toward intuition is also evident in her dissection and formulation of new and original intellectual ideas, as Rand's thinking remains unhindered by the constant intrusion of sensory experiences that auxiliary extroverted sensation would bring. Instead, her extroverted intuition allows her thinking to delve deeper and function more intensely.

One quintessential quote from Rand that illustrates her use of intuition followed someone complimenting her for her courage in speaking out against communists. She replied: "I'm not brave enough to be a coward. I see the consequences too clearly."

---

[182] (Jung 1923, 139)

Kant's Altruism versus Rand's Reason: A Philosophical Showdown

We now move on to Rand's position on Kant's influence on modern philosophy, which compels us to perform an extended and detailed exploration that examines thinking styles, theories of concept formation, and psychological compensation for a full comprehensive understanding.

Kant's Influence and Rand's Critique

If you ask me to name the man most responsible for the present state of the world, the man whose influence has almost succeeded in destroying the achievements of the Renaissance—I will name Immanuel Kant. He was the philosopher who saved the morality of altruism, and who knew that what it had to be saved from was—reason.

This is not a mere hypothesis. It is a known historical fact that Kant's interest and purpose in philosophy was to save the morality of altruism, which could not survive without a mystic base. His metaphysics and his epistemology were devised for that purpose. He did not, of course, announce himself as a mystic— few of them have, since the Renaissance. He announced himself as a champion of reason—of "pure" reason.[183]

Jung's Typology in Philosophical Discourse

Before we can accurately digest Rand's critique of Kant as it relates to this discussion, there is a need to elaborate on the distinction between Jung's thinking types, as the function of thinking is always at the forefront of any intellectual debate or disagreement.

---

[183] (Rand, Faith and Force: The Destroyers of the Modern World 1960, 94-95)

Jung uses the examples of Darwin and Kant to contrast extroverted and introverted thinking types. Kant is an example of the introverted thinking type. The distinguishing characteristic is the attitude of the subject toward the object and objective data. The extroverted type, because they empathize with the object, speaks of facts for the sake of facts, while the introverted type abstracts from the facts and speaks of them as they relate to the subject. Jung writes,

> *Just as we might take Darwin as an example of the normal extroverted thinking type, the normal introverted thinking type could be represented by Kant. The one speaks with facts, the other relies on the subjective factor. Darwin ranges over the wide field of objective reality. Kant restricts himself to a critique of knowledge.*[184]

Jung characterizes the introverted thinking type through the dominant form of thought, as previously explained. Unlike the extroverted thinker who draws ideas from external sources, the introverted thinker bases his ideas on internal, subjective foundations. This type pursues their ideas inwardly rather than outwardly, seeking depth over breadth. This inward focus distinctly sets apart the introverted type, who maintains a stronger connection to internal experiences, from the extroverted type, who engages more intensely with external objects. The introverted type, in contrast, often shows a lack of interest or even a dislike toward objects, a trait common to all introverts. This detachment from objects makes it challenging to describe the introverted type. Jung explains the introverted thinking type further:

> *His judgment appears cold, inflexible, arbitrary, and ruthless, because it relates far less to the object than to the subject. One can feel nothing in it that might possibly confer a higher value*

---

[184] (Jung 1923, 354)

on the object; it always bypasses the object and leaves one with
a feeling of the subject's superiority.[185]

To advance our understanding of type and its manifestation in Rand's psychology, we take a significant step by recognizing her approach: Rand consistently speaks from the standpoint of the subject. She uses objects and objective data as mere evidence to validate the logical consistency of a principle or concept.

Examining Altruism through Introverted Thinking

Building on this understanding of the introverted thinking type's cognitive approach, let us now return to Rand's original argument and examine the validity of altruism as a concept.

As established in our examination of "The Comprachicos," logic dictates that only a subject can bestow value on an object, meaning that objective facts have no inherent value outside their relationship to a human life. In fact, human life is the only thing that makes the concept of value possible.

To illustrate, imagine a bottle of water sitting on a table in a room. In the absence of any human observers or consumers, the bottle of water has no inherent "value." It is merely a container filled with liquid. Now, introduce two different individuals into the room: One is extremely thirsty after a long walk, and the other just drank a large bottle of water.

For the thirsty individual, the bottle of water takes on significant value—it can quench thirst and provide immediate relief. For the person who has just hydrated, the bottle has much less immediate value. The key takeaway here is that the bottle of water did not possess

---

[185] (Jung 1923, 354)

intrinsic value; rather, the needs and states of the interacting subjects conferred value upon it.

Applying this to the concept of altruism, the altruistic perspective, which empathizes with the object (or person in need), erroneously assumes that the need or value is an intrinsic quality of the object itself (such as the bottle of water) or the recipient of altruism. This perspective is illogical because value does not intrinsically reside within the object; instead, the subject confers value upon the object through its own needs or judgments. Value thus becomes a relational concept between the subject and the object, emphasizing the importance of the individual's role in ascribing value, thereby questioning the premises upon which altruism is based.

By recognizing that value is subjective and derives from the relationship between subject and object, one can then recognize that altruism loses its logical grounding. This is because value cannot be universally determined solely by the mere existence of need or utility in the object; a subject must assess and confer it.

Extroverted judgment never segregates the subject's perception of facts from their evaluation of them, which is inherent in the subject's (i.e., perceiver or valuer's) judgment. Using this clearer understanding of introverted thinking—which distinguishes between the subject's perception and evaluation of facts—we can more accurately assess Kant's philosophy in Jung's terms, and how it relates to Rand's critique, the root of which lies in the extroverted method of concept formation.

The Problem of Universals: Rand's View on Conceptual Consciousness

Digging deeper into the area of concept formation, Ayn Rand's critique of post-Renaissance philosophy zeroes in on what she perceives as a fundamental assault on the human mind's conceptual faculty. She identifies the failure to solve the "problem of universals"—the nature, source, and validity of abstractions—as the linchpin in the philosophical undermining of the conceptual level of consciousness. According to Rand, this failure led to the bifurcation of philosophers into two camps: Rationalists, who believed in deriving knowledge from internal concepts; and Empiricists, who believed in acquiring knowledge from sensory experience. Rand sees this as a false dichotomy that forces a choice between reality (body) and the mind (consciousness), a choice that she deems both unnecessary and destructive.[186]

Jung's analysis of the nominalism and realism debate complements Rand's perspective by providing a psychological dimension to this philosophical conflict. Jung's typology, which includes both introverted and extroverted attitudes, offers a framework for understanding the inherent biases that can lead to such a dichotomy. He sees nominalism and empiricism as extroverted attitudes that focus on the concrete and singular, while realism and rationalism exhibit introverted attitudes, emphasizing the abstract and universal.

The Evolution of Human Thought: From Sensory to Conceptual

Jung's insight into the psychological underpinnings of these philosophical positions highlights the natural human tendency to concretize abstractions, a process that has been integral to the development of human thought. He points out that for early humans, conceptual thought was not an abstract activity but a vivid, sensory experience. This historical perspective sheds light on the difficulty contemporary individuals may have in separating thought from sensory perception, a challenge that remains relevant in psychological analysis today. To illustrate this point, Jung provides a striking example of the concretization of thought in early human experience:

> Among primitives, for instance, the imago, the psychic reverberation of the sense-perception, is so strong and so sensuously colored that when it is reproduced as a spontaneous

---

[186] (Rand, For the New Intellectual 1963, 28)

memory-image it sometimes even has the quality of an hallucination. Thus when the memory-image of his dead mother suddenly reappears to a primitive, it is as if it were her ghost that he sees and hears. We only "think" of the dead, but the primitive actually perceives them because of the extraordinary sensuousness of his mental images. This explains the primitive's belief in ghosts and spirits; they are what we quite simply call "thoughts." When the primitive "thinks," he literally has visions, whose reality is so great that he constantly mistakes the psychic for the real. Powell says: "The confusion of confusions is that universal habit of savagery—the confusion of the objective with the subjective."[187]

Jung's theory distinguishes between the process of abstraction, which he associates with introversion, and his psychological function of thinking. It is important to clarify that these two concepts are not synonymous. Introverted thinking involves abstract thought that operates independently of external, empirical data or sensory perception. Other introverted functions blend perception of the external, empirical world with thought, resulting in a more concrete approach. This distinction is important because it underscores the unique human ability to engage in abstract thinking, which has been a driving force in societal progress.

The Origin of Concepts: Mind and Reality in Harmony

Jung's reference to Abelard and his conceptualism offers a historical example of an attempt to reconcile the conflict between nominalism and realism. Abelard's approach suggests that concepts originate in the mind and are subsequently confirmed by reality, presenting a balanced perspective that does not negate the existence of universals

---

[187] (Jung 1923, 26-27)

or the reality of individual things. Jung emphasizes the significance of psychological types in this context, stating:

> *If one disregards the existence of psychological types, and also*
> *the fact that the truth of the one is the error of the other, then*
> *Abelard's labors will mean nothing but one scholastic sophistry*
> *the more. But if we acknowledge the existence of the two types,*
> *Abelard's efforts must appear to us of the greatest importance.*[188]

In the psychological landscape painted by Jung, we see the philosophical approaches of realism and nominalism mirrored in the introverted and extroverted attitudes of his typology. These attitudes represent the two necessary and mutually exclusive viewpoints that apply to each psychological function. Introversion shows a preference for the idea of the thing, an abstract inclination that seeks to understand the essence behind the tangible. In contrast, extroversion gravitates toward the tangible object itself, valuing the immediate and sensory reality that objects present.

Jung echoes Rand's critique of the dichotomy between rationalists and empiricists when he observes that the essence of ideas ("esse in intellectu") lacks tangible reality, while the essence of things ("esse in re") lacks mind. This observation underscores the inherent flaw in one-sided attitudes which either disregard the tangible world, or ignore the realm of the intellect. In life, neglecting neither reality nor the mind is tenable, as humans must navigate the physical world, prompting their psyche to abstract and form concepts from it. This necessitates a dual recognition and respect for both the intellect and reality.

For Jung, the psyche, or the "esse in anima" (essence of the soul), serves as the reconciling force that unites intellect and reality within everyone. He identifies this unifying process as fantasy, which is not

---

[188] (Jung 1923, 43-44)

mere escapism but a vital psychological activity. Physical existence supplies the raw material from which our intellect shapes ideas, and it is through the psyche's autonomous activity that these ideas gain vitality and the impressions of the world gain significance.

Rand and Jung's analyses converge on the importance of acknowledging and integrating both the conceptual and the sensory, the abstract and the concrete, in our understanding of the world. They both argue for an integrated approach that respects the power of the human mind to form concepts and the necessity of grounding those concepts—in reality. This balanced engagement with life is essential for a complete grasp of reality and for the healthy functioning of the individual and society.

Kant's A Priori Reasoning and Its Implications

In a section of his book titled "The Problem of Universals," Jung restates Kant's logic as a means to exploring the so-called "power of illusion"—which we can understand as the innate, enchanting influence that words exert over ideas or concepts. This captivating power traces its origins to primitive human psychology. It took a long time for people to understand that words alone do not always correspond to things that are real. However, the belief in the power of words persists in our minds, due to a kind of instinctive superstition that we cannot easily shake.[189]

Kant takes this idea further. He introduces the notion of "**a priori**" reasoning, a kind of understanding that exists independently of empirical, sensory experience. He argues that when it comes to sensory objects, we can confirm their existence through our perceptions and empirical laws. However, when we deal with abstract concepts or objects of pure thought, there is no empirical way to confirm their existence. Understanding these objects relies solely on reasoning

---

[189] (Jung 1923, 38-40)

which is a priori, or without the need for sensory experience. Kant restricts our awareness of existence to what we can connect to our sensory experience.[190]

To elucidate this point, consider Kant's perspective on the concept of "justice." He would argue that our understanding of justice is a priori, not derived from empirical observations but from innate structures of the human mind. Justice, then, would be a "universal concept," existing independent of empirical laws. His philosophical approach opens him up to criticism, particularly concerning the validation process. If no one empirically validates a concept like justice, then how can we ascertain its universality, and how can we be sure it is not merely a construct of the mind?

Kant argues that there are certain core ideas or entities that are so essential that we cannot even think about existence without them. He uses this line of reasoning to argue for the concept of God—not God as a real being, because being is not a predicate to the concept of God—but God as an idea. In Kant's view, just the idea of God is powerful enough. He contends that "existence" is not an additional quality you can add to an object or concept. Saying "God is omnipotent" does not add anything new to the concept of God; it simply positions God's omnipotence in relation to our own understanding. Therefore, the idea of God does not require Him to exist in reality; it is sufficient that the idea exists only in relation to our thoughts.[191]

In the above, what we witness from Kant is his achievement in validating a mystical base. In his quest to posit God as a postulate for moral reasoning, suggesting that the mere idea underpins ethical principles and guides human actions, Kant's logic leverages the magical power of words via the intrinsicist method. What Kant has done

---

[190] ibid
[191] ibid

with his reasoning is use the phenomenon experienced in universal concepts for his own purposes, by completely separating perception of reality from thought and implying that universals lie beyond empirical verification. But Kant's assertion that understanding universals requires transcending empirical laws introduces a problematic disconnect because it risks detaching concept formation from reality, potentially leading to baseless assumptions or fantasies.

In the process of concept formation, empirical knowledge requires direct interaction with the object via one's perception, always taking place retrospectively. In other words, it is what happened. One's abstraction from this empirical knowledge leads them to a thought. However, a thought can take one of at least three forms from a statistical perspective: One that is highly likely based on experience; one that is moderately likely or possible based on experiential inference; and one that gives free rein to fantasy—having little to no connection to experience at all.

Kant disregards the process of accurately linking one's perception of reality to concept formation in evaluating a concept's validity. Without a validation process, Kant insinuates that humans need only create concepts at the perceptual level. For him, active directed thinking and passive intuitive thinking are equivalent. This separation is problematic, however, because it does not offer a method to ensure that our concepts are indeed valid, rather than merely assumptions or fantasies. Take the concept of "freedom" as an example. Without linking this concept to real-world experiences and perceptions, how can one evaluate its validity?

Kant's Phenomenal World: The Collective Delusion

In "For the New Intellectual," Rand draws attention to Kant's assertion that life as we perceive it is merely a delusion. However, as Kant explains it, a delusion held together by collective subjectivity:

The "phenomenal" world, said Kant, is not real: reality, as perceived by man's mind, is a distortion. The distorting mechanism is man's conceptual faculty: man's basic concepts (such as time, space, existence) are not derived from experience or reality, but come from an automatic system of filters in his consciousness (labeled "categories" and "forms of perception") which impose their own design on his perception of the external world and make him incapable of perceiving it in any manner other than the one in which he does perceive it. This proves, said Kant, that man's concepts are only a delusion, but a collective delusion which no one has the power to escape.[192]

Rand's interpretation of Kant's philosophy suggests that our conceptual faculties distort reality, rendering our basic understanding of the world a shared illusion. This collective delusion, according to Kant, limits reason and science to dealing with a predetermined, phenomenal world, shifting the criterion of reason's validity from the objective to the collective. However, Rand argues that this is a negation not only of man's consciousness but of consciousness itself. She asserts Kant's argument as essentially stating: Man is limited to a consciousness of a specific nature, which perceives by specific means and no others—therefore, his consciousness is not valid; man is blind, because he has eyes—deaf, because he has ears—deluded, because he has a mind—and the things he perceives do not exist, because he perceives them.[193]

Building on Rand's critique, Jung's analysis again introduces a psychological dimension to this philosophical discourse, echoing her concerns from a different vantage point. He concurs with Rand regarding the limitations inherent in the extroverted philosophical stance, which I assert corresponds to the domain of rational judgment in his typology. Consciousness is inherently subjective and unique, a

---

[192] (Rand, For the New Intellectual 1963, 31-32)
[193] ibid

215

reality that introversion accepts, while extroversion pursues illusory objectivity, pushing subjectivity into the unconscious, leaving behind a consciousness devoid of self-awareness.

From a subjective standpoint, Rand rightly criticizes Kant's negation of consciousness as impractical and devoid of actionable insights. Philosophy is a tool to guide living, not just an abstract exercise. A philosophy that fails to influence our actions and decisions falls short of its purpose in helping individuals navigate life's complexities.

Kant's conclusions are immune to evidence-based refutation, leading to the ultimate question, if we are to accept his claims at all: "So what?" The phenomenal world is our reality; our perceptions are bound to the tools we possess. Our subjective viewpoint still confines any speculation about a world beyond our perception.

Without a standard for comparison, how can Kant claim knowledge of human limitations? The only conceivable standard he could be using is based on his own conceptual constructs—his fantasies. If man cannot achieve perfection, then it is the concept of perfection itself that is flawed.

Fantasy and Consciousness: The Origins of Religious Beliefs

Jung's exploration of the nature of fantasies and their role in the genesis of religious beliefs provides a tangible framework for understanding our psychological processes. Fantasy, arising from the unconscious, incorporates conscious elements, but distinguishes itself through its involuntary nature and its contrast with conscious thoughts. This involuntary aspect is also present in dreams, although fantasy exhibits a less pronounced divergence from conscious thought. The individual's relationship with their fantasies is determined by their relationship with the unconscious, which is itself influenced by the spirit of the age and the prevailing degree of rationalism.[194]

Closed religious systems, such as Christianity, tend to suppress the unconscious in the individual as much as possible, thereby paralyzing fantasy activity. These systems offer generalized and familiar symbolic concepts intended to totally and ultimately replace the individual's unconscious content. The symbolic concepts of religions are re-creations of unconscious processes in a universally binding form, providing absolute answers about the metaphysical and the world beyond human consciousness. When we observe the birth of a religion, we witness doctrinal figures emerging from the founder's unconscious fantasies as revelations. These revelations are subsequently considered universally valid and replace the individual fantasies of others.[195]

Kant's philosophical approach mirrors this religious methodology by attempting to define a universal essence of the soul, which, as in religious doctrine, limits the scope of subconscious activity to affirm only those fantasies that align with the established doctrine. The result of this process is indoctrination. This indoctrination is not a mere alignment with shared values but a fundamental restriction on the psyche's creative engagement with the subconscious.

The Psychological Realm and Moral Postulates

Jung emphasized the necessity of revisiting Kant's foundational arguments because they clearly illustrate the difference between intellectual concepts (esse in intellectu) and actual entities (esse in re). According to Jung, the psyche, or "anima," fills this gap between intellectual concepts and reality, obviating the need for ontological proof of God's existence. Kant himself delved into this psychic realm

---

[194] (Jung 1923, 46)
[195] ibid

in his *Critique of Practical Reason*, proposing God as a necessary postulate for moral reasoning.[196]

In this realm of the psyche, Jung argues, God becomes a psychological concept that varies across individuals. It is the highest psychic value, or the "esse in anima," that directs our thoughts and actions. Depending on where an individual places their highest value, God can be anything from money to power to sex. Therefore, a psychological theory rooted in a single instinct like power or sexuality cannot fully account for human behavior.[197]

Kant's attempt to necessitate the idea of "God" as the universal essence of the soul mirrors fellow introverted thinking type Tertullian's concept of "anima naturaliter christiana," which translates to "the soul is by nature Christian."[198] Tertullian, known for his intellect, offers the drastic example of sacrificing intellectual faculties in favor of faith. This act symbolizes the relinquishment of human reason (the recognition of causality) for divine revelation (the acceptance of duty), embodying Jung's concept of the need for psychological compensation in the Christian process of development.

The reality that Kant and Tertullian arrive at similar conclusions regarding the nature of the human soul is no mere coincidence. This becomes clear when we consider what Jung describes as the Christian process of development, as witnessed in the following statement:

> *The idea-oriented man is by nature logical... Compensation of his type makes him, as we saw from Tertullian, a man of passionate feeling, though his feelings still remain under the spell of his ideas.*[199]

---

[196] (Jung 1923, 37)
[197] ibid
[198] (Jung 1923, 12)
[199] (Jung 1923, 45)

Jung's theory illuminates the need for psychological compensation, enabling individuals to function in both personal and societal contexts. This psychological compensation represents a sacrifice of the "**one-sided attitude**." Unlike the complete amputation of the most valued function seen in historical figures like Tertullian, Jung's concept of compensation aims for a psychological equilibrium. However, the dominant (differentiated) and inferior (undifferentiated) functions become interchangeable when one prioritizes the latter over the former. If an introverted thinking type gives the passive extroverted feeling function the intensity usually reserved for the active introverted thinking function, it becomes the dominant faculty and supersedes it—giving way to a secondary type. This role reversal leads to a state where the individual becomes deeply merged with the object of their perception, losing their personal identity, and becoming engulfed in a kind of collective consciousness. This archaic state of extreme relatedness, or inferior extroversion, is markedly different from the extroversion of an extroverted type.[200]

Diverging Philosophical Pathways

From what Jung articulates, Kant engages in an act of mysticism, where his concept of God postulates a subjectively held moral sense that, if universally valid, would make Jung's psychological types irrelevant, as all individuals would perceive the highest good in the same way. This illustrates how an ill-formed and indefinite concept can profoundly influence people's thinking, particularly a concept that lacks empirical evidence and even negates the need for such evidence. When society at large adopts the concept of God as a secondhand idea, it obscures crucial differences between individuals, as well as key details. As Jung emphasizes, a universal view of the highest good conflicts with individual experience because God means different things to different people.

---

[200] (Jung 1923, 91)

However, Jung commends Kant for proposing that some universal concepts inherently do not require empirical validation, a position with which I suspect Rand would vehemently disagree. Nevertheless, the key questions then become: What is the nature of that element, and how does that element manifest in different individuals?

The Role of Psychological Types in Ethical Decision-Making

As we have seen, individuals must integrate intellect and reality, yet Kant and Rand diverge significantly in their understanding of what serves as this crucial integrating mechanism. Kant believes that this mechanism goes beyond mere cognition, driven by a mystical moral quality. Rand advocates for reason, rejecting the idea that mystical elements should take a leading role.

Imagine two individuals faced with a moral dilemma. According to Kant, both would consult a universally valid moral law inscribed in their souls. Rand would argue that one should make decisions based on reasoned self-interest. Despite these being mutually exclusive philosophical approaches, Jung suggests that the individual's unique psyche, comprising both rational and irrational elements, would guide their decision. In this context, both Kant's moral universality and Rand's rational empiricism offer complementary pathways for the integration of intellect and reality.

Delving deeper, Rand identifies a process where the rational mind actively shapes cognitive abstractions to guide subconscious emotions, leading to normative abstractions that are both empirical and logical. This conscious endeavor aligns one's values and judgments with a deliberate engagement with reality.

Consider the moral dilemma faced by Sarah, a seasoned nurse, when she must decide whether to allocate a limited supply of a life-saving drug to a young patient with a promising future or an elderly patient with a terminal illness. In a scenario guided by Rand's philosophy,

Sarah would use rational self-interest and empirical evidence to shape her cognitive abstractions about life's value and the potential outcomes of her actions, thereby informing her emotional response to this ethical crossroad.

In contrast, Kant introduces a model in which the soul's essence transcends empirical cognition, guided by innate moral imperatives—categorical imperatives—that can sometimes bypass rational processes. These imperatives suggest an understanding that is not fully accessible to conscious reasoning, a mystical moral quality that drives the integration of intellect and reality.

In Sarah's case, Kant might argue that her decision should be based on a universal moral law that she recognizes within herself, one that dictates her duty irrespective of the consequences or her personal feelings about the patients.

Jung's analytical psychology, however, posits that an individual's psychological type profoundly influences their approach to such dilemmas. Rather than suggesting that Sarah might arbitrarily align with Rand's rationalism or Kant's moral imperatives, Jung would argue that her psychological type predisposes her to a particular mode of decision-making.

For example, if Sarah is an introverted thinker, her decision-making process would lean toward Rand's emphasis on rational self-interest. Conversely, as an extroverted feeler, she would tend to resonate with Kant's categorical imperative, feeling an inherent duty to consider the community's needs or the well-being of the patients collectively.

Jung's perspective suggests that Sarah's ultimate decision reflects her psychological orientation, which dictates whether she prioritizes empirical evidence and rational analysis (as Rand would advocate) or a sense of universal moral duty (as Kant would suggest). Her type does not force her into one perspective or the other, but indicates a natural inclination that will guide her as she grapples with the moral complexity of her situation.

This nuanced view acknowledges that within a larger psychological framework, an individual's type orientation critically influences how they weight and integrate cognitive functions and normative abstractions. Thus, Sarah's decision-making process integrates intellect and reality; influenced not only by a balance of empirical evidence and intrinsic moral sense but also by the inherent predispositions of her psychological type.

Rand's Critique of Kant's Methodology

Finally, I argue that Rand's scathing critique of Kant is a result of their shared typology, which diverges sharply in their application, particularly in their distinct methods of concept formation. According to Jung, Kant is an introverted thinking type, and I contend that Rand also falls into this category. However, their philosophical paths could not be more opposed.

Rand vehemently condemns Kant, viewing his surrender to mystical and collective emotional elements as an abdication of intellectual integrity and a betrayal of reason itself, as Kant's philosophical approach strips all rational power from the subject. For Rand, this is an unforgivable transgression that undermines the individual's capacity for rational judgment. This, she cannot accept.

Objectivism versus Altruism: The Political Implications

As we return to Rand's essay, she explains the necessary political system that must result from the rational egoism of Objectivist ethics. She states,

Ladies and gentlemen, capitalism and altruism are incompatible.

Make no mistake about it—and tell it to your Republican friends: capitalism and altruism cannot coexist in the same man or in the same society.

Tell it to anyone who attempts to justify capitalism on the ground of the "public good" or the "general welfare" or "service to society" or the benefit it brings to the poor. All these things are true, but they are the by-products, the secondary consequences of capitalism—not its goal, purpose or moral justification. The moral justification of capitalism is man's right to exist for his own sake, neither sacrificing himself to others nor sacrificing others to himself; it is the recognition that man—every man— is an end in himself, not a means to the ends of others, not a sacrificial animal serving anyone's need.[201]

Rand's core ethical stance serves as a foundation for political systems. She contrasts altruism, which mandates serving others as one's moral duty, with capitalism, a system born from the ethics of rational egoism. This conflict mirrors deeper psychological tendencies—rational extroversion and introversion—that influence individual perceptions and judgments.

Rand's argument is logically sound, while being simultaneously rooted in her psychological perspective; whereas other psychological orientations, while aiming for outcomes akin to those of rational egoism, often resort to indirect and less efficient methods. These approaches tend to grasp at the byproducts of capitalism—its societal benefits—without recognizing or prioritizing its core moral justification or essential factor, which underpins its success: the individual's right to self-interest.

---

[201] (Rand, Faith and Force: The Destroyers of the Modern World 1960, 98-99)

The Practical Contradictions of Capitalist Principles

Rand's declaration on the true nature of capitalism and government intervention exposes inconsistencies in real-world political dichotomies, revealing a lack of principled judgment. For example, Mitt Romney, a Republican, implemented a healthcare reform in Massachusetts that included an individual mandate to buy health insurance. While defending this as a market-friendly solution, the mandate restricts free choice and thus counteracts the pure capitalist ideology he claims to uphold. This reveals a contradiction that undermines the integrity of his claimed principles.

Similarly, Republican politicians—such as, for example, Donald Trump—who support trade tariffs to protect American industries and who intervene in markets to do so, act on decisions in a manner incongruent with pure capitalism. The 2008 financial crisis serves as another striking example. Politicians from both sides of the aisle supported bank bailouts, justifying them as necessary for economic stability. However, this approach contradicts the capitalist principle that cautions against government intervention to prop up failing businesses. In the same vein, politicians who profess to have capitalist leanings sometimes advocate for raising the minimum wage or engaging in public-private partnerships, both of which involve considerable regulation and government oversight.

In each of these instances, the decision-making reveals a compromise of principle, undermining the politicians' claims of adhering to capitalist tenets. This act of compromising serves as a practical manifestation of what Rand identified as a "perceptual consciousness" in her essay "Selfishness Without a Self," a mentality reflective of individuals' inability to believe that ideas can have any personal importance to anyone. Such compromises dilute the very principles they espouse, calling into question the usefulness of holding these principles at all.

The Intellectual Dilution of Capitalist Ideals

This dilution affects not only politicians; several intellectuals also attempt to dissect and reinterpret capitalist principles to reach different conclusions, such as the notion of "late-stage capitalism," which posits that capitalism's flaws necessitate a move toward a different economic system. Instead of recognizing and respecting the fixed principles of capitalism, these intellectuals, also displaying the traits of a perceptual mentality, believe they need to augment or alter the principle in some way. Viewers can perceive these attempts as efforts to avoid the stringent implications of pure capitalism, and an overall evasion of principles as such.

Critics such as Thomas Piketty, the author of *Capital in the Twenty-First Century*, argue that capitalism inherently causes inequality, and suggest revising or replacing it with a system that includes more redistributive policies. This line of thinking, while intellectually intricate, often serves to muddle the clarity of capitalism's basic principles rather than to enhance understanding of its fundamental tenets. Thus, whether it is politicians who compromise principles for short-term gains or intellectuals who seek to modify the core tenets of capitalism, the result is the same: an undermining of the system's integrity and the dilution of its foundational principles.

Mysticism and Force in Political Judgment

Bridging Rand's earlier declaration on the incompatibility of capitalism and altruism with her subsequent remarks on mysticism and force, an unsettling connection emerges. Politicians who say they support free markets but then intervene to set tariffs or minimum wages disregard the natural mechanisms that govern free markets—saying, "It is so because I say it is so."

This appears as an exercise in extroverted judgment, as witnessed in a collectivized mind, driven by mysticism—a form of "I say so" bereft of individual-oriented reasoning. By substituting their judgment for the aggregate choices of individuals in the marketplace, they are indeed reaching for the metaphorical gun: using legislative force to bring about their vision, regardless of whether it aligns with the principles they claim to uphold. In this way, they reflect Rand's warning regarding the inevitability of force arising when arbitrary assertion supplants reason.

When society primarily employs mysticism, expressed through extroverted judgment, as its means of communication, Rand asserts that it inevitably leads to a single outcome: the use of force.

She posits that reliance on faith and the use of force go hand in hand, with mysticism invariably leading to a regime of oppression. This happens because reason is the only way people can objectively communicate and understand each other; when they resort to claiming supernatural insights, no true persuasion or mutual comprehension is possible. To the question, "Why do we kill wild animals in the jungle?" she would respond by saying that we cannot communicate with them in any other way. And this is the condition mysticism brings humanity to—a state in which only violence can resolve disagreements. Furthermore, no individual or group can enforce their arbitrary edicts upon society without resorting to force. Anyone who falls back on the claim "It's true because I say it's true" will inevitably have to use force to uphold their assertions. Communists, as with all materialists, who are neo-mystics, whether they deny the mind for revelations or conditioned responses, end up at the same conclusion.[202]

What Rand uncovers here is that force is the necessary and ultimate result of altruism. It does not matter what version of altruism because both mysticism and collectivism are its corollaries—its cause and expression. They are both a result of the rejection of reason—the refusal to use or even acknowledge one's independent judgment. This

---

[202] (Rand, Faith and Force: The Destroyers of the Modern World 1960, 103)

understanding necessitates a much more thorough look at the concept of force, something which I will attempt in Part III.

Mysticism's Regression to Primitive Psychology

According to Jung, mysticism serves as a reversion to humanity's more primitive psychological states. In this view, the medieval mystical focus on the relativity of God is a step back to these primal conditions. This contrasts with Eastern philosophical ideas, which are not so much a reversion but a sophisticated evolution from this primordial base. Jung argues that this reversion or continuous connection is vital, as every effective religious system incorporates some aspects of primitive instinct, connecting us back to the primal energies of Mother Earth. He further notes that these instinctual, or "impure" forces, have their own vitality, cautioning that excessive pursuit of rational or ethical purity can deplete life's essential vigor, which comes from a blend of both clear and muddy sources.[203]

Jung's thoughts on mysticism and its primitive nature support Rand's claim that western civilization's basic contradiction is mysticism versus reason. One glaring example being Christianity—as the dominant religion of America—versus capitalism. Christianity is a result of mysticism: the psycho-epistemological root of altruism. Capitalism is a political derivative, resulting from a psycho-epistemology of reason and an ethics of rational egoism.

The Prerequisites of Human Survival and Conscious Thought

As Rand points out, mysticism, as the cause of altruism, and capitalism, as an expression of reason, cannot coexist. We conclude this section with her assessment of the natural requirements of human survival,

---

[203] (Jung 1923, 228)

His mind is given to him, its content is not. To remain alive, he must act, and before he can act he must know the nature and purpose of his action. He cannot obtain his food without a knowledge of food and of the way to obtain it. He cannot dig a ditch—or build a cyclotron—without a knowledge of his aim and of the means to achieve it. To remain alive, he must think.[204]

Rand's statement shows conscious thinking is necessary for an elevated standard of living, for anyone who wants to achieve a higher standard of life must consciously think for themselves or benefit from the thinking of others. But all thinking is not conscious and, as we have seen, Rand sees the conflict as one between conscious and unconscious thinking.

---

[204] (Rand, Faith and Force: The Destroyers of the Modern World 1960, 106)

SUMMARY

In the previous section we used several sources related to Objectivism as material to contrast with the principles of Carl Jung's psychological types. And in this summary section we will look at the major takeaways of importance from this comparison in reference to our overall theme of proper ethics for America.

Psychology

In carefully reviewing the journey so far, as laid out in "Philosophy and Sense of Life," the analysis began by looking at the perceiving axis in isolation. The discussion identifies this level of the psyche as the essence of an individual, and the text provides examples of irrational types to illustrate the manifestation of these psychological orientations in everyday life. In doing so, we also set the groundwork for understanding the distinction between an irrational and rational orientation. We then examined three case studies to demonstrate how one's "sense of life" could conflict with one's personal rational philosophy, and began our case for using Jung's framework to facilitate a better understanding of Rand's psycho-epistemology.

In carrying this theme into "The Psycho-Epistemology of Art," we aimed to establish the connection between Rand and Jung's theories, demonstrating how psychological type can clarify one's psycho-epistemology. Cognitive abstraction and concept formation

229

proved crucial in this exploration because it is at the heart of the types' alternative approaches to reason and rationality. This is where we first encounter an implicit relationship of psychology to ethical philosophy, in relating these concepts to normative abstractions and objective values.

With "The Comprachicos," we use Rand's essay to examine how one's type's "cognitive style" develops during one's early years, aiming to better understand the contextual underpinnings of our newly formed framework of psycho-epistemology and psychological types. Education methods were central in this examination, while other factors also play a role in this development. This section allowed us to examine the dynamics of objectivity and subjectivity in psychological interpretation. The discussion also covers abstract and concrete thinking in relation to one's psychological type and how they contribute to the development of tribal mentalities. We concluded the section by highlighting how tribal mindsets manifest in numerous areas of society.

"The Missing Link" allowed us to further elucidate the underlying characteristics of Jung's types through Rand's concept of an "anti-conceptual mentality," and we find that Jung's conceptualization of concrete thinking—which he traces back to primitive origins—and Rand's concept exhibit extreme similarities. Once again, we examine education to understand both its role in contributing to concretistic thinking and how educational methods can perpetuate this type of thinking into future generations. We further discuss the tribal and collective perspective, demonstrating that those who unquestionably embrace their beliefs respond negatively when encouraged to be more intellectually critical.

Psychology to Ethics

As a first step in transitioning from psychology to ethics, "The Psychology of Psychologizing" allowed us to narrow the scope of the discussion. Establishing that, while psychology is the discipline that provides a window into the human mind, moral philosophy is concerned with humans as conscious beings, we began to limit our focus to rational types only. This is where we morally judge the implicit ethical philosophy of each psychological type.

"Selfishness Without a Self" uses the essay Rand authored to detail the societal effects of an isolated member of a tribe. She contends that individuals with perceptual mentalities lack a genuine sense of self, and we explore the ethical implications of this mindset, providing several examples that illustrate its real-world tribal manifestations. Importantly, how the mindset appears in politics is of significant relevance to our main theme. Furthermore, we examine philosophies resulting from what Jung labels negative thinking, such as pragmatism. Individuals use this type of thinking not to achieve comprehensive understanding, but rather to diminish or negate complex experiences or perceptions, often simplifying them into reductive explanations.

In "Mental Health versus Mysticism and Self-Sacrifice," we explored the intersection of rationality, self-perception, and moral reasoning, emphasizing how one's psychological type influences their view of reality. It delves into the impact of feeling and extroverted types on this dynamic, providing examples to illustrate these effects. The analysis then examines mysticism within the framework of individual psychological types, with a specific focus on how these types relate to self-concept and the inclination toward self-sacrifice. The section thoroughly examines the influence of Jung's psychological functions on the formation of one's ethical and epistemological stances.

In "Causality Versus Duty," the text contrasts lives guided by duty, linked to external authorities and societal norms, with those informed by an awareness of causality. This section explores how these psychological foundations affect ethical decisions, highlighting the impact of a distorted self-perception on ethics. It critically examines the concept of duty, as seen in Rand and Immanuel Kant's philosophies, and discusses the role of education in fostering mystical or collective thought. The analysis reinterprets duty as a concept emerging from one's psychological orientation and examines hypothetical cases to expose that what people commonly accept as an innate sense of duty is, in fact, a widely accepted mystical construct: an ethical and psychological consequence of a duty-bound upbringing.

In "Collectivized Ethics," the essay explores the impact of extroverted rational types on ethics, particularly their inclination toward altruism and the concept of a "collectivized soul." It addresses how concretistic cognition challenges individualism in modern political thought. The work contrasts Rand and Jung's perspectives to unravel collective ethical consciousness, focusing on the implications for individual rights and political philosophy. The section delves into the psychological underpinnings of collective mentalities and their societal effects, particularly in the context of altruistic government projects and policies.

Ethics to Politics

In "Faith and Force: The Destroyers of the Modern World," we brought all of what we have learned together from psychology's application to ethics, up to ethics' application to politics. This exposes the inferiority of a political system hinged on the ethics of altruism while said to be protecting freedom and individual rights.

PART III

THE PROPER ETHICS
FOR AMERICA

The primary aim of Parts I and II was not only to establish a framework integrating the comprehensive systems of Objectivism and Jungian psychology but also to define and contextualize key terms and concepts crucial for a profound exploration of the issues facing the nation. This endeavor originates from a recognition of the United States' significant departure from its foundational principles—a departure that has led to a societal misalignment. This misalignment, characterized by a persistent shift toward policies and cultural norms that undermine the very essence of rights. These laws, policies, and norms also deviate from the fundamental principles of capitalism— the only social system that truly supports a society of free and thriving individuals.

This section aims to articulate the proper ethical framework for America, grounding these principles in the context of political discourse to make them accessible and applicable to our societal structure. Objectivism and Jungian psychology provide the theoretical underpinnings for this, offering insights into the relationship between individual psychology and collective ethics. This synthesis provides a nuanced understanding of ethics, not as abstract principles detached from real life, but as the very foundation upon which a just and effective political system must stand. In this analysis, the stage is set for a conclusion with my views on what constitutes the proper politics for America—a politics that is deeply rooted in and reflective of the ethical framework outlined in this examination.

In the following text, I advocate for a fundamental realignment of American culture and politics. By critically examining contemporary trends through this combined psychological and philosophical lens, this work proposes a path forward that both acknowledges and respects the need for individual rights and rational governance. This realignment calls for a reexamination of America's core values, aiming to recapture an essential element of its ethos that was never fully grasped on its inception.

I do not claim this as a solely independent discovery. I credit Rand, and Objectivism, which together provide the philosophical foundation which catalyzes my argument. One can witness the true significance of Rand's accomplishment and its contribution to America in the following statement from Leonard Peikoff:

> *Objectivism is preeminently an American viewpoint, even though most people, here and abroad, know nothing about it. It is American because it identifies the implicit base of the United States, as the country was originally conceived.*[205]

My contribution, through creating a triangulation of sorts, is in unlocking the deeper psychological underpinnings of the American ethos and individualism by using Jung's framework, enabling the combined use of these long-established systems as tools for practical action.

---

[205] (Peikoff 1991, 460)

When viewing Objectivism's philosophical framework, we must first backtrack to its antecedent philosophical branches: metaphysics, epistemology, ethics, politics, and esthetics. When we do this analysis, we see that Objectivism's political philosophy is the successor of its ethical philosophy, and if we backtrack again to its epistemological, and once again to its metaphysical philosophies, we reveal that these philosophical layers have a psychological parallel in Jung's concepts of rational and irrational functions.

By beginning with an examination of human psychology—the bedrock of both individual behavior and collective societal norms—we can trace how ethical considerations should inform the evolution of our political landscape from its most basic origins to its current complexity. This exploration is not an academic exercise; it is a necessary endeavor to identify and advocate for ethical standards that can guide America toward a future that respects rights and upholds the principles of capitalism as the bedrock of a free society.

Individuation and the American Spirit: The Journey to Independence

$=\!\!=\!\!=\!\!=\!\!=\!\!=\!\!=\!\!=$ ★ ★ ★ $=\!\!=\!\!=\!\!=\!\!=\!\!=\!\!=\!\!=$

Carl Jung introduced the concept of **individuation** as the process through which a person evolves into a distinct, indivisible entity, developing a unique personality apart from society's collective unconscious. This understanding of "individuality" is modern, marking a significant psychological achievement over the historically predominant collective attitude.

The evolution of individuality mirrors the transformative journey that the U.S. Constitution demands of its citizens, which necessitates one's transition from a collective orientation, to one in which individuals become autonomous. This alignment underscores the Constitution's role in fostering liberty, individual rights, and self-governance, acknowledging the critical importance of individuality within the nation's framework.

Individualism is foundational to Americanism which finds its explicit articulation in Objectivism. Rather than merely aligning with American principles, Objectivism crystallizes the essence of what was implicit in the nation's philosophy. The implication is that only upon reaching the level of an individual—achieved through a profound psychological evolution—can one consciously hold a rational set of ethics suitable for human beings.

Jung's process of individuation describes the journey from a collective beginning, to achieving personal autonomy, a transformation honed over millennia facilitated by various forms of education. Initially rooted in perception, individuation advances toward conceptual understanding, paving the way for one's rational independence. Jung explains it like this:

> *A conscious process of differentiation, or individuation, is needed to bring the individuality to consciousness, i.e., to raise it out of the state of identity with the object. The identity of the individuality with the object is synonymous with its unconsciousness. If the individuality is unconscious, there is no psychological individual but merely a collective psychology of consciousness. The unconscious individuality is then projected on the object, and the object, in consequence, possesses too great a value and acts as too powerful a determinant.*[206]

Physical existence alone does not produce a psychological individual. In the initial stage of individuation, perception plays a key role as a child recognizes their physical separateness, marking the beginning of their journey toward individual consciousness. This stage, however, is just the start. Full individuation, which is crucial for achieving rational independence, demands a more volitional, conscious effort. In the absence of this effort, one's judgment remains primarily a byproduct of sensory experiences and instinct. This limited state of psychic freedom often manifests in mystical beliefs or a deterministic worldview, reflecting a lack of developed individuality.

---

[206] (Jung 1923, 411)

To state this simply and in the clearest terms possible, individuality *is* rational independence. It is one's ability to make choices for themselves and generate personally chosen values. Without developing one's rational independence, a person has not truly become an individual in the psychological sense.

However, as to rational independence, it is my assessment society will never arrive at a fully rational world, nor would I say that is my desire. The mental health of each person rests on their ability to achieve a psychological balance that fulfills their unique needs. A healthy society allows for diverse types, under the same principles as free markets and division of labor.

The Birth of Individuality: From Primal Instinct to Rational Thought

The evolution from primal, instinct-driven beings to entities capable of rational thought, distinguishes humans as the quintessential "rational animal." However, unlike instinct, which operates automatically, rationality necessitates active engagement and development. It is a choice rather than an innate attribute.

Initially, humans were perceptual beings with undifferentiated thinking and feeling. They experienced the world as a cohesive whole with no clear distinction between judgment and perception. Over time, we developed the ability to differentiate these functions, marking a pivotal point in our evolution toward rationality.

It was the emergence of abstraction that facilitated this significant leap. Abstraction acts as a critical mechanism for managing overwhelming floods of sensory information, enabling humans to focus on essential details by filtering out the non-essential. This process is inherently subjective, rooted in the individual's understanding and internal processing.

The Primacy of Existence: Sensory Input and Objective Reality

Rational decision-making begins with the perception of facts through sensory input, followed by subjective analysis and valuation. This principle highlights the necessity of acknowledging the object's existence prior to engaging in rational judgment. For example, when a person encounters a painting for the first time, the immediate sensory experience—the colors, textures, and composition—is a prerequisite to any subsequent rational analysis or interpretation of the painting, such as understanding its artistic style or evaluating its quality.

Abstraction versus Empathy: The Repressed Individuality of the Rational Extrovert

Based on what we have learned about these concepts and their application to modern humans, an especially important distinction emerges. An introverted irrational function requires an act of abstraction by the subject; the process itself engages judgment. On the other hand, extroverted rational processes require empathy from the subject, and empathy necessitates non-judgmental acceptance. Thus, the fusion of judgment and perception seen in extroverted rational types is what causes the repression of the subject's individuality. Jung alludes to this dynamic when he classifies the thinking of the introvert as rational and the thinking of the extrovert as programmatic.

Nurturing Individuality: The Essence of Conceptual Education

A conceptual education is the only type of education worthy of the title because it does not aim to dictate what you think, but instead offers the method for you to arrive at your own conclusions. One can learn everything else on their own. Although this approach influences the development of type, it will not produce a specific type because type results from a large set of existential and relative circumstances. The natural and nurtured skills one possesses uniquely orient, position, and incentivize them to develop certain functions to a higher proficiency above others.

Fostering Rational Individuality through Conceptual Education

Any formal education that does not prioritize the development of a child's conceptual capacity amounts to indoctrination, as it aims to instill the child with collective values instead of facilitating their ability to generate self-determined values. This indoctrination compromises the individual's lifelong ability to separate thinking from feeling by blurring the distinction between sensations, which are immediate responses to physical stimuli, and emotions, which are complex reactions arising from cognitive processes and interpretations.

A conceptual education is a purely independent method focused exclusively on the psychological function of thinking, which promotes a person's development from the primitive or infantile state toward rational individuality. However, the collective method of indoctrination relies solely on emotion and feeling, hindering this individuation process. Any refusal to acknowledge the notion that indoctrination substitutes collective values for a set of personally chosen individual values, is a misrepresentation of the fundamental differences between individual thinking and collective conditioning.

The Self-Fulfilling Prophecy of Collective Thinking

Indoctrination presents an existential threat to the individuality, independent thinking, and personal autonomy of a society's members when done coercively, but in cases in which an outside party has limited means to persuade the individual, the personal acceptance of collective values is a matter of the individual's choice. Yet, it is the act of choice that is problematic for the deterministic, collectively oriented personalities because popular opinion appears coercive to the collective mentality.

It is almost impossible for these types to perceive popular opinion as anything other than a form of coercion because of their psychological orientation. But their collective orientation is frequently a result of the indoctrination they have received, masked as education. Therefore, indoctrination is an anti-conceptual education that perpetuates the primitive tribal mentality. It reinforces the collective way of thinking, to the point that it becomes a self-fulfilling prophecy.

In modern educational settings, the case of a student named Jordan vividly illustrates the challenges of navigating a curriculum shaped by emotional avoidance and selective debate. In Jordan's school educators teach subjects like history and social studies with an emphasis on avoiding discomfort, resulting in a curriculum lacking depth and evading critical evaluation of sensitive topics. This selective openness, under policies labeling certain views as too extreme based on potential emotional responses, not only discourages intellectual curiosity but also prioritizes cultural indoctrination over educational diversity and critical thinking. Jordan's story underscores the pervasive challenge of fostering an educational environment that truly encourages conceptual thinking, individual autonomy, and the development of a personal set of values.

Assimilation and Indoctrination: Mechanisms of Social Integration

Social cohesion is crucial to the survival of any healthy society and its culture. While indoctrination is often a means to creating cohesion using the individual's blind and passive acceptance, assimilation, on the other hand, is the means to achieve the same cohesion through an active process of one's will. Assimilation involves an individual integrating into a larger group, but this integration does not necessarily require the abandonment of personal values or independent thought.

Assimilation allows for the individual to retain their sense of self and agency, choosing which aspects of the collective to adopt and which to reject or modify based on personal judgment. In contrast, indoctrination seeks to override this individual agency, promoting a uniform acceptance of beliefs without room for critical assessment or personal interpretation. Thus, indoctrination and assimilation are two sides of the same coin with different underlying mechanisms, rooted in one's psychological perspective. This difference in opinion highlights a recurring theme when understanding an individual's interpretation of such dichotomous concepts: "choice defines perspective."

Jung comments on the individuality stunted by indoctrination and its relationship to collective values,

> *Any serious check to individuality, therefore, is an artificial stunting. It is obvious that a social group consisting of stunted individuals cannot be a healthy and viable institution; only a society that can preserve its internal cohesion and collective values, while at the same time granting the individual the greatest possible freedom, has any prospect of enduring vitality.*[207]

Integrity of the System: Upholding Philosophical Principles

In American political philosophy, the intent behind federal laws and institutions should be to embody the philosophy's principles, aiming to balance collective values with individual freedom. Crafted by experts, these laws and institutions translate philosophical concepts into governance, ensuring the system's integrity. Altering them risks the philosophical foundation they support, highlighting their role in sustaining the political system's coherence and the dynamic between personal choice and societal values.

---

[207] (Jung 1923, 411-412)

Balancing Collective Values with Personal Freedom

Indoctrination, by its very nature, suppresses personally chosen values, favoring instead a rigid adherence to predetermined beliefs. This reality highlights that it is crucial for those in authority to restrict the application of coercive laws and enforcement to situations that are essential for preserving the foundational collective values upon which the country's doctrine is based. Such restraint ensures that the enforcement of law and order serves to protect the country's core values, without unnecessarily infringing on the individual's right to personal value formation and autonomy. This careful balancing act is crucial in preventing the legal system from becoming an instrument of indoctrination, thereby allowing for the coexistence of a cohesive societal structure with the preservation of individual freedoms and choices.

The key to maintaining a healthy balance between individual autonomy and collective cohesion is to make the distinction between necessary legal coercion and unnecessary infringement on personal values logical and explicit. This clear demarcation serves to reduce societal polarization, and ensures limits on the number of concretizations in concepts such as nationalism, Christianity, liberalism, and other similar ideologies. These ideologies concretize their moral values within their ideas and teachings, leading to ease of conflation and taking the form of what Jung terms "negative thinking."

For instance, consider the concretization of values in nationalism. Nationalism often elevates the concept of national identity to an extent where it overshadows individual identities and perspectives. This can lead to the conflation of patriotism with a rigid adherence to national policies, regardless of their ethical implications. People might feel compelled to support their nation's actions unquestioningly, conflating loyalty with uncritical acceptance. One can view such a perspective as an instance of Jung's "negative thinking," where it oversimplifies complex social and ethical issues into a binary of nationalistic loyalty versus disloyalty. Jung uses the example of theosophical thinking—defined as a philosophy that aims to explore the divine and mystical elements within various religious teachings—to illustrate the characteristics of reductionist thinking:

> *Theosophical thinking has an air that is not in the least reductive, since it exalts everything to a transcendental and world- embracing idea... We have only to open a theosophical book to be overwhelmed by the realization that everything is already explained, and that "spiritual science" has left no enigmas unsolved. But, at bottom, this kind of thinking is just as negative as materialistic thinking... The only difference is that materialism reduces everything to physiology, whereas theosophy reduces everything to Indian metaphysics... Not only are both methods of explanation futile, they are actually destructive, because by diverting interest away from the main issue, in one case to the stomach and in the other to imaginary vibrations, they hamper any serious investigation of the problem by a bogus explanation. Either kind of thinking is sterile and sterilizing. Its negative quality is due to the fact that it is so indescribably cheap, impoverished, and lacking in creative energy. It is a thinking taken in tow by other functions.*[208]

Conceptual Education's Role

A cultural education best classifies an education focused on social adjustment, whereas it should only contain the essential elements necessary for the group's association. For America, the essential tenets of American philosophy, central to the country's formation, would serve as the only cultural principles allowed in a classroom delivering a conceptual education, because as citizens, we are all unified under the country's fundamental principles. The additional benefit of coupling the country's essential principles, such as liberty, equality,

---

[208] (Jung 1923, 328)

individual rights, and capitalism, with a conceptual education, for instance through practices like reciting the Pledge of Allegiance, singing the national anthem, or studying the Constitution, is that it forces an ongoing cogent examination of why these principles are correct. These activities not only instill a sense of national identity but also invite critical engagement with the foundational values they represent, further strengthening their validity by exposing and extracting philosophical weaknesses identified under intellectual scrutiny. All other more specialized cultural training should take place via institutions reserved solely for that purpose, such as the religious institutions of Christianity, Islam, or Judaism, or non-government organizations like cultural associations, community centers, and specialized educational groups.

Embracing Individuality: Mental Health and Knowledge for Self

According to renowned neuroscientist and psychologist Lisa Feldman Barrett, humans are not born with emotions; we create them.[209]

Crafting Emotions: The Transactional Nature of Affect

Emotions are guesses and a product of the way a person thinks. This core aspect makes humans inherently transactional because emotions result from judgments, and these judgments continually occur at both the subconscious and conscious levels. One cannot avoid this process. Rand expands on this aspect of life further, via the character of John Galt,

> As there can be no causeless wealth, so there can be no causeless love or any sort of causeless emotion. An emotion is a response to a fact of reality, an estimate dictated by your standards.[210]

---

[209] (Barrett 2018)
[210] (Rand, Atlas Shrugged 1957, 1033)

Navigating the Cognitive Landscape: External versus Internal Decision-Making Frameworks

Rand's philosophic principle, delivered through *Atlas Shrugged's* protagonist, exposes the importance of attitude toward judgment because it sets the cognitive standard for all decisions that follow. When one exercises rational extroversion, personal judgment is repressed, leading external factors to determine decisions. In contrast, introverted judgment consciously employs subjective reason, taking the side of individualism. Hence, for extroverted feeling types, the implicit principle equates to: "What result do most people I identify with feel is good?" An example might be a civic leader who aligns their actions with the emotional consensus of their community. When deciding on organizing a local event, they might choose a theme that they believe will resonate with the majority's feelings, even if there is not concrete evidence to support the event's success.

Similarly, for extroverted thinking types, their implicit principle equates to: "What result do most people I identify with think is true?" For example, a corporate manager might adopt a new business strategy because it is popular and widely accepted in their professional network, relying on the collective logic of their peers rather than individual, in-depth analysis.

For introverted feeling types, their implicit principle equates to: "What result do I feel is good?" An artist might choose to work on a project that deeply resonates with their personal values and emotions, rather than what is commercially popular. This decision is based on their internal assessment of what feels authentically meaningful to them, rather than external validation.

Similarly, for introverted thinking types, the implicit principle equates to: "What result do I think is true?" An example here could be a scientist who develops a theory based on their meticulous analysis and logical reasoning. Despite the theory not being immediately accepted widely, or popular, they pursue it because their rational process leads them to believe in its truth. They rely on their internal logical framework to arrive at a conclusion, independent of external opinions or consensus.

In the dichotomy of introverted and extroverted judgment, one must always choose, consciously or subconsciously, if they are to measure things by their own standards or by the standards of others. The implicit principle of one's rational process highly influences their perception of a fact, with the subject serving as the sole controller of the thinking side. This is what makes active thinking so important because it is the only means to impart any sort of conscious input in the continual process of judgment that takes place, whether conscious or not.

Unveiling the Roots of Psychological Distress

Galt continues,

> *Thinking is man's only basic virtue, from which all the others proceed. And his basic vice, the source of all his evils, is that nameless act which all of you practice, but struggle never to admit: the act of blanking out, the willful suspension of one's consciousness, the refusal to think—not blindness, but the refusal to see; not ignorance, but the refusal to know. It is the act of unfocusing your mind and inducing an inner fog to escape the responsibility of judgment—on the unstated premise that a thing will not exist if only you refuse to identify it.[211]*

The root of psychological issues always rests in the way one thinks—because all psychological issues for a human originate with thinking.

---

[211] (Rand, Atlas Shrugged 1957, 1017-1018)

The Emotional Byproduct of a Disconnected Mind: A Journey from Faith to Fear

The default methods of the irrational, and rational, extrovert are faith, trust, and belief, and the refusal to acquire knowledge. Knowledge is requisite of understanding, and the flaw demonstrated by the previously mentioned types is they attempt understanding without it. However, it is crucial to identify how these tendencies manifest at a deeper psychological level.

In "The Comprachicos," Rand offers insight into this phenomenon, particularly focusing on the role of the subconscious. Her exploration into the psycho-epistemology of an "anti-conceptual" mind reveals how the subconscious, when not consciously directed, continues to integrate experiences in its own way. This process, often unrecognized and unchecked, leads to a significant emotional byproduct that is a constant in the person's mental flux: fear. Rand captures this idea as follows:

> *The secret of his psycho-epistemology-which baffles those who deal with him—lies in the fact that, as an adult, he has to use concepts, but he uses concepts by a child's perceptual method. He uses them as concretes, as the immediately given—without context, definitions, integrations or specific referents; his only context is the immediate moment. To what, then, do his concepts refer? To a foggy mixture of partial knowledge, memorized responses, habitual associations, his audience's reactions and his own feelings, which represent the content of his mind at that particular moment. On the next day or occasion, the same concepts will refer to different things, according to the changes in his mood and in the immediate circumstances.*
>
> *He seems able to understand a discussion or a rational argument, sometimes even on an abstract, theoretical level. He is able to participate, to agree or disagree after what appears to be a critical examination of the issue. But the next time*

one meets him, the conclusions he reached are gone from his mind, as if the discussion had never occurred even though he remembers it: he remembers the event, i.e., a discussion, not its intellectual content.

It is beside the point to accuse him of hypocrisy or lying (though some part of both is necessarily involved). His problem is much worse than that: he was sincere, he meant what he said in and for that moment. But it ended with that moment. Nothing happens in his mind to an idea he accepts or rejects; there is no processing, no integration, no application to himself, his actions or his concerns; he is unable to use it or even to retain it. Ideas, i.e., abstractions, have no reality to him; abstractions involve the past and the future, as well as the present; nothing is fully real to him except the present. Concepts, in his mind, become percepts—percepts of people uttering sounds; and percepts end when the stimuli vanish. When he uses words, his mental operations are closer to those of a parrot than of a human being. In the strict sense of the word, he has not learned to speak.

But there is one constant in his mental flux. The subconscious is an integrating mechanism; when left without conscious control, it goes on integrating on its own—and, like an automatic blender, his subconscious squeezes its clutter of trash to produce a single basic emotion: fear.[212]

Fear of others does not motivate rational introversion, but a mentality hinged on rational extroversion cannot expect anything beyond it. Fear, to varying degrees, will be the driving force in their lives.

Ignorance is the root cause of fear, and addressing it fundamentally hinges on how individuals acquire knowledge, specifically their

---

[212] (Rand, The Comprachicos 1970, 76-77)

psycho-epistemology. The prioritization and orientation of a type's rational axis represents one's psycho-epistemology, and this logically dictates that thinking and feeling are responsible for fear.

The Spectrum of Belief: Knowledge versus Trust

In Jung's theory, there are only four rational types with the proclivity toward decision-making. The introverted feeling type makes decisions based on subjective feeling and secondarily considers the thinking of others. The extroverted feeling type makes decisions based on objective feeling and secondarily considers the thinking of themselves. The extroverted thinking type makes decisions based on objective thinking while secondarily considering their personal feeling, and the introverted thinking type makes decisions based on subjective thinking and secondarily considers the feeling of others.

If we accept that knowing and trust are, respectively, the ultimate and penultimate points on the spectrum of belief, then we can say, because the rational introvert's basis for judgment always remains internal, it retains the greatest potential strength of belief, enabling knowledge. Alternatively, the rational extrovert reaches the pinnacle of trust because they surrender the basis for judgment to the external factor. Thus, we can conclude that the rational introvert seeks to know; while the rational extrovert only seeks to trust in others, who know.

The Primacy of Thinking in Knowledge and Identity

As knowledge relates to the differences between introverted thinking and feeling types, my interpretation of Jung's theory is that the thinking function is the primary source of conceptual knowledge. This is because it directly engages with identity, logic, and analysis, which are essential for intellectual understanding. Therefore, I conclude that knowledge is a function of one's subjective thinking and consequently, the only direct means by which to address fear.

251

Ti-Fe versus Fi-Te: A Comparative Analysis of Guilt and Shame

Fear manifests in various forms, including guilt and shame, influenced by an individual's psychological type. For those who primarily use the introverted thinking and extroverted feeling axis, moral issues often surface as guilt, stemming from a conflict between their logical analysis (Ti) and sensitivity to others' feelings (Fe). Conversely, individuals aligned with the introverted feeling and extroverted thinking axis tend to experience shame in moral contexts, due to a clash between their personal values (Fi) and external societal norms (Te). The introverted thinking and extroverted feeling axis predisposes one to guilt over perceived emotional neglect, while the introverted feeling and extroverted thinking axis inclines one to shame resulting from discrepancies between internal values and external standards.

The All-Knowing Other: From Fear to Tribalism

The method by which the rational extrovert chooses to alleviate their fear is increased adherence to the object—which often is the group—seeking protection through the validation and sacrifice of others. This exercise in the archaic style of the primitive, results from what Jung frequently refers to as Lucien Lévy-Bruhl's concept of participation mystique, whereas individuals embrace a mystical idea or collective subjectivity that automatically "mis-integrates" them into an inseparable whole. This dynamic is evident in all instances of tribalism seen in human groups. God(s) and society are commonly-used examples of such secondhand concepts, which only serve as code words for the group. These concepts represent the all-knowing "other" that holds the ultimate power. The group is what they believe in, is their means to, and what they except as, knowledge, on faith—because, for this mentality, only the group can know.

Concrete judgment is the fundamental source of mysticism, the driver in all attempts at altruism, and instances of collectivism—where one always substitutes belief for knowledge and effectively substitutes people for ideas.

The Critical Link: Applying Thought to Action

Though we have identified irrational fear originates from a lack of knowledge, we must also identify the focus of that knowledge. The complete issue is lack of knowledge in applying thought to action to obtain objective results.

People must obtain physical resources to ensure their survival, and they engage in thinking to address this challenge to a progressively more efficient level. But when people use God, love, empathy, and similar concepts such as those Jung categorizes as negative thinking, as answers to everything, frustration ensues when the individual finds they cannot apply these concepts to the physical world. The sole remaining possibility then becomes to live in a duplicitous and contradictory manner, leading to a psychological split of ideas versus reality, rather than, ideas—for, reality.

The Diminishing Role of Independent Thought: Navigating Modern Education

The current American education system places significant emphasis on social adjustment in children, often neglecting the development of their independent thinking and decision-making skills. This social adjustment includes programs and curricula focused on teaching children to accept specific viewpoints on topics like sexuality, religion, and politics, often under the guise of promoting inclusivity and openness. For instance, schools may introduce comprehensive sex education programs that emphasize certain attitudes toward sexuality, or they might provide one-sided perspectives on political and religious matters, implicitly discouraging students from exploring a range of viewpoints or forming their own opinions.

253

While learning institutions frequently aim to foster a more accepting and diverse environment, they often condition children to unquestioningly embrace these ideas, stifling debate, and the exploration of alternative perspectives. The education system's shift toward group consensus over individual inquiry subtly instills the notion that knowledge is unattainable by the individual; only the group can know. Critical thinking and the pursuit of objective knowledge take a backseat to fitting into pre-established social molds.

Undermining Independence: The Sure Road to Mental Distress

The consequence of this approach is not just academic but also psychological. Students learn to distrust their own judgment and rely heavily on group thinking.

The inability to think independently and sustain one's own survival leads directly to poor mental health. Yet, there is a noticeable rise in mental health struggles among the youth, which, under these educational practices should not be the least bit surprising. The resulting psychological impact of these educational practices aligns with Rand's critique of intellectual dependency, as she eloquently asserted about the products of this system,

> *He has no concept of knowledge: he does not know when he knows and when he does not know. His chronic fear is of what he is supposed to know, and his pretentious posturing is intended to hide the fact that he hasn't the faintest idea.*[213]

From schools, to religion, to politics, people openly promote poor mental health by promoting its cause—rational extroversion, or simply, "rule following." While claiming to combat mental illness,

---

[213] (Rand, The Comprachicos 1970, 75)

those offering the cure are often the ones responsible for inflicting the disease.

Though psychological adaptiveness protects against its complete eradication, the tendency toward rational extroversion is certainly not a goal for a developed society premised on independence; it is merely an outcome. Humans capable of making decisions for themselves are at least aware of what life requires whether they choose to practice this requirement or not.

Undermining Self-Esteem: The Consequences of Group Dependency on Individual Worth

As a result of all this, one never develops or else loses self-esteem, an indispensable characteristic of a mentally healthy individual; and there is no pathway to regaining or attaining it when the primary tool for survival—the ability to think—is defective. Educators have taught people to place trust in the group, not themselves, the method of the rational extrovert. It is no wonder why they believe they cannot exist without the group at that point.

The attitude of rational extroversion undermines self-esteem by fostering dependency on the group as the primary source of value. This dynamic is evident across social contexts: businesspeople who prioritize service over profit and personal success, religious followers who find value solely in devotion, and politicians who cater to public whims instead of personal convictions neglecting individual rights in the abstract. Such dependency on group approval diminishes the individual's intrinsic worth, making personal value contingent on utility to the group rather than inherent virtues.

The Building Blocks of Self-Esteem: Achieving Personal Values

The path to improving quality of life and mental health lies only in the rational pursuit of personal values, and relatedly in recognizing the inherent risks and struggles in such a pursuit. Success in this pursuit serves as evidence of competence in achieving values, the foundation of self-esteem. One cannot experience true love or fulfillment in life without this journey of self-discovery and valuation—no matter the inherent risks and struggles therein. Rand encapsulates this principle in the following,

> To love is to value. Only a rationally selfish man, a man of self-esteem, is capable of love—because he is the only man capable of holding firm, consistent, uncompromising, unbetrayed values. The man who does not value himself, cannot value anything or anyone.[214]

The sentiment that individual self-esteem is foundational to valuing others has gained wide acceptance beyond the confines of Randian philosophy. However, what often remains less acknowledged in mainstream discourse is the depth of thought preceding this recognition. Valuing oneself is not merely an act of affirmation but the result of a rigorous, rational pursuit of personal values. This journey, essential for genuine self-esteem, involves not only recognizing but also overcoming the external pressures that sway one's self-perception.

The popular understanding emphasizes the outcome—self-esteem's role in fostering healthy interpersonal relationships—without fully engaging with the underlying philosophical challenge: the need for intellectual independence and a personal value system developed through deliberate self-examination.

In contrast to the rational introvert, whose values and judgments are self-determined, the changing expectations of the group sway the extrovert, leading to an inconsistent self-value because of the overreliance on external validation. This distinction highlights the

---

[214] (Rand, The Objectivist Ethics 1964, 40)

importance of internal over external criteria in determining one's values and sustaining self-esteem.

A Tale of Two Prides: Group Deference in Religious and Secular Contexts

When examining the concept of pride through the lens of certain religious and secular groups, a stark contrast and glaring similarity emerges. Religious groups, for example Christians, often condemn pride in oneself, equating one's prioritization of personal concerns over others with arrogance or sin, while many secular groups, such as those in the LGBTQ community, celebrate "pride" as a symbol of self-acceptance.

Despite their apparent differences, both approaches reveal a deference to group dynamics: Religious adherents exhibit this through their abstract submission to divine will, emphasizing a spiritual alignment, while secular members demonstrate it through their concrete identification with a collective identity, marked by visible symbols and shared behaviors. The former, while maintaining a definition of pride that aligns closely with its classical meaning, leads to a complete erosion of one's self-esteem, extirpating personal significance, while the latter voids the concepts of pride and self-esteem of their genuine meaning, rendering them both a hollow façade.

Those lacking genuine pride or self-esteem are susceptible to manipulation, making it easy to persuade them to believe anything. Furthermore, those who adopt a superficial sense of pride, without genuine self-worth, recognize their own deceit, leading to internal conflict. This duplicity undermines the individual's sense of self, driving them further into group dependency as their sole source of perceived security.

The approach of these groups toward actions and consequences further illustrates this dichotomy. Where one side imposes strict prohibitions in the name of sin, the other advocates a form of boundless freedom, neglecting the importance of cause and effect. Where one side oversteps boundaries in the name of order, the other side displays no order whatsoever. However, both sides overlook a balanced approach that values reasoned choice and personal accountability, where individuals freely make informed decisions and accept their consequences.

Prioritizing Outcomes over Insights: A Surface-Level Approach

A consistent theme observed in the extroverted mindset is the prioritization of effects over causes, a tendency to focus on outcomes rather than seeking to understand their underlying reasons. This approach aligns with the concept of "regression to the mean," where extroverts often aim for objective outcomes, overlooking the individual subjective experiences that contribute to this known average. Such an approach, over time, leads to a distortion and eventual loss of all meaning. By neglecting the unique variables that shape outcomes, this mindset oversimplifies complex situations, resulting in a superficial understanding that lacks depth and accuracy.

The Perils of Emotion-Driven Conceptualization

In concept formation, ignoring causality leads to ill-conceived concepts that defy both logical constructs and reality. For instance, the term "birthing people" seeks inclusivity but ends up contradicting biological realities by implying birth is not exclusive to women, unlike the term "surrogate," which aligns with biological facts. Similarly, Modern Monetary Theory overlooks basic economic principles by proposing increases in money supply—often to fund government spending—without anticipating negative repercussions. The persistent defense of such terms often shows a preference for emotive over logical abstraction, presenting progressive ideas that stem more from subjective feelings than objective facts.

This preference highlights the complex interplay between thinking and feeling. While thinking provides the foundation for understanding, feeling often guides the development of thought, prompting deeper inquiry; however, when feeling overshadows thinking in conceptualization, particularly regarding language, it leads to ambiguous terms that obscure rather than clarify meaning, contributing to increased confusion, frustration, anxiety, and fear. A distorted understanding of reality resulting from such clumsy and inarticulate concepts fosters a nihilistic worldview because it negates objective truths—truths which one must still navigate and reconcile with daily.

Thus, to ensure grounding and adherence to logical consistency it is crucial to prioritize critical thinking when creating and validating concepts. This approach prevents the development of concepts that, while subjectively appealing, fail to accurately reflect the world, underscoring the inadequacy of relying primarily on feeling for meaningful conceptualization.

Beyond Extroversion: The Introverted Thinker's Dilemma

It is not only the extrovert who must contend with the phenomenon of rational extroversion, as all types possess an extroverted rational function in their ego, along with the potential to fall into the same method of rationalization or external validation—especially as extroversion is the general style of the public.

As this book delves into philosophical matters related to the thinking function, it is important to raise an issue commonly seen with the introverted thinking type: the frequent lack of courage. The profound impact of this tendency will become increasingly clear as my argument for the administration of proper ethics builds.

Cowardice, although not an emotion, is another product of fear. External criticism or attacks often result in a hesitancy and inaction, and for the introverted thinker, the risk of confrontation or misinterpretation when expressing their ideas can result in a reluctance to take decisive action. Consequently, concepts not applied in action lose their value, as the thinker retreats from the practical implementation of their ideas.

For those who understand the power of ideas and the intellect, neglecting to follow through with actions in line with your thinking renders your thinking inconsequential: "To think and not to do is not to think at all."[215]

Perceiving it unsafe to act on your thoughts only signals a crucial moment for deeper reflection. It is a call to strategize and strengthen your resolve, ensuring that you not only align your actions and thoughts but also execute them effectively.

Extroverted types do not inherently possess this cowardice and are often more willing to act. In fact, action is often the extrovert's most effective tool, while often overlooking the negative results of their actions on themselves and others. Their proficiency in group adjustment bolsters their willingness to act, with their comfort and skill in navigating social dynamics often empowering the extrovert to take decisive actions, as they are more attuned to the collective feedback and less swayed by introspective analysis. The neglected ego is less revered.

---

[215] (Covey 2013)

THE ESSENCE OF LEADERSHIP:
INTEGRATION AND INFLUENCE

★ ★ ★

While individuality forms the bedrock of personal ethics and rational independence, leadership demands a translation of these personal virtues into actions and decisions that shape the collective destiny. Comparable to how an individual integrates facts into a singular focus for a purpose, leadership is integration done with individuals. It sits at the highest level of contextualized abstraction and is a hierarchy that funnels up from individual contributors to leaders, and from those leaders to the leaders of leaders.

A leader can be formal or informal; implicit or explicit; and while some followers may seek out leadership in order to avoid responsibility for the consequences of their actions, this is not its purpose. A rational choice of leader is about volitionally choosing someone you think competent enough to lead your associated group and to make decisions on your behalf. Just as division of labor allows people to free up time to focus on other important things in their lives, leadership allows them to outsource decision-making for the members of the group to a person specializing in or focusing on strategic direction, critical decision-making, and achieving collective goals.

Defining Competent Leadership: The Synergy of Intelligence and Courage

The main components of competent leadership are intelligence and courage. When a leader exhibits these traits, it opens opportunities for group members to fill roles better suited for them, such as specialized experts, creative thinkers, operational managers, tactical planners, or frontline workers. These roles leverage individual strengths and contribute to the group's collective success, allowing each member to focus on what they do best within the framework set by the leader.

In leadership, intelligence manifests in a leader who makes broad abstractions from the facts to determine one integrative approach for all involved. They demonstrate this ability through what I describe as either a macro- or micro-minded method, of which the basic principle is as follows: The macro approach considers all stakeholders, whereas in the micro approach, shareholder concerns need be the only focus. Leading groups in an ethical capacity resulting in normative action for the population (e.g., federal government) requires a macro approach. Leadership that succeeds in narrower segments of the population (e.g., state and local government, businesses, families) typically thrives when employing the micro approach, where leaders make decisions with a closer, more immediate social fabric in mind.

Courage allows leaders to implement ideas for the group in the face of perceived social pressure while simultaneously maintaining group cohesion. Good leaders must be able to stand their ground with conviction even when receiving pushback from members. This can be a point of anxiety for those who find it unsettling to go against what others say. Members of the group, while seeking cohesiveness, still desire results; and for a person who prioritizes harmony or agreement with others, it can be difficult for them to make the decisions necessary to achieve the results desired when others openly disagree.

Authority versus Influence: The Leadership Paradigm

It is important to understand that leadership and management are not synonymous terms, though they are frequently used as if they are. Management typically refers to a role or position within an organizational hierarchy, achieved through positional power. It involves the administrative and operational oversight of resources, processes, and tasks. Organizations appoint managers to their positions and invest in them with formal authority.

Leadership, on the other hand, transcends positional power. It is not just about holding a title or a managerial role. Leadership embodies the ability to inspire, influence, and guide others, regardless of formal authority. A leader is someone to whom group members naturally look for direction, motivation, and guidance. This can happen in formal settings, where the leader is also a manager, but it is equally common in informal scenarios, where an individual becomes a leader through their actions, behaviors, and ability to rally others toward a common goal.

While all managers are in positions of authority, not all managers are true leaders. Similarly, not all leaders are formally recognized managers. Leadership is about the impact, influence, and inspiration one has on others, and it often emerges organically based on a person's qualities and actions.

Asserting Agency in Leadership Decisions

You can decline to accept leadership from a person you think is unfit to lead. In politics, voters accomplish this through casting their ballots. At work, your employment in most cases is at-will, and you can choose to vacate a position under the leadership of an incompetent leader through transfer or resignation.

The Imperative of Vocal Leadership: Why Leaders Must Speak Up

Group members anticipate receiving direction, so good leaders must verbalize methods, conclusions, and next steps, even if these are only guidelines—not instructions or rules. This is an area in which the introvert tends to err when they accept the unspoken as assumed, neglecting to communicate verbally.

Harnessing Individual Strengths: The Leader's Role in Achieving Collective Aims

Introverts are also sometimes confused about the nature of leadership, thinking that following a leader is akin to relinquishing their autonomy, but this is not the case. A group voluntarily chooses to form an alliance to achieve a shared goal, and a competent leader directs the perspectives, skills, and abilities of group members toward a singular focus to attain that shared goal, or fosters an environment that enables its accomplishment.

Maximizing Potential: The Synergy of Diverse Thinking Types in Leadership

Considering that the rational principles of the Constitution are the sole unifying factor among the citizens of America, and leadership is essential in maintaining those principles and executing actions in line with them, it follows that rational types are best equipped to lead the country politically. Logic at this point compels me to focus on the rational types for the remainder of this section while classifying the irrational types into the category of "still in the process of assimilating."

Though feeling is an indispensable function in the process of creating a rational set of principles, it is not as crucial as thinking when it comes to forming the conceptual connections that lead to these principles.

Thinking, in accordance with the laws of logic, is the function that primarily enables us to link ideas conceptually and to communicate these principles objectively in words.

Contrasting Thinking Styles: From Theory Formation to Practical Application

The NERIS Analytics Limited[216] study referenced earlier provides a detailed breakdown of personality types within the population. According to their findings, 49.5% of the participants fall into the category of rational types. Within this group, thinking types make up 22.5%. This subset of thinking types divides further into extroverted and introverted thinking types. Extroverted thinking types are more prevalent, comprising 14.5% of all psychological types. In contrast, introverted thinking types account for 8%. This distribution aligns with Jung's observations, noting extroverted thinking as the more commonly encountered thinking orientation, which he describes as:

> *It seems to be constantly affected by the objective data and to draw conclusions only with their consent. Hence it gives one the impression of a certain lack of freedom, of occasional short- sightedness, in spite of all its adroitness within the area circumscribed by the object.*[217]

The intense focus on the object restricts the extroverted thinker's breadth of thought, channeling their full mental energy into the area specified by the object. However, this focus limits their capacity for abstract thinking, necessary for accurately integrating information across varied conceptual domains easily. For extroverted thinkers, abstractions manifest as feelings, sensations, or intuitions rather

---

[216] (16personalities.com 2016)
[217] (Jung 1923, 320)

than thoughts, and their reasoning is inductive, often employing secondhand concepts.

Despite these limitations in abstract thought, Jung highlights that the extroverted thinking type is remarkably productive. Their thinking is constructive and leads to the discovery of new facts or the formulation of general concepts from a range of empirical data. It is typically synthetic in nature, constantly moving beyond mere analysis to create new combinations or ideas that reorganize the analyzed material in innovative ways, or which augment it. The term "predictive" characterizes this kind of thinking, always substituting a new value for a devalued one. It is never wholly depreciative or destructive because the thinking process is a major channel for the individual's vital energy. This energy flow imbues their thinking with a progressive, creative nature, ensuring that it is dynamic and forward-moving, rather than static or regressive.[218]

In contrast, introverted thinking is more subject-oriented, focusing on subjective data. It starts from the individual and, although it may venture far into the realm of reality, circles back to the subject. Jung elucidates this by noting that introverted thinking is not primarily concerned with external facts, but rather with the formation and elaboration of subjective ideas. It poses questions, crafts theories, and opens new vistas of understanding, treating facts more as illustrative than foundational. For introverted thinkers, facts serve to support theories, and are not ends in themselves. This thinking style, driven by its goal to transform the "dark image" of reality into a "luminous idea," endeavors to determine how external realities align with the framework of an idea. The true prowess of this thinking lies in its ability to generate an idea that, while not directly derived from concrete facts, aptly abstracts them, proving its validity through the facts it encompasses.[219]

---

[218] (Jung 1923, 326)
[219] (Jung 1923, 351-352)

The intense focus on the idea of the introverted thinking type creates the danger of losing strength of relationship to objective facts. In this way, the attitude is reminiscent of rationalists and subjectivists. Their thinking is abstract, and their logic is deductive. Additionally, the bulk of mental energy dedicated toward the idea can lead to practical application becoming a mere afterthought. Jung states,

> But no more than extroverted thinking can wrest a sound empirical concept from concrete facts or create new ones can introverted thinking translate the initial image into an idea adequately adapted to the facts. For, as in the former case the purely empirical accumulation of facts paralyzes thought and smothers their meaning, so in the latter case introverted thinking shows a dangerous tendency to force the facts into the shape of its image, or to ignore them altogether in order to give fantasy free play.[220]

Strategic Alliances: Maximizing Efficiency through Diverse Strengths

Jung's exploration of extroverted and introverted thinking types lays the groundwork for understanding the dynamics of leadership and decision-making in a society guided by rational principles, such as those enshrined in the Constitution. Rand's work, particularly in "For the New Intellectual," further delineates these types into the pragmatic, result-focused businessman, and the introspective, theory-oriented intellectual. These distinctions, supported by Jung's typology, highlight how these archetypes' divergent psychologies and methods can complement each other in leadership roles, enhancing decision-making through their combined strengths.

Collaboration between the types represents the optimal approach for mitigating the drawbacks inherent to these natural tendencies. An

---

[220] (Jung 1923, 352)

organically cultivated balance of powers allows for each type's strengths to complement the others': Where one excels in abstraction, another thrives in practical application; one may gather facts, while another interprets them meaningfully. This synergy is not merely for the sake of harmony; it is a purposeful and beneficial alliance, founded on the principle of leveraging diverse strengths to achieve shared objectives. This rational approach to collaboration maximizes efficiency and innovation.

Education or Indoctrination? Diverging Approaches between Thinking Types

Keeping in mind that external influences and criteria shape extroverted judgment, we observe that this orientation creates confusion between the types on the issue of education versus indoctrination. Parents, groups, systems, institutions, or any outside authority, "program" the extroverted thinking type—whose primary connection to ideas is secondhand—to think what they want them to think. They do not evaluate the inner logic of objective ideas themselves, thus their default method of validating such ideas to be through popular acceptance or consensus.

In educational settings, this often manifests in specific ways. For example, extroverted thinkers often prioritize memorization of facts in subjects like history or science rather than engaging with overarching theories (recall the use of mnemonics by those learning in the medical field); they prefer courses with clear, straightforward messages and visually appealing presentations that garner their attraction. They engage best with interactive activities like quizzes, polls, or debates, and favor practical, structured frameworks for decision-making, such as SWOT analysis—a strategic planning tool used to identify Strengths, Weaknesses, Opportunities, and Threats in management— due to their concrete nature.

Moreover, extroverted thinkers often adjust their study or project approach based on external feedback or grading metrics. Group activities, for which the emphasis is on achieving a concrete goal, can also be where they excel. An overabundance of concrete examples, along with a heavy focus on messaging, optics, engagement, modeling, and adjustment, marks their educational experience, aligning with their natural cognitive style.

Conversely, the introverted thinking type sees education as a demonstration of external possibilities based on logical principles. Their method is to evaluate the inner framework of an idea, the fundamental principle, to see if it holds true over multiple iterations when applied. If the principle does not hold up to their test, they reject it or restrict the validity of the principle to a more specified or appropriate context.

The Essence of Rights: Laying the Foundation for Political Theory

★ ★ ★

The final foundational element we must establish in this section before engaging in a more complete discussion on American ethics, is the concept of morality. This begins with understanding morality's essence and then the fundamental means to secure it.

Morality and Ethics

In discussing morality and ethics, it is essential to recognize their distinct but interconnected roles.

Morality, as viewed in this context, is fundamentally about discerning what is good for the individual. It is a personal compass, guiding one's decisions and actions based on what they perceive as beneficial or detrimental to their well-being. This individual-centric approach to morality emphasizes self-interest and personal values as the core drivers of moral judgment. It is a process of internal deliberation, where each person evaluates what is right and wrong based on their own needs, experiences, and perspectives.

Ethics, in contrast, extend beyond the individual to the collective. It encompasses the norms and standards that govern behavior within a group or society. While ethics can enrich our understanding of right and wrong, they do not exclusively shape our moral beliefs. Instead, they provide a broader context, helping individuals understand how their actions and decisions resonate within the wider social fabric. Ethics serve as a guide, offering insights into the collective understanding of right and wrong, which can in turn influence an individual's moral reasoning. This influence, however, does not override the individual's primary focus on what is personally good in their own lives.

From Personal Conviction to Social Doctrine: Tracing the Ethical Continuum

One can clearly differentiate morality from ethics with two simple questions. Morality or personal ethics asks the question: How should "I" live? Ethics or moral philosophy asks the question: How should "*we*" live?

The answers to these questions have opposing natures and through contrasting the "I" and "we" in these statements, we are able to illuminate the difference between introversion and extroversion. The introvert approaches the question as an individual and indivisible primary, while the extrovert approaches it as a fraction of a whole. This fundamental difference drives every decision one makes, as well as those one expects others to make.

Logically, there cannot be a question of how we should live together without first answering the question of how the individual should live, as the collective can only develop from a group of individuals. A rational set of ethics only evolves out of one's awareness of the effects of their actions on others, which one can only understand through their awareness of others' actions upon themselves.

Morality is the learning, understanding, and formation of rules for life one makes for oneself, backed by the penalty of psychological discontent. In other words, it is the positive or negative emotion one experiences regarding their efficaciousness in the pursuit of survival and purpose.

Ethics, in its proper sense, are principles devised by the group to protect the individual's ability to pursue a moral existence from the actions of others. In applying ethics to politics, a collective, in turn, backs these principles through collectivized force, imposing explicit corporal penalties like fines, imprisonment, community service, or probation.

A moral compass is implicit, guiding one internally based on personally derived ideas about right and wrong or the ideas about right and wrong one has accepted from others.

Morality and ethics, though closely related, necessitate distinct approaches in abstract reasoning due to their inherent differences. Morality undergirds the "social sphere," is rooted in personal choice and a subjective interpretation of right and wrong. It acts as an independent variable and is the bedrock from which societal ethics emerge. Ethics, in contrast, function as a dependent variable—a collective manifestation of individual moral standards. This symbiotic relationship underscores the notion that personal moral judgments directly inform and shape societal ethical frameworks. By understanding morality as the precursor to ethics, we acknowledge a dynamic interplay in which individual choices not only contribute to, but also define the ethical boundaries that govern society.

From Belief to Behavior: How Religion Shapes Ethical Decision-Making

In the context of Jung and Rand's theories, religion emerges from a collective subjectivism, making it akin to a group's shared perception,

273

or simply mysticism. This collective subjectivism, where people ascribe mystical powers to physical or mental objects, plays a pivotal role in forming the moral and ethical standards within religious groups. Therefore, we can perceive religion not only as a set of beliefs about the supernatural but also as a guiding framework for moral and ethical decision-making.

This framework often defines what the religion considers morally right or wrong, exerting influence on an individual's behavior and choices. For instance, the moral codes derived from religious doctrines typically govern a wide range of actions and decisions, from interpersonal conduct to lifestyle choices. Similarly, the ethical principles espoused by religions often extend to how adherents interact with the broader society, influencing social norms and collective behaviors.

Like every form of mysticism, organized religions seek obedience to their teachings irrespective of understanding. This phenomenon leads followers to adhere to practices without fully grasping their reasons, beyond the explanation that "it is a rule." When questioned, the rationale provided is tautological, saying the rule exists because it is the rule, which suggests an external locus of authority—e.g., God, society, the greater good—as the justification for obedience. However, it is crucial to recognize that within these groups, it is only the living members who interpret, communicate, and enforce these rules. This dynamic raises questions about the source of religious and mystical authority and the role of individual agency in spiritual adherence.

In considering the critique of religion as tautological, it is also crucial to recognize a broader philosophical context. The nature of judgment itself, at its most abstract level, involves circular logic— where the cause is also the result, and the result becomes the cause. This phenomenon does not only apply to religious reasoning but constitutes a fundamental aspect of how humans conceptualize and justify their beliefs and actions. Consider the statement often found in religious contexts: "This practice is sacred because it is commanded by the divine." Here, divine command justifies the sacredness of the practice, yet the acceptance of divine authority is based on the presupposition of its sacredness. This forms a circular argument where the practice's sanctity and the divine command justify each other without an external anchor in rational justification.

The circular reasoning witnessed within religious contexts not only illustrates the complexities of faith and obedience but also leads us to a deeper, more introspective, and philosophical inquiry: the critical question of the foundation of our judgment. What is the basis of one's judgment? Is it rooted in the self, derived from personal insights and experiences, or is it based on the "other"—external authorities or collective beliefs? This distinction is paramount, as the choice between self-based versus other-based judgment frames one's entire approach to understanding and navigating the world. Such a choice is mutually exclusive, profoundly influencing whether one autonomously constructs their own beliefs or adheres to externally imposed beliefs.

Humans naturally question why they should engage in any action, effectively asking, "For what reason do I do this?" This necessitates a philosophical framework, whether consciously chosen or not. For Christians, the motivation behind actions is aligned with service to God, providing a clear framework for making decisions. Objectivists, on the other hand, find their motivation in the pursuit of life and happiness, guided by principles of rational self-interest and individual rights. Meanwhile, those who have not deeply contemplated their own philosophical stance are frequently driven by a mix of societal expectations, fleeting emotions, and unexamined beliefs, which leads to inconsistency and confusion in decisions ranging from career choices to personal relationships and ethical dilemmas, as they lack a stable foundation.

Therefore, to act with purpose and consistency, it is crucial for one to explore and articulate a philosophical foundation. Regardless of the specific philosophy adopted, this underlying belief represents one's interpretation of life, influenced by their inherent rational orientation—whether introverted, focusing on personal judgment, or extroverted, deferring to external guidance.

Religion, regardless of its pros or cons, is an explicit philosophy of morality; it is a simplified concept of life, allowing a person to easily identify whether something is good or bad, with a single question: Does it aid that concept, or go against it?

God, the Soul, and Psychology: Unraveling the Connections with Kant and Jung

As Jung went through Kant's philosophy, he identified Kant's attempt to evaluate the soul, which for all humans sits intermediate to reality and the intellect. Juxtaposing these concepts with Jung's theory, we see the way in which reality is sensation, intellect is thinking, and the soul is the psychology of the subject, which brings these elements together, always in the middle. What is clear is the soul permeates through the entire process.

This would make one think the answer to the question of the essence of life clearly rests on the individual's psychology, but this is not the conclusion we see coming from Christianity, or Kant. What we see is a universal prescription of the "essence of the soul" conceptualized as God. God, as the highest good, according to Jung, is equivalent to the psychological phenomenon of maximum libido, also referred to as the God-concept in analytical psychology. However, when people use the term "God" informally, viewing it externally, it exists as a secondhand concept defined by the group. In other words, an outside party can dictate the values of the subject's psychology through that objective idea.

The important thing to remember here is that psychology—the locus of all cognition—always has the subject as its referent. Psychoanalysts appropriately recognize this in the God-concept because the judgment of good is always subjective. One can never circumvent one's own psychology, hence, one should never disregard it in matters of judgment. Thus, logically, we must conclude, if we are to accept the term of God and its definition of the highest good, it can only be the highest good for the subject and nothing more.

Accordingly, the psychological preference of rational introversion or extroversion also answers the fundamental question: "The highest good for whom?" And more importantly, implied in that answer is the answer to the question of the subject's identity: "Who am I?" The introvert correctly identifies the highest good for themselves, always subordinating the object to the subject and assuming the subject's primacy. The extrovert answers with the highest good for the object to the extent they have subconsciously identified with it. The latter is what we see throughout the history of religion and in Kantian philosophy—submission to the object.

Blurring Boundaries: How Participation Mystique Fosters an Altruistic Ethos

Participation mystique describes the transcendental state of identification with an object, leading to one's loss of individual distinction. This profound merging of self with something beyond individual identity naturally paves the way for altruism, an ethical stance that necessitates a prioritization of the interests or well-being of others over one's own self-interest. In this light, mysticism, manifested through participation mystique, acts as the psychological impetus for altruism by blurring the individual's sense of self with that of others, thereby making the interests of the collective appear as one's own. This method of judgment, embodied in rational extroversion by Carl Jung, serves as the psychological foundation for what Ayn Rand critically refers to as the "altruist's morality," where moral decisions are extroverted, prioritizing external needs over individual rational self-interest.

This dynamic within mysticism, whereby the individual is inclined to merge their sense of self with a larger collective or divine will, illustrates not just a pathway toward altruism but also mirrors a deeper mystical conviction: that individuals do not discover knowledge and truth independently, but knowledge and truth are already known and only independently experienced. The mystical doctrines of religious philosophies underscore this stance by positing that we hold the answers within the depths of our collective consciousness. The universal truth they seek to educate others about is, therefore, only the subjectivity we experience psychologically—namely, consciousness itself.

Consciousness manifests itself as a personal moral struggle, highlighting the profound, albeit archaic understanding in religious philosophies of our innate psychological experiences. Despite our efforts toward objectivity, these philosophies recognize that our identity and worldview are deeply rooted in the essence of our "souls"—our consciousness shaped significantly by our thoughts and perceptions. This underscores the importance of thinking in shaping our perception of the world, highlighting the intricate interplay between consciousness, morality, and philosophical belief.

Philosophy rooted in mysticism often falls into what Ayn Rand termed the "fallacy of the frozen abstraction." This logical fallacy occurs when a concept is isolated from its broader context and treated as an absolute. Such philosophies condition success on the acceptance of prechosen values, which are merely the abstractions of the philosophy's creator. In this way it is remarkably like the statement, "for nature to be commanded, it must first be obeyed," where the philosophy's creator presents their own interpretation of nature: their metaphysics. Thus, adhering to the philosophy is framed as equivalent to obeying nature itself.

However, the best philosophies must allow for the widest abstractions if they are to preserve free choice. The wider the abstractions, the more autonomy for humans to choose. Freedom of thought enables the subject to think in a new or alternate way that sharpens their view of nature, adding clarity, detail, and definition. In other words, the subject can think about nature in a unique or original way in order to achieve values more efficiently. Limiting one's ability to think independently necessarily destroys their ability to improve their condition.

In the context of religion, especially Christianity, the philosophy determines the essence of the soul, and it dictates that a moral existence is only permissible within the constraints of its rules. The subject cannot choose values for themselves or live for their own purpose. Their value can only increase as an appendage of God: the object. The philosophy places a focus on the salvation of each individual soul, allowing each person to feel a small sense of personal significance. However, in alignment with the overall philosophy, that significance remains just a fraction of the whole.

Authority over Nature: A Comparative Analysis of Christian and Objectivist Ethics

A crucial aspect of Christianity that distinguishes it from other religions is its unique perspective on humanity's relationship with nature. In Christianity, God grants his subjects authority over all of nature, granting them dominion over the Earth and its contents. This empowerment elevates the individual above the natural world, framed within a doctrine that dictates adherence to divine will. This viewpoint starkly contrasts with other religious teachings, such as Hinduism and Buddhism, which promote a more harmonious and stewardship-oriented relationship with nature, advocating for balance, non-violence, and respect for all forms of life. Similarly, Indigenous spiritualities often view humanity as an integral part of a larger web of life, charged with a sacred duty to care for and preserve the natural environment. In these traditions, people revere nature as a partner or a being, rather than something to be dominated as a resource.

Objectivism offers a parallel yet fundamentally unfamiliar perspective by also placing the individual above nature. However, it achieves this position through recognition of rational self-interest and the assertion of the individual's right to use reason to master the natural world. Unlike the Christian doctrine of divinely granted dominion, Objectivism's unique stance is rooted in the belief that the individual, empowered by logic and reason, naturally assumes a position of superiority over the object—that is, the natural world, in alignment with the subjective nature of psychology. This philosophical approach is inherently non-mystical, promoting a vision of the individual as inherently self-reliant, self-interested, and independent.

Building on this philosophical discourse, the mind creates all gods and mystical forces as conceptual objects, and any obedience to these constructs is obedience to the values embedded within another person or entity's moral philosophy. This insight underscores a critical view of the mysticism found in traditional religions, including Christianity, from an Objectivist standpoint. The essence of the "soul," according to Objectivism, lies in the subject's intellect, leaving the subject free to choose their own values because the tenets of Objectivism do not impair independent judgment by fettering them with external dictates. In this way, Objectivism is a rationally introverted philosophy—the proper orientation of a free and enlightened human being.

While both Christianity and Objectivism elevate the individual above nature, they do so from vastly different premises. Christianity's elevation relies on divine authority and the fulfillment of God's will, implying a stewardship guided by moral and spiritual obligation. On the other hand, Objectivism champions the sovereignty of the individual's intellect and rational capacity as the basis for asserting dominion over nature, emphasizing autonomy and the pursuit of personal values. Consequently, these philosophies offer distinct interpretations of the individual's place in the world, shaped by differing views on authority, morality, and the role of the natural environment.

In delineating the sources of value that underpin the two moral philosophies that explicitly acknowledge rights and freedom of the individual, a clear divergence emerges. Christianity sets God as the ultimate standard of all value, implying that the individual's actions and choices should align with divine will. Objectivism, conversely, places the subject's life at the center of its value system, advocating for a moral philosophy where the individual's life and their concept of it form the core of all value judgments. This fundamental difference highlights the contrasting ways in which Christianity and Objectivism conceptualize rights, freedom, and the essence of value, offering two distinct pathways for understanding the relationship between the individual and the broader universe.

Rational Egoism versus Altruism: A Comparative Ethical Analysis

The implicit doctrine on which the Objectivists' ethics rests is that of **rational egoism**: the theory that treats one's rational self-interest as the foundation of morality. Altruism is rational egoism's antithesis.

When examining the ethics of rational egoism and altruism, one pertinent question arises: Which of these ethical frameworks can sustain and promote life in accordance with logical principles? A related question is: Which of these ethical approaches can address both individual and collective needs within a civilized society? Interestingly, both approaches can meet these criteria. One can address individual needs while adhering to the ethical premise of altruism, just as one can address the needs of others while adhering to the ethical premise of rational egoism.

The more critical question then becomes: Which of these ethical philosophies can one practice exclusively? On closer inspection, rational egoism emerges as the only viable option. This is because, under rational egoism, fulfilling social needs by attending to others— when done of one's own free will—does not conflict with rational self-interest. In contrast, the ethics of altruism offer no moral justification for individuals to address their own needs if others simultaneously require their specific assistance. According to this premise, one must prioritize the needs of others over one's own when those others require something that only the individual can provide.

The Ethics of Self-Sacrifice: A Critical Examination through Jung and Rand's Eyes

Altruism is, psycho-epistemologically, the preferred moral code for rational extroverts, and Jung's observations bolster Rand's depiction of the duality of altruism and egoism by explicitly identifying egoism in the introverted function. Both he and Rand align on the brutal nature of the extrovert due to the repressed "self," or subjective reason, of those types, as evidenced by the following observation from Jung,

> Thus with every repressed impulse a considerable amount of energy ultimately remains, of an instinctive character, and preserves its potency despite the deprivation that made it unconscious. The more complete the conscious attitude of extroversion is, the more infantile and archaic the unconscious attitude will be. The egoism which characterizes the extrovert's unconscious attitude goes far beyond mere childish selfishness; it verges on the ruthless and the brutal.[221]

Jung revisits Schiller's insights to underscore the tension between individual and collective needs within one's psychology. He elaborates on the "profound lack" or "inner division" that emerges when one unduly suppresses personal needs and functions. This theme aligns closely with Rand's discussions on the absence of a sense of self or personally chosen values. Both Schiller and Jung, through their emphasis on individual values and their emotionally rich, introspective language, indicate an inclination toward an introverted perspective.

---

[221] (Jung 1923, 315)

This inclination toward introversion is also evident in Rand's own writings, which emphasize individualism. Interestingly, the trajectory of human intellectual evolution that Jung outlines through his analysis of Schiller aligns with the broader trends of humans shifting from extroverted societies to a more introverted focus.

Schiller, whose ideas Jung reinforces, argues that an overemphasis on collective functions can create individuals with extraordinary talents, but leaves them with a sense of emotional and psychological fragmentation. He poses a moral question about the ethics of such a system, asking whether mankind is destined to be mere "bondslaves of humanity," sacrificing their individual wholeness for some greater, collective aim. Schiller strongly argues against this notion, stating that this kind of sacrifice not only leaves a painful, inner division in individuals but also goes against what reason dictates for human completeness. He further questions the long-term implications of such sacrifices, asking whether it would be fair for one generation to benefit at the expense of another. Schiller also poses a poignant question: "Can man really be destined to neglect himself for any end whatever?"[222] Both Schiller and Jung advocate a more balanced psychological approach in which individuals cultivate their values alongside their collective responsibilities. They argue that this balance is essential for genuine happiness, fulfillment, and the preservation of civilization.[223]

Having established the relationship of morality and ethics to the abstract concepts of rights and freedom, we now proceed to explore how individuals actualize and safeguard these ideals in human experience. This examination necessitates a foundational inquiry into how individuals and societies navigate and uphold the delicate balance between personal conviction and collective responsibility.

---

[222] (Jung 1923, 67-68)
[223] ibid

Force: The Theory of Everything

In this work, we posit morality as undergirding our understanding of ethics. But what undergirds our understanding of morality? Epistemology—the nature of concepts and conceptual knowledge. And what undergirds our understanding of conceptual knowledge? Metaphysics—our basic understanding of the world. And what undergirds this basic understanding of the world? Force—its meaning to humans, as perceived through sensation being what we see, hear, touch, taste, and smell.

The Role of Perception in Shaping Ethics and Morality

In modern civilization, we often overlook the fact that our perception of the physical world fundamentally shapes not just our concepts of good and bad, but our entire conceptual framework, as we aim to not detach but transcend our primitive beginnings, leveraging the full scope of our evolved capabilities. However, by viewing everything through that basic contextual lens, we can present a clearer, more inclusive, and intelligible view of our existence. This helps us bridge the communicative gap created by a diversity of cognitive styles and aids us in addressing that diversity in the arenas of ethics and politics.

In examining our advanced conceptual framework, contrasting this with the instinctual world of animals serves to enlighten us. This reveals our shared biological impulses and emphasizes the significant evolution from mere instinct to complex thought and moral reasoning.

Animals operate primarily on an irrational, perceptual level, relying on concrete sensations and instincts rather than abstract reasoning. They have limited awareness of the immediate environment, with pain serving as a critical indicator of potential threats to their survival. Consequently, animals instinctively avoid pain, guided by an inherent understanding of purpose that, like pain, is not a matter of choice but a metaphysical given.

Humans share this layer of instinct with animals, driven by a similar compulsion toward survival and purpose. However, what distinguishes humans is the evolution of a conceptual faculty from these irrational, perceptual beginnings. This unique capability enables us to not just react to our immediate environment, but to reflect on and understand it through abstract thought and rational deliberation, thereby distinguishing us from other species and giving rise to the very concept of morality.

Conceptualization to Actualization: The Human Quest for Purpose

Conceptualization is fundamental in translating our immediate physical experiences (sensation) into abstract cognitive processes (thinking). The strength of our rationality, and consequently our ability to navigate and thrive in life, however, depend significantly on maintaining a strong and accurate relationship between these elements. If this relationship becomes too tenuous or disjointed, our decision-making and actions become unmoored from reality, compromising our ability to fulfill our purpose and needs.

Thought operates via mental constructs derived from physical and tangible objects, existing not in the physical realm but within the psychic domain—a realm that runs parallel to yet dependent on the physical. This mode of cognition allows humans to psychically transcend the immediate constraints of time and space, employing concepts to make conscious, long-range decisions from which to take appropriate action. Our capacity for conceptualization mirrors the sensory world of objects in an intellectual realm of ideas, enabling us to navigate and interpret our experiences beyond the immediate moment.

Because this conceptual development does nothing to change the fact that humans are sensual animals, the two most important aspects to consider with our conceptual capabilities are the same two aspects of any animal's life: survival and purpose. We can see a popular example of these concepts in the levels of Maslow's hierarchy of needs. Our physical survival rests on the elements found within physiological needs, such as food, water, and shelter; however, individuals can only discover purpose within the realm of the higher, psychological needs, which include love, belonging, and self-esteem. The combination of these two results in the highest form of living for a rational being: **self-actualization**.

What we may observe in Maslow's concept of self-actualization is that it is identical to the concept of value. Physiological needs in combination with psychological needs equal self-actualization, just as the product of survival and purpose equals **value**. All value originates in this way.

While our fundamental purpose, driven by the emotions constituting our deepest values, is beyond our control, through thinking, humans possess a unique capacity. We can—if we choose to—identify and consciously pursue our perceived purpose. This pursuit involves a selection of personally chosen methods, both physical and psychological, that align with our individual understanding of purpose. Unlike non-human animals, whose pursuit of purpose is instinctive, humans have the distinct ability to reflect, adapt, and modify our approach to fulfilling our purpose based on self-awareness and rational thought.

Our ability to conceptualize and use those concepts to strategically navigate and plan our lives also enriches our perception of harm, and this process ensures that we are not merely reacting to immediate threats but are also capable of anticipating potential dangers through the lens of our experiences and knowledge. Such foresight, grounded in the tangible world, extends our understanding to the abstract, highlighting the interconnectedness of physical and psychological realms.

Yet, this long-range conceptual understanding carries with it the risk of misinterpretation, particularly with one's use of feeling or emotion as a primary cognitive tool. While ideas empower us to identify and react to potential threats proactively, an overreliance on the feeling aspect of these ideas can foster false associations, whereby perceived harm may not accurately reflect tangible threats, leading to either overestimation or underestimation of danger. Such misalignment underscores the vital need for precise conceptualization that accurately integrates psychological perceptions with physical realities. It highlights the importance of distinguishing genuine threats from benign situations through a balanced approach that avoids letting emotional responses dictate our perception of harm, ensuring our responses are rooted in the factual aspects of our environment.

Force and Reality: The Inextricable Bond of Psychology and Physical Existence

Though objective reality is absolute and independent, human psychology is an ever-expanding and elastic entity that is fundamentally anchored in this reality. When we interact with the metaphysically given elements of our existence, we must conform to the characteristics of these elements and learn how to adapt to them. This dynamic interplay results in a situation in which either the physical world imposes its force on the individual, or, because applying thought to external reality necessitates one's use of force, the individual learns how to exert force on the physical world. In either case, there is an act of physical force applied.

This fundamental dynamic makes physical force—perceived through the sensation function of Jung's psychological types—the bedrock of all human conception, underpinning the very fabric of action and thought. This intrinsic linkage between sensation and force profoundly impacts decision-making, echoing Ayn Rand's principle of causation, which underscores the significance of actions and their consequences in defining reality. The perception and influence of force, whether direct or implied, shape our interactions with the physical world, highlighting the fundamental role of sensory information in our conceptual understanding.

Thought as Psychological Force: Communicating with Impact

All thought is psychological force deriving its value from physical force—force's most fundamental form. The relationship of psychological force to physical force parallels those of idea to action and thought to sensation. Consequently, recognizing the inherent physical force behind a thought or argument is crucial in understanding its use and implications within the complex web of human communication.

For example, if a lover tells their partner that they cannot continue a relationship where their lifestyle needs remain unfulfilled, and they feel their partner is not currently meeting those needs, this constitutes a psychological statement with tangible consequences. The lover is psychologically threatening to physically leave the relationship, and all the power in the statement comes from the final act. Without the final act of leaving, the statement is otherwise meaningless, beyond the partner's irritation at having to hear an empty threat.

In the realm of argumentation, validity hinges on a connection to actionable outcomes, and without a tangible, physical consequence, a concept lacks substantive intellectual weight. However, the mere perception of impending physical force suffices to make a thought psychologically significant, because our intuition and emotional responses, influenced by these sensory experiences, are projections and anticipatory guesses about potential physical outcomes.

Further complicating this dynamic is the diversity in cognitive processing styles, particularly seen between Jung's thinking types. Introverted thinking types prefer communicating through abstract concepts, often leading to misunderstandings with extroverted thinking or irrational types, who rely more on concrete concepts derived from direct sense-experience. Introverted thinkers regard ideas to be as real as the concrete experiences from which they have abstracted those ideas. Conversely, an extroverted thinking type is likely to dismiss ideas as simply words or what Nietzsche derisively referred to as "speech metaphysics." The latter always seeks to understand in concretes, not concepts.

In their communication with each other, one type frequently finds themselves asking the other: "What is your point?" For the introvert, the answer lies within the concept, while for the extrovert, it lies in the concrete. For the extrovert, knowledge is determined from without, and for the introvert, from within.

This fundamental difference in cognitive orientation can lead to challenges across various domains. In academia, causing misunderstandings between empirical and theoretical disciplines; in education, skewing teaching methods; in professional settings, creating communication barriers; and in public debates, like those on climate change, leading to misinterpretation of scientific theories. The dislike or preference for abstractions fundamentally shapes the way we use and perceive others' use of psychological force and has a profound impact on our everyday communication. However, the potential weakness of the introvert is in losing sight that sensation is closer to reality than abstract thought.

Cognitive Styles and the Challenges of Abstract versus Concrete Thinking

The finite range of human consciousness limits our ability to focus on more than a small number of percepts and objects at once. Percepts being the raw data of experience prior to any conscious interpretation or categorization—our basic understanding of existence; and objects being the entities that exist, available for us to perceive. The tools we use to overcome the limitations of our consciousness are concepts, and the method by which we create these concepts is through conceptualization: the act of compressing the percepts of our direct experience with objects into a generalized idea, using thinking. That idea then becomes a singular object, freeing up mental resources for additional analysis, innovative ideas, or further cognitive tasks.

The process of abstraction in basic conceptualization helps us categorize and organize our sensory experiences and observations. It involves identifying common features or patterns among different items and grouping them under a single conceptual umbrella. For example, recognizing that apples, bananas, and oranges all share the characteristics that define the concept "fruit." It is about moving from the specific to the general within the realm of our direct experiences and knowledge of the world.

Abstract thinking, on the other hand, represents a broader and more complex application of conceptualization, enabling us to reason about, imagine, and understand concepts and relationships that go beyond what is concrete and observable. It is a more advanced cognitive capability to think about complex ideas, hypothetical scenarios, principles, patterns, and concepts like justice, freedom, or infinity. Through abstract thinking, we can comprehend the vastness of space and the principles of physics governing the universe, despite never directly experiencing these realities. This illustrates how abstract thinking grounds us in a reality that extends beyond our immediate perception, proving its essential role in human cognition.

While basic conceptualization removes us from the singularity of real, tangible objects to the intangible idea of the general, abstract thinking extends this psychological separation from reality even further. It formulates longer chains of conceptual connections that facilitate advanced problem-solving, creativity, and theoretical reasoning. This level of thinking requires individuals to generalize more extensively and to engage with ideas that are more abstract and distant from the sensory and concrete.

In Jung's writings, he explored the difficulties in communication seen between introverted and extroverted thinking types throughout history. Yet, the introverted thinking type can overcome this difficulty simply by altering their mode of communication when dealing with other types.

When facing difficulties in achieving mutual understanding, the most effective method is to communicate in terms that directly appeal to the senses—"speaking to sensation." This solution emphasizes conveying the direct, tangible consequences of actions or situations, rather than relying heavily on abstract concepts. By grounding communication in concrete experiences, it becomes more accessible and less susceptible to misinterpretation, facilitating clearer understanding between parties.

If we use the example of the lover mentioned above, the lover presents an idea that requires their partner to infer multiple layers of meaning before arriving at the actual consequence. These connections include understanding the dissatisfaction, interpreting the potential seriousness of the situation, and realizing that this dissatisfaction could lead to the end of the relationship. However, by speaking directly to sensation and focusing on the final physical act, communication becomes more effective. Instead of saying, "I cannot remain in a relationship where my lifestyle needs are not being met," it is more effective to explicitly state, "I will leave this relationship if I do not receive whatever specific lifestyle need is desired." This approach makes the final physical consequence—ending the relationship—readily apparent to the other party with minimal logical connections for them to make.

The Human Psyche: A Leverage Point in Behavior and Decision-Making

The human psyche is a critical leverage point for influencing behavior, with its impact manifesting in both positive and negative ways. Consider the division of labor principle, the core of which is trust in specialization. This principle is founded on the belief that when individuals concentrate on their areas of expertise, they increase overall efficiency and productivity. This belief in turn is rooted in the abstract concept of interdependency, suggesting that collective specialized efforts surpass individual ones. This principle, though complementary to self-reliance, necessitates a change in mindset from one centering reliance solely on oneself to one centering collaborative work and trade. Its effectiveness is evident in various fields, providing tangible evidence that supports the belief in specialization. Critically, the capacity to conceptualize the unseen connections of specialized roles within a broader framework enhances one's commitment to this system.

On the other hand, a fraudulent Ponzi scheme exemplifies negative psychological manipulation. It operates on the concept of high returns, enticing investors with the promise of future financial prosperity. Engineers of these schemes manipulate perception by linking the abstract promise of wealth with fabricated evidence of profitability, exploiting the idea of future benefits. This deception underscores the psychological leverage point where belief in future returns can disconnect from the reality of non-existent tangible returns. The eventual collapse of such schemes, when returns fail to materialize, starkly demonstrates the dangers of an incongruity between abstract expectations and physical reality.

These examples illustrate that persuasion techniques aim to manipulate the psychological space between abstract thought and concrete sensation, leveraging the dynamic and expansive nature of human psychology against the fixed nature of reality. The success of such manipulation depends on how well our thoughts and real-world sensations align. A close alignment leads to grounded decisions and actions, while a disconnect makes us more prone to manipulation and mistakes. Understanding this interplay is crucial for effective decision-making and resistance to deception.

Elevating the Human Experience: Aligning Sensation, Thought, and Action

Though thinking abstracts reality into thought, its ultimate value lies in concretizing thoughts (back into sensation) through action, echoing the relationship between psychological and physical force: Thought is the derivative; sensation, the source. The common mistake of many philosophers, theorists, and the public alike is to see sensory experience and thinking as opposing, either-or forces. This view leads to confusion and overlooks the fact that the thinking human is the descendant of the sensual human who evolved—as all humans, not just animals, have evolved to be sensual—while only some humans consciously employ their thinking capacity in a directed fashion.

Action is the experience of life, but conscious and directed thought converted into action facilitates life on an elevated plane. This blend combines sensory experience with our thoughts and ideas, bridging the gap between perception and concept.

The Ethical Dimensions of Force: Shaping Society and Morality

The development of civilizations, particularly in the West, marks a progression from reacting to the metaphysically-given with instinct, to the establishment of moral principles that guide our reasoning and behavior. In this light, the concept of force is foundational not only to our interactions with the natural world but also to our interpersonal relationships and the structure of our societies. Our capacity for abstract thought and deliberation enables us to formulate moral frameworks that dictate the rightful use of force with respect to social harmony, commonly known as right. Politically, we refer to these principles as rights.

Understanding the pivotal role of force within the human experience highlights the shift from instinctual survival strategies to the creation of these ethical principles, underlining the significance of rights as a moral standard in navigating the complexities of human interactions and societal organization. Through abstract reasoning, we confront the task of correcting widespread misconceptions about the nature of rights and the ethical application of force, aiming to foster a society that upholds the dignity and freedom of each person.

In this context, our journey from instinctual existence to rational understanding, from the perceptual to the conceptual, is not merely a distinguishing feature of humanity; it is the very foundation upon which our notions of morality and ethics stand. This evolution reflects a profound comprehension of the role of force in shaping human morality and underscores the critical importance of individual rights in establishing a just and ethical society.

Bridging the Gap: Fostering Ethical Engagement
in a Diverse Psychological Landscape

There are many people who sense something amiss in the country today, yet struggle to pinpoint the issue or formulate a response. This challenges the effectiveness of the Objectivist exhortation to "think for oneself" when addressing the masses. This message, inherently abstract and focused on independent, critical thinking, primarily appeals to those already inclined toward such introspection—typically introverts. For others, especially those who base their understanding more on tangible experiences and immediate consequences, this message lacks relatability. It is not that independent thought is not a worthy aim, but rather that the message's abstract nature fails to engage those who experience life more immediately, for whom the physical force and direct consequences of actions are more influential in shaping their worldviews and responses. The sensation of life is absent in the message: the consequence, the experience, the physical force.

For the irrational, anti-conceptual, and extroverted types, learning comes through experience. Meaning, they must experience a sensuous consequence from their actions to learn a lesson that others may be able to learn conceptually. This approach does not pose an ethical challenge when dealing with the physical reality of inanimate objects but has ethical implications when the object is another human.

Humans are not inherently born with an understanding of ethics; rather, a combination of learned behavior and personal reflection cultivates empathy toward others and a sense of right and wrong. This learning process is particularly crucial for individuals who grasp concepts best through direct experience. For these individuals, tangible consequences for actions that society deems unethical serve as irreplaceable catalysts for moral development. However, the effectiveness of such consequences in promoting ethical behavior hinges on a clear societal consensus about what constitutes ethical and unethical actions. Education, cultural norms, and legal frameworks typically establish this consensus, collectively guiding individuals in recognizing and correcting behaviors that negatively impact others. Therefore, fostering ethical behavior involves not just levying appropriate consequences but also ensuring that individuals understand the ethical framework that defines those actions as unethical in the first place, thus supporting moral development through a combination of experience, education, and societal norms.

What are the effective consequences one can impose? Options include dissociation, legal penalties, withdrawal of financial support, or the use of physical force as a defensive last resort. On the contrary, what consequences do people often attempt to impose today? Insults, ridicule, badgering, and the initiation or threat of physical force are common yet ineffective methods for persuading the minds of others or maintaining a healthy society long-term. These approaches often fail to yield the desired change and can exacerbate conflicts or misunderstanding, highlighting the need for more constructive methods of addressing wrongdoing and promoting learning.

The Intersection of Psychological Types and Legal Ethics:
Crafting Laws for a Diverse Society

According to NERIS Analytics Limited,[224] 49.5% of all study participants tested as rational types, leaving 50.5% as irrational types in the context of Jung's psychological framework. What are the societal implications of these results? This classification suggests that half of the population primarily process information through perception, as opposed to the evaluative and decision-making processes that characterize rational types. Jung asserts that for these irrational types, conscious reasoning does not primarily govern the initial responses to information or situations.

The societal implications of this finding are notable, particularly in the realm of politics and decision-making. It indicates that a substantial number of individuals, many of whom currently hold governmental office, naturally lean toward perceiving and interpreting the world in a way that is less immediately influenced by logical analysis. This inclination can affect how they engage with political issues, form opinions, and make decisions, frequently leading to a more instinctual or perception-based approach which our previous examinations reveal hark back to tendencies characteristic of primitive psychology.

We see in the types that what separates the rational from the irrational is the primacy of reasoned judgment, but regardless of one's attitude toward judgment, a healthy and viable society built on individual rights requires that each person be accountable for their choices. Therefore, proper ethics that lead to the corresponding applicable politics are of the utmost importance in a just society. The rational and irrational cannot peaceably coexist without an enforceable code of conduct—laws with associated penalties and consequences. No psychological type has exclusive right to existence in a society that

---

[224] (16personalities.com 2016)

recognizes the intrinsic value of every individual. Consequently, law must serve as the bare minimum, objective standard of behavior when interacting with others.

Laws must also be sufficiently broad—encompassing enough to apply universally yet adaptable to individual circumstances—to meet the varied needs of a psychologically diverse population and require ethical grounding in high-level abstractions—a realm in which introverted thinkers excel. Their natural orientation toward deep, analytical contemplation makes them uniquely equipped for the task of law development, as they inherently value and engage with abstract concepts more rigorously than other types. This distinction is crucial, as the crafting of legal codes is less about drafting specific, tangible rules and more about embedding these abstractions into the fabric of society in the form of ethical principles.

People often misunderstand a commitment to moral principles over practical constraints as impractical. However, the perceived impracticality of ethically grounded laws reflects an intellectual shortfall, where the challenge lies not in a conflict between morality and practicality but in a shared commitment to embrace complex moral reasoning. Thus, the essence of effective lawmaking lies in recognizing the indispensable role of moral abstractions and the unique capacity of introverted thinkers to navigate these complexities, ensuring laws are not just practical but are rooted in a profoundly ethical vision.

This is a task that other types are less capable of, given their psychological orientations. The challenge for introverted thinkers then becomes devising a code of law broad enough to serve the psychological diversity of the masses.

A key concern in this context is the potential for laws to become overly restrictive, influenced by the type-orientation of those who enact them. History provides insights into this dynamic. Irrational, feeling, or extroverted types might introduce laws that severely limit freedom of thought, akin to the Soviet Union's control over education and media or Nazi Germany's propaganda policies. These examples illustrate how those in power can use laws to suppress alternative viewpoints and exert control over public opinion.

Conversely, introverted thinking types might enact laws that overly restrict freedom of action. A historical illustration of this is the Prohibition era in the U.S., an attempt to legislate morality that made bootlegging an extremely profitable venture, thereby empowering the underworld and organized crime syndicates. This period vividly demonstrates how policies intended to improve public morality and health can paradoxically foster a culture of lawlessness and corruption, as ordinary citizens and criminal organizations alike circumvented the law. This outcome reflects the ineffectiveness of poorly contrived laws, especially those with paternalistic bents.

The mere introduction of overly restrictive laws represents an immediate erosion of freedom of action, a principle whose compromise begins not with the manifestation of consequences but at the very moment of enactment of such laws. This erosion is not contingent on empirical evidence of harm or a perceptible sequence of events but is inherent in the very act of imposing constraints that exceed what is strictly necessary to maintain social order. The moment a law infringes upon individual autonomy beyond this threshold, it transgresses a fundamental principle of human freedom, setting into motion a process of degradation that affects the fabric of society itself. The nature of this violation does not demand objective proof through its consequences but is evident in its discordance with the concept of human action. A framework that justifies ends without regard to the means cannot be reconciled with human nature, especially when those means compromise individual autonomy. Over time, this approach can lead to a societal shift where the norm becomes one of compliance and conformity, driven by an ever-expanding web of regulations that dictate not only the outer bounds of legal behavior but also the inner scope of personal decision-making.

Moreover, the implications of such an approach extend beyond the historical context of Prohibition to the present day, where the tendency to legislate extensive controls persists in various forms. While the specifics of the regulations might differ, the underlying issue remains: a paternalistic approach to lawmaking that prioritizes perceived collective good at the expense of individual freedoms. In this environment, diminishing the value placed on freedom of action not only stifles the capacity for innovation, economic growth, and societal progress by immediate practical barriers but also fundamentally undermines them.

The nature of the irrational, feeling, or extroverted types do not typically allow for the nuanced thought required in lawmaking that adequately balances freedom of thought and action. Alternatively, the virtue of introverted thinkers' analytical and conceptual tendencies better position them to develop a legal system that accommodates the full spectrum of human psychology. Thus, if introverted thinkers truly value a society where all humans possess intrinsic value, it becomes their responsibility to develop and maintain a legal system that reflects this ideal. They must create laws that neither excessively restrict thought nor action, thereby fostering a just and functional society. This responsibility is logically incumbent upon those who can deeply understand and navigate abstract concepts—and as such, understanding is crucial for crafting laws that effectively embody principles like liberty, justice, and freedom.

The Price of Collectivism: Sacrificing Individual Values for Group Demands

The clash between individuality and collectivism often manifests in the actions of extroverts who, driven by their subconsciously subjective interpretation of "greater good," attempt to impose their will on others. This coercion undermines the independence of the individual, who has the inherent right to resist such impositions. The extrovert's preference for collective values—which are mystical in nature and rooted in altruism—over personally chosen values, demands that the individual make sacrifices whenever the group needs it. Meaning, in other terms, whenever the extrovert secretly wants it. This dynamic, however, is not sustainable or objective as an ethical standard, especially when it leads to government intrusion that extracts resources from individuals without considering their essential needs for survival and purpose.

Excessive regulation and high taxation, for example, severely limit the ability of professionals to produce and contribute to society. Consider a dedicated doctor who faces not only the intrinsic challenges of her profession but also the added pressures of bureaucratic oversight and mandatory compliance with ever-changing regulations. In addition to exposing her to increased risk for potential legal claims and the financial and reputational damage that may ensue, these regulations also impose a significant administrative burden, diverting time and resources away from patient care toward compliance efforts. These additional burdens can lead to burnout, potentially causing her to reduce her patient load or leave the practice altogether, thereby diminishing the community's access to quality healthcare. Similarly, a small business owner, despite creating jobs and contributing to the local economy, might find the regulatory environment and tax obligations so onerous that they decide to shutter their business, leading to job losses and reduced economic vitality. In both cases, the government's attempt to harness and direct individual contributions undermines the very resources it sought to exploit, illustrating the flawed logic at the heart of such extractive approaches.

Further complicating this dynamic is the government's monopoly on legalized force, which attracts those who wish to exploit this power for personal gain or to impose their choices on others. Historical and contemporary examples, ranging from Stalin's authoritarian regime to modern leaders who enforce censorship and suppress dissent, reveal the dangers of governmental authority used to dominate and control. Similarly, government interventions, such as the bailouts during the 2008 financial crisis, illustrate how public funds can subsidize the personal choices of specific entities, impacting the broader populace. These actions bring into question the ethical basis of using collective resources to support selected businesses, blurring the lines between individual responsibility and market forces.

The Essence of Liberty: Navigating the Spectrum of Persuasion and Coercion

The essence of valid argumentation and the autonomy to disregard baseless claims underscores a foundational principle in a rational society: the liberty to engage or disengage based on the merit of arguments presented. This freedom is pivotal to maintaining personal autonomy and fostering a culture of critical judgment, particularly to one's right to consent or dissent in the face of persuasion.

Persuasion based on invalid premises—lacking ties to concrete consequences—manifests as posturing or bluffing. This is an attempt to exploit the ignorance of others or their neglect to judge independently. However, as we transition from persuasion to coercion, the line between urging and enforcing marks the precise moment where individual choice vanishes. Coercive tactics betray a disregard for voluntary exchange and mutual respect, highlighting the importance of vigilance against such overreach. The significance of this dynamic marks the gateway into political discourse, notably in debates over rights and governance, where the distinction between persuasion and imposition reflects broader concerns about freedom, autonomy, and the role of the individual versus the collective.

Recognizing the paramount importance of liberty and autonomy, as delineated through the distinction between persuasion and coercion, underscores the need for policies that respect these principles at their core. By focusing on individual-centered policymaking, we extend these foundational values into the realm of practical governance. This approach not only respects the individual's right to informed consent or dissent but also ensures that policymakers craft policies in a manner

301

that is accessible and relevant to every citizen, thus reinforcing the societal fabric with informed participation and respect for autonomy.

The essence of individual-focused policymaking lies in distilling complex ideas down to actionable, personal levels, thereby engaging the survival instinct and rational capabilities of every citizen. This approach magnifies the relationship between abstract ideas and tangible reality, ensuring that even those with limited intelligence or foresight can effectively participate in society. It capitalizes on the natural tendency of people to respond swiftly to local consequences, which directly impact their lives, in that way fostering a more responsive and informed community. This methodology underscores the importance of subjective reason in creating a robust, agile society where localized decision-making leads to meaningful participation.

In parallel, the capitalistic system champions individual autonomy, offering the freedom to make choices that reflect personal values within free markets. This autonomy is foundational, enabling people to navigate their preferences and decisions independently, a principle that resonates with the goal of individual-focused policymaking. However, a challenge arises when deterministic mindsets, particularly found in extroverts, confront the uncertainties of a free market. The discomfort with variability often leads to attempts to curtail these freedoms, either by making choices for others or by advocating for restrictive policies that limit available options, thus clashing with the ethos of capitalism.

Such attempts not only contradict the principle of individual autonomy but also weaken the system's inherent strength—its ability to adapt and evolve through the aggregated choices of its participants. When external interventions, such as government interference, restrict this freedom, they diminish the capacity of individuals to express their preferences naturally. The capitalistic and individual-focused approach advocates for minimal interference, suggesting that the best way to contest a product or practice is simply by choosing not to buy, sell, endorse, or engage with it, preserving the integrity of choice and market dynamics.

By embracing the rational ability of each person and the principle of autonomy, society can ensure a dynamic equilibrium where individual choices drive collective progress, uninhibited by unnecessary constraints. This integrated approach to policymaking and economic participation not only honors individual autonomy but also secures a foundation for a resilient, thriving society.

Intrinsic Value and Self-Defense: Defining the Political Landscape of Force

The extroverted approach to human value often attempts to justify an individual's right to exist through external validation. This approach always consists of some utility to the group, such as economic or environmental benefit. However, these justifications, even when done with scientific rigor, always rest on a false premise: that an individual's right to existence requires external proof. This belief is often tied to concepts such as God, the greater good, society, or planetary well-being. Rejecting collectivism for individualism—which parallels choosing reason over mysticism, and consciousness over unconsciousness—underscores that an individual's right to existence is intrinsic and requires no external validation. In this light, securing one's rights hinges solely on their survival instinct: the defense of their values with force. This consists of the thinking they are capable of and willing to do, along with the physical consequences they are capable of and willing to impose.

In Objectivism, the initiation of force against others is immoral, but when someone initiates force against you, it is morally correct for you to defend yourself with force. However, philosophy can offer increased value by identifying and isolating exactly what, when, where, and by whom an initiation of force upon the individual originates, as this is not always immediately apparent or detectable to the average person.

In human relations, aggression and defense are fluid and opposing states, along the continuum of force. This dynamic, transcending the physical, influences individual behaviors and societal structures alike. Understanding this interplay sheds light on the causality governing our responses to external challenges and internal motivations. Such exploration is crucial, not just academically, but in comprehending how we navigate survival, purpose, and the pursuit of value in our lives.

Humans, like all living beings, are subject to natural forces—tornadoes, earthquakes, and thunderstorms represent such uncontrollable events, inherently distinct from human-made phenomena. These forces, alongside the instinctual actions of animals, constitute the metaphysically given aspects of our existence. Consequently, we consider it natural for animals to employ their innate defense mechanisms for protection, driven by the fundamental pursuit of purpose and survival, which underpin all organismic behavior.

Understanding the nature of inanimate objects comes naturally to humans. For instance, when confronted with the task of lifting a heavy object like a large rock, people instinctively recognize its inherent nature—its heaviness—and adjust their approach accordingly. This recognition is due to the clear, unambiguous physical characteristics of the object, which dictate the need for caution and appropriate measures, if harm is to be avoided. We accept the nature of the heavy object without question because its possible physical ramifications are immediate and predictable if handled recklessly.

Contrast this with encountering a bear in the wilderness. Unlike the static, predictable nature of a rock, a bear presents a dynamic and potentially lethal threat. Instinctively, humans recognize the danger posed by such a powerful animal, not because of a detailed understanding of its biology or psychology, but because of an intrinsic awareness of the bear's capacity for harm. This immediate perception of threat does not stem from a conscious analysis but from a deep-rooted instinct to protect oneself from harm. The bear's presence activates an understanding of risk and the need for caution or avoidance, highlighting an instinctual response to a living being's potential for aggression.

This straightforward understanding of a rock or bear contrasts sharply with the complexity of recognizing the nature of living humans. Unlike an inanimate object or even a formidable animal like a bear, human nature is not immediately apparent or defined by simple physical characteristics or the potential to inflict harm. Instead, humans manifest their nature through judgment and action. It is through these processes that an individual's essential nature becomes perceptible to others.

The fundamental principle of a human life is the pursuit of personal purpose, alongside the survival necessary to achieve this purpose. The concept of "value" encompasses both these aspects. In a society that acknowledges and safeguards individual rights, people understand that each person has the right to live according to their personal values, given they do not infringe on the rights of others. Imposing the values of others onto an individual mirrors the fundamental principle of slavery, hindering the individual's pursuit of their own values and compromising the very purpose of their life. Such a situation is especially intolerable for the fully individuated rational introvert, for whom autonomy and self-direction are paramount.

Therefore, the fundamental characteristic of an individual is not simply what they claim, but what they are truly willing to fight and risk death for. Each person has a threshold that, when breached, triggers a warranted physical response. This is the juncture at which individuals must either surrender or fight for their values. This underlying threat of violence is the ultimate physical consequence underpinning all human interaction. Without it, there would be no deterrent against taking whatever one desires from another, as there would be no consequence to face.

Thus, humans recognize the acts of a firefighter who rushes into a burning building to save lives as an exemplification of a nature defined by bravery, courage, and compassion for others. These qualities, which are implied through actions rather than static characteristics, illustrate how individuals perceive and define human nature. Similarly, the way individuals or societies respond to threats to their core values or existence, the nature of their response—whether to stand and fight, or surrender—reveals the essence of their collective or individual character. This principle, that actions informed by judgment reveal true nature, underlies all human interaction; without these actions and without the readiness to face the consequences of these actions, human nature remains a mere abstract concept. Thus, understanding humans requires observing their actions, through which we discern the intrinsic qualities that define their essence.

Upholding Constitutional Rights in the Face of Government Coercion

Frequently, and typically by way of government, the function of rational extroversion ignores the rights of, and attempts to impose its will on, the individual coercively. This dynamic, detailed in the discussion on "Collectivized Ethics," highlights the conflict between collective orientation and individual autonomy.

When faced with collective demands that require the individual to surrender their rights to the desires and choices of others, the individual may best communicate their position by emphasizing the physical consequence they intend to impose in response to such rights violations. Crucially, he or she should direct these consequences toward those orchestrating the coercive actions—not merely those executing them—underscoring the accountability of decision-makers in scenarios of imposed collectivism.

For example, a significant debate occurs over restricting the Second Amendment rights of Americans, with some policymakers entertaining the opinion that they can and should be able to restrict these rights.

This attitude threatens the American right to bear arms and protect oneself. However, these policy propositions, deemed arbitrary because they bypass the constitutional process and reinterpret the Bill of Rights based on personal or collective desires, overlook a fundamental constitutional principle: the right of the people to abolish a government that becomes destructive of the ends for which the people established it.

While those planning to institute the policy amendment are attempting to force Americans to adhere to these edicts, the persistence of such actions eventually triggers a constitutionally recognized defense mechanism. This mechanism is not merely an inherent instinct to protect oneself from harm or death, as seen across various species, but also a constitutional acknowledgment of the right to resist and, if necessary, overthrow a government that ceases to respect and uphold its constitutional mandates. We recognize and formally sanction this instinct through self-defense laws, which justify the use of reasonable force in defense against threats, and with the constitutional tenet that empowers citizens to defend their liberties against tyrannical governance.

This understanding of potential conflict is the ultimate physical consequence that must be stressed by concerned citizens when communicating with government officials on the issue of Second Amendment infringement. The unfortunate reality, however, is that while the physical conflict would arise between individuals and law enforcement, the true accountability lies with the offending officials responsible for enacting such illegitimate policy. This scenario underscores the importance of adhering to constitutional processes and respecting established rights, including the explicit constitutional provision that empowers citizens to act against a government that fails to abide by its foundational principles.

A civilized person often desires to avoid physical conflict by way of thinking, and an individual may first attempt this by engaging in debate. However, engaging in debates over fundamental constitutional rights, such as the Second Amendment, poses a significant risk. Such discussions implicitly validate a premise that undermines these inviolable protections and consequently lends credence to arguments aiming to limit them. This not only diverts attention from enforcing these rights but also allows officials to leverage their authority, all while lacking a constitutional basis to do so.

The Constitution clearly defines certain rights, including the right to bear arms, as fundamental and beyond infringement. Despite the complexities of interpreting and applying these rights, it mandates that officials uphold them unequivocally. Engaging in debates over the very existence of these rights thus grants unwarranted legitimacy to those who challenge them, allowing government officials to benefit by delaying the enforcement of constitutionally guaranteed freedoms. This situation emerges from a reluctance to firmly reject any contention over these established rights, thereby empowering a narrative that weakens constitutional safeguards and the principle of individual autonomy.

The Ethical Imperative of Defense against Aggression

Whenever someone coerces an individual to surrender their values, it constitutes an act of aggression and an initiation of force. In such situations, imposing consequences in one's defense becomes a moral imperative. Failing to act in the face of wrongdoing leads to a cycle of continuous and escalating harm. This not only affects the individual initially wronged but can also create broader societal issues, empowering perpetrators to act without fear of repercussion.

Therefore, the imposition of appropriate consequences tailored to each specific situation is crucial. This action serves to protect the individual directly affected and upholds the ethical standards of society. By holding wrongdoers accountable and clearly demonstrating that actions carry real and tangible consequences, we deter future transgressions and reinforce a framework of justice. This approach to force and consequences—whether it involves legal, social, economic, or physical means—is fundamental in a society that respects and protects individual rights and values.

It is particularly important to recognize that in certain dire situations, extreme responses, such as the use of lethal force, may be necessary. While the civilized nature of many in society often leads to an instinctive aversion to this harsh reality, it is imperative to understand that protecting one's life and values requires actions as severe as the threat faced. Acknowledging and preparing for such responses is a critical aspect of ensuring justice and security in a society that upholds individual rights.

Having now traced the concept of ethics back to morality, and then the concept of morality further back to the principle of force, we uncover a foundational aspect of human interaction. This progression underscores that when an individual resorts to force solely in defense against threats to their values, they are neither an aggressive brute nor an initiator of force. Rather, such an individual is fundamentally defending their life.

THE PROPER POLITICS
FOR AMERICA

$$\equiv \star \bigstar \star \equiv$$

The concept of **life**, as explored in this work, is what I express as the sum of all **value**.[225] This encompasses both survival and purpose, which are fundamental to human existence.

Survival operates on the level of instinct and necessity, compelling us to secure food, shelter, and safety—elements essential for our biological continuity. It is a reactive state, guided by the immediacy of physical needs. Purpose, in contrast, transcends these basic needs, rooted in our capacity for self-reflection, aspiration, and the pursuit of meaning. While survival ensures we live, purpose decides why we live, imbuing our actions with intention and direction with the goal of fulfillment.

Often, these two realms of needs intersect and influence each other, leading to a nuanced convergence that can blur the lines between purely physical and purely psychological requirements. For instance, the pursuit of a career (a psychological need for accomplishment and purpose) directly impacts one's ability to fulfill physical needs (financial resources for food and shelter). Understanding this intersection is

---

[225] See Appendix

crucial for a holistic view of what constitutes life and how we assign value to its various components.

One can illustrate the difference between survival and purpose by posing two simple questions. Survival asks the question: "How can I continue to live?" In contrast, purpose asks the question: "What kind of life do I wish to lead?" The former is irrational instinct, and the latter, rational choice, with each relying on the other for achieving a balanced and fulfilling existence.

While it is true that one necessarily (though not sufficiently) achieves purpose through survival, since survival constitutes a fundamental component of purpose, the reverse relationship—that one accomplishes survival through purpose—does not hold in the same manner. Unlike the direct contribution of survival to purpose, the influence of purpose on survival is more indirect, shaping one's motivation and drive rather than directly ensuring physical existence. This asymmetry arises because survival is a necessary but insufficient condition for purpose. Purpose extends beyond mere survival, encompassing broader aspirations and meanings that an individual seeks in life. The broader concept of life unifies both concepts, suggesting a symbiotic but not identical relationship between them. Therefore, any human who chooses life, thus chooses to bear the responsibility of sustaining their own survival, and they partially achieve their purpose by attaining the goal of maintaining life and ensuring continued existence. The more efficiently one secures survival, the more resources—both physical and psychological—are available for pursuing purposes that go beyond the mere act of survival.

External factors dictate physical survival, whereas individuals can alter and adjust the pursuit of psychological purpose in their minds through their thought processes. This is why a major function of purpose is to think; to mitigate the amount of time and energy required for physical survival. For instance, consider the evolution of home appliances like washing machines, refrigerators, and dishwashers. These innovations have significantly reduced the time and effort once needed for basic household tasks, thus freeing up mental and physical resources for more fulfilling pursuits. Similarly, the development of vehicles has transformed transportation, once a significant survival challenge, into a less time-consuming and physically demanding task. This reduction in effort required for mobility allows individuals to focus more on intellectual, social, and personal growth activities. In both cases, purposeful thinking—in the form of technological innovation—has played a pivotal role in minimizing the energy expended on survival needs, thereby enhancing the capacity to pursue higher psychological purposes.

Once one comprehends the fundamental role of purpose in individual life, it becomes crucial to understand how this concept interacts with the political sphere. Here, we confront a stark contrast: the individual's pursuit of purpose versus the primitive collective mentality that permeates the upper echelons of American politics.

Ayn Rand vividly captured the essence of this mentality in "The New Intellectual," where she depicts the philosophical archetype "Attila," an extrovert, as a figure who sees others not as individuals with their own purposes but as mere resources for exploitation. Such a mentality, devoid of understanding the intrinsic value of individual purpose, threatens the very fabric of freedom inherent in American individualism by regarding human life as a means to "society's" end.

The portrayal of Attila underscores the grim consequences of reducing human beings to mere resources—a reality echoed across historical and contemporary authoritarian, totalitarian, and statist regimes. Such governments, by prioritizing state or collective goals over individual aspirations, starkly contrast with environments that foster personal purpose. However, this systemic suppression of individual freedoms and aspirations, often exacerbated by physical hardships, may not stem from a conscious strategy aimed at the regime's own survival and progression. Rather, it reflects a subconscious conflation of the regime's

313

survival with that of the collective. Leaders and enforcers within these systems may not fully distinguish between the well-being of the group and their own power dynamics, genuinely believing they are acting in the collective's best interest. However, it is their political actions, rooted in this lack of self-awareness, which create an environment in which individuals are increasingly unable to seek and fulfill their own purposes. This, in turn, not only diminishes the will to live among those individuals but also, ironically, undermines the cohesion and sustainability of the society these leaders intend to preserve.

Individuals deprived of independence, freedom, and liberty fail to meet the minimum level of purpose necessary to incentivize further survival. Failing to meet this minimum level does not supply enough reason for one to exert the energy required to go on; at that point, the person just gives up on life. Rises in homelessness, substance abuse, mental illness, and suicide are all symptoms of and metaphors for this surrender in the face of increased deprivation. Therefore, deprivation of one's personal purpose to the point where there is no reason to continue survival, renders that person no longer of value to those wishing to extract resources from them—there is nothing left to deplete. The experiences of people living under these regimes illustrate how political conditions, by continually suppressing or negating personal purpose, can erode the will to live.

"The Zero": Unraveling the Rational Extrovert's Dilemma

In John Galt's pivotal speech in *Atlas Shrugged*, Rand explores a concept she refers to as "the zero," which I interpret as symbolizing the rational extrovert. This type, implied by Rand, bases decisions on averages, lacking consciously-chosen personal values and relying upon a mystical collective. This collective, devoid of intrinsic value, is merely a sum of individual perspectives, yet the extrovert aims to assimilate into it, at the cost of their individuality.

For the rational extrovert, the average, or their subconscious impression of what others do is the obvious answer for all, ignoring that averages derive from multitudes of subjective perspectives and there would be no average if the subjective perspectives did not exist. Accordingly, they are not averse to forbidding others from choosing anything other than what is "generally accepted" as rational. These external standards or norms are the objective "rules" they live by, and these rules must come from outside, a view we have seen stated by Jung, and—though not so explicitly—by Rand as well. When an average of the average is the ideal, over time, the result can only be a regression. Society cannot logically expect an upward motion by any other means but through the sacrifice of some individuals to the collective. The group discourages the individual from thinking differently and views their selfish desire for personal achievement negatively.

Rand's exploration of conceptual understanding challenges the prevalent approach toward knowledge and ethics, particularly critiquing the external orientation—a hallmark of the extrovert—that prioritizes collective norms over individual reasoning. This external focus often neglects the importance of logical connections, leading to a superficial understanding of concepts, which Rand identifies as a form of "unconsciousness." This unconsciousness manifests most detrimentally in the realm of morality and ethics, where the absence of a logical, conceptual framework undermines the individual's capacity to navigate complex ethical landscapes with clarity and principle.

For instance, Rand writes, "Joy is not 'the absence of pain,' intelligence is not 'the absence of stupidity,' light is not 'the absence of darkness,' an entity is not 'the absence of a nonentity.'"[226] Through this, Rand emphasizes the inadequacy of negative definitions—defining values or entities by what they lack—particularly criticizing the rational extrovert's tendency to anchor understanding in the absence or

---

[226] (Rand, Atlas Shrugged 1957, 1024)

negation of traits. This approach, she argues, leads to the "reign of the zero," a philosophical void which diminishes values to non-values, such as weakness or incompetence, reflecting a collective average-oriented perspective that fails to recognize the richness and autonomy of individual existence.

Rand's critique extends to the impact of this perspective on individuality, suggesting that those with an extroverted orientation, who place less importance on their own ego or individual reasoning, are more susceptible to embracing mysticism and altruism. This susceptibility stems from their tendency to overlook or deny the existence of abstract concepts and causal connections, culminating in a denial of consciousness itself. Such a stance not only weakens their individuality but perpetually distances them from a true understanding of morality and ethics, areas where the absence of individual reasoning and logical connections leads to ethical ambiguity and moral relativism.

In contrast, Rand champions a "conceptual consciousness" that is characteristic of a rational individual who uses reason as the foundation of knowledge and places utmost importance on the ego. This approach, she suggests, leads to rational egoism—an ethical theory that champions the individual's rational interest as the moral good.

Rationally speaking, ethics can only go in one of two directions: either toward egoism, which prioritizes the individual with group benefits as a byproduct, or toward altruism, which focuses on the group often at the expense of individual concerns. These ethical stances are politically mirrored by individualism and collectivism, respectively, and are philosophically incompatible. The choice lies between individuals making rational decisions with group benefits as a secondary consideration, or the group making rational decisions with a reckless disregard for individual rights. This conclusion is exhaustive, leaving no other logical possibility.

The Birth of American Individualism and Free Markets

Extroverted types are antithetical to the principles of free will and free choice, and thus to free markets, which serve as both the conduit and a reflection of the individual's capacity to make choices based on personal judgment and values. This paradoxical nature of the rational extrovert becomes evident as they subconsciously indulge in their own values while simultaneously attempting to limit the value choices of others through coercion and force. However, such attempts at control only work if others accept them.

This is what made the concept of the U.S. so groundbreaking at its time of inception. Instead of coercing and forcing the public to follow the edicts of elites, individuals were free to make choices of their own in pursuit of their own happiness. Free markets, characterized by the unhampered functioning of supply and demand, are and will always be the direct conduit to this outcome. They operate on the principle of voluntary exchange, whereby individuals and businesses are free to trade goods and services based on their own assessments of value without undue interference from external authorities. This system inherently fosters innovation, efficiency, and choice, leading to the greatest amount of opportunity possible through natural competition.

Individual Choice and Collective Culture: Understanding the American Ethos

In this context of individual choice and opportunity, the insights of Jung on the development of collective culture and its psychological implications become particularly relevant. Jung's analysis elucidates how collective cultures affect and often limit individual psychological functions. This perspective is crucial for comprehending the complex dynamics between individual liberty and collective norms, which is at the heart of the American ethos.

Jung insightfully addresses the evolution of collective culture and its effects on individual development. He notes,

> *A high level of individual culture was undoubtedly reached by certain exemplary personalities, but a collective culture was quite unknown to the ancient world. This achievement was reserved for Christianity.*[227]

This shift, according to Jung, led to a form of collective culture where the individual's value was redefined, focusing on a singular dominant function. This change marked a significant transition from the external suppression of the masses, as seen in ancient societies, to an internal psychological process within the individual.

Jung further elucidates this internalization as a psychological enslavement, where the individual becomes subjugated to their dominant function, neglecting their other capabilities in the process. He states,

> *Just as the enslavement of the masses was the open wound of the ancient world, so the enslavement of the inferior functions is an ever-bleeding wound in the psyche of modern man.*[228]

This observation uncovers a deep-seated conflict inherent in collective cultures: the tension between preserving one's individuality and conforming to the prevailing cultural norms. Drawing from Schiller's insights, Jung suggests that collective culture measures the individual's worth not by their holistic being but by a single, distinguished function.[229] This perspective highlights a dilemma in modern society: While collective culture has advanced, progress has often come at the

---

[227] (Jung 1923, 64-66)
[228] ibid
[229] ibid

cost of individual development. Schiller's view complements this, suggesting that cultural advancement necessitates a kind of internal opposition, a battleground of capacities within the individual. Jung explains how this internalization of collective culture results in a dominant function that defines the individual's value in society. Schiller's insights reveal that not everyone navigates this transformation successfully, struggling to maintain their individuality while trading with society based on their dominant function. As Schiller puts it,

> *There was no other way of developing the manifold capacities of man than by placing them in opposition to each other.*[230]

Considering this, the "rights of man" protected by the collective culture of Christianity represent a double-edged sword—a protection that simultaneously fosters a collective mindset at the expense of individual development. This leads to the eternal philosophical conflict between extroverted and introverted types, as Jung suggests. The extrovert tends to surrender to collective culture, often failing to fully realize their individual potential, while the introvert strives to maintain individuality within the cultural framework, embodying the true essence of an American citizen.

While it does appear evident that a collective culture must be at the forefront of a civilized society with some tradeoff between culture and individuality, from what Jung mentions, however, an additional tradeoff must take place within the subject's psychology. If the tradeoff exists at the societal level only, it results in a dominant minority having power over a subordinate and slave-like majority.

To achieve equilibrium, society must find a balance with the individual, and the subject's psychology must also establish an internal equilibrium point. Ethics exemplifies this equilibrium point between

---

[230] (Jung 1923, 65)

society and the individual. The equilibrium point in the subject's psychology reveals itself in morality. Free choice is the key factor in this process because only through free choice can individuals fully experience both their personal moral development and the ethical benefits of collective culture.

The Ego's Tightrope: Balancing Personal Judgments and Societal Influences

In both Rand's psycho-epistemology and Jung's psychological types, there is a shared recognition that human psychology must reconcile individual and collective lives, that is, the judgments made on a personal level and those influenced by the society they identify with. Rand argues that contemporary individuals often fail in this respect; they are paradoxically both social and antisocial, lacking a clear understanding of what forms a rational association among humans.[231] Her insight sheds light on the inherent conflict between a person's individual and collective functions within the ego. To achieve a healthy balance between these two aspects, a process of equalization is essential, which involves a balancing act between one's dominant and inferior psychological functions.

Jung adds nuance to this idea by suggesting that to achieve a more balanced state, one must consciously integrate one's less developed psychological functions into their dominant mode of functioning. He explains that achieving this equalization demands a serious commitment to recognizing and addressing these weaker functions, creating an energy gradient that provides an opportunity for these latent aspects of the psyche to activate and develop. Jung elaborates on this internal struggle:

---

[231] (Rand, The Missing Link 1973, 68)

From all this it is abundantly clear that any attempt to
equalize the one-sided differentiation of the man of our times
has to reckon very seriously with an acceptance of the inferior,
because undifferentiated, functions. [232]

To clarify, in Jung's perspective, our psychological landscape is a blend of stronger, more distinct functions, and weaker, less developed, or undifferentiated ones. While the dominant functions guide most of our conscious decisions, the inferior functions are like the untapped potential within us, still influencing our behavior subconsciously. These inferior functions require nurturing to prevent them from becoming sources of internal conflict or distress.

Jung further elaborates that transforming an underdeveloped function into a dominant one is an unattainable goal. This transformation can only occur if the dominant function cedes some of its power, but even then, the lesser function cannot fully reach the level of the dominant one. Instead, we must strive for an optimal balance at an intermediate level of functionality. For those who have overly concentrated on one specific function, this will initially feel like a regression but will lead to a more balanced psychological state. Any educational approach aspiring to create a harmonious human nature must take this complex dynamic into account.[233]

Christian Ethics and Their Impact on America's Collective Culture

Christian ethics heavily influenced America's politics from inception, serving as a historical steppingstone that improved the human condition for the masses. But a system rooted in mysticism leaves it intellectually defenseless against charges of arbitrary dogmatism. As

---

[232] (Jung 1923, 78)
[233] (Jung 1923, 78)

knowledge builds and technology makes information more widely accessible, people can identify much of their traditional outlook as being rooted in nothing more than make believe. Resentment builds from antiquated restrictions placed on the individual which leads to people's underdevelopment in other cognitive areas.

Consider the shift in attitudes toward certain social issues, such as LGBTQ+. In societies where traditional views, often grounded in religious beliefs, have historically marginalized these groups, there is growing resentment, especially among younger generations who, with access to global information and diverse perspectives, find such marginalization incongruent with contemporary understandings of human rights and equality. This resentment is not just about the specific issue but also reflects a broader frustration with being bound by belief systems that no longer resonate with an increasingly informed and globally connected populace.

The culture of Christianity never provided a pathway to rational independence because it requires that one make a specific choice: complete submission to Christian metaphysics. This doctrine led to the emergence of counter-culture groups like Satanists, who, in their rebellion against Christian norms, believe they are embracing freedom through alternative possibilities. However, these groups fail to recognize that the culture they oppose fundamentally shapes their reactionary stance. By defining themselves in direct opposition to Christianity, they inevitably remain tethered to it. Their opposition, rather than representing a true departure from underlying philosophical constraints, mirrors the same lack of rational independence they seek to escape.

The culture of a society reveals itself in extroversion, and with that understanding, it becomes clear that much of the division we see in America stems from a conflict between extroverted thinking and feeling. One could argue that the Christian influence on the U.S.'s founding documents demonstrates that the country is deeply rooted in collective feeling; Jung certainly alluded to that connection. However, backlash from the oppressiveness and intellectual poverty of such a culture has now come to a head, creating a fork in the road. We are now at a point where the dominant culture is leaning toward either collective thinking, which—incapable of conceiving a rational set of ethics on their own—it finds to be the only pathway to ethical behavior through a dominant culture of collective feeling; or, a permutation of collective feeling, which applies kindness for kindness' sake, disconnected from reason and a conceptual understanding of the term. Ironically, the intellectual bankruptcy of the latter makes way for the ethical ineptitude of the former.

In real thinking, an individual abstracts concepts from facts and critically engages with each step to attain a desired outcome. In this process, one must inherently comprehend the reasons for their actions because each step causes a specific effect. Extroverts use concepts secondhand, flippantly considering the underlying reasons and assumptions as they perform this action. For instance, instead of understanding the ethical reasons behind treating people in a manner that fosters moral cohesiveness within a group, extroverts may focus primarily on the resulting feelings, such as kindness. They might try to apply this feeling of kindness without comprehending that it is merely the outcome of an intellectual process designed to achieve group harmony. The further out this process goes, the more disconnected from reason this mentality becomes, and the more impoverished, ineffective, and meaningless concepts, words, and ideas become.

Deconstructing the Mystical Origins of Rights in America

Many people champion America for the influence of Christian principles on the Constitution, crediting God—an abstract mystical being—as the grantor of individual rights. For those oriented to believe the State grants rights to citizens, their mystical beings of choice are the sensuously perceptible members of government.

Both God, and when viewed from the perspective above, the State, are secondhand and mystical ideas. Both views express a stance on the essence of nature, and whether one believes rights originate from God or from the State, in both cases, some mystical and supernatural force bestows rights upon humans. Ironically, these mystical forces only communicate with certain living spokespeople, leaving both approaches to culminate in people deriving their rights from the spokespeople who enjoy this privilege.

We must also keep in mind that because God or the State is the source of human rights in this case, verifying the validity of this premise is important because subsequent logical conclusions must be based on the correctness of that view of nature.

Contrary to both views, the fact is that humans grant themselves rights. By rooting rights in mysticism, we detach them from their logical underpinnings, introducing ambiguity into the core of ethical reasoning that should otherwise be clear and objective. The source of human rights is the individual, and those rights are intrinsic in them, not granted to them by any group, external object, or mystical being. In fact, the human mind is the creator of all mystical beings, including those believed to grant rights, and all thus beings are results of psychological fantasy. The creative process, while inherently capable of fantasy, also possesses the profound ability to abstractly conceive of rights, anchoring them in principles derived from objective reality beyond our immediate perceptions.

Mysticism is a threat to the very idea of individual rights because it negates rational independence and, with that, one's conscious individuality. This reliance on an imagined intermediary distorts the direct recognition of rights as inherently ours, obscuring the true source of autonomy and rational independence. There is nothing to judge for oneself because the outcome is already determined, however, determined by the unconscious individuality in the subject's psyche. As this relates to the types I have limited this discussion to thus far, this quality, seen in rational extroversion, results in the "negative thinking" that Jung juxtaposes with theosophical thinking.

True autonomy emerges from questioning and critically evaluating societal norms, a testament to the strength of individual judgment against the backdrop of collective pressures.

Choosing Reason over Mysticism: A Philosophical Imperative for American Politics

Humans inherently possess both psychology and, consequently, an implicit philosophy, the latter being a conceptual reflection of the former. The critical distinction lies in the application of thought: While all have the capacity to think, actively employing this capacity to explicitly shape one's philosophy is a deliberate choice. In the absence of a consciously chosen philosophy driven by deliberate thought, one defaults to a philosophy shaped by their immediate emotions. This subconscious philosophy adopts the principle that "good is whatever I feel at this moment." Such a philosophy, absent an overarching rational set of societal ethics, and corresponding governance informed by a coherent political philosophy, reveals its inadequacies when confronted with the societal implications of actions based solely on individual whims—highlighted by the critical question, "What if others do not feel like being subjected to the consequences of your actions?" This underscores the distinction between possessing the capacity to think and choosing to employ this capacity in a manner that guides our philosophical outlook. In making this choice, we determine whether we actively construct our philosophy through rational thought or passively form it by instinct, intuition, or emotion which, if left unchecked, lead to an irrational and potentially harmful set of beliefs.

If the politics of America remain influenced by the waning ethical culture of Christianity, the default ending place will be a regression to some rendition of the Greek system Jung claims Christianity replaced—featuring classes of serfs and elites. Furthermore, this scenario exposes the poverty of aligning oneself with Christian ethics because, as a secondhand arbitrary idea, there can be no intellectual defense provided for it, and against opposing arbitrary ideas. This outcome is not in line with the intended purpose of a political system designed to safeguard individual rights and freedoms. The necessity for a clear transition to a philosophy grounded in reason has always existed and remains essential. Any culture built on mysticism necessarily restricts free choice which is the freedom to think and act for oneself—the essence of an individual. Slavery is the result of restricting free choice since it denies individuals the opportunity to choose and live by their own values.

While a collective thinking approach to governance most resembles a monarchical, dictatorial, or totalitarian format, a collective feeling approach to governance resulted in America's Constitutional Republic. Although this system was developed highly dependent upon Christian principles, the mysticism of Christianity renders it inherently collective and altruistic. This underlying collectivism presents a contradiction: America promotes individualism at its philosophical core, yet practices a form of collective spiritual mysticism. For this reason, America will consistently struggle with defending itself against other forms of collectivism, such as socialism, if it continues to uphold this spiritual collectivism. The inherent contradiction between advocating individualism while practicing spiritual collectivism results in a hypocrisy that undermines the country's philosophical consistency and defense against other collectivist ideologies.

Individuals exercise true individualism through reason, a process whose outward cultural expression manifests as collective feeling.

Given the inherent contradictions and challenges presented by a foundation built on Christian ethics and its mystical underpinnings, the question then becomes how a society, especially one as diverse as

America, can effectively defend the individual rights and freedoms it purports to uphold. The answer lies both within the philosophical domain and the practical mechanisms that safeguard these rights. It is here that we encounter the role of force as a fundamental aspect of societal interaction and governance.

Force: The Final Backstop in Society

The essence of defending one's values lies in the individual's inherent capacity to exert force, understood in its broadest sense as the imposition of perceptible consequences for those who act to violate these values. This fundamental principle underlies not only personal defense mechanisms but also the collective enforcement of shared values. As individuals, the ultimate recourse to safeguard what we hold dear is the readiness to employ physical force, including the willingness to fight or kill, should all other means fail. An underlying threat of violence serves as the ultimate guarantee of personal values. This reality does not depend on societal constructs or government enforcement but on the primal right of self-preservation and value protection. When individuals with aligned values come together, this individual capacity for force naturally extends into a collective capacity, leveraging societal structures to enforce norms through a wide array of consequences. This collective expression of force can manifest in legal systems that impose penalties, social norms that ostracize, economic measures that penalize, and, if necessary, physical measures to protect the group's values.

Thus, the collective's ability to enforce its values through non-violent means or societal norms still fundamentally relies on the underlying individual readiness to use physical force as a last resort. This individual and collective readiness to use physical force, therefore, acts as the final backstop against violations of deeply held values, transcending organized systems of governance, and reaching into the core of human nature and interpersonal relations.

If the prevailing culture fails to impose negative consequences on individuals who violate society's rules, this indicates that the final backstop for upholding collective values remains intact. This is the very reason people look for societal outrage in cases where they conclude a wrong has been committed. It is a call to the group, urging them to impose consequences that clearly show that the group will not tolerate the violative actions. Although rarely stated in these terms, the end of this tolerance inevitably leads to the use of some form of physical force.

The 2020 Reaction to George Floyd's Death: A Case Study in Collective Response

An illustrative example of this dynamic, for better or worse, was the widespread reaction to the death of George Floyd on May 25, 2020, in Minneapolis, Minnesota. During an arrest, Derek Chauvin, a police officer, knelt on the neck of George Floyd, a Black man, for over nine minutes, leading to Floyd's death under highly controversial circumstances. Many people perceived this incident as a glaring example of police brutality and a symbol of systemic racial injustice. It ignited nationwide protests that, in some cases, escalated into riots in various cities.

People engaged in these protests and riots as a collective response to what they perceived as a longstanding pattern of injustice. In some communities, the intensity of the reaction crossed into violent expressions, with incidents of vandalism, arson, and looting. Some protestors turned to force because they believed that the traditional avenues of justice had failed to address the grievances of racial inequality and police misconduct.

When some individuals perceive the legal system as failing to hold those responsible for injustices accountable, or when they view it as not aligning with the collective values of justice and equality, they may feel compelled to take matters into their own hands. This was evident in the 2020 riots, where the absence of immediate and formal legal consequences for Floyd's death led some people to enforce their sense of justice through direct action.

Setting Societal Standards: The Convergence of Ethics, Law, and Force

Under normal circumstances, we distinguish politics from social actions by examining how each side employs force. People use the civil acts of persuasion and choice in social settings, while they reserve coercion and force for politics. However, any superficial limitations imposed through politics not aligned with the country's ethics will eventually become evident in this process.

Individuals drive the social realm, but a civilized society must have a governing body implementing an objective code of laws, rooted in ethics. This is the area of politics. For as much as people desire freedom, there must be objective laws to protect people and set standards for behavior. The overall governing body creates and enforces those laws, along with determines who has the right to legitimate force. For this reason, it behooves citizens to have an interest in ethics because ethics drive the politics that set the laws by which courts judge them.

Philosophy and Law: Crafting Ethical Foundations in America

As mentioned previously, humans cannot live without a philosophy, and this consists of the ever evolving personally held moral philosophy the individual governs themselves by, and which, in America, informs the ethics driving the politics in the State for which they seek a moral existence within. In the individual, a consciously chosen moral philosophy sets a personal standard by which to judge what is good and right. When individuals do not consciously choose this philosophy, they invariably adopt the fluctuating belief that "good is whatever they feel like it is." People actively choose the former motion through their volition, while they passively accept the latter.

A person or entity must explicitly state an ethical doctrine thereby consciously choosing it. However, this does not exempt it from being poorly constructed insofar as containing inconsistencies and therefore being the equivalent of an subconsciously chosen personal moral philosophy. Politics resulting from ethics constructed in this way can only equate to a principle of, "at some point." This is why constructing an ethical philosophy requires the utmost logical rigor because the answer cannot justly be, "at some point." For a just society, the answer must be at a specific point, stated explicitly because ethics underpin the laws that people must follow; when suspected of violating these laws, individuals face penalties that jeopardize their liberties. Authorities must exercise objectivity because, without it, they will act based on their ever-shifting emotional and subjective perspectives when passing judgment on others without accountability—which is an unjust stance to uphold within society.

Furthermore, a principle of, "at some point" translates to "whenever 'we' do not like it," raising the crucial question: Who exactly defines "we" in this context? In America, citizens expect the "we" to include them equally alongside their fellow citizens. However, individuals do not always realize this ideal, effectively leaving a back door open that undermines objectivity in decision-making. When reasons for laws or actions become ambiguous, bias is often revealed on the part of lawmakers or government officials, whether conscious or subconscious.

The concept of bias highlights a fundamental divergence in the thinking types, due to the way each approaches and interprets information. Extroverts, often slow to understand how disparate facts and experiences undergird universal principles, tend to view situations from a pluralistic standpoint, reflecting their subconscious biases. The introvert prefers long-term logical consistency, often perceived by extroverts as lacking practical use. The extrovert's perspective leads to prioritizing immediate, concrete responses over broader ethical considerations, as witnessed in New Mexico Governor Michelle Lujan Grisham's 2023 emergency order banning both open and concealed firearms in Albuquerque. This order, which she defended as a necessary measure despite acknowledging it might not stop criminals and facing questions about its constitutionality, exemplifies this extroverted approach to problem-solving, prioritizing immediate action over abstract rights. Jung articulates this dichotomy, explaining,

> *Intellectualism is always monistic. It begins with the whole, with the universal, and unites things; empiricism begins with the part and makes the whole into an assemblage. It could therefore be described as pluralistic.*[234]

The ambiguity which often results from subconscious bias shifts the country away from governance by impartial laws, to governance by the subjective judgments of individuals. A subtle transition from a government of laws to a government of men occurs when personal biases and unequal representation cloud objectivity.

The law must be objective, and there can justly be no enforceable part of it that is unwritten because a citizen cannot readily align themselves with, or even protest a law to avoid future penalties if that law is not stated explicitly. This objectivity is also necessary to provide clarity on when the law exceeds its bounds. Inconsistencies in written law create situations where the same action is both lawful and unlawful within the same context, a byproduct of a poorly constructed system.

We can see a prime example of this issue in how antitrust law address it. Regulatory authorities intend these laws to control and prevent monopolistic practices and ensure fair competition. However,

---

[234] (Jung 1923, 279)

their interpretation and enforcement can often be ambiguous and inconsistent. For instance, ambiguity in what constitutes a "monopoly," or "anti-competitive behavior" leads to different interpretations and applications of the law. This ambiguity creates uncertainty among businesses, whose leaders may not understand whether their actions keep them in compliance with the law. It also provides excessive discretion to those enforcing the law, potentially leading to arbitrary or inconsistent application.

While lawmakers are frequently conflated with law enforcement agents, the members of the legislative governing body hold the responsibility to formalize the standards to which citizens and law enforcement agents must adhere. The lack of explicitness in antitrust law highlights how challenges and potential injustices arise when legislators do not clearly define laws. Lawmakers must ensure that laws are precise, unambiguous, and consistently applicable to effectively guide both citizen behavior and law enforcement actions.

A well-constructed ethical philosophy aids in creating sound and consistent law. However, lawmakers sometimes opt not to follow this approach, a point highlighted by the Legal Information Institute at Cornell University, which notes that the law does not simply codify ethical norms.[235] This raises a pertinent question: If laws are not based on ethical norms, on what, then, are they founded? It is understandable that lawmakers do not codify every unethical action as illegal, given that laws, though broad, have a narrower scope than ethical principles. However, law in America is only meant to explicitly delineate prohibited actions, so anything unlawful should undoubtedly share the designation of unethical. This unintelligible stance often arises in a mysticism-driven culture, which results in the mind-body split, thereby disconnecting the theoretical aspects of ethics from their practical application in law.

---

[235] (Wex Definitions Team 2022)

Theoretical principles are broad abstractions meant for practical application. The natural scope of a principle extends beyond that of its practical application, but the practical application should never extend beyond the scope of the principle. If a deviation from this guideline is ever necessary, one must revisit and reevaluate the theory, and, if needed, adjust, or, if it is found to be fundamentally flawed, discard it.

Navigating the Complexities of Choice and Freedom in America

The issue at the core of the impasse between the types as it pertains to freedom is their opposing views on choice. In America, freedom of choice is not oppression, it is one's responsibility as a citizen to think for oneself and make decisions. But if one does not possess the psychic freedom necessary to make choices for oneself, that disposition causes one to evade that responsibility and conflate persuasion with coercion.

The primary barrier to freedom in a country where the government's proper role is to protect its citizens, is the restriction of free choice. This is crucial because, out of necessity, it is the relationships among citizens—optimized through the mechanisms of free-market capitalism—that most efficiently fulfill everyone's needs. When someone restricts free choice, they hinder these relationships and, as a result, impede the efficient fulfillment of needs.

Restriction of free choice frequently results from the government allowing some citizens to elevate their personal concerns to the level of legislation, a strategy many use to leverage the government against their fellow citizens. A prime example of this is the advocacy for excessive consumer protection laws. While the intent to protect consumers is vital, overreach in this area can stifle innovation and create overly burdensome regulations for businesses. Such laws can inadvertently hamper the development of new products or services, limiting consumer choice and market dynamism.

This desire to ensure safety and fairness often overshadows the need for a balanced approach, one that assumes the personal agency of citizens to make decisions, which would automatically mitigate negative impacts on innovation and business growth. Furthermore, individuals who advocate for such legislation typically do so without fully accepting responsibility for their personal choices, instead forcing others to conform and support their initiatives regardless of consent.

A relevant example of this issue is California's 2019 legislation, the CROWN Act, which addresses discrimination based on natural hair. This law amends the California Education Code and the Fair Employment and Housing Act's definition of race to include traits historically associated with race, such as hair texture and protective hairstyles, including but not limited to braids, locks, and twists. Lawmakers introduced the legislation to address and prevent discrimination in workplaces and schools, particularly targeting Black individuals, based on hair texture and styles associated with their race. The CROWN Act makes it illegal for employers and school officials to enforce dress codes or grooming policies that disproportionately affect individuals based on their natural hair.

While aiming to protect individuals from discrimination, this and other similar laws pose significant challenges in enforcement and proof. Demonstrating that one did not get a job specifically due to natural hair is extremely difficult, leading to legal complexities with little tangible benefit. Despite laws like these, which infringe on the rights of private citizens and companies to exercise free choice, legislators could more effectively address them through social awareness or internal organizational policies. These laws give the false impression that legislators are actively working for the public good, while they are filling bills with unnecessary restrictions, regulations, and language that do not significantly benefit the people in terms of protection or freedom.

Our failure as a country lies in increasingly allowing the politicization of personal grievances over the years which give a false sense of accuracy due to historical precedent. Issues that do not reach the level of ethical violations should remain within the social realm, where individuals can work out their differences among themselves. When disagreements occur, and if a citizen becomes dissatisfied with the outcome, the judicial system stands ready to address these situations because that is precisely its societal function.

From Market Freedom to Political Reliance: A Vicious Cycle

It would be a failure for people to consider free markets strictly an economic concept because free markets are a core foundation of freedom in every aspect of life. But free-market dynamics invoke fear in those who despise the activities of judgment and choice. This fear results from a sense that the world is leaving them behind, that they will be at a disadvantage, and lose their ability to survive; this is necessarily true for those who do not make a concerted effort to think. People commonly experience these phobias, such as the fear of technology, monopolies, other countries, outsourcing, and lack of diversity—all examples of fear resulting from the tribal mentality.

Using the fear of monopolies as an example, I want to demonstrate how these fears lead to paradoxical political actions restricting the free choice of the individual. Ironically, the claim is that this intervention is for the individual's protection.

People often face a paradox in wanting both free choice and protection against monopolies. A key distinction lies between organic monopolies, which arise naturally in a free market due to consumer preferences, and artificial monopolies, created through government

335

intervention. In a free market, a monopoly that forms because of consumer choices reflects the collective will of the people. However, when the government steps in, for example, with stringent regulations in industries like pharmaceuticals, health care, or green energy, it creates artificial monopolies. Such regulations can prevent smaller companies from competing, leaving consumers with limited choices.

Many citizens may not fully grasp this dynamic, and when politicians argue that they are restricting free choice for the public good, people often do not easily recognize the absurdity of this claim. What regularly goes unnoticed is how these politicians use policies to channel business toward their preferred organizations, shifting the freedom of choice from the people to the policymakers. This transfer of decision-making power represents a fundamental misunderstanding of the political role: Politicians should act based on rights granted by the people, not as though they are bestowing rights on them.

However, what is more puzzling is the circular effect that emerges from people's reliance on political actions over market-driven choices. Many wonder why they have not yet seen the benefits of past political actions, not realizing that by opting for political solutions—casting their vote by ballot instead of casting it with their dollar—they have forfeited their most efficient and effective means of influencing outcomes. This reliance on political decision-making creates a feedback loop: As people perceive a lack of progress, they increasingly turn to politicians to make more decisions on their behalf, further ceding their individual power and influence.

Each time this cycle repeats, it reinforces the perception that solutions must come from governmental action rather than individual choices in the market. This perpetuates a growing dependency on political interventions, which often leads to expanded government control over various aspects of life. As government power increases, individual autonomy in influencing outcomes diminishes, leading to a sense of disenfranchisement and frustration among the populace.

Government Run Amok: How Political Ignorance Facilitates Corporate Manipulation

In many cases, politicians, ironically lacking a fundamental understanding of the source of rights—which is central to their role—become vulnerable to manipulation by corporate lobbyists and lawyers. These external influencers, claiming to operate in the best interest of the people, often sway political decisions. However, they designed their proposals—ostensibly or potentially good intentions notwithstanding—primarily to serve the interests of their respective companies. This is because the reasoning behind these proposals stems from corporate decision-makers, not from a dispassionate concern for public welfare—not that this should be their obligation.

As a result, the laws shaped by these corporate cohorts end up benefiting those groups, rather than individual citizens. This dynamic creates a disconnect between the intended purpose of political roles, which is to safeguard the rights and interests of the populace, and the reality of policymaking often skewed in favor of corporate interests. The ultimate consequence is legislation that prioritizes the needs of specific groups over the broader needs and rights of individual citizens.

Special interest groups pushing for public policy assume it is the duty of their fellow citizens to financially support the initiatives they push for. It is worth noting that individuals could accomplish this privately without government involvement; however, this approach would only grant both the government and these groups the opportunity to gain control over other people's resources through persuasion, rather than their preferred method of coercion. When the government facilitates these activities, it permits the members and affiliates of the special interest group to seize control over resources extracted from taxpayers. The government acts as an intermediary in the transaction and must receive compensation for administrative costs. The entire process bloats budgets and props up government with state-created jobs. When anyone points out this fact, politicians then play on people's fears because many believe that any job creation is good. Yet, decisions made in the free market are the key to achieving a well-functioning and efficient economy. Without addressing this issue, wages distort, and industry cannot accurately assess the need for jobs. If a need exists in society, entrepreneurs will organize with willing members of the labor force to provide that value to consumers in the market in pursuit of the profit they deem appropriate.

Private versus Public: Aligning Collective Types with Effective Leadership Roles

The types driven by collective feeling are perfect candidates for leadership of charitable organizations in the private sphere, such as non-profit organizations focusing on environmental conservation, where they cannot compel other citizens to contribute to their cause. They must organize their special groups with funds provided only by willing donors. Similarly, individuals guided by collective thinking make ideal candidates to lead companies, such as tech startups that prioritize innovative solutions, where they cannot impose government mandates or appropriations on other citizens to support their businesses. They must organize their companies with funds provided only by willing customers and investors.

The two situations just described—individuals driven by collective feeling leading charitable organizations and those guided by collective thinking leading companies—inherently rely on the activity that rational extroverts fear most: personal choice. The relationships between charity organizers and donors, and between business owners, labor, customers, and investors, exhibit the same forces as supply demand dynamics in free-market principles. Willing participants must step forward to fulfill any genuine need, but conflict arises when someone initiates force to compel others to conform to their desires without obtaining consent. A consensual relationship makes it win-win.

Unfortunately, many individuals with these inclinations, who could significantly benefit the country through industry and private charity, have taken the route of government force. They often occupy positions in government agencies, where they attempt to pursue their noble intentions through governmental coercion. This trend has a "brain drain" effect on private industry, redirecting talents and energies that could be more effectively and ethically employed in the private sector.

I recently attended a talk where a local congressman discussed his role in ensuring America's competitiveness with China; this struck me as a fundamental misunderstanding of the legislator's job. Politicians, thinking they are akin to CEOs, seem confused about their actual responsibilities. Their duty is to protect the people, not to engage in the intricacies of running a business or managing market competition. The people themselves, with their innovative spirit and competitive drive, are exponentially more adept at these tasks than any legislator could be. Politicians often mistakenly believe they are steering the economy like a corporate entity, overlooking the fundamental differences between government and industry.

Economic Choice and Political Voice: Understanding America's Dual Voting System

There are two ways to vote in America, separated into political and social realms. In the social realm, you exercise your vote through your dollar. Money enables the individual to make personal interest and self-preservation choices in parallel with their moral outlook. In the political realm, you cast your ballot vote for political representatives and propositions. These representatives—who act as intermediaries between you and the producers who enhance your ability to survive and pursue purpose—seek your vote. With this, there is a tendency to place more emphasis on, and emotion in, the ballot vote, steering attention but not importance away from your dollar because your dollar carries greater importance than your ballot. The dollar vote is your daily and primary means of personal choice while the ballot vote is the occasional and supplementary measure to apply coercion and force in specified areas of society.

Rational extroversion emphasizes the political process for the exact reason it is an effective means to dictate the choices of others. It diverts attention from the personal choices made through the daily dollar vote, where individuals hold the greatest influence, but a massive portion of the population fails to act in alignment with this dynamic.

The tendency of many is to demonize companies while companies only possess the power people willingly hand over in a free market. In free markets, companies can only accumulate power through their interactions with consumers and labor. However, in mixed economies, which is what we have in America today, companies can also acquire power through government intervention, which often allows them to operate independently of your daily purchasing and labor decisions.

Individuals wield their power to attain outcomes aligned with their values through commerce. Yet, because rational extroversion grounds its decision-making in external factors, it overlooks personal choice in this procedure. Consequently, the tribal mentality fuels a desire to "legally" extract resources from citizens via government action—through coercion and force, mirroring fascist principles. In line with Rand's depiction in *The New Intellectual*, Attila and the Witch Doctor symbolize the archetypes of brute force and mysticism, respectively. Attila uses physical coercion to achieve his ends, representing the ultimate pragmatist who disdains intellectual pursuits. In contrast, the Witch Doctor manipulates through spiritual and intellectual intimidation, advocating for irrational beliefs to control the masses. Together, they represent a world where coercion, either physical or psychological, is the standard operating procedure—neither of them can conceive of a world where this is not the case.

Capitalism emerges as the only political and socio-economic system that can accommodate a country of rational individuals at scale. The social realm of the country is more significant to an individual because their daily choices correlate most closely with the psychological experience of their lives. Even individuals with average to moderately below-average intelligence can engage in rational thinking when making decisions within the constraints of the immediate moment. Individuals exercise personal choice and responsibility through the capitalistic activities of working for, investing, and spending money. This system enables everyone to participate actively, underscoring the universal applicability and benefits of living in a society that values and replicates these principles.

Capitalism and Psychology: Understanding Relationships among Rational Individuals

Beyond economics, at its core, capitalism is simply relationships between and among rational individuals. It is a system in which each person's contributions, based on their unique strengths and inclinations, add significant value to a society that respects their right to exist and operate freely. In such a society, relationships are based on mutual benefit, with individuals engaging in trade to deliver value that neither could produce independently. This dynamic creates value that would not exist without these interactions, embodying the principles of supply and demand seen in free-market economies.

In psychological terms, these interactions mirror the dynamics between different psychological functions. For instance, the most differentiated function in an individual's psyche operates with greater ease and consumes most of their psychic energy or libido. Introverted functions tend to be source-oriented, generating ideas or solutions, while extroverted functions are more outwardly focused, seeking to apply or consume these ideas. This leads to a variety of relationships

341

between psychological types, some based on similarities, others on differences, and yet others on the interplay of these functions.

For example, an introverted thinking type might find a profound sense of understanding and fellowship with another introverted thinker. They can relate on a level unique to their type, sharing a common approach to processing information and problem-solving. In contrast, an introverted thinker and an extroverted feeler (see Jung's analysis of the extensive correspondence between Schiller and Johann Wolfgang von Goethe) may share certain functions, but their prioritization differs, leading both to common ground and potential conflicts in decision-making and value judgments.

A classic American example is the relationship between an extroverted thinker and an introverted thinker, akin to the dynamic between "the businessman" and "the intellectual" described by Rand. You can understand this relationship by applying the economic theory of comparative advantage, which states that trade benefits each party the most when they specialize in producing what they can do most efficiently. Introverted thinkers generate abstract concepts with ease, concepts which the extroverted thinker can then apply in a business context, benefiting both parties.

The common thread in all these examples is the perceived value by each participant, giving the relationship purpose from their perspective. Whether it is intellectual understanding, practical application, or a combination of both, each person gains something they value from the interaction. These relationships, when built on mutual respect and voluntary exchange, always result in a positive outcome, fulfilling needs and enhancing lives.

Capitalistic (i.e., rational) relationships are those not backed by physical force and rely solely on free choice; therefore, the nature of these relationships has an ethical implication. Although individuals in groups often engage in political debates with the aim of imposing their subjective views on others, through government—meaning backed by physical force—there exists a clear middle ground before reaching that stage. In capitalism, individuals can more effectively and peacefully address societal voids in ways more effective than any political action ever could.

Choice Defines Perspective: Shaping Ethics and Decision-Making

In a society that values free choice and autonomy, the concept of "owing" without explicit agreement is not an objective fact but a perception. It arises from an undefined feeling, not a factual obligation. This is a vital distinction for understanding properly ethical relationships, especially in a capitalistic framework. While individuals may feel gratitude or a sense of acknowledgment toward others, this does not translate into a debt or an obligation. True recognition and appreciation can only emerge from a personal choice to understand and value these contributions, not from any forced sense of indebtedness.

Consider the generational contributions to society. One might suggest that younger generations should acknowledge older generations for their societal contributions. However, it is a mistake to assume that someone can impose understanding or elicit any sort of genuine appreciation from someone without it. In reality, understanding is a personal journey; one cannot achieve it through the concept of obedience or duty. People must choose to understand and appreciate the contributions of others. Only through this personal choice can they genuinely acknowledge and value what others have done for them.

This principle aligns with the idea that "choice defines perspective." Imposing a sense of debt where there is no voluntary agreement contradicts the principles of autonomy and individual choice. Properly ethical relationships emerge from mutual consent and voluntary

343

interaction, contrasting sharply with those based on perceived obligations that bypass the essential process of personal understanding.

In societal dynamics, this means that there is no obligation for individuals in groups with a higher quality of life to diversify or dilute their efficiency. Any assistance or collaboration they offer should be at their discretion, based on their values and choices, not from a coerced obligation.

This principle is equally relevant in the workplace as it is in market interactions. For instance, an employer should not misconstrue their gratitude toward an employee for their contributions as an owed debt beyond the agreed-upon compensation. For example, if an employee voluntarily works overtime to complete a project, the employer might express appreciation through a bonus or recognition. However, this should not create an expectation that the employee will always work overtime without additional compensation, or that the employer will always issue a bonus for overtime worked, as either act goes beyond the original agreement. Both parties should govern the relationship based on the terms of employment and their personal choice to genuinely acknowledge each other's contributions.

The Ethical Dimensions of Diversity, Equity, and Inclusion: Freedom of Choice in Relationships

Though individuals can experience great benefit to their lives through relationships, it is never morally appropriate to force this choice on others. The purpose of America was to create a nation where individuals are free to make choices for themselves. The necessities of life will lead them toward choices in their own best interest, provided coercive forces do not interfere in the process. For many, the benefit gained from relationship leads to relationships with anyone who adds value to their lives, but there are others who may only want to pursue relationships with members of their perceived tribes regardless of shared or surplus values delivered through trade.

In any free market, competency gets compensated, and the market will eventually push out those who are non-competitive. If you intentionally limit the pools you choose from, to members of your perceived group regardless of value provided, you put yourself at a disadvantage—limiting your ability to compete with others who form relationships based strictly on value exchange.

The ethical implications here are significant. True freedom allows individuals to choose associations and interactions based on their values, leading to natural consequences. Any attempt to force interactions or obligations without consent and personal understanding is an infringement of personal autonomy and an ethical transgression. It is essential to recognize that true understanding and ethical relationships stem from voluntary choice, not from imposed obligations. This understanding is fundamental in building a society that respects individual autonomy and cultivates genuine appreciation among its members.

Some individuals, recognizing disparities in quality of life among diverse groups, advocate for forcing diversity as a political strategy. Their goal is to implement diversity, equity, and inclusion (DEI) initiatives to ensure more equitable opportunities and access to resources. Such efforts often stem from a belief in a societal debt or obligation to level the playing field. Counterintuitively, this approach to forced diversity aimed at enhancing equity reduces the overall quality of life for all, due to its inefficiency.

In this discussion, we use "equity" in its fundamental sense, emphasizing fairness in the distribution of costs and resources among individuals. This interpretation aligns with the traditional understanding of equity as fairness in transactions and interactions. It is important to note that this differs from how organizations often represent "equity" in the context of DEI, where they may imply a redistribution of resources to address historical imbalances. While the DEI context seeks to expand the term to encompass social justice objectives, here we maintain its core principle—that of ensuring fairness without compromising its underlying logic.

In this fundamental sense, the individual must bear the burden of all equity, and evading this responsibility implies asking someone else to carry these costs. When one withholds consent for this exchange, obtaining the resources in question can only occur through an act of aggression. However, the acquisition of resources from others in this way, rather than through consensual agreement, is morally reprehensible and warrants resistance. Maintaining this definition of equity is crucial to upholding the values of fairness, a cornerstone of ethical interactions in a free society where each person is accountable for their choices and actions.

The beauty of America lies in how diversity and inclusion naturally emerge from competitive free markets. In a capitalist system, people choose to engage with members from diverse groups to achieve shared goals, benefiting all involved. Individuals form these relationships willingly, free from coercion. In contrast, forced relationships encourage engagement without reason. While forced diversity may increase interactions among individuals of diverse backgrounds, these interactions lack cohesiveness in the absence of shared values.

In a noncoercive relationship, a person must identify for themselves the benefit of interacting with others. Conversely, when diversity is forced, a person is in turn forced to act in accordance with the rules while not understanding what personal benefit this diverse relationship brings. Some external authority chooses their values, which constitutes the essential characteristic of both collectivism and slavery.

In a free society it is incumbent on the individual to identify the personal characteristics which need improvement, in order for them to achieve a higher quality of life; it is not the responsibility of a person who is already enjoying a higher quality of life to bestow upon other individuals a path to that reality. This removes the struggle it takes to achieve a higher level, and, as we have seen, will not result in the necessary process that builds knowledge and self-esteem. The pursuit of values entails risk and struggle; the process must contain these elements. Only in this manner can individuals build self-esteem and, consequently, lead a healthy life.

Bridging Minds: Understanding the Psychological Diversity in Political Philosophy

To effectively bridge the gap between different psychological types, as outlined in Jung's concept of eight types each with a dominant function, a form of communication compensation is necessary. This adjustment is especially crucial in the realm of political philosophy, where implicit respect for diverse perspectives is required to coexist with minimal conflict. Understanding and respecting these differences is vital for mitigating potential disputes and ensuring a healthy, cooperative society.

To promote a healthier, more functional and cohesive society, people would do well to understand the nature of objectivity because it is where most of the conflict in opposing philosophy lies. Objectivity is only necessary in our dealings with others because communication with others is only possible through external objects. Throughout history, the idea versus the thing, or concept versus the concrete, were fierce debates between nominalism and realism, the resolution of which—credited to the French philosopher Peter Abelard—was conceptualism, which takes place in one's psychology: the subjective perspective. Before psychology, there was no understanding of a perspective. To each side, one was clearly right and the other wrong, as witnessed in the differences between the nominalist and realist views.

347

The concrete object has properties, yes; and it benefits humans to acknowledge and understand these properties, but this understanding is valuable primarily because it allows these properties to be intellectually represented as concepts. A person's psychology is the place where they engage in conceptualization, deriving concepts from their perception of concretes.

While those with extroverted perspectives contribute valuable insights, especially in fields such as research and science, it is crucial to recognize the inherent limitations of human objectivity. The notion that a human can be completely objective is a misconception. True objectivity in human endeavors is not about personal detachment or impartiality, as individual biases and perspectives invariably influence our understanding and interpretations.

However, one can approach objectivity by employing objective methods, such as the scientific method. This process operates externally to the individual, manifesting in a manner that allows others to verify and communicate the results independently. For instance, different researchers can replicate and verify the results of a scientific experiment conducted using the scientific method, regardless of their subjective views. This external validation is what lends credibility and objectivity to scientific findings, transcending individual subjectivities.

Jung notes that intellectual methods of describing personality types are inherently limited, especially when it comes to introverts accurately portraying extroverts. His reflections reveal the limitations of Abelard's one-sided approach to the nominalism-realism conflict. Abelard's failure to find a satisfactory resolution stems from his reliance on purely logical-intellectual expression, which inherently lacks the vitality of concrete reality. Jung elucidates this notion when he states:

> *There is no possibility, therefore, of finding any satisfactory, reconciling formula by pursuing the one or the other attitude. And yet, even if his mind could, man cannot remain thus*

divided, for the split is not a mere matter of some off-beat
philosophy, but the daily repeated problem of his relation to
himself and to the world. [236]

Jung also adds that while the introvert's nature lends itself well to intellectual explanation, given their focus on reason and conscious motivation, the extrovert does not exhibit the same characteristics. An extrovert's true value emerges from their engagement with the external world, a process that intellectual analysis alone cannot fully encompass. Lived experience alone fully illuminates the worth of the extrovert, as intellectual analysis falls short in this task.[237]

In this context, the parallels between the logical dichotomy of "yes or no" in rational decision-making and the moral binary of "right or wrong" from an ideational standpoint, become evident. Both realms operate within the framework of universal concepts, where decisions or judgments are not merely subjective preferences but reflections on overarching principles that transcend individual perspectives. This connection underscores a fundamental disconnect between introverts and extroverts in their approach to universal ideas. Introverts are more inclined to navigate these universal concepts through deep, reflective thought, considering the broader implications of "yes or no" and "right or wrong" within a cohesive ideological framework. Conversely, extroverts, focusing more on external realities and interactions, often find themselves at odds with this mode of conceptual thinking. They tend to engage with these binaries more in terms of immediate, practical outcomes rather than abstract principles, leading to potential misalignments in understanding and valuing the universal underpinnings of these ideas.

This dichotomy not only illuminates the diverse ways introverts and extroverts relate to the world but also the challenges in bridging

---

[236] (Jung 1923, 45-47)
[237] (Jung 1923, 150)

their perspectives, especially in matters where logical and moral judgments intersect. Introverts deeply intertwine the logical and moral dimensions of "yes or no" and "right or wrong," with each decision reflecting a broader, principled stance. For extroverts, these decisions are more about navigating the concrete realities of the moment, where the universality of principles may take a back seat to the pragmatics of action. This disparity highlights the necessity for mutual understanding and respect for differing approaches to life, acknowledging that both perspectives bring valuable insights into the collective discourse on ethics and rationality.

Jung acknowledges the contributions of extroverts in modern society:

> *We can, of course, establish that the extrovert is socially useful, that he has made great contributions to the progress of human society, and so on. But any analysis of his resources and motives will always yield a negative result, because his specific value lies in the reciprocal relation to the object and not in himself. The relation to the object is one of those imponderables that an intellectual formulation can never grasp.*[238]

Jung's comment drives home the point that rational beings only find value in concepts when these abstractions from perception relate back to tangible experiences. However, the extroverted mentality never fully ventures beyond the realm of sensations and perceptions to consciously formulate solid and valid concepts, in which, although they never become great users of their conceptual ability, their object-oriented approach retains a direct psychological relationship to the basic everyday experience of life. Jung continues,

> *Intellectual criticism cannot help proceeding analytically and bringing the observed type to full clarity by pinning down its motives and aims. But this, as we have said, results in a picture*

---

[238] (Jung 1923, 150)

> *that amounts to a caricature of the psychology of the extrovert,*
> *and anyone who believes he has found the right attitude to an*
> *extrovert on the basis of such a description would be astonished*
> *to see how the actual personality turns the description into a*
> *mockery. Such a one-sided view of things makes any adaptation*
> *to the extrovert impossible. In order to do him justice, thinking*
> *about him must be altogether excluded, while for his part*
> *the extrovert can properly adapt to the introvert only when*
> *he is prepared to accept his mental contents in themselves*
> *regardless of their practical utility. Intellectual analysis cannot*
> *help attributing to the extrovert every conceivable design,*
> *stratagem, ulterior motive, and so forth, though they have no*
> *actual existence but at most are shadowy effects leaking in from*
> *the unconscious background.*[239]

While Jung offers a detailed explanation about the limitations of intellectual criticism in accurately assessing extroverts, let us focus and elaborate on the final part of his statement. The phrase "Intellectual analysis cannot help attributing every conceivable design, stratagem, ulterior motive, and so forth," to the extrovert, illustrates how intellectual scrutiny tends to project its own interpretative framework onto the subject, thereby creating an image that may diverge significantly from the subject's true nature. This projection by analytical thinking often introduces unnecessary and unwarranted assumptions, constructing a narrative of complex motivations or strategies where simpler, more direct intentions may exist.

For instance, consider the tendency to make over-generalizations about individuals based on a single aspect of their identity or behavior. One may unjustly assume a gay person a pedophile, or they may deem someone who eschews cultural norms to be a bad person, simply because their actions or identities diverge from the norm. These prejudiced judgments, much like the caricatures created by intellectual

---

[239] (Jung 1923, 150)

criticism of extroverts, arise from an inability or unwillingness to appreciate the depth and diversity of human experience. They reveal a failure to understand that deviating from the norm is not inherently indicative of malintent or moral failing but is often a manifestation of genuine individuality and personal choice. Such examples underscore the critical importance of approaching each person with an active, inquisitive mind, free from unwarranted assumptions, to truly grasp the richness of their character and motivations.

The phrase "shadowy effects leaking in from the unconscious background" implies that, if an extrovert does exhibit complex motives or designs, these are often not the result of deliberate or conscious planning but are more likely incidental, arising from subconscious impulses. They are not central to the extrovert's approach to life; they are peripheral, almost accidental.

The implication here is that to understand an extrovert, one must move beyond intellectualization and appreciate the value that extroverts place on direct engagement with the external world. It is not that an extrovert lacks depth or complexity, but their modus operandi typically involves a more direct, spontaneous interaction with their environment rather than meticulously planned actions. Therefore, intellectual attempts to dissect and categorize extroverts often produce a distorted image that makes meaningful interaction and understanding difficult.

The passage also suggests that for effective adaptation and understanding between extroverts and introverts, there needs to be a mutual acceptance of the other's mental contents "regardless of their practical utility." In other words, the introvert needs to appreciate the extrovert's spontaneous, direct engagement with the world as a legitimate approach to life, while the extrovert needs to accept the introvert's more deliberate, analytical perspectives even if they do not immediately perceive the practical utility of such viewpoints. This mutual respect is what is meant by protecting freedom of action and thought.

Transitioning from the insightful reflections provided by Jung, we approach a crucial consideration for the structuring of ethical and political systems within American society. Jung's observations suggest a nuanced understanding of extroverts, cautioning against imposing a purely intellectual or introverted perspective on those whose engagement with the world fundamentally differs from the introverted approach. This understanding brings us to a critical juncture in our examination of American political philosophy, particularly in the formulation and application of decisions that shape our societal fabric.

Thinking at the Forefront: Shaping Ethical and Political Systems

The reality that America is a country founded for individuals and yet is mostly comprised of those who have yet to fully embody this ideal, necessitates a political leadership imbued with a deep personal understanding of the abstract concept "rights." Based on my interpretation of Jung's typology, only one psychological type possesses a firsthand and intellectual relationship with that concept, rendering them uniquely qualified to protect and uphold this principle. Thus, we should select our political leadership with this psychological compatibility in mind, ensuring the preservation of America's philosophical foundation.

Although the introverted thinker of Jung's types is best oriented to deduce and understand the principles of an objective code of ethics, the preservation of individualism and American freedom necessitates a cautious, arm's-length approach. This tempered psychological approach to ethics leaves room for independent judgment, safeguarding the necessary freedom for people to learn from their own experiences through reality, rather than taking it on faith from an external opinion or belief.

Holding individuals to an objective ethical standard without accounting for the nuanced complexities of personal understanding can be psychologically detrimental. It can lead to increased levels of stress, anxiety, and feelings of inadequacy, undermining the ego's critical function as a mediator between the internal and external worlds.

Therefore, when introverted thinkers attempt to impose their personally held moral standards as universal ethical truths, their well-intentioned efforts can paradoxically have the same coercive impact as the proselytizing methods of any purveyor of a mystical religion, thereby negatively affecting both individual and collective mental well-being. Thus, for the sake of both individual well-being and societal cohesion, we must grant individuals the freedom to make choices and learn from their experiences because true morality cannot exist in the absence of such freedom.

We must also acknowledge and apply the orientation toward individualism or collectivism in shaping any country's ethics and subsequent politics. While all the types have a right to existence, thinking, as a function, is the predominant activity required by government officials to maintain a healthy and well-functioning country; this is their primary duty to the citizenry. It is only through thinking that they can conceptualize and construct a noncontradictory, logical political system for individuals to operate within and fulfill their respective duties effectively. There is, however, a distinction between legislative and executive positions in the American system of government—lending to optimal psychological types for these distinct roles.

Abstract Thinking in Legislation: The Need for a Macro View

The American system of government consists of three branches providing a balance of power. Each branch—executive, legislative, and judicial—is different both in nature and in the thinking types which best fit these positions. Consequently, the introverted view in which abstract thinking predominates must take leadership in pursuing and maintaining the proper ethical system for America.

To perform its function properly and to its best ability, the legislative branch of government requires abstract thinking in the creation and maintenance of ethics, or what I call a **macro view**.[240] For the legislative branch to function effectively and fulfill its role, it must adhere to this macro-minded approach, a perspective that considers all stakeholders. This approach is essential for lawmakers, whose duty is to protect the interests of all citizens, whether at the federal level or within their respective districts. Operating under the principles of freedom and equality for all, macro-mindedness in legislation ensures logically consistent decision-making that aligns with the ideals of choice and individual rights.

Introverted thinking types are the ideal candidates to fill America's legislative positions. This is because individuals create law from a blank slate. The Constitution itself notwithstanding, there is no set framework or objective justification for rights beyond human imagination, and even the Constitution is amendable in certain circumstances. The introverted thinking type is most naturally capable of upholding the logical and ethical discipline required to perform these duties.

The finite range of human consciousness limits the ability to focus on more than a small number of objects at once, underscoring the importance of abstract thinking and conceptualization. Concretistic

---

[240] Macro and micro-mindedness are terms I associate with the abstract and concretistic thinking of the introverted and extroverted thinking types.

thinking confines the range of consciousness to what is directly perceivable and immediately given. Conversely, abstract thinking allows individuals to compress multiple objects, percepts, and lower-level abstractions into higher-level concepts, thereby freeing up mental capacity and enabling abstract thinkers to think accurately about an ever-increasing number of issues simultaneously. This integrated type of thinking, grounded in the adherence to guiding principles, enables long-term logical consistency. It is particularly vital for the fields of ethics, and politics, where legislators must weigh an infinite number of factors for a limitless number of people. By basing decisions on sound principles, abstract thinking facilitates the consideration of broader ethical implications and the consistent application of these principles across varied scenarios, ensuring that legislative actions align with overarching ethical standards.

Most people, by nature, tend to be micro-minded, often focusing narrowly on specific groups or immediate concerns, a mindset that leads to fragmented and inconsistent thought, behavior, and policies. An example of this is the classification of crimes into categories such as "hate crimes" or "war crimes," which are subcategories of broader offenses such as murder or assault. While the intention behind creating these categories—such as hate crimes—is to recognize and address the particularly egregious motivations behind these offenses, this approach is largely aspirational. Lawmakers have already comprehensively addressed murder; categorizing crimes based on the assumed motive of hate aims to elevate societal condemnation and deter specific harmful attitudes. However, this is often more aspirational than practical due to the inherent difficulties in reliably determining a perpetrator's exact motivations, a task often fraught with uncertainty and subjectivity. This approach risks overshadowing the actual criminal act, which should remain the primary focus of legal judgment.

In the realm of rights, similar fragmentation occurs with the division of rights into categories like "gay rights," "women's rights," or "state's rights." Such categorizations overlook the fundamental principle that rights are, and can only be for individuals, not groups. Acknowledging that children, as not yet full individuals, warrant different considerations, it is crucial to remember that rights and legal judgments should focus on individual actions and responsibilities rather than becoming entangled in the subjective interpretations of motive or group identity. An approach such as universalism, which advocates for the uniform application of rights and responsibilities to all individuals regardless of group identity, leads to more consistent and equitable legislative outcomes, aligning more closely with the principles of justice that prioritize the act or individual over perceived intentions or identities.

Two things are characteristic of this micro-minded type. The first is the difficulty those with this type pose to those aiming to validly integrate their ideas, leaving contradictions throughout their formulas, systems, and resulting worldview. The second thing is the inability to allow for the grasping of higher-level abstractions.

A proper ethical code must be general and broad, leaving space for individual choice because morality cannot exist without it. The introverted thinking type is naturally systematic, and principle based, making them the ideal thinking type for the creation and maintenance of an ethical system. The extroverted thinking type, with their inclination for concrete thinking, is a poor candidate for this role. They gravitate toward micromanaging and limiting people's choices, imposing the collective perspective on the individual. The subconscious and collective thinking of the extrovert introduces tribal mentality into ethics, systematically undermining the country's foundational principles because the extrovert neglects to acknowledge or fully comprehend the universal abstract concepts upon which only a document like the Constitution can rest. However, this is a non-issue to the concretistic thinker. They rely on others in their rationale to fill the voids resulting from their persistent violations of logic. Contradictions and inconsistencies are features of their systems, not bugs. "Somehow," or, "something"—which invariably implies "someone"—becomes the scapegoat for the systematized failures that are bound to occur.

An unprincipled ethical code results in a cyclical back and forth between personal interest groups. As each group gains political power, they pursue policies that extract resources from groups who do not elicit their empathy, in order to re-appropriate those resources to those who do. Regardless of whether they are aware, this is the ultimate result of their actions and the reason the concretistic thinking of the extrovert is undesirable in the creation of American ethical or political philosophy. The micro-mindset fails to adhere to any consistent principles beyond empathy toward the objects of their own interests. In other words, micro-minded thinkers are inclined to increase the portion of the pie for those who are of their interest, while macro-minded thinkers are inclined to increase the size of the pie for all. Both mentalities have their benefits, but where those mentalities are employed in politics makes all the difference.

Concretistic Thinking in Politics: Understanding Its Limitations

Executive roles, with their inherent structural boundaries, align well with the extroverted thinking type's aptitude for navigating and executing tasks within defined frameworks. These boundaries are essential; they provide a safeguard that counterbalances the extrovert's tendency to inconsistently uphold principles, encompassing not only ethical standards but also operational, strategic, and personal guidelines. Jung illuminates the nuances of this type, noting that their often-remarkable conscious altruism can paradoxically undermine itself due to hidden self-interest. This contradiction can lead to unprincipled actions or situations that contradict their overtly ethical intentions. They frequently find themselves entangled in the very dilemmas they aim to resolve. Their intense commitment to causes, even noble ones, can sometimes drive them to questionable methods, including deceit or manipulation, rationalized by a belief that their ends justify their means.[241]

---

[241] (Jung 1923, 323)

While such micro-mindedness might not be ideal for legislative roles, it is uniquely suited for executive and judicial positions. In fact, both extroverted and introverted types can effectively serve as judges, tasked with interpreting and applying the law. The concrete-focused mindset is well-equipped for judgment based on clear rules, while an abstract thinker excels in legal interpretation. This dynamic balance ensures that the legal system remains grounded and adaptable to various contexts.

The extroverted thinking type also excels at campaigning, generating funding, stoking emotion, engaging with the people, and decisiveness in immediate decision-making situations. These qualities, though vital in certain political arenas, do not align seamlessly with the demands of a legislative position, which requires a high degree of intellectual rigor to maintain a sound ethical-political framework. Unlike executive roles, legislative positions demand less immediate action and more thoughtful deliberation.

The extrovert is more likely to grandstand, or engage in constant criticism, characteristic of political mudslinging. Mudslinging, or the practice of making unverified, derogatory allegations to undermine opponents, is often not rooted in substantial reflection or factual analysis but instead a quick, emotionally charged reaction aimed at swaying public opinion. One can view this approach as an extension of their natural inclination to engage more with the emotive and social aspects of politics, rather than the introspective, ethical contemplation required in legislative processes.

Jung writes on the nature of extroverts, engaging with and responding to studies by Furneaux Jordan, who classifies various characterological types within his broader work, *Character as Seen in Body and Parentage*. Jordan, credited as F.R.C.S.—a title denoting his medical expertise as a Fellow of the Royal College of Surgeons—offers insights that Jung encountered through his esteemed colleague Dr. Constance Long. In "The Less Impassioned Woman," Jordan's portrayal, interpreted by Jung as the extroverted woman, sheds light on why those with extroverted tendencies might gravitate toward activities such as mudslinging. Jung notes,

> *Her whole demeanor indicates a character that by its very nature must be called extroverted. The continual criticizing, which is never based on real reflection, is an extroversion of a fleeting impression that has nothing to do with real thinking. I remember a witty aphorism I once read somewhere: "Thinking is difficult, therefore let the herd pass judgment!" Reflection demands time above everything: hence the man who reflects has no opportunity for continual criticism. Incoherent and inconsequential criticism, dependent on tradition and authority, reveals the absence of any independent reflection; similarly the lack of self- criticism and the dearth of independent ideas betray a defect in the function of judgment.*[242]

Here Jung emphasizes the extrovert's aversion toward independent thought, highlighting a preference for responding critically—often baselessly—while dedicating little time to reflective thinking, which is crucial for the introverted thinking type. The dependence on tradition and authority underscores the extrovert's reliance on existing frameworks, which provide the external basis that justify their fleeting impressions of the collective ethos.

Jordan's portrayal of "The Less Impassioned Man," interpreted by Jung as the extroverted man, offers another comprehensive view of the extrovert's typical characteristics, a view that was significant enough for Jung to include in his analysis within *Psychological Types,* despite some disagreements with Jordan's interpretations. To better understand these characteristics and their implications in a political context, let us consider a paraphrased overview of Jordan's observations, which Jung found noteworthy for their insights into the extroverted mindset:

---

[242] (Jung 1923, 146)

The individual in question often exhibits a temperamental and unpredictable demeanor, characterized by irritability, fussiness, and a tendency to complain, and criticize. Despite frequently making harsh judgments about others, he remains self-satisfied. His confidence in his judgment and projects remains unwavering, even when they are flawed or fail. Reminiscent of a remark by Sidney Smith about a notable statesman, this individual believes himself capable of any task, regardless of its relevance or his expertise. He tends to dismiss ideas either as false or as common knowledge and struggles to share the spotlight with others.

This person typically shows maturity at an early age and has a strong inclination toward administrative roles, often excelling as a public servant. He shows equal interest in minor details as in major decisions within his organizations. Socially, he is known for his alertness, wit, and ability to respond sharply. He actively seeks to be visible and involved, driven by a belief in his own dynamism and eloquence.

Although not often the originator of innovative ideas or paths, he is adept at following and implementing existing ones. His preferences lean toward traditional or widely accepted beliefs and policies, though he may occasionally admire his own non-conformist thoughts. His intellect, less swayed by emotion, allows him to form broad and just views in various areas of life. His conduct is moral and principled, but his eagerness for immediate impact can sometimes backfire.

In public settings, if not given a specific role, he seeks attention through trivial requests or actions, revealing a need for recognition. He often takes on tasks outside his expertise, convinced of his public image as a devoted servant of communal welfare. He is skilled at influencing others through his rhetoric, even if he personally remains unaffected by it. Quick to grasp the nuances of his era or political party, he adeptly addresses threats, organizes efforts, and confronts adversaries. He is always busy with various initiatives and plans, aiming to impress or startle society. Viewed as a savior by some, he relishes this role, believing deeply in his importance to the public.[243]

The goal of this examination was to focus on ethics because it directly influences the country's politics. The important ethical implication to remember when understanding the nature of the two thinking types is that extroverted thinking rests on the altruist premise, and collectivity is an automatized feature of this type. Their decision-making falls victim to the fallacy of the frozen abstraction and projects their subconsciously abstracted ideals on all. They fail to distinguish between the man-made and the metaphysical and make ethical decisions within a vacuum where they ignore the individual—the source of all value. To this type, the individual can be sacrificed for the group if they believe the group will be objectively better off, ignoring the fact that better off for the group necessarily means better off for the individuals who comprise it, and ignoring the fact that people must choose from the options they have preselected in order for their plans to succeed.

The fundamental limitation of concretistic thinking, characteristic of the extroverted thinking type, particularly in leadership roles within American politics, lies in their inherent struggle with interpreting facts in relation to the individual. Jung observes:

> *So far as the recognition of facts is concerned this orientation is naturally of value, but not as regards the interpretation of facts and their relation to the individual. Concretism sets too high a value on the importance of facts and suppresses the freedom of the individual for the sake of objective data.*[244]

---

[243] (Jung 1923, 148-149)
[244] (Jung 1923, 388)

This limitation is particularly problematic in the context of American governance, where the understanding of how facts impact individuals is essential for creating policies that respect and uphold individual rights and freedoms. This mindset cannot align with a morality of individual rights, which means we cannot reasonably expect individuals with this mindset to behave ethically in governmental roles without strict guidelines and restrictions.

Unalienable Rights: The Non-Negotiable Foundation of American Ethics

Contrary to the widely held belief that the foundational ethics of America, as encapsulated in its founding principles, are open to debate, these ethics are firmly rooted in the concept of unalienable rights. This core principle asserts that an individual's right to existence is beyond the purview of others' opinions or decisions, manifesting in practical terms that a person's life and choices must remain free from the imposition of others' preferences or desires.

This principle applies equally to various scenarios, ranging from a man's refusal of vaccines to a woman's assertion of her reproductive choices, underlining that each person's autonomy is paramount. Indeed, while people may naturally gravitate toward separate groups, the healthiest society is one in which a robust ethical system prevents the initiation of force against individuals, with strict legal penalties for transgressions. In cases where individuals cross these boundaries, it is imperative for authorities to act and impose penalties, including severe ones, if necessary, because self-defense constitutes the highest moral right. This stance finds its foundation in the stark reality echoed in Founding Father Patrick Henry's impassioned declaration, "Give me liberty, or give me death!" vividly encapsulating the essence of American ethics: a resolute affirmation that the pursuit of liberty, as a manifestation of one's right to life, is paramount and indomitable. This perspective underscores that the right to life, backed by the inherent force of self-preservation, is fundamental and non-negotiable, guiding not only individual choices but also shaping the ethical system that governs society.

In cases of disagreement over these foundational ethics, a standoff becomes the only viable option, reflecting the seriousness with which these rights are, and must be, upheld in American society. The right to life and autonomy forms the bedrock of American ethics, ensuring that we respect and protect individual freedom, even in the face of conflicting opinions or societal pressures.

What sets America apart from other countries in the world and makes it transcendent is the fact its foundation rests on the rationally introverted view of ethics. These psychological types have a definite sense of self, leading such individuals to value freedom and personal choice highly, qualities not seen across all the types. Anyone desiring to live in and maintain America as a free country rooted in individual independence—as an embodiment of the principles explicated within its founding documents—can never compromise on this perspective, because introverted thinking is both the method and source of the logical principles securing political freedom for its citizens. Any compromise on this for any non-evidentiary reasons (i.e., mystical beliefs) is a complete compromise of the country's ethics. There can be no debate about this because America is the result of a fundamental arbitrary choice vis-à-vis how its citizens desire to live in a state with others. This choice is incontrovertible. Americans choose individualism; counter to the orientation toward collectivism associated with primitive groups. Any coercive attempt to convert, or even subvert that choice without an appeal to reason, constitutes an act of aggression, requisite of extreme prejudice because the ideologies are antithetical and incompatible.

Guardians of Rationality: Introverted Thinking's Role in Shaping America

In Ayn Rand's essay, "The Comprachicos," she explains that the goal of the modern-day comprachicos is to produce a child who functions in a concretistic manner; even when this objective fails, the process often yields rational adults who are disinterested in engaging in societal functions, such as participating in government:

> *The comprachicos succeed in either case. The independent children, who resist the conditioning and preserve some part of their rationality, are predominantly shunted, or self-exiled, into the physical sciences and allied professions, away from social, philosophical or humanistic concerns. The social field—and thus society's future—is left to the "adjusted," to the stunted, twisted, mutilated minds the comprachicos' technique was intended to produce.[245]*

I submit that ethics is the most vital of societal functions because it defines the proper role for a country's politics, and a society where people must interact with each other is the only thing that makes a discussion of psychological orientation relevant. This is because people must use both introverted and extroverted functions to function.

However, this does not imply that one perspective is incorrect while the other is correct from the standpoint of the individual. Yet, a government must establish and enforce an objective definition of right and wrong within the state it governs. In doing so, through politics, it must clearly outline the unlawful behaviors through which citizens can interact with one another.

While negotiation is a part of everyday interaction between people—where one chooses to deal or not deal with others according to their

---

[245] (Rand, The Comprachicos 1970, 75)

own free will—a political philosophy cannot justly have this arbitrary character. The institution of government exercises a monopoly over legalized force, and because of this responsibility, those in charge of politics must take the ethics at its core very seriously if they are to prioritize and maintain respect for individual rights. Many people of all of Jung's psychological types will be concerned, as they should, but most do not possess the logical discipline to think about the abstract concept of rights properly, and thereby keep the tribal tendencies of concretistic thinking at bay.

It is for these reasons that the introverted thinking type must engage in and bear the burden of thought for American politics because concretistic thinking in that area poses a direct threat to the country's ethics. Accepting this burden is no selfless act of benevolence on their part; it is in defense of their right to free thought and action. Any benefit to others is merely a byproduct of an individual's fight for rights as a rational human.

In a rational society, the people entrust political leadership to those who demonstrate reasoned and principled governance. Americans who value reason and individual rights naturally gravitate toward leaders who reflect these values. Sadly, the current American political landscape often falls short of these ideals. The ideal ethical framework for America aligns with the principles of introverted thinking, emphasizing logic, individual rights, and a system that respects the autonomy of every citizen.

There is only one set of ethics proper for America, and they are the ethics of the introverted thinking type.

An Alternative Perspective

I would like to ask the conceptual thinker to consider an alternative perspective of my argument for a moment. If we are to accept that individuals reduce life to a power game with others because they believe it has no inherent meaning, we may comprehend the perspective that existence primarily revolves around bias and power dynamics. This perspective is gaining ground in today's public discourse, which increasingly lacks a commitment to full-fledged individualism or Christian ethics.

Traditional individualism, emphasizing moral worth and autonomy, and Christian ethics, providing a moral compass, counterbalance such nihilistic views by offering frameworks for meaningful personal growth and choices. However, the current societal trend, which adopts selective aspects of American individualism while neglecting core tenets like personal responsibility and individual happiness, leads to a fragmented and inherently nihilistic worldview. In this context, people perceive life simply as a series of power struggles, without attributing deeper meaning to it. Thus, the absence of a comprehensive embrace of individualism or Christian ethical structure inevitably steers us toward viewing life through the lens of bias and power dynamics.

Engaging with this alternative perspective requires us to momentarily adopt the skeptic's viewpoint, not to endorse it but to dissect and understand its implications. While I affirm the values of individualism, exploring skepticism serves as a method to illuminate the reasoned foundations beneath this construct. It is through this lens that we challenge the skeptic's dismissal, revealing the depth of understanding that supports individualism, and, though to a lesser extent, the construct of Christian ethics as well. This approach is not a concession to skepticism but an affirmation of the robustness of American individualism's framework when scrutinized with rigorous logic.

If I adopt the skeptic's perspective, I will affirm my bias toward the producer of goods and services, because without them, no life can sustain itself—most importantly, not even my own. This is why I play the role of producer for myself. But because I can also consume what others produce, my affinity for, and bias toward the producer extends to the productive: all those who produce a surplus of goods and services made available to me, aiding in sustaining my life. The more production they are responsible for organizing, the higher my bias, as the more they enable me, and subsequently others, to sustain life in general.

Accordingly, I hold a bias against individuals who aim to take from me and offer an unsatisfactory return. These could be non-contributing members of society who rely on others' efforts, unfair traders engaging in exploitative practices, or overreaching governments or bureaucracies that impose disproportionate burdens. Such entities decrease my ability to sustain my life and treat my production as their property to do with as they please.

Before delving deeper into the societal shifts influenced by production and consumption, it is crucial to acknowledge why these concepts are central to our discourse. At the heart of human existence, production and consumption are not merely economic terms; they are the most fundamental aspects of life, underpinning everything from our daily survival to the complexities of global economies. They represent the primal actions of creating and utilizing resources, actions upon which all societies rest. This intrinsic link between production and consumption and the fabric of human life forms the foundation of our argument. Recognizing their primacy helps us understand not just the economic, but also the ethical, social, and psychological dynamics that govern human interactions and societal structures. It is against this backdrop of fundamental necessity that we explore the evolving nature of community and individual responsibility, highlighting how these elemental forces shape our values, relationships, and collective futures.

Given that production is one of the two most essential motions in life, why would anyone ever want to destroy a producer who creates value that would otherwise not exist? That production can only aid in their lives or at the very least have no negative bearing on their lives at all. It is for these reasons that any desire to destroy a producer is irrational, but oddly, this is what we see when a producer is unwilling to provide their production at the price the consumer desires. If the consumer is unwilling to pay the price set by the producer, they are free to obtain production through other means.

The only argument one can provide at this point is that the producer must produce for others, whether he or she chooses to or not. Hence, we are back to the fundamental moral choice between individualism and collectivism. Is the individual an end in themselves? Or is the individual the means to others' ends? Is it right for the group to dispose of the individual as if they were a sacrificial animal whenever they do not receive what they want from that individual? The answer to these questions is either yes or no; and whichever you conclude is the moral premise from which all your views on economic, social, and political structures will inevitably stem.

This pivotal choice between valuing the individual's autonomy, versus subsuming it under the group's needs, leads us to examine the broader implications of our beliefs and the systems we uphold. It is here that skepticism emerges as a critical stance in any questioning of the validity and origins of these societal constructs.

Skepticism, when employed constructively, urges us to scrutinize and understand the deeper reasons behind our beliefs and systems. Yet, when skepticism turns cynical and overly critical, dismissing the value of these constructs without seeking to understand or engage with their foundational logic, it veers toward nihilism. This brand of skepticism views the constructs of individualism and Christian ethics not as frameworks developed through reason but as arbitrary impositions lacking inherent meaning.

Alternatively, when individuals fail to challenge these foundational beliefs and accept them without scrutiny, they pave the way for a more insidious transformation. The uncritical acceptance of pre-packaged beliefs or ideas without individual examination lays the groundwork for what becomes mysticism. Mysticism, in this context, arises when these unexamined ideas, filled with a mixture of essential and non-essential elements, start to take on a life of their own, guiding beliefs and actions in a way that disconnects from rational, individual analysis.

For example, the principles of Christian ethics, intended to guide moral behavior within large communities, reveal how a gap can emerge between the foundational reasons for actions and the actions themselves. This gap, bridged by a mystical teaching approach, prioritizes adherence to doctrine over understanding, leading individuals to follow commandments without fully grasping their purpose. The directive from 2nd Thessalonians: 6-12 embodies this phenomenon, encapsulating the fundamental concepts of production and consumption within a moral and traditional context. It exemplifies the shift from rationale-driven teachings to commands that require obedience, thereby highlighting the drift toward action without understanding.

> But we command you, brethren, in the name of our Lord Jesus Christ, that you withdraw from every brother who walks disorderly and not according to the tradition which he received from us. For you yourselves know how you ought to follow us, for we were not disorderly among you; nor did we eat anyone's

bread free of charge, but worked with labor and toil night and day, that we might not be a burden to any of you, not because we do not have authority, but to make ourselves an example of how you should follow us.

For even when we were with you, we commanded you this: If anyone will not work, neither shall he eat. For we hear that there are some who walk among you in a disorderly manner, not working at all, but are busybodies. Now those who are such we command and exhort through our Lord Jesus Christ that they work in quietness and eat their own bread.[246]

This Bible story serves as a poignant lesson on the ethics of production and consumption, while giving instruction on the social obligations of community members regarding how to treat those who consume without producing. However, when teaching becomes commanding, the student accepts the commandments as duty rather than reason; and without intellectually connecting reason to action, one remains ignorant.

The magical experience of ideation, deeply embedded in mysticism, arises from the psychological processes that serve as a bridge between the sensory and intellectual realms—linking the objective with the subjective. One can choose to revel in the mystical allure of how an idea spontaneously appears, overlooking the intricate details beneath, or alternatively, delve into these underlying details to demystify the idea, thereby embracing a rational approach that dispels the magical aspect.

The tendency toward mysticism, particularly resonant in the psychology of extroverts, reflects a departure from critical examination, favoring feeling over reasoned thought. Conversely, skepticism, while posing as a guardian of rationality, mirrors this departure by adopting a stance

---

[246] (Holy Bible - New King James Version n.d.)

of perpetual doubt. As Leonard Peikoff astutely observes, the mystic "just knows" whatever he wishes to believe, while the skeptic "just doesn't know" whatever he chooses to doubt.[247] Both rely on feeling as a guide rather than evidence or reason, highlighting a crucial denial of reason's capacity to grasp reality. This parallel between mysticism's acceptance without evidence and skepticism's rejection without examination underscores the complex interplay of understanding and belief, challenging extroverts to navigate these waters with a mindful embrace of reason.

The extrovert, because of their tendency toward concretism, prioritizes the object in the subject object relationship. When they identify themselves with an object, they work to increase the value of that object and believe their value increases as a result. Altruism, and the closest humans can come to it, collectivism, results from the mysticism in such ideas as God, the State, society, the global community, etc. This is why Rand arrives at the conclusion that reason conflicts with mysticism as well as with altruism; these are contradictory concepts that cannot coexist.

Furthermore, it is possible for individuals to rely solely on reason, unlike mystical perspectives which oscillate between rational thought and mystical belief. Only through abstract thinking can individuals diagnose these contradictions, yet such abstraction is challenging for those predisposed to concrete thinking, highlighting the enduring struggle between concretism and the pursuit of reasoned personal understanding.

Understanding the dynamics of production and consumption required to sustain life underscores the significance of one's immediate surroundings. For instance, in a tight-knit community, the support of others may mitigate the loss of a job by one member, illustrating the practical application of these philosophical concepts. This realization

---

[247] (Peikoff 1991, 183)

brings into focus the crucial role played by those in proximity—family, community, and acquaintances—who contribute directly and regularly to one's well-being. These are the individuals and groups with whom we build reciprocal relationships, the value they bring often referred to as "social equity." Social equity is the value accumulated from mutual support, trust, and cooperation. It is this social equity that makes these groups more likely to provide support in times of need, such as when one faces a shortfall in personal production and requires assistance for survival. What we begin to see here, from this mutual interdependence and support, evident in the dynamics of production and consumption, are the key reasons why many people, when asked about their core values, give the immediate response of "family" and "community." Thus, we do not just experience emotional connections with family and community; we construct these emotional connections based on the dynamics of survival and prosperity, blending our deepest affections with the practical necessities of life.

"**Package deals**" are bundles of concepts and associated details that are often accepted without full awareness or understanding of all their components. Accepting a package deal is like accepting a preselected set of beliefs or ideas without examining each element individually. Rational extroversion accepts these packages while maintaining obliviousness to the full and necessary detail of their contents. For example, when a person says they value family, a concept, what they mean even without understanding the underlying detail, are the essential reasons I have listed above: the benefits of mutual support, trust, and cooperation that define social equity. However, non-essential contents, such as the belief that a traditional family structure is the only valid one, might also exist in the package of that idea in their minds. These non-essentials are not integral to the core value of "family" but are often subconsciously associated with it. This person has automated their response, and if they are unable to limit the underlying detail to essential information only, these non-essential contents will continue to be a part of their conceptualization of family until they consciously correct it. Abstract thought enables individuals to extract such non-essential information from concepts, leaving only the essentials, thus enhancing one's ability to apply ideas.

In package dealing, what we see is mysticism in its embryonic form: concepts filled with inaccurate and non-essential information. The idea of "self" first extends to the immediate family, and then beyond mother and father to extended family, and then to immediate community, and then out into all relevant points in between, until reaching the individual's own world-embracing idea: God, society, human race, nature, etc. These are all examples of Lévy-Bruhl's participation mystique: where one experiences partial identity with objects or groups they identify with and begins to lose the ability to distinguish themselves from others. All forms of mysticism exhibit this, but each type has distinct preferences.

One type gravitates toward the idea, via concretistic feeling, while the other gravitates toward the sensuously perceptible, via concretistic thinking. These groups can be interpreted, drawing on Ayn Rand's concepts, as the "mystics of spirit" and "mystics of muscle." "Mystics of spirit," or concretistic feelers, prioritize ideas to such an extent that they overlook the tangible world, viewing abstract concepts as the only reality. Conversely, "mystics of muscle," or concretistic thinkers, focus on the physical realm, disregarding the significance of abstract ideas that shape and give meaning to the physical world. Both groups, in their extremes, exhibit a form of mysticism that neglects part of reality—the "mystics of spirit" by floating away from the concrete, and the "mystics of muscle" by adhering too closely to it. Each fails to fully embrace reason's capacity to bridge the abstract and the concrete, leading to a skewed perception of reality that lacks the integration offered by a balanced, reasoned approach. Succinctly, their reliance on either aspect to the exclusion of the other displays a departure from reason, highlighting the need for a harmonious balance that fully acknowledges both the ideational and the tangible. All who lack the ability to track the details packaged within an idea directly back to themselves, engage in mysticism of some sort.

This juxtaposition of extroversion against the backdrop of skepticism and mysticism reveals the challenge in understanding the complex interplay of societal constructs. Through this exploration, it becomes evident that skepticism, much like mysticism, emerges from a similar root—a departure from reason that can lead to a nihilistic worldview. However, by adopting a reasoned, skeptical lens, we not only dissect the superficial layers of these worldviews but also affirm the robustness of individualism as a foundational pillar of modern civilization. Grounded in reason, this framework requires individuals to engage in transactional interactions, consciously acknowledging and exchanging value. Herein lies the essence of our societal constructs: a balanced negotiation between the producer and the consumer, the introvert, and the extrovert, each playing their role within a rational framework.

The extrovert lacks personal identity, or otherwise stated—in Jungian terms—their personal identity is unconscious while their conscious identity is collective. Given this, if we are to embrace extroversion as a personal identity, it is only the introvert's desire to trade with the extrovert that can provide a sustainable balance of value exchange within a rational country. The government should not negotiate terms universally, as with the example of entitlement programs, especially not from the extrovert's perspective, because the extrovert is the consumer of personal values, and the introvert, the producer. Negotiations should only occur directly between the beneficiary and benefactor of values, where the benefactor perceives something in the beneficiary that inspires them to invest in the recipient as an act of will. The extrovert must earn everything they desire on the open market through direct negotiation with the introvert because those who do not produce for themselves exist at the mercy or pleasure of those who do.

So, in conclusion, the answer to whether America should allow the perspectives of nihilists, skeptics, or mystics to dictate its norms and values in a top-down manner is, no. America must not permit these perspectives to dictate its trajectory. Hence, our discourse advocates not for rigid mandates that shape America's contours or for the undue scrutiny of any specific group, such as extroverts; instead, we call for the establishment of basic, universally applicable standards. However, these standards should be set from the introvert's perspective, insofar as they rest on reason, and can act as ethical guideposts. The intent of these standards is that they are sufficiently broad enough to accommodate a diversity of expressions and behaviors that, although they may not seem aligned with these principles on the surface, do not fundamentally contravene them. Through this balanced methodology, we aim to construct an American societal framework that both respects the individual and guides the collective toward a more ethical, productive, and understanding future.

Artificial Intelligence Domination

★ ★ ★

With the increase of machine learning, generative artificial intelligence (AI), automation, and algorithm-driven processes used today, there is much hand-wringing about the impacts of these technologies on society. An abundance of journalistic pieces focuses on the fears people have about these processes and their ethical implications. My assumption is there is concern about removing so-called human decision-making from the loop, with people fearing that computers will replace humans at some point. However, the takeover they envision will not result from robots or technology. The greatest threat of AI to American culture lies within the extroverted thinking type.

A computer cannot engage in valuation; it can only execute the processes programmed into it. Unlike machines, humans possess the ability to value—to assess, judge, and prioritize based on subjective experiences, profoundly shaped by the awareness of one's mortality. This awareness of life's finitude instills a sense of urgency and significance in human choices, a necessity that not only distinguishes but will always differentiate humans from technology, ensuring that machines will never fully replace human judgment.

The extroverted thinking type, like technology, is programmatic; but unlike a device constructed of transistors, circuit boards, and microprocessors, extroverted thinkers are also mortal beings, who must inherently engage in valuation. This psychological type is the original and most sophisticated AI ever to exist. While people may not perceive the extroverted thinker as technology, this mirrors their underlying functionality, and if the introverted thinking type does not assume the role of ethical programmer, the extroverted thinking type inadvertently programs themselves, leading to automated rather than reflective decision-making processes.

Human survival depends on intelligence, and quality of life depends on the magnitude and multitude of ideas sustaining and improving it. Societies witness improvements only when individuals or organizations create and apply innovative ideas or enhance the efficiency of existing ones. The possibility of innovative ideas is limitless, but increased efficiency is finite. Without innovative ideas, groups experience a regression toward the mean. There are examples throughout history where societies became stagnant, reaching points where the dominant culture was unable to maintain its progressive state and direction, causing an overwhelming minority to bring about some sort of revolution. The Enlightenment era is one of these examples.

A group's culture, manifested through either extroverted thinking or feeling, reveals itself in the dominant method in which the group approaches objects and objective data. But because the nature of rational extroversion is collective and appears in culture as oppressive to the individual, it is often difficult to distinguish one rationally extroverted type from the other. Furthermore, when observing this relationship regarding only the thinking function, extroverted thinking sits opposed to introverted thinking because extroverted feeling is the cultural expression of introverted thinking. Thus, introverted thinking gives direction to the culture while extroverted thinking receives direction from it.

The extroverted thinker often presents as individualistic, but this impression is misleading; they rely on the dominant culture because of their object-oriented attitude. In other words, they do not impose themselves on culture, they result from it. They organize ideas obtained from others to acquire the objects of their desire rather than abstracting concepts from the raw facts themselves. Adherence to ethical principles is only a result of their compliance with the dominant culture, not necessarily from any understanding of the underlying reasons behind these ethical principles. Real thinking does not occur in their conscious mind, only memorization of the steps used in the borrowed idea applied to achieve their goal.

In many cases, the extroverted thinker often becomes more proficient than the concept's creator in executing the steps, but they do not create anything new in the world of thought. Instead, they repeat the same steps until they adopt another method from someone else. With this attitude, the type is proficient at obtaining material goods. The status associated with material objects carries all the meaning for this type, because for them, there is little distinction between the concrete object and the abstract ideas leading to or associated with it.

For example, if one were to enter a bank with nothing and exit with a bag of cash, the material object—cash, without context, carries with it the symbol of success. Who is to say this is not a legitimate businessperson or wealthy individual? But if you learn that the person robbed the bank at gunpoint and shot two people in the process, your perception of the situation may change. However, this change in perception is a result of your ethical development, reflecting a complex interplay of thinking about others' feelings or feeling in response to others' thoughts.

I am not at all insinuating that the extroverted thinking type is inherently evil, only that they do not make the logical connections necessary to construct or understand a full ethical framework. A deep understanding of ethical nuance is not instinctively apparent to them, just as it is not to a child who never learned the reason it is important to respect others. They need the rules and associated penalties of the culture to continually condition and program them, in the same way we must teach and reinforce the concept of rights to new generations and immigrants. Because all cultures do not share the same reverence for independence, American culture requires assimilation. While the extroverted thinking type's execution of the culture's program can come off as synthetic, or even theatrical at times, they can achieve ethical behavior in no other way.

Culture and education, rather than biology, shape ethics. The traditions of the group condition us to treat each other in certain ways due to the lessons learned throughout history, and many of these traditions have roots in reason. Therefore, to ensure respect for human life and the attainment of ethical behavior in a society, society must always guide the extroverted thinking type through laws and consequences.

One could never say there was a time when America was a fully rational country, but what is disappointing is that conceptual, abstract thinking in the country's leadership has been on the decline since its inception. Without an education rooted in reason, or simply, a moral education, learning institutions increasingly promote extroverted thinking to produce more extroverted thinkers.

Through education, the goal should be to produce a person who can employ a conceptual thinking process, not necessarily to create an introverted thinking type. This sets the expectation for conceptual thinking in the culture regardless of the person's preferred functions, establishing a standard from which logically consistent laws originate. Some will gravitate toward reason, but history shows us many will not, and that is why those who choose reason must retain the role of ethical programmer for America.

PART IV

APPLICATION

In society, individuals divide into two groups: those who think, and those who do. However, full actualization of potential lies in uniting the two.

In this book, the objective has been to juxtapose the theories of Rand and Jung in Part II, then delineate my own insights in Part III. This concluding section focuses on bridging theory with practice, demonstrating the application of concepts introduced earlier.

I recognize that while some readers may value the presentation of abstract ideas, there are others who seek actionable steps to execute. My aim here is to unite theory and practice, challenging the commonplace yet flawed notion of severing and isolating the two.

Much of my inspiration in authoring this book has been to engage those keen on exploring how psychology underpins ethics and politics, showcasing pathways for personal and societal betterment. My approach is rooted in conceptual thinking, the most lucid means possible. Furthermore, it is not my intention to coerce or impose authority, instead, I only offer methods and suggestions for individual and collective action.

Until now, I have minimized personal anecdotes to maintain an objective stance. However, in this section, I share firsthand experiences to illustrate the practical application of the concepts that inform my philosophy. Herein, I detail techniques I employ in my life and in interactions with various psychological types.

It is my belief that all humans are in pursuit of a fulfilling life, and the most effective means to achieve this end will always be of interest. This book aims to provide a foundation for such a pursuit, blending deep theoretical insights with practical steps for living a principled and purposeful life.

Embrace a Non-Mystical, Objective Moral Philosophy

A moral philosophy steeped in mysticism fails to equip individuals for navigating the complexities of our modern, technologically advanced reality. Such philosophies foster a dichotomy between reality and spirituality, suggesting no intersection exists between the two realms. Religious discourse often echoes this division, which contrasts the material with the spiritual. Kantian philosophy also delineates these realms similarly through the distinction between the noumenal and phenomenal worlds.

Moral philosophy serves as a guiding framework for daily decision-making. Absent a coherent philosophy, individuals lack a defined identity; without an objective foundation, they resort to an incoherent amalgamation of disparate beliefs. Adopting an objective moral philosophy empowers individuals to anchor their lives in consistent principles, facilitating unified and coherent decision-making.

Mysticism-based moral philosophies compel adherence to externally derived precepts, disrupting the direct engagement with reality. This approach restricts individuals to lives constrained by pre-established boundaries, rather than lives crafted from personal reasoning.

Historically, mysticism has dominated American moral thought, its preference being Christianity.

However, human judgment, inherently subjective and influenced by individual perspective, necessitates a rational approach to survival; reason stands as the sole reliable tool for navigating and understanding the world. Thus, it is imperative to choose not just an objective moral philosophy, but one free from mysticism and rooted in reason. To this end, I advocate for Objectivism—a philosophy that champions reason, individualism, and rational self-interest as the cornerstone of ethical living.

Some People Require Direction: Give It to Them

It is a challenging notion for conceptual thinkers to embrace, but not everyone operates on a conceptual level. Some are far from doing so, and yet this does not necessarily decrease their value in any other area except in the realm of thought, because to this type, thought can only be mystical. Demonstrating the practical application of your ideas through lived experiences is the most effective way to bridge the gap between the abstract and the tangible for such individuals. Thoughts gain value only when transformed into actions; without action, they remain abstract and untested—nothing.

Moreover, it is never morally appropriate to force someone to adopt your values. Coercion transforms what could be a meaningful adoption of principles into mere dogmatism, where the individual acts without understanding or personal conviction—merely following orders. However, there is a place for intuitive action, which, even when initially vague, can lead to a deeper, conscious understanding over time. This progression from intuition to insight is a crucial aspect of learning.

Given the propensity of those struggling with ethical concepts to latch onto any presented idea, it behooves conceptual thinkers to offer direction, doing so as a form of preemptive self-defense. Lay it out for them, explain it, judge them by it, but never force them to adopt it. For some, this guidance may kickstart a journey toward solving more complex problems. For others, it might mean adopting these concepts secondhand, merely as tools for navigating an ethically structured society.

Speak to Sensation

The responsibility of bridging the communicative gap between different thinking types often falls to the conceptual thinker. This is because, regardless of one's orientation toward thinking, all thought processes must maintain a relationship with sensation. Introverted thinking engages with ideas on a conceptual level, constructing theories from observations or experiences. In contrast, extroverted thinking is more concretistic because of its object-oriented approach, operating directly with tangible precepts and focusing on the external assembly of facts.

Avoid the trap of projection; do not assume the person you are communicating with shares your intellectual approach. While commonalities may exist, there are instances in which aligning your communication with sensory details can significantly enhance understanding.

To achieve this, emphasize the tangible: objects, actions, and their consequences. For an extroverted thinker, factual contexts often interweave with the essence of an idea, making abstract discussion seem aimless. This mode of communication, while natural to them, can be mentally exhausting, banal, and dull to the introvert, whose preference is for ideas to convey specific points directly.

In discussions where abstract concepts fall short, leverage the tangibility of your ideas by relating them to sensory experiences or concrete examples. This method effectively communicates the underlying impression of your thoughts to an extroverted thinker, using their affinity for sensation to your advantage and creating an "idea equivalent."

Always Judge on Consequences

Always judge people on the logical conclusions of their statements and actions. Never suspend disbelief to ignore the inevitable result of what they are saying and doing. Even if they do not see the flaw in their argument, you do. Even if you are in error, a fully rational person is willing to forgo a potential benefit when the validity or logic of the benefit is not clearly understood or rationalized. Rand encapsulates this principle eloquently, stating,

> *When I disagree with a rational man, I let reality be our final arbiter; if I am right, he will learn; if I am wrong, I will; one of us will win, but both will profit.*[248]

This perspective champions the notion that, regardless of the outcome, both parties stand to gain through learning and adaptation.

You are the only person directly aware of what matters to you; when faced with propositions that work against your interests, remember that acquiescence serves only the proposer. It is only they who benefit from your suspended judgment. Those seeking a compromise often employ this stalling tactic when you have nothing to gain. Subsequently, not only can they benefit from you elevating their judgment above your own, but they also benefit from your unwarranted deliberation, and many times on a false premise. It is critical to trust your discernment, not theirs, and cut them off at the pass, swiftly addressing the logical or tangible implications of their suggestions.

---

[248] (Rand, Atlas Shrugged 1957, 1023)

This approach is particularly pertinent in political discourse, where special interest groups, disconnected from your concerns, may claim to act in your best interest. Actively evaluate their arguments based on the anticipated consequences, compelling them to address the practical outcomes of their proposals. By insisting on this direct confrontation, you not only accelerate the dialogue but also ensure that the implications of their ideas are personally relevant, even if it means you must enforce these consequences. Such scrutiny tests the integrity of their logic and hastens the revelation of any hidden agendas.

Always Impose Consequences

Proper ethics dictates one should never initiate force against another person, but it is important to remember force undergirds everything, including defense in addition to aggression. It is morally appropriate to defend yourself at any time, and you should never hesitate to do so, issuing suitable consequences when necessary.

Individuals learn in diverse ways; whereas conceptual learners integrate knowledge through both conceptual understanding and perceptual experience, perceptual learners depend on direct experiences and tangible examples. For those heavily influenced by tangible examples and cultural norms, experiencing consequences is crucial for their understanding of acceptable behavior. Shielding individuals from the repercussions of their actions does them a disservice, reinforcing a dependency on others to rectify their mistakes, and inhibits their personal growth and understanding of responsibility. This reliance implies that individuals who primarily rely on cultural norms and personal interactions to evaluate acceptable behavior often require consequences more frequently to facilitate their learning process.

When people exhibit undesirable behavior, you are not benefiting them or anyone else by shielding them from consequences. When people are shielded from the consequences of their actions, especially with an irrational or concrete bound mentality, they experience you, or "people," being the fix for any problem they encounter. If you are willing to take sole responsibility, that is fine, but that person will not recognize the elements of responsibility because you have failed to let them learn them. Due to your actions, they will always expect you, or—unfortunately for others who never consented to bear that responsibility—someone else, to do so and fill the gap for their shortcomings going forward.

If always shielded from consequences, how will that person ever learn? What makes that person irrational when you have conditioned them by stepping in to protect them from consequences each previous time?

The person with the expectation that something, somehow will fix everything for them, someway, is not the irrational one. It is the person who believes anything different could or should occur when never allowing the person to experience the consequences that would teach them. They will continue to do the same thing that has been successful for them in the past.

It is for these reasons that you should always impose consequences when someone acts in a manner that infringes upon your rights or well-being. Crucially, you must exercise judgment in determining the most appropriate response, ensuring it aligns with both the severity of the act and the principles of justice. The nature of these consequences should be proportionate to the wrongdoing and could range from social distancing and expressing disapproval to seeking legal recourse, all the way up to and including lethal force, always within the bounds of justice and with respect to legality. Consistently applying this approach not only establishes clear boundaries for interactions but also promotes a culture of accountability and respect for rights.

The evil and morally agnostic feed on pity and mercy. Those who value goodness should never compromise or sacrifice any part of it or be afraid to defend it by any means necessary, at any time.

Always Identify the Good and Pursue It

All value, or "the good," stems from independent judgment. Good is inherently subjective, defined by what is beneficial or valuable to the individual. This concept champions a proactive stance, grounded in reason, which requires one's judgment to continually assess the merit or lack thereof in the various aspects of life. Therefore, to abstain from exercising independent judgment is to abstain from engaging with the concept of goodness itself. Reason furnishes direction, and only through our judgments can we navigate our understanding and pursuit of what is good.

Apply this principle by limiting your focus to pursuing only the things that matter to you, such as achieving your career goals, fostering personal growth, and nurturing meaningful relationships.

Reflexively responding to everything people say and do, particularly those things that have no direct consequence on your life or are outside your control, drains you of your finite energy and decreases your ability to focus on better identifying and achieving your values. Learn to recognize the difference between situations that necessitate your attention and those you can avoid. This discernment enables you to conserve your energy, ensuring you are fully present and can vigorously defend your values when confrontation becomes necessary. By applying this principle, you ensure that you invest your efforts in pursuits that genuinely enhance your life, thereby leading to greater fulfillment and effectiveness in accomplishing your unified goals across the span of your lifetime.

Never Support the Anti-Good

The anti-good is everything not consciously concluded to be good. For something to be good, it must both be good, and true, for in the case of good but not true, or true but not good, both result in not good.

In a perfect world, where everyone were to make full use of their rational and conceptual faculties, only pursuing either good or bad, there would be no need to discuss this. However, in our current world, we must make a clear distinction to explain everything that constitutes the anti-good and why you should never support it. Rand very eloquently states the nature of this issue,

> There are two sides to every issue: one side is right and the other is wrong, but the middle is always evil.[249]

It is common to hear someone state, "nothing is only black or white," and this is a quintessential statement reflecting the differences in type, because logic, is in fact either black or white. Rational judgment is either good or not good; true or not true, based on your perception. There is no in-between, and the rational mind makes this so. For irrational types, this statement is perplexing for obvious reasons but there exists a twist in rational types that makes the introvert and extrovert fundamentally different. Jung explains this difference when writing about the extroverted thinking and feeling types:

> This gives a peculiar stamp to the unconscious of both our types: what they consciously and intentionally do accords with reason (their reason, of course), but what happens to them accords with the nature of infantile, primitive sensations

---

[249] (Rand, Atlas Shrugged 1957, 1054)

and intuitions. At all events, what happens to these types is irrational (from their standpoint) ...

The rationality of both types is object-oriented and dependent on objective data. It accords with what is collectively considered to be rational. For them, nothing is rational save what is generally considered as such. Reason, however, is in large part subjective and individual. In our types this part is repressed, and increasingly so as the object gains in importance.[250]

This fundamental difference ties the rational extrovert to what society collectively deems as good or true, as it hinders their capacity to remain faithful to their own subjective reasoning. Thus, at best, the rational extrovert can only provide a rational conclusion based on the logic or subjective feelings of others, while the irrational character of their perception never sees things as black or white. The rational introvert, however, does not operate in this way, because their rational processes work to bring everything in their perception into accordance with reason. Therefore, by staying true to the subjective nature of reason throughout the complete cognitive process, they can apply logic properly.

This means that there is no middle ground between good and evil, and individuals must use reason to distinguish between them. Once you have identified the good, you must align your actions and keep aware to not mistakenly support anything that goes against it. That support can come in many forms and fuel what you judge as anti-good, enabling its survival.

The personality traits of the rational extrovert incline them to be enforcers of collective culture, but this is only their impression of the culture, of course, and here you see how the collective mind works. It internalizes its impression of the external object and projects that

---

[250] (Jung 1923, 334)

impression onto the greater society. In other words, a collective mentality only acknowledges and accepts the culture it identifies with, labeling anyone falling outside it "other."

This creates a tendency toward scolding others whenever there is a point of disagreement, meaning, when others do not obey the extrovert's tribe's rules. However, in the highly diversified and mobile society of today, this approach is useless because insults, by themselves, provide no meaningful consequence to members of other tribes. There is no threat of backlash from their fellow tribe members because the group values differ, and social lines rarely in fact need to cross.

Yet, there are two areas of modern society where the lines must cross regardless of social affiliation: commerce and law. These are the two areas available for a significant reprisal of consequence when others do not align with your values.

In commerce, companies supply goods and services for dollars. Additionally, entertainers, advertisers, and influencers receive payment for attracting attention. When provided with the opportunity, consumers actively contribute to their success. If you continuously consume the goods and content of those whom you judge as anti-good, you do not issue any negative consequence to them through insult because you continue to purchase their products and enable them to cash in on your attention.

If you wanted to affect them negatively you would withdraw your business and attention from them altogether, because with business, if the dollars come in, it indicates the value proposition was valid and the customer satisfied.

We find that many people want to break up companies when their purchasing decisions are exactly what have enabled these companies to become so large in the first place. It never occurs to them to edit their own behavior to change the result, they always want to edit the resulting effect of their behavior. This mimics the collective function because it always wants to use the object to change the subject. It wants business, government, culture, world—to change—to force them to be better people. This paradox highlights a lack of self-awareness and responsibility in consumer behavior, where the desire for change in the external world does not align with personal actions that contribute to the status quo.

For example, Amazon has grown exponentially over the years, expanding far beyond its origins as an online bookstore to become a colossal player in retail, cloud computing, digital streaming, and more. Its success stems from the convenience it offers, with a vast selection of products, competitive pricing, fast shipping, and the Prime membership program, which provides a variety of benefits.

As Amazon's dominance became more apparent, concerns over its impact on local businesses, worker treatment, market competition, and even its influence on consumer behavior began to emerge. Critics argue that Amazon's practices may stifle competition, potentially leading to a monopoly in certain sectors. There have been calls for regulatory action to address these concerns, including antitrust investigations and proposals to break up the company.

Yet, the paradox lies in the behavior of consumers themselves. Many of those who express concerns about Amazon's market dominance continue to shop on Amazon due to the unmatched convenience and value it offers. They may lament the closing of local bookstores and the challenges faced by small businesses, yet their purchasing decisions—opting to buy from Amazon for quick delivery and competitive prices—contribute to the very dominance they critique.

This situation highlights the disconnect between the desire for a more competitive marketplace and the individual actions that favor convenience and efficiency. It illustrates a broader societal trend where consumers seek change in external entities without reflecting on how their personal behavior contributes to the status quo, underlining a lack of self-awareness and responsibility in consumer behavior.

Trying to address culture itself directly is a flaw of the rational extrovert's psychology because they attempt to achieve a result without leveraging or even acknowledging its causes. Their programming encourages them to safeguard culture, yet culture consists of judgments made by the individuals within it. As individuals arrange their personal lives, the outcomes of their actions shape culture, and this constitutes the full extent of anyone's influence on it.

The Montgomery Bus Boycott of the 1950s Civil Rights Movement, sparked by Rosa Parks's courageous refusal to give up her seat, stands as one of the greatest American examples of leveraging economic actions to express and advocate for values. This boycott effectively used the withdrawal of patronage from a bus system to protest racial segregation, showcasing the power of collective action in commerce to enforce social change. A voluntary change in personal behavior forced a change in collective attitude because it levied an economic consequence.

In a free country, individuals must be willing to invest in the common good by changing their personal behavior in ways that demonstrate to businesses and corporate entities that they do not align with their values. These entities will see they cannot obtain the resources you provide them with voluntarily, without providing you with what you require, either doing what it takes to retain your support or finding the resources they desire elsewhere.

This exercise of personal accountability works similarly in government but instead of voting with your dollar, you vote with your ballot. If your ballot supports bills or elects politicians who support bills that do not align with your values, you have voluntarily contributed to the anti-good.

In the pursuit of holding all parties accountable in the context of the anti-good, it becomes imperative not only to dissociate from those who blatantly violate rational ethical principles but also to impose penalties on those who choose to remain morally agnostic. This category notably includes middlemen—entities or individuals who, by refusing to take a clear stance, become complicit in the spread of the anti-good. Their moral agnosticism, under the guise of neutrality, often places an undue burden on society. By abstaining from judgment, they contribute to a landscape where the consequences of ignorance are not solely theirs to bear but are diffused across both the informed and the uninformed. This diffusion distributes the "price" of ignorance—be it in the form of societal, economic, or environmental costs—across the entirety of society, unfairly burdening both those who have engaged in thoughtful consideration of these issues and those who may remain unaware of the underlying principles at stake.

To address this, it is incumbent on the wise and the principled not just to dissociate from these middlemen but to actively ensure they fully bear the consequences of their inaction. We witness an illustrative case in the handling of the migrant crisis, where states or entities that have historically voted for or supported lenient immigration policies must confront the direct outcomes of such decisions. Governors sending migrants to states advocating for lax policies exemplify a tangible form of retribution, forcing a direct encounter with the consequences of their legislative choices. Similarly, moral agnosticism in the face of critical issues demands a rigorous response—refusing to share the burden their indifference imposes on society. By making those who advocate or decide these policies "pay the full price," we underscore a refusal to enable or support a system that allows the ignorant—those unable to grasp the conceptual breadth of the issue unless they experience its direct impact—and the agnostic to offload their share of responsibility onto those who actively engage in and promote ethical reasoning. This real-world example illustrates the broader principle that individuals and entities must hold themselves accountable not only in theory but in practice, ensuring that the repercussions of their actions lead to a reflective and, ideally, corrective course.

There is one more aspect I would like to address in connection with this topic and it concerns the most detrimental and increasingly seen offerings to the anti-good possible: children. Because many people derive their path from secondhand concepts rooted in rule-following, where they do not know or understand the reasons for the rules they follow, their aspirations and the moral guidance they present ring hollow to their children and new generations; especially in religions that denigrate pride. Why would or how could a child develop pride in themselves following such empty, unexplained prescriptions?

Everything in a religion—such as the emphasis on original sin, the notion of inherent unworthiness, the suppression of personal desires in favor of divine commandments, or rituals that prioritize submission over individual autonomy—removes a person's self-confidence; by that point, there is no wonder they can be swayed by virtually anything. The failure of the culture approach is that, once accepted, there is no individual at its foundation. And if the person does not take the leadership of the culture you agree with, they take leadership from another culture, something that could be far more sinister.

A lack of balanced structure—being overly rigid in some areas while completely unstructured in others—and superficial parenting approaches set children on a negative trajectory by neglecting to steer them toward positive directions. We are currently offering up children to a life of depravity because of ineptitude as parents and leaders. The result is the type of culture we have today.

When we give children nothing to live for, they believe us, and live for nothing. When you present a child with the sole option of believing that they are an extension of a secondhand concept and then remove the concept of God from their thoughts, you leave them with only the concept of society to worship. Both are bad options, though the former is closer to a conceptual understanding of ethics.

Anyone oriented by a secondhand idea accepts the act of rule-following, but choice forces us to become true individuals. Reason guides an individual through a life built on personal values. Rules are for those who prefer not to think.

The quality of character of those who amass vast resources in a free society directly reflects the character of the individuals within it, because the only way resources can flow to businesses, entertainers, or influencers promoting anti-good, is through the active support and endorsement of no-good individuals. The more prominent these idols become, the clearer the indication that we have failed to raise new generations with the understanding they have something to live for: themselves.

By raising children with no moral education rooted in reason whatsoever, which is the only path to a free and independent ethical society, we have effectively created monsters; and because we have conditioned them to expect support from others: entitled little monsters. Raising children in this manner is both the greatest and worst show of support to the anti-good there can be.

Defend Yourself from Third Party Attacks

Though it is easy to identify direct attacks on you, it is more difficult to identify those done via third-party, where your fellow citizens leverage the government against you, to force your support of their special interests.

You, the special interest group, and the politician, all have your own interests and each one plays against the other in the modern-day shambles of American politics. The special interest group is looking for funding or a bill passed for an issue that does not benefit you in any way. The politician is looking for votes for reelection and contributions to their campaign funds, not to mention good optics. But if you are someone who believes in personal responsibility, you are simply the mark in this game of three-card monte, a mere trick that has you focusing on what is going on with the left hand so they can do things with the right.

Many people overlook the fact that when they cast their ballot, they themselves relinquish the ability to vote with their dollar later, as the subsequent destination of that dollar is effectively already determined for them. When government funds go to organizations and initiatives that do not align with your values, you are supporting the anti-good, third-party, and you must defend yourself from these attacks.

When people support anti-good through personal choice, it does not affect you directly. They must bear the burden of that choice themselves and that does not consist of an initiation of force on you. That is why, when there is a difference of opinion between me and others, if it does not pertain to law, I do not care about it; it is simply a matter of choice. However, once a government initiates a law or passes a bill, it ceases to be a matter of choice; it becomes a decision imposed on you, backed by legalized force.

Due to the nature of rational extroversion, there is a tendency toward an altruistic attitude, embracing responsibility not only for oneself but inherently for others as well. This perspective often extends to projecting a sense of responsibility onto others, driven by identification with the group. However, this universal application of responsibility is problematic, as not everyone shares the same values. Despite this, the political lean toward collectivity allows for the redirection of resources extracted from individuals to fund those with whom they may have fundamental value disagreements.

In many cases, individuals find that the political system leverages their own virtues against them. There are people who criticize and express disapproval of certain ways of life yet use the government to extract resources generated by those very lifestyles they condemn. Those extracted resources then go to support the lives that these people refuse to sustain on their own. Instead of learning from the virtues that have enabled others to thrive and seeking to emulate these virtues to improve their own lives, they would rather receive benefits derived from the work of those they criticize.

It is within the rights of Americans to declare, "Just leave me alone. You are free to think whatever you want but not free to force me to be complicit in it." This stance underscores a fundamental tension within the political landscape between collective responsibility and individual autonomy, emphasizing the right to live free from conflicting collective ideals.

It is not a right if you need something from someone else nor is it your right to take it from them. Moreover, it is morally correct to compensate them in some way. This principle of fair exchange does not always involve offering monetary or material compensation, but it necessitates presenting something of equal value to the person, and they must willingly accept it in exchange for what you desire.

Vote No for Extroverted Thinking

The legislative branch of government, comprised of Congress, creates laws from nothing, an endeavor that demands the utmost in abstract thinking aimed at upholding a sound and consistent ethical framework. Legislators inherently limit the judicial and executive branches through the laws they enact. However, they face a unique challenge as they also create the laws that govern their own proceedings and responsibilities.

The extroverted thinking type shows a tendency toward being a pragmatist but while pragmatism is a desired trait of a legislator, they should never be pragmatists. The distinction lies in the ability of a truly effective legislator to apply real-world applications of broader principles, as opposed to a pragmatist who might sidestep or ignore principles altogether in favor of expedient action.

Given these considerations, as discussed in Part III, it is advisable to minimize the presence of extroverted thinking types within the legislative branch, especially where practicality permits a more selective approach. The U.S. House of Representatives, due to its size and operational dynamics, presents challenges to such selectivity. However, its very nature and smaller size ideally position the U.S. Senate to act as the bastion of reason. It should be composed, if not exclusively, of introverted thinking types better equipped to prioritize principles and reasoned analysis over expediency.

When evaluating senatorial candidates, it becomes crucial to discern traits indicative of extroverted thinking—or any type not introverted thinking—as these could detract from the Senate's role as a final defense for reason. Voters should carefully consider excluding such candidates, favoring those whose cognitive orientation promises a commitment to principled governance and the maintenance of a consistent ethical framework.

Convert Thoughts into Action Quickly

To effectively counter the predominance of concretism in today's culture from an intellectual standpoint, conceptual thinkers must enhance the intensity and efficiency of their intellectual function. The rapid pace at which the concrete mind operates can lead to exponentially compounding errors if conceptual thinkers are slow to formulate ideas and implement them. This delay allows poor thinking to create complex problems in need of disentanglement before one can even return to a good starting point.

To remain relevant and amplify the impact of quality thinking, three metrics require optimization: **thought quality**, which ensures the integrity and applicability of ideas; **thought velocity**, or the speed of abstraction; and **thought conversion**, defined as the rate of successfully turning ideas into tangible outcomes as its explicit goal.

Conceptual thinking is essential for achieving objective values over the long term, building principles and systems that secure these values more effectively than concrete thinking, which may achieve short-term goals but lacks sustainability. The exponential impact of both positive and negative thinking underscores the importance of what I term "**thought turnover**"—the rapid generation and application of innovative ideas for the continued success of an ethical society.

To counter the swift proliferation of flawed thinking, a structured approach to the thinking process is necessary, uniting the strengths of both introverted and extroverted thinking into a cohesive rational method. This principle posits that by actively incorporating more constructive, ethical, and innovative ideas into our societal fabric, we inherently diminish the prevalence and influence of detrimental or flawed thinking, thereby achieving what I call "subtraction by addition." This holistic approach involves a collaborative cycle of observing, abstracting, implementing, validating, and repeating, with each thinking type contributing their strengths to the process. The goal is to elevate the frequency of this iterative process, thereby increasing the rate of thought turnover.

This is an area where extroverted and introverted thinkers can align and join forces—reminiscent of "the businessman" and "the intellectual" from Rand's writings. The introverted thinker can focus on observation and abstraction, while working with extroverted thinkers to implement those ideas and validate the results. The method caters to each type's natural traits.

Reflecting on the synergy between diverse cognitive approaches, Ayn Rand eloquently captures the essence of collaboration between thinkers and doers, a concept that resonates deeply with the cooperative dynamic necessary for progress. She states:

> *In this complex pattern of human co-operation, two key figures act as the twin-motors of progress, the integrators of the entire system, the transmission belts that carry the achievements of the best minds to every level of society: the intellectual and the businessman.*[251]

Protect Yourself from Savages

Two major scenarios will always provoke a person who refuses to acknowledge reason or accept judgment by any standard. A person like this will always experience frustration with reality and those who possess intellect or high moral character. Because they are incapable of accepting the responsibilities of personal agency ascribed to an American citizen, their only option to obtain the necessities for survival, at some point, becomes an initiation of force upon others. It is for this reason you must be sure to protect yourself because violence is the inevitable language of the savage, who, lacking the tools of discourse and persuasion, eventually turn to force.

The first of these scenarios is when you deny someone access to your property based on terms that you, as the owner, deem unreasonable. The other is when, by embodying high moral standards, you inadvertently highlight the shortcomings in others.

When this happens, do not give them the benefit of the doubt, and if you do, speak on your own behalf, and accept the consequences of your actions solely. Savages do not reason, they only take and keep taking.

---

[251] (Rand, For the New Intellectual 1963, 26)

Investing: A Social Engineering Exercise in Reframing Language

People behave in accordance with their beliefs—a concept well-understood by social scientists and engineers. This understanding motivates them to alter public perception, often by initiating campaigns that change the language we use to describe various aspects of life. These efforts are not just for enhancing brand images; they fundamentally aim to shift public perceptions and increase sales through enhanced goodwill.

For example, consider how renaming can change public perception:

- **Asian Carp to Copi**: This change aims to shift the view of Asian carp from "an invasive species" to "a sustainable food source," thereby increasing the fish's consumption.
- **Mother to Birthing Person**: This alteration in terminology reflects a shift in recognizing diverse parental identities and roles.
- **Sexual Transformation to Gender Affirmation or Gender Confirmation Surgery**: This replacement aims to reframe the narrative around the medical procedures involved in gender transition.

These campaigns, launched by organizations or individuals, specifically aim to change people's attitudes toward social norms. Renaming is not merely cosmetic but a strategic tool to influence behavior and perceptions. Similarly, the way we conceptualize broader abstract terms can profoundly influence societal attitudes and personal behavior.

The term "sacrifice" is a prime example. Defined as "an act of offering to a deity something precious"[252] and "something given up or lost,"[253] the term is frequently used in daily conversation, and based on this frequency, the perception and expectation of many is that sacrifice is a necessary part of life. However, this view can be traced back to mystical traditions that do not emphasize independent judgment, an essential component of rational thought. Without the exercise of reason, individuals passively accept "sacrifices" without critically evaluating their necessity or benefit.

On the other hand, the term "invest," defined as "to make use of for future benefits or advantages"[254] and "to involve or engage especially emotionally,"[255] suggests a more deliberate and reasoned engagement with our goals and priorities. Individuals who engage in "investment" consider future benefits along with emotional commitments.

Building on this, what is evident is that the term "invest"—including related terms "investing" and "investment"—must come from a place of knowledge, because one must know not only what one is investing in, but also why. This requires one's use of reason, supported by the psychological process of individuation or introversion, in which the individual actively pursues personal values.

Sacrifice, however, is a misleading term, a "package deal," or concrete concept that obscures one's perception of expected benefits without conscious acknowledgment. Also known as a "covert contract," this perspective is detrimental when it becomes a habitual mode of thought, as it renders individuals oblivious to the reasons behind their perceived "sacrifices."

---

[252] (Merriam-Webster.com n.d.)
[253] ibid
[254] ibid
[255] ibid

I have stated multiple times throughout this work the crucial assertion that "choice defines perspective," and I recognize that the above terms, though originating from opposite premises, converge on the same fundamental concept of decision-making. From the pervasive perspective of mystical belief, individuals must make sacrifices, whereas, from the standpoint of introverted thinking and reason, this notion proves false. In fact, the terms "sacrifice" and "compromise" are both unnecessary once one embraces the premise of human agency—in which individuals possess the capacity for choice and personal judgment.

Thus, to rectify this glitch in rational attitude and thought, I propose replacing any current or future use of the word "sacrifice" or "compromise" with the word "invest," thereby relegating these terms to obsolescence. For example:

- Instead of saying "I sacrificed my time for the project," say "I invested my time in the project, expecting professional growth and success in return." This reframing shifts the perspective from passive surrender to active contribution with a purpose.
- Rather than "I compromised my interests for the relationship," use "I invested in our mutual happiness by aligning our goals and working toward a shared vision." This implies a thoughtful decision rather than a reluctant concession.
- Replace "I sacrificed my personal hobbies for my children" with "I invested in my children's upbringing, knowing the long-term benefits it brings to our family." Here, the term "invest" communicates a deliberate choice made with foresight and understanding of the value it brings, rather than a loss endured.

In conclusion, by replacing terms like "sacrifice" and "compromise" with "invest," we can transform the narrative frameworks that shape

APPLICATION

our daily decisions and societal norms. This linguistic shift does not merely alter vocabulary but redefines our approach to personal and collective challenges. Instead of perceiving actions as losses or concessions, viewing them as investments can encourage a more proactive and optimistic engagement with our goals and the challenges we face. Imagine a society where individuals and institutions adopt this mindset, fostering a culture that values deliberate, informed decision-making and long-term planning. Such a change could lead to more sustainable and positive outcomes in various aspects of life, from personal relationships to professional projects and beyond. Therefore, I urge readers, leaders, and policymakers to consider this reframing seriously, recognizing the profound impact that our words have on our thoughts, actions, and the fabric of society itself. Let us invest in this change—not just in terminology but in the underlying attitudes that drive our world forward. This notion of investment leads us directly into the concept of "high-risk investing," where the stakes are not just theoretical but intensely personal and philosophically grounded.

High-Risk Investing: A Philosophical Approach to Need

In the realm of social contribution and personal engagement, I adhere to a principle I term "high-risk investing" (HRI), which diverges significantly from traditional charity. This approach is not just about allocating resources—it is a deliberate gamble, grounded in the belief that every investment must align with my personal desires and values, rather than guaranteeing a monetary return. The "high risk" comes from the potential for significant impact or even failure, which I willingly embrace. I invest in people, and initiatives that resonate with me, those I believe have the potential, albeit uncertain, to realize outcomes that I find desirable. This stance arises from a conviction that a clear objective should drive every contribution, ensuring that each investment, whether of time, resources, or effort, promotes measurable improvements aligned with my values and interests.

405

Investment Criteria and Impact Measurement

My approach to selecting and evaluating HRI investments is deeply personal and combines both rational assessment and intuition. I focus on the potential of individuals to reach their full capabilities, choosing investments where I see genuine promise and a likelihood of significant personal development, avoiding those who may not effectively utilize the resources provided. This contrasts with traditional charity models that often prioritize immediate relief over transformative, long-term impacts.

I measure the success of my investments by blending objective outcomes and intuitive insights. While I employ tools like the scientific method to measure tangible results, such as employment outcomes from funding a career training program, intuition is crucial for gauging the less tangible aspects of personal growth and societal impact. This combination allows me to capture the full spectrum of an investment's influence, acknowledging that not all valuable outcomes are immediately quantifiable.

Investing on My Own Terms and Rejecting Traditional Contributions

Grounded in the principles set forth in my investment criteria and measurement strategies, I engage in HRI not out of a sense of obligation but from a deliberate choice to invest in the world as I envision it, expecting returns that contribute to this vision. I am unapologetic in seeking outcomes that align with my terms, which foster advancements that resonate personally rather than conforming to external expectations.

For example, when considering a contribution to a scholarship fund, my support is contingent on objective evidence that the investment yields a positive outcome, such as the recipient's graduation and their subsequent contributions to society in areas of personal significance.

This approach ensures that my investments are not merely acts of goodwill, but strategic actions aimed at cultivating a better social fabric, distinctly departing from traditional philanthropy by always seeking a return, whether it is an improvement aligned with my vision or an external validation of the investment's impact.

Simultaneously, my approach to HRI categorically rejects mandatory contributions to entitlement or welfare programs, which, in my view, fail to address the foundational challenges of cultivating a society that fosters fully individuated citizens. By pursuing a deeper sense of purpose, these citizens can achieve self-actualization, the ultimate goal of human psychological development. Entitlement programs often perpetuate dependency and fail to tackle the underlying issues that inhibit personal and societal growth. This not only undermines personal agency but also contradicts the ethos of HRI, which advocates for empowering individuals through strategic, voluntary investments aimed at achieving specific, meaningful outcomes. The cycle of dependency, if unaddressed at its roots, leads to a society increasingly reliant on external support rather than one that cultivates its own potential.

Philosophical Foundations and Future Vision

It is my belief that individuals should contribute to causes they find worthy based solely on personal conviction and commitment— effectively putting their "money where their mouth is." This approach is an extension of my philosophical commitment to actively engaging with reality and pursuing what I consider the good. Over time, I envision this model of HRI encouraging more individuals to engage actively with societal challenges, fostering a shift from passive charity to a more engaged, purpose-driven form of contribution. By redefining what it means to invest in society, HRI prompts a deeper, more personal connection to the causes one chooses to support, aligning closely with a world where personal conviction and strategic investment go hand in hand.

The Protector

We stand at a pivotal moment, tasked with weaving the fabric of a culture fit for America. However, it is imperative that we better utilize our understanding of psychology to achieve a healthy culture. Whereas in a moral education of the past, Christianity was the culture of collective feeling used to bring about reason, in educating future generations of Americans, we must reverse this practice and rationalize it. This approach will not only preserve our values but also guarantee that they serve the collective good effectively and resonate with our evolving societal needs.

With this said, I am committed to leading this charge, and assume role of protector and defender for an ethical culture rooted in reason, in addition to capitalism's protector and defender as well. Anyone holding these values but afraid to speak out, can get behind me, as I am unwavering in my defense; plus, I am willing and able to handle all that will undoubtedly come with it. I accept and will endure the backlash. Furthermore, I am unwilling to concede to or conform with mystical leadership of any kind, regardless of shared goals; but all are welcome to follow my lead. Whether you choose to aid in this endeavor or be transported in its wake, I urge you to engage actively. As we stand on the precipice of change, I leave you with the words from Rand that have ignited my resolve and guided my thoughts, hoping they will inspire and challenge you in equal measure:

If you are seriously interested in fighting for a better world, begin by identifying the nature of the problem. The battle is primarily intellectual (philosophical), not political. Politics is the last consequence, the practical implementation, of the fundamental (metaphysical-epistemological-ethical) ideas that dominate a given nation's culture. You cannot fight or change the consequences without fighting and changing the cause; nor can you attempt any practical implementation without knowing what you want to implement.

In an intellectual battle, you do not need to convert everyone. History is made by minorities—or, more precisely, history is made by intellectual movements, which are created by minorities. Who belongs to these minorities? Anyone who is able and willing actively to concern himself with intellectual issues. Here, it is not quantity, but quality, that counts (the quality—and consistency—of the ideas one is advocating) ...

Man cannot exist without some form of philosophy, i.e., some comprehensive view of life. Most men are not intellectual innovators, but they are receptive to ideas, are able to judge them critically and to choose the right course, when and if it is offered. There are also a great many men who are indifferent to ideas and to anything beyond the concrete-bound range of the immediate moment; such men accept subconsciously whatever is offered by the culture of their time, and swing blindly with any chance current. They are merely social ballast—be they day laborers or company presidents—and, by their own choice, irrelevant to the fate of the world.

Today, most people are acutely aware of our cultural-ideological vacuum; they are anxious, confused, and groping for answers. Are you able to enlighten them?

Can you answer their questions? Can you offer them a consistent case? Do you know how to correct their errors? Are you immune from the fallout of the constant barrage aimed at the destruction of reason—and can you provide others with antimissile missiles? A political battle is merely a skirmish fought with muskets; a philosophical battle is a nuclear war.

If you want to influence a country's intellectual trend, the first step is to bring order to your own ideas and integrate them into a consistent case, to the best of your knowledge and ability. This does not mean memorizing and reciting slogans and principles, Objectivist or otherwise: knowledge necessarily includes the ability to apply abstract principles to concrete problems, to recognize the principles in specific issues, to demonstrate them, and to advocate a consistent course of action... What is required is honesty—intellectual honesty, which consists in knowing what one does know, constantly expanding one's knowledge, and never evading or failing to correct a contradiction. This means: the development of an active mind as a permanent attribute...

If you like condensations (provided you bear in mind their full meaning), I will say: when you ask "What can one do?"—the answer is "SPEAK" (provided you know what you are saying).

...Speak on any scale open to you, large or small—to your friends, your associates, your professional organizations, or any legitimate public forum. You can never tell when your words will reach the right mind at the right time. You will see no immediate results—but it is of such activities that public opinion is made...

The opportunities to speak are all around you. I suggest that you make the following experiment: take an ideological "inventory" of one week, i.e., note how many times people utter the wrong political, social and moral notions as if these were self-evident truths, with your silent sanction. Then make it a habit to object to such remarks—no, not to make lengthy speeches, which are seldom appropriate, but merely to say: "I don't agree."...Most particularly, do not keep silent when your own ideas and values are being attacked...

It is a mistake to think that an intellectual movement requires some special duty or self-sacrificial effort on your part. It requires something much more difficult: a profound conviction that ideas are important to you and to your own life. If you integrate that conviction to every aspect of your life, you will find many opportunities to enlighten others.[256]

---

[256] (Rand, What Can One Do? 1972, 272-276)

Appendix

$$* \bigstar *$$

$$V = Value$$

$$L = Libido$$

$$S = Libido\ devoted\ to\ self\ survival\ (in\ time)$$

$$P = Libido\ devoted\ to\ personal\ purpose\ (in\ time)$$

$$S_{min} = Minimum\ libido\ required\ for\ self\ survival$$

$$P_{max} = Maximum\ libido\ available\ for\ personal\ purpose$$

$$S_{eff} = Survival\ efficiency$$

$$P_{util} = Purpose\ utilization$$

$$L = S + P$$

$$S_{eff} = \frac{S_{min}}{S}$$

$$P_{util} = \frac{P}{P_{max}}$$

$$V = S_{eff} * P_{util}$$

$$Life = \sum V_i$$

$$Fulfillment = V_\mu$$

Acknowledgments

───────── ★ ★ ★ ─────────

There are people I would like to thank who are unaware they have contributed to this book:

C. S. Joseph and Michael Pierce for their in-depth online content which first showed me that there was far more to personality types than the MBTI, and that I needed to learn more to fully understand them.

Dr. Harry Binswanger for his lectures on psycho-epistemology that led to my initial awareness of the connectivity between psychology and philosophy.

And Peter Schwartz for my favorite essay of his that made me say, "I may want to do that thing." In my own way, of course.

Thank you for reading my book!

I view this material as the introduction to a conversation and would very much love to hear your feedback as a reader. Please take a couple minutes to leave a review on Amazon to let me know what you think about the book.

If you have any questions or would like to discuss the content further, please email americasethicalarchetype@damientdubose.com.

Thank you so much!

Damien Terrence Dubose

WORKS CITED

16personalities.com. 2016. NERIS Analytics Limited.

Associated Press. 2023. *New Report Points to Homicide Rate Declines in US Cities After Pandemic-Era Spike.* July 21. Accessed April 25, 2024. https://www.usnews.com/news/us/articles/2023-07-21/new-report-points-to-homicide-rate-declines-in-u-s-cities-afterpandemic-era-spike.

Barrett, Lisa Feldman. 2018. "You aren't at the mercy of your emotions -- your brain creates them | Lisa Feldman Barrett." TED, January 23. https://youtu.be/0gks6ceq4eQ.

Blumgart, Jake. 2021. *After a Violent Year, a Search for Answers.* March 19. Accessed April 25, 2024. https://www.bloomberg.com/news/articles/2021-03-19/the-u-s-homicide-rate-spiked-in-2020-why.

Branden, Nathaniel. 1964. "Mental Health versus Mysticism and Self-Sacrifice." In *The Virtue of Selfishness*, by Ayn Rand and Nathaniel Branden, 45-54. New York: Penguin Group.

—. 2011. *The Vision of Ayn Rand: The Basic Principles of Objectivism.*

Congressional Research Service. 2020. "COVID-19 and Other Election Emergencies." July 16. Accessed April 24, 2024. https://crsreports.congress.gov/product/pdf/R/R46455.

Covey, Stephen. 2013. *The 7 Habits of Highly Effective People.* Simon & Schuster.

Emre, Merve. 2018. *The Personality Brokers.* New York: Doubleday.

Ghate, Onkar. 2022. "Dismantling Roe." Washington DC: Ayn Rand Institute, July 9.

Herby, Jonas, Lars Jonung, and Steve H. Hanke. 2022. "A Literature Review and Meta-Analysis of the Effects of Lockdowns on COVID-19 Mortality." *Johns Hopkins University.* January. Accessed April 25, 2024. https://sites.krieger.jhu.edu/iae/files/2022/01/A-Literature-Review-and-Meta-Analysis-of-the-Effects-of-Lockdowns-on-COVID-19-Mortality.pdf.

n.d. "Holy Bible - New King James Version." *Bible Gateway.* https://www.biblegateway.com/passage/?search=2%20Thessalonians%203&version=NKJV.

Jung, C. G. 1923. *Psychological Types.* Translated by H. G. Baynes. New York: Routledge.

Merriam-Webster.com. n.d. *Dictionary.* Accessed April 8, 2024. https://www.merriam-webster.com/dictionary.

Peikoff, Leonard. 1991. *Objectivism: The Philosophy of Ayn Rand.* New York: Penguin Group.

Rand, Ayn. 1957. *Atlas Shrugged.* New York: Penguin Group.

Rand, Ayn. 1974. "Causality Versus Duty." In *Philosophy: Who Needs It*, by Ayn Rand, 133-141. New York: Penguin Group.

Rand, Ayn. 1964. "Collectivized Ethics." In *The Virtue of Selfishness*, by Ayn Rand and Nathaniel Branden, 106-112. New York: Penguin Group.

Rand, Ayn. 1960. "Faith and Force: The Destroyers of the Modern World." In *Philosophy: Who Needs It*, by Ayn Rand, 87-110. New York: Penguin Group.

—. 1963. *For the New Intellectual.* New York: Penguin Group.

Rand, Ayn. 1966. "Philosophy and Sense of Life." In *The Romantic Manifesto*, by Ayn Rand, 14-22. Berkley.

Rand, Ayn. 1974. "Selfishness Without a Self." In *Philosophy: Who Needs It*, by Ayn Rand, 71-77. New York: Penguin Group.

Rand, Ayn. 1970. "The Comprachicos." In *Return of the Primitive: The Anti-Industrial Revolution*, by Ayn Rand and Peter Schwartz, 51-94. New York: Penguin Group.

Rand, Ayn. 1973. "The Missing Link." In *Philosophy: Who Needs It*, by Ayn Rand, 56-69. New York: Penguin Group.

Rand, Ayn. 1964. "The Objectivist Ethics." In *The Virtue of Selfishness*, by Ayn Rand and Nathaniel Branden, 15-44. New York: Penguin Group.

Rand, Ayn. 1965. "The Psycho-Epistemology of Art." In *The Romantic Manifesto*, by Ayn Rand, 3-13. Berkley.

Rand, Ayn. 1971. *The Psychology of Psychologizing.* Vol. 5, in *The Voice of Reason: Essays in Objectivist Thought*, by Ayn Rand, Leonard Peikoff and Peter Schwartz, 23-31. New York: Penguin Group.

Rand, Ayn. 1972. "What Can One Do?" In *Philosophy: Who Needs It*, by Ayn Rand, 271-277. New York: Penguin Group.

Wex Definitions Team. 2022. *Ethics.* December. https://www.law.cornell.edu/wex/ethics#:~:text=In%20the%20legal%20context%2C%20ethics%20defines%20how%20individuals,principles%2C%20law%20and%20ethics%20are%20far%20from%20co-extensive.

www.ingramcontent.com/pod-product-compliance
Lightning Source LLC
Chambersburg PA
CBHW062129040426

42335CB00039B/1835